XML

A Beginner's Guide

Go Beyond the Basics with Ajax, XHTML,
XPath 2.0, XSLT 2.0, and XQuery

About the Author

Steven Holzner is an award-winning author of many computer books. He's been writing about XML since it was born, and this is his fifth book on the topic. He's written on all aspects of XML, and his books have sold millions of copies and been translated into 18 languages. He's been on the faculty of MIT and Cornell University, as well as a contributing editor to *PC Magazine*.

About the Technical Editor

Guy Hart-Davis is the author of many computer books, including *Word 2007 Macros & VBA Made Easy, How to Do Everything: Microsoft Office Excel 2007,* and *Word 2000 Developer's Handbook.*

XML
A Beginner's Guide

Go Beyond the Basics with Ajax, XHTML,
XPath 2.0, XSLT 2.0, and XQuery

Steven Holzner

New York   Chicago   San Francisco
Lisbon   London   Madrid   Mexico City
Milan   New Delhi   San Juan
Seoul   Singapore   Sydney   Toronto

The McGraw·Hill Companies

Library of Congress Cataloging-in-Publication Data

Holzner, Steven.
  XML : a beginner's guide : go beyond the basics with Ajax, XHTML,
XPath 2.0, XSLT 2.0, and XQuery / Steven Holzner.
      p. cm.
  Includes index.
  ISBN 978-0-07-160626-4 (alk. paper)
  1. XML (Document markup language) I. Title.
  QA76.76.H94H65145 2009
  006.7'4—dc22

                                                2008048100

McGraw-Hill books are available at special quantity discounts to use as premiums and sales promotions, or for use in corporate training programs. To contact a special sales representative, please visit the Contact Us page at www.mhprofessional.com.

XML: A Beginner's Guide: Go Beyond the Basics with Ajax, XHTML, XPath 2.0, XSLT 2.0, and XQuery

1 2 3 4 5 6 7 8 9 0 DOC DOC 0 1 9 8

ISBN 978-0-07-160626-4
MHID   0-07-160626-2

Sponsoring Editor   Jane K. Brownlow
Editorial Supervisor   Patty Mon
Project Manager   Arushi Chawla, International Typesetting and Composition
Acquisitions Coordinator   Carly Stapleton
Technical Editor   Guy Hart-Davis
Copy Editor   Robert Campbell
Proofreader   Manish Tiwari, International Typesetting and Composition
Indexer   Kevin Broccoli
Production Supervisor   George Anderson
Composition   International Typesetting and Composition
Illustration   International Typesetting and Composition
Art Director, Cover   Jeff Weeks
Cover Designer   Jeff Weeks

To Nancy!

Contents at a Glance

1 Creating Well-Formed XML 1

2 Creating Valid XML Documents: Document Type Definitions 33

3 Creating Valid XML Documents: XML Schemas 73

4 XML Schemas: Creating Your Own Types 105

5 Formatting XML with Cascading Style Sheets 137

6 Finding Your Way with XSLT and XPath 175

7 Formatting XML with XSL Transformations 211

8 Extending XML with XHTML 245

9 XML and Data Binding 281

10 XML and JavaScript 319

11 XML and Java 353

12 Ajax and XQuery 389

Index 423

Contents

ACKNOWLEDGMENTS xv
INTRODUCTION xvii

1 **Creating Well-Formed XML** 1
   All about Markup Languages 3
      Using HTML 4
      Using XML 5
   Formatting XML 9
   Extracting Data from XML 10
   Applications: XML Dialects 12
   Well-Formed and Valid XML Documents 14
   Writing a Well-Formed XML Document 15
      Start with an XML Declaration 16
      Putting in a Prolog 17
      Adding Comments 17
      Handling Processing Instructions 18
      Checking Syntax with a DTD 18
      Storing Your Data in XML Elements 19
      Adding XML Attributes 26
      Use Only the Predefined Entity References 29
   CDATA Sections 31

2 Creating Valid XML Documents: Document Type Definitions **33**

Validating XML Documents 35
Creating a DTD 39
Declaring Elements in DTDs 40
    Content Model: ANY 41
    Content Model: Child Elements 41
    Content Model: Text 42
    Content Model: Multiple Children 43
    Content Model: EMPTY 47
Choices in DTDs 49
Handling Attributes in DTDs 52
    Setting Default Values 55
    Setting Attribute Types 60
External DTDs 62
Divide and Conquer: Namespaces 66

3 Creating Valid XML Documents: XML Schemas **73**

Creating an XML Schema 83
Declaring Elements 84
    Declaring Simple Elements 84
    Declaring Complex Elements 85
Specifying the Minimum and Maximum Number
    of Times an Element Can Occur 95
Declaring Anonymous Types 97
Declaring Elements by Reference 101

4 XML Schemas: Creating Your Own Types **105**

Declaring Attributes 106
Specifying Attribute Use 113
Restricting Simple Types 116
Making Selections with XML Schema Choices 123
Creating Empty Elements 126
Creating Element Groups 127
Creating Attribute Groups 129
Creating All Groups 131
Schemas and Namespaces 132
Annotating Schemas 133

5 Formatting XML with Cascading Style Sheets **137**

Using *The Jungle Book* 138
Introducing CSS 140
Connecting a Style Sheet to an XML Document 142
Understanding Style Sheets 144

Creating Style Sheet Selectors 145
   Selecting by Element 145
   Grouping Elements 146
   Selecting by Pseudo-Element 146
   Selecting by ID 148
   Selecting by Class 150
Using Inline Styles 155
Using CSS Styles 157
Creating Block Elements 157
Formatting Text 157
Styling with Colors 162
Styling with Margins, Indentations, and Alignments 167
Styling into Lists 168
Styling with Borders 171

6 Finding Your Way with XSLT and XPath **175**
Creating a Sample XML Document 176
First Formatting of the Sample XML Document 183
Creating Our First XSLT Style Sheet: Replacing the Entire Document .. 187
Applying XSLT Templates 188
Replacing <friend> Elements 193
Applying New Templates 195
Extracting the Value of <name> Elements 199
Using <xsl:value-of> 201
Extracting Multiple Elements Values 205

7 Formatting XML with XSL Transformations **211**
Working with the Match Attribute 212
   Matching the Root Node 213
   Matching Element Nodes 213
   Matching Child Element Nodes 214
   Matching Attributes 217
   Matching by ID 223
   Matching XML Comments 224
   Matching XML Processing Instructions 229
   Matching Either/Or Expressions 230
   Matching with [ ] 230
Using XPath 234
   XPath Axes 234
   XPath Node Tests 236
   XPath Predicates 236
Some XPath Examples 243

8 Extending XML with XHTML **245**

Getting Started with XHTML 247
Validating XHTML 252
Understanding XHTML 254
The Differences Between HTML and XHTML 255
Using <html>, the Document Element 257
Using <head> to Create Head Sections 258
Using <title> to Hold the Document's Title 259
Using <body> to Hold the Document's Body 260
Using Headings: <h1> Through <h6> 263
Using Plain Text 265
Using <b> to Make Text Bold 266
Using <i> to Make Text Italic 267
Using <font> to Specify Text Font 268
Using <img> to Display Images 271
Creating Tables 272

9 XML and Data Binding **281**

Getting Started with DSOs 282
Storing Data in HTML Format 282
Binding Data in HTML Format 287
Navigating from Record to Record 293
Binding XML Data 297
Using XML Data Islands 298
Extracting Data from DSOs Yourself 303
Binding XML Data into HTML Tables 308
Handling Nested Records 314

10 XML and JavaScript **319**

Reading XML and Extracting Data from It 322
Creating a DOMDocument Object 324
Getting a Document's Document Element 329
Searching for XML Elements by Name 338
Extracting Data from XML Attributes 342
Using XML Data Islands 351

11 XML and Java **353**

Working with Java and XML 354
Creating a Document Builder Factory 357
Creating a Document Builder 359
Parsing an XML Document 362
Accessing XML Data That You've Read in 365
Extracting All the Data in an XML Document Yourself 370
Walking over XMLNodes 374

Handling the Root Node 376
Handling the Opening Tag of Element Nodes 378
Handling Attribute Nodes 380
Handling CDATA Nodes 381
Handling Text Nodes 382
Handling Processing Instruction Nodes 383
Handling the Closing Tag of Element Nodes 383

12 Ajax and XQuery **389**
Getting Started with Ajax 390
Understanding ajax.html 393
Creating an XMLHttpRequest Object 395
Opening an XMLHttpRequest Object 398
Connecting to the Server 399
Displaying the Download 402
Making the Download Happen 404
Downloading Some XML 405
Writing ajaxxml.html 406
Configuring XMLHttpRequest Objects to Handle XML 407
Recovering the Downloaded XML 408
Using XQuery 414
Putting XQuery to Work 416
Using XQuery Functions 418

Index **423**

Acknowledgments

The book you hold in your hands is the work of many people. I'd particularly like to thank Jane Brownlow, Carly Stapleton, Arushi Chawla, and Bob Campbell.

Introduction

XML is the lingua franca of the Web. Since its birth, it has spread to all parts of the Web—anywhere there's data, you'll find XML.

That's because with XML, the name of the game is data. While HTML can let you format Web pages for display, XML lets you store your data for easy retrieval. We're going to see just how that works in this book, including seeing every major way of retrieving the data in XML documents.

We're going to see how to use Cascading Style Sheets to format your data, how to use browsers to display it in plain text, how to format and manipulate it with Extensible StyleSheet Language Transformations (XSLT), even how to grab it using some easy programming with JavaScript and Java. It's all in this book.

What's in This Book

Here's an overview of the contents of this book:

Chapter 1: Creating Well-Formed XML

- Introducing XML

- Handling the different dialects of XML

- Understanding well-formed XML

- Formatting XML

- Parsing XML

Chapter 2: Creating Valid XML Documents: Document Type Definitions

- Creating valid XML documents
- Introducing DTDs
- Creating a DTD
- Declaring elements
- Declaring attributes
- Using an XML validator

Chapter 3: Creating Valid XML Documents: XML Schemas

- Introducing XML schemas
- Creating valid XML documents using XML schemas
- Declaring elements
- Declaring elements by reference
- Using an XML schema validator

Chapter 4: XML Schemas: Creating Your Own Types

- Declaring attributes
- Restricting attribute values
- Using XML facets
- Creating XML schema choices
- Annotating XML schemas

Chapter 5: Formatting XML with Cascading Style Sheets

- Introducing CSS
- Connecting CSS to XML documents
- Formatting XML
- Creating style rules

Chapter 6: Finding Your Way with XSLT and XPath

- Introducing Extensible Stylesheet Language Transformations (XSLT)
- Introducing XPath
- Extracting data from XML documents
- Reading element values
- Finding attribute values

Chapter 7: Formatting XML with XSL Transformations

- Matching the root node
- Matching elements
- Matching element descendants
- Matching attributes
- Matching comments

Chapter 8: Extending XML with XHTML

- Using Extensible Hypertext Markup Language
- Introducing XHTML
- Creating XHTML documents
- Using text, images, and more
- Validating your XHTML document

Chapter 9: XML and Data Binding

- Introducing data binding
- Binding HTML data
- Binding XML data
- Creating bound tables

Chapter 10: XML and JavaScript

- Introducing XML and JavaScript
- Using the W3C DOM
- Navigating through XML documents
- Searching for XML data

Chapter 11: XML and Java

- Introducing XML and Java
- Using the W3C DOM
- Navigating through XML documents with Java
- Searching for XML data

Chapter 12: Ajax and XQuery

- Introducing Ajax
- Creating XMLHttpRequest objects
- Fetching Text
- Fetching XML
- Working with XQuery

All this and more is coming up in your guided tour of XML.

What You'll Need

You won't need to buy anything to be able to work through the examples in this book. To start, you'll need a text editor (Windows' built-in WordPad works fine) and a browser (one that supports JavaScript).

There are many browsers out there, but Microsoft Internet Explorer comes with a great deal of XML power already in it—and that's power we can't ignore. If you want to work through the chapters on Data Binding (Chapter 9) and the Extensible Stylesheet Language (Chapters 7 and 8), you're going to need Internet Explorer.

There are other freebies that we'll use in this book, such as the Java programming language and the Saxon XQuery processor, and we'll show you where to get them for free.

And that's it—you're ready to enter the world of XML by turning to Chapter 1.

Chapter 1

Creating
Well-Formed XML

Key Skills & Concepts

- Introducing XML

- XML dialects

- Well-formed XML

- Valid XML

- Formatting XML

- Parsing XML

Welcome to the wild and wooly world of XML! This book is going to give you a guided tour of that world, and it's a large world to explore.

XML has gotten into everywhere you have computers these days. Everywhere you go, it's XML-this, XML-that. What's all the hype about?

You're going to see in this book. The name of the game in XML is *data,* and it excels at handling that data. Originally, XML became popular because it offers you a text-based way of storing your data, and the World Wide Web is text-based—that is, the kind of data you sling around on the Internet is usually text-based. Web pages were originally constructed to be pure text, so the Web developed around them—and that meant doing everything in terms of text.

That's where XML comes in—it provides you a way of storing text-based data in a way that's easily searchable, and easy to work with. If Web pages are the magazine pages of the Internet, XML makes up the phone books, tax returns, spreadsheets, and so on—everything that is all about storing data, not about presenting that data.

There are many ways of working with that data, as you're going to see in this book. You can use existing programs to read XML data. You can write programs yourself to read and report that data. You can format that data for display. All those are possible, and they're all coming up in this book.

HTML is a great language, as far as it goes. But it might not be your first choice when you're thinking of sending a thousand bank statements over a secure Web connection, or the records of a thousand employees. HTML has all kinds of tags, such as <html>, <head>, and <h1> built in, but it doesn't have any <account_number> tags, or <beginning_balance> tags, or <hire_date> tags.

That's what XML is all about—giving you maximum freedom to structure your data into documents, because, using XML, you can create your own tags. Want an <account_number> tag, or a <beginning_balance> tag? Just create 'em!

HTML was fine for a long time, but as the Web grew up, its needs changed and got more advanced. You probably can't picture international banking and investment corporations storing their internal data in HTML—that is, HTML is great to present text and images in browsers, but not so great to structure pure data that's not meant to be displayed directly.

That's why XML has taken off—your data has its own structure, and you can construct your own data documents using XML. As the Internet became more and more trusted—and central—to moving data around, the XML revolution was born.

All about Markup Languages

Take a look at the browser display you see Figure 1-1.

That's an HTML Web page you see in Figure 1-1, and here's what the corresponding HTML, named hello.html in the downloadable code for this book, looks like:

```
<html>
    <head>
        <title>Hello From HTML</title>
    </head>
    <body>
        <center>
            <h1>
                Hello From HTML
            </h1>
        </center>
        Welcome to HTML!
    </body>
</html>
```

Figure 1-1   An HTML page

Using HTML

As you know, an HTML document like this is meant to be displayed in a Web browser. The part that's meant to appear in the browser is stored in the HTML document's body element, which is created with an opening <body> tag and ended with a closing </body> tag:

```
<html>
    <head>
        <title>Hello From HTML</title>
    </head>
    <body>
          .
          .
          .
    </body>
</html>
```

Inside the body element, you can enclose other elements, using formatting tags like <center> and <h1> to center text and make it appear on its own line, in large bold font, as here, where we display the heading "Hello From HTML":

```
<html>
    <head>
        <title>Hello From HTML</title>
    </head>
    <body>
        <center>
            <h1>
                Hello From HTML
            </h1>
        </center>
          .
          .
          .
    </body>
</html>
```

And you can also display simple text in a Web page, as with the text "Welcome to HTML!":

```
<html>
    <head>
        <title>Hello From HTML</title>
    </head>
    <body>
        <center>
            <h1>
                Hello From HTML
            </h1>
        </center>
        Welcome to HTML!
    </body>
</html>
```

Using elements like the body element and the center element to enclose the data in your document is a hallmark of a *markup language.*

HTML is a widely known markup language, and the tags (both opening and closing tags) in it, like <body> and </center>, are called *markup.* Markup is what gives structure to your documents and allows you to give instructions to programs like browsers on how to display your document.

XML is a markup language too—except that you're more free to create your own tags. That's great, because as good as HTML is, it has only a few more than 100 tags, and that's not going to fit all types of data needs. For example, there is no <street_address> or <phone_number> tag in HTML.

What does XML actually look like? Let's take a look.

Using XML

So what's all this about being able to create your own markup in XML? Yep, it's true, as we'll see now—and although you get more freedom than in HTML this way, you also have more responsibilities, as we're going to see.

Every XML document starts off with an XML declaration, which looks like this:

```
<?xml version="1.0" encoding="UTF-8"?>
        .
        .
        .
```

This line isn't considered markup—it's the XML declaration, which the organization responsible for creating XML, called the World Wide Web Consortium (or W3C, www.w3.org—more on them is coming up throughout the book), has decreed shall begin every XML document. The XML declaration informs the world that this is an XML document, and it announces the version of XML (currently, only XML 1.0 and 1.1 are allowed) and the character encoding (which matches numerical codes with the characters they stand for). More on the XML declaration is coming up in this chapter when we get into XML formally.

After the XML declaration, you can create your own markup. For example, say that you wanted to create an XML version of our HTML page:

```
<html>
    <head>
        <title>Hello From HTML</title>
    </head>
    <body>
        <center>
            <h1>
                Hello From HTML
            </h1>
        </center>
        Welcome to HTML!
    </body>
</html>
```

How can you cram this data into an XML document? You might start off by creating a new element named <document>, with opening and closing tags that look like this:

```
<?xml version="1.0" encoding="UTF-8"?>
<document>
      .
      .
      .
</document>
```

And in fact, we've made a good move here, because each XML document must actually have one and only one element that contains all other elements in the document.

That element is called the *document* element—which is why we've named it <document> here. In fact, you can give it any legal XML name—you might have called this element <data> or <my_document>, for example.

The document element can contain other XML elements. For example, we want to store the greeting "Hello From XML" in our document, so we might create a new element greeting, with a <greeting> opening tag and a </greeting> closing tag, just as in HTML—except that here, we've named this element ourselves:

```
<?xml version="1.0" encoding="UTF-8"?>
<document>
     <greeting>
           .
           .
           .
     </greeting>
</document>
```

And inside the greeting element, we can store the actual text of the greeting, like this:

```
<?xml version="1.0" encoding="UTF-8"?>
<document>
     <greeting>
           Hello From XML
     </greeting>
</document>
```

Is it really this easy? Are we just making up elements as we go along?

Yes, it really is almost this easy. In fact, we're following a few rules the W3C has created for XML, which we're going to see later in this chapter.

In addition to the greeting, let's put the message "Welcome to the wild and woolly world of XML!" into our document, using a new message element:

```
<?xml version="1.0" encoding="UTF-8"?>
<document>
     <greeting>
          Hello From XML
     </greeting>
```

```
<message>
     .
     .
     .
</message>
</document>
```

And here's how we store the text of the message:

```
<?xml version="1.0" encoding="UTF-8"?>
<document>
    <greeting>
        Hello From XML
    </greeting>
    <message>
        Welcome to the wild and woolly world of XML!
    </message>
</document>
```

Okay, that's our data in the XML document, hello.xml. Is it really true that XML isn't designed for browsers—that there's no way to see this document in a browser?

Well, yes and no. Here's the thing about XML—because you make up your own markup, browsers won't know how to handle that markup, unless you tell them. It's not like HTML, which the browser has all kinds of built-in knowledge of, enabling it to use the HTML elements you've specified to format the document and display it.

However, you can still look at an XML document in a browser like Internet Explorer. That browser will note that the extension of the document is .xml, and will display the document as an XML document, as you see in Figure 1-2.

So you actually can display an XML document in a browser—insofar as you only want to see the text-based data in that document. Note also the little minus sign (–) next to the <document> opening tag in Figure 1-2. That's Internet Explorer's way of saying you can expand or collapse XML data as *nodes*—for example, clicking the minus sign in Figure 1-2 collapsed the document

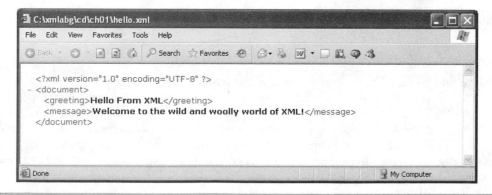

Figure 1-2 An XML document

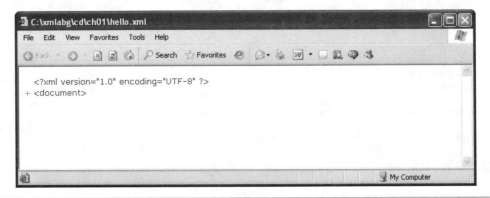

Figure 1-3 A collapsed XML document

element, as you see in Figure 1-3—note the plus sign (+) next to that element now, which indicates that there's collapsed content that can be displayed when you click the plus sign.

Displaying an XML document like this also works in the Firefox browser.

Try This   Creating an XML Document

Try creating your own XML document now. Use a text editor that is on your computer, such as WordPad if you have Windows, and store your name and title (make the title up—give yourself a good one), something like this:

```
<?xml version="1.0" encoding="UTF-8"?>
<data>
    <name>
        Steve
    </name>
    <title>
        CEO
    </title>
</data>
```

Make sure you save the document in simple text format, with the extension .xml.

Next, open your XML document (navigate to it in your browser—use the File | Open menu item in Internet Explorer (in Internet Explorer 7, first display the menu bar by selecting Menu Bar in the Tools drop-down menu) or the File | Open File menu item in Firefox). Make sure you can see all the data in the XML document displayed. (If Internet Explorer gives you a security bar saying "To help protect your security, Internet Explorer has restricted this web page . . .", right-click the security bar and select Allow Blocked Content and click Yes.)

Okay, so you can see the data in an XML document in a browser. Is there really no way to format the XML document so that you get a more appealing display than the one in Figure 1-3?

Formatting XML

It turns out that modern browsers like Internet Explorer and Firefox do indeed let you format XML documents for display. At this point, we have this document, with these elements:

```
<?xml version="1.0" encoding="UTF-8"?>
<document>
    <greeting>
        Hello From XML
    </greeting>
    <message>
        Welcome to the wild and woolly world of XML!
    </message>
</document>
```

How can you tell the browser how to format the greeting element the way you want it? Or the message element? As we're going to see in this book, you can do that with Cascading Style Sheets (CSS). Here's how you might format the text in the greeting element to appear on its own line, in 24-point font, in red, using CSS:

```
greeting {display: block; font-size: 24pt; color: #ff0000; text-align:
center}
                .
                .
                .
```

And here's how you can format the text in the message element to appear on its own line, in 18-point font, in blue:

```
greeting {display: block; font-size: 24pt; color: #ff0000; text-align:
center}
message {display: block; font-size: 18pt; color: #0000ff; text-align:
center}
```

These two lines are called *style rules,* and you can store them in a CSS file named, say, formatted.css.

You also need to connect formatted.css to the XML document containing the greeting and message elements, and you can do that with an <?xml-stylesheet?> processing instruction, of the kind that we're going to get more familiar with in this book. Here's how to use that processing instruction to tell the browser that the CSS file that has the formatting information it should use is formatted.css:

```
<?xml version="1.0" encoding="UTF-8"?>
<?xml-stylesheet type="text/css" href="formatted.css"?>
<document>
```

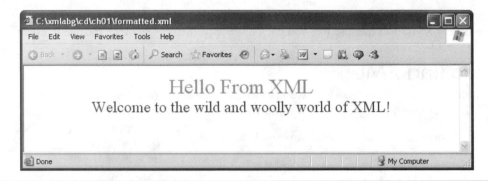

Figure 1-4 A formatted XML document

```
<greeting>
    Hello From XML
</greeting>
<message>
    Welcome to the wild and woolly world of XML!
</message>
</document>
```

And what's the result? You can see that in Figure 1-4, where the data from the greeting and message elements appears—nicely formatted, as you can see.

So it turns out that you can format the data in XML for display, a process that we'll see more of in this book.

But what if you didn't want to simply display the data in an XML document, but to read it?

Extracting Data from XML

It turns out that there are many ways to extract the data from an XML document and make use of that data. After all, that's usually the whole point—you store your data in XML documents; then you extract that data and make use of it.

For example, we'll use both the JavaScript scripting language and the Java programming language in this book to extract data from XML documents. JavaScript runs in browsers, making it particularly handy; here's a JavaScript example in a Web page that reads the text from the greeting element in hello.xml and displays that text in a Web page:

```
<html>
    <head>
        <title>
            Retrieving data from an XML document
        </title>

        <xml id="firstXML" src="hello.xml"></xml>
```

```
<script language="JavaScript">
    function getData()
    {
        xmldoc= document.all("firstXML").XMLDocument;

        nodeDoc = xmldoc.documentElement;
        nodeGreeting = nodeDoc.firstChild;

        outputMessage = "Greeting: " +
            nodeGreeting.firstChild.nodeValue;
        message.innerHTML=outputMessage;
    }
</script>
</head>

<body>
    <center>
        <h1>
            Retrieving data from an XML document
        </h1>

        <div id="message"></DIV>
        <p>
        <input type="button" value="Read the greeting"
            onclick="getData()">
    </center>
</body>
</html>
```

We'll see how this JavaScript code does its stuff later in this book. When you open this example, javascript.html, in a browser, you can see a button displayed, as appears in Figure 1-5.

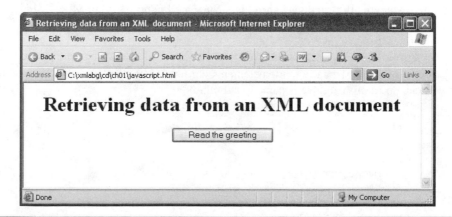

Figure 1-5 An XML-reading JavaScript example

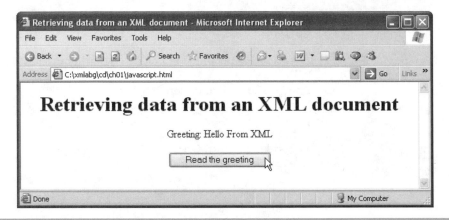

Figure 1-6 Reading XML data using JavaScript

Clicking that button causes the JavaScript in this example to read the text from the greeting element and display that text, as you see in Figure 1-6. Not bad.

Don't like programming? That's okay—we'll also see how to extract data from XML documents using Extensible Stylesheet Translations (XSLT), which are easy—and no programming is required to read and work with data from XML documents.

Applications: XML Dialects

Because you make your own tag names in XML, there are many XML dialects that already exist. That is, some XML languages have already been created—in fact, thousands of them—using their own tag names. These XML dialects are called XML *applications* (an unfortunate name, because "application" also refers to a computer program, but there you are).

For example, one prebuilt XML application is MathML—math markup language—which you use to display math equations in browsers capable of handling MathML.

Say for example that you wanted to display this equation using MathML:

$$5x^2 - 2x + 8 = 0$$

You could use the specially written elements in MathML to display that equation. Here's how you can do it; this example is named mathml.ml:

```
<?xml version="1.0"?>
<math xmlns="http://www.w3.org/1998/Math/MathML">
    <mrow>
        <mrow>
            <mn>5</mn>
            <mo>&InvisibleTimes;</mo>
            <msup>
                <mi>x</mi>
                <mn>2</mn>
            </msup>
```

```
            <mo>-</mo>
            <mrow>
                <mn>2</mn>
                <mo>&InvisibleTimes;</mo>
                <mi>x</mi>
            </mrow>
            <mo>+</mo>
            <mn>8</mn>
        </mrow>
        <mo>=</mo>
        <mn>0</mn>
    </mrow>
</math>
```

Want to take a look at the actual MathML document in a browser? You can't use Internet Explorer or Firefox, since they don't understand MathML, but you can use the World Wide Web Consortium's test browser, named Amaya, which does. Amaya is free for download at www.w3.org/Amaya, and it's often used as a testing ground for new things the W3C is doing.

You can see mathml.ml in the Amaya browser in Figure 1-7, where the equation $5x^2 - 2x + 8 = 0$ is displayed in all its glory.

Applications like MathML consist of an agreed-upon set of XML elements, and there are thousands of such applications, ranging from XML documents that are used to exchange financial information between banks to applications used to store genealogical data in an easily accessible way.

Programs that use these XML applications can either display the XML in browser fashion, as you see in Figure 1-7, or make use of the data in them without displaying it directly, such as financial data exchanged between banks. For example, there's a famous dedicated browser named Jumbo that you can use to read ChemML—chemistry markup language documents—to display complex molecules.

That gets us started with an overview of XML—let's start digging into XML deeper.

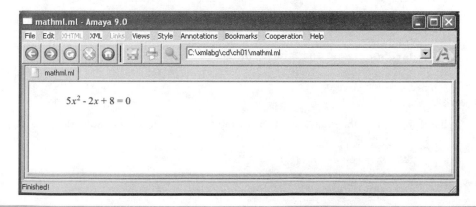

Figure 1-7 A MathML document

Well-Formed and Valid XML Documents

It turns out that there is more to say about XML documents than simply that they're XML documents. In fact, the W3C doesn't even consider a document an XML document unless it's *well formed.*

What's a well-formed XML document? Such documents follow a number of rules, such as rules that specify the legal names you can use for elements, rules that say you must start an XML document with an XML declaration, rules that say XML elements must be nested properly—for example, you can't mix opening and closing tags on the same level, like this:

```
<?xml version="1.0" encoding="UTF-8"?>
<?xml-stylesheet type="text/css" href="formatted.css"?>
<document>
    <greeting>
        Hello From XML
    <message>
    </greeting>
        Welcome to the wild and woolly world of XML!
    </message>
</document>
```

As you can see here, the message element starts before the greeting element is done, and that's obviously a problem.

The W3C puts great stress on using XML to accurately transmit data, which means that it doesn't even consider a document an XML document unless it's well formed. We're going to see the rules for well-formed XML documents in this chapter.

Making an XML document well formed is just the beginning. It can't be considered an XML document unless it's well formed, of course. But using XML, you can also check if your data is in the correct format. For example, say that you had this element in an XML document, and it gave a date:

```
<document>
    <customer>
        <name>
            <last_name>Grant</last_name>
            <first_name>Cary</first_name>
        </name>
        <date>October 25, 2009</date>
        .
        .
        .
```

What if the data in the <date> element wasn't a date at all, but was something like this?:

```
<document>
    <customer>
        <name>
            <last_name>Grant</last_name>
```

```
      <first_name>Cary</first_name>
</name>
<date>Donuts are good to eat.</date>
  .
  .
  .
```

It turns out that you can specify the syntax for XML documents—down to the type of data and even the range of data values you'll allow. For example, what if you had an element named <day_of_the_week> like this:

```
<day_of_the_week>6</day_of_the_week>
```

That's fine, because the day of the week can vary from 1 to 7. But what if you had this element?

```
<day_of_the_week>9</day_of_the_week>
```

Clearly, the data here, 9, is out of the legal range of values for the <day_of_the_week> element.

Using XML, you can specify the syntax of the XML dialect you're creating using either of two mechanisms—a Document Type Declaration (DTD) or an XML schema—and we'll see these two mechanisms at work in the next few chapters. You create a DTD or a schema for an XML document yourself, to allow the software reading that document (called an XML processor) to check the document, avoiding such errors as the ninth day of the week, for example.

If your XML document is checked against its DTD or schema and it checks out okay, your document is called *valid* (in addition to well formed).

So here's how to think of this: an XML document is *well formed* if it follows the W3C rules for well-formedness (legal element names, no nesting errors, and so on). Documents have to be well formed before they can be read by XML processors (such as the XML processor built into Internet Explorer or Firefox when it reads your document). In addition, if you specify the legal grammar or syntax of the document using a DTD or schema, and the XML processor confirms that your document adheres to that grammar or syntax, the document is considered *valid*.

So XML documents can be well formed, or both valid and well formed. You don't have to supply a DTD or schema when you write an XML document, but you do have to make sure the document is well formed.

Well-formedness will be covered in this chapter, and validity (DTDs first, then XML schema) in the next couple of chapters.

Let's start by taking a look at how to write a well-formed XML document, according to the W3C rules.

Writing a Well-Formed XML Document

The World Wide Web Consortium not only says that a document must be well formed before it can be called an XML document, it even says that an XML processor is supposed to quit, dead in the water, if it finds that a document is not well formed. The XML processor specifically isn't supposed to guess at what you meant in an XML document—if it finds a well-formedness error, it's just supposed to quit. Optionally, it can inform you of the error.

That's different from HTML browsers, which go to great lengths to correct the errors people make when writing HTML Web pages. By some estimates, over half the code in modern browsers is there to handle errors in peoples' Web pages. If your Web page has an HTML error, the browser is supposed to figure out what the problem is and fix it.

Not so in XML. An XML processor will just stop at the first sign of a well-formedness error. Frankly, this gives XML a more prickly and choosy feeling than HTML. That's because XML is considered more of an advanced language than HTML—there are fewer hobbyists writing XML, for example. The W3C puts great weight on accurate transmission of your data using XML, so there's no room for error. That's both good and bad—and it means that until you learn that, writing XML can feel frustrating. But making your XML error-free is definitely worth the effort.

Okay, let's start writing our well-formed XML document. This document will be a simple one, designed to keep track of the purchases of a number of customers. We'll have <first_name> and <last_name> elements, for example, and <price> elements.

Note that there are many, many rules about what makes an XML document well formed, and we're not going to be able to cover them all here—but we will cover all the rules that you're likely to ever need. Many of the rules are technical and do not concern us here, such as what advanced Unicode character may be used in a certain place (more on Unicode is coming up soon).

For the full well-formedness rules, or if you ever have any question, take a look at the official W3C XML 1.0 specification at: www.w3.org/TR/xml/, or the XML 1.1 specification, which you'll find at www.w3.org/TR/xml11/. You'll see all the well-formedness constraints in those documents.

What's the difference between XML 1.0 and 1.1? Thankfully, those differences don't concern us a great deal here. When XML 1.0 was written, the W3C didn't really have the rest of the world in mind, so it used a somewhat restricted character set for the characters that are considered legal in XML. XML 1.1 was all about making other, more advanced, characters legal. So in practical terms, the differences between XML 1.0 and 1.1 won't concern us in this book, with one or two small exceptions. Most XML processors are still written in terms of XML 1.0, in fact, as we're going to see.

Okay. The first well-formedness rule is that every XML document must start with an XML declaration, and we'll start our well-formed XML document, customers.xml, from there.

Start with an XML Declaration

Our goal is to write a well-formed XML document here that keeps track of the purchases made by various customers, and we'll call that document customers.xml. We'll start customers.xml out as we should, with an XML declaration:

```
<?xml version = "1.0" standalone="yes"?>
    .
    .
    .
```

The XML declaration isn't an XML element—it's just the XML declaration, which has a special form all its own, starting with <?xml and ending with ?>. There are three attributes in the XML declaration:

● **version**   The XML version; currently, only 1.0 or 1.1 are possible here (we'll be using 1.0 in this book). *This attribute is required if you use an XML declaration.*

● **encoding**   The language encoding for the document. As discussed next, the default here is UTF-8. You can also use Unicode, UCS-2 or UCS-4, and many other character sets, such as ISO character sets. *This attribute is optional.*

● **standalone**   Set to "yes" if the document does not refer to any external documents or items, "no" otherwise. *This attribute is optional.*

Note that the version attribute is required, but the other two are not. Note also that the encoding attribute sets the character set for the document. Here are a few words about encoding: the default encoding—if you omit the encoding attribute—is UTF-8 (Unicode Transformation Format 8).

The original computer character set was ASCII, which contained only 256 characters—but there are a lot more character sets out there in the world—such as Bengali, Armenian, Hebrew, Thai, Tibetan, Japanese Katakana, Arabic, Cyrillic, and others. So the W3C turned to Unicode, and in particular UTF-8, which expands the number of characters available into the millions. UTF-8 was built so that the first 256 characters corresponded to the ASCII set, however, which means that if you use a text editor like WordPad, you're writing in ASCII—which is also UTF-8 due to that overlap. (Note that WordPad can also save documents in Unicode.)

Besides UTF-8, there are also UTF-16, and iso-ir-126 (which is Greek), and ISO-10646-j-1 (Japanese). More character sets are available than those mentioned here; for a longer list, take a look at the list posted by the Internet Assigned Numbers Authority (IANA) at www.iana.org/assignments/character-sets.

So that's the XML declaration, which must be the first line in any XML document. It also turns out that the XML declaration can also be used as the first line of a *prolog*.

Putting in a Prolog

In XML documents, the prolog is made up of everything that comes before the document element. In general, prologs can contain XML declarations, comments, processing instructions, and doctype declaration(s).

XML documents don't need a prolog—they just need an XML declaration before the document element. But you can include prologs in any XML document. We'll take a look at the items that can appear in prologs next: comments, processing instructions, and doctype declaration(s).

Adding Comments

XML comments are just like HTML comments. You can use comments to include explanatory notes in your document that are ignored by XML processors; comments may appear anywhere in a document outside other markup. As in HTML, you start a comment with <!-- and end it with -->.

Here's an example of two comments:

```
<?xml version="1.0" encoding="UTF-8"?>
<document>
<!--Here is the greeting-->
    <greeting>
        Hello From XML
    </greeting>
<!--Here is the message-->
    <message>
        Welcome to the wild and woolly world of XML!
    </message>
</document>
```

Besides comments, you can also have XML processing instructions in the prolog.

Handling Processing Instructions

XML processing instructions are, you might not be surprised to hear, instructions to the XML processor. They start with <?xml-*name,* where *name* is the name of the processing instruction, and end with ?>.

Because these instructions are processor-specific, there are no processing instructions built into XML. However, there are a number of popular processing instructions that have been agreed to by various processors, such as the <?xml-stylesheet?> processing instruction we used earlier in this chapter to connect a CSS stylesheet with an XML document:

```
<?xml version="1.0" encoding="UTF-8"?>
<?xml-stylesheet type="text/css" href="formatted.css"?>
<document>
    <greeting>
        Hello From XML
    </greeting>
    <message>
        Welcome to the wild and woolly world of XML!
    </message>
</document>
```

What processing instructions can you use? Any that are supported by the XML processor that you're working with. The most popular processing instruction is <?xml-stylesheet?>, and we'll see it in use throughout the book.

Checking Syntax with a DTD

The other item that can appear in a prolog—that part of an XML document that appears before the document element—is a DTD, which, as you know, is used to check the syntax of a document.

DTDs can take a whole chapter by themselves—and in fact, they do, because that's what Chapter 2 is all about—but let's get an advance thrill by taking a look at what the DTD for the customers.xml document we're writing looks like. A DTD uses its own elements to declare what's legal in the syntax of the rest of the document—and here's what the DTD for customers.xml would look like, were we giving it a DTD (which we won't, in this chapter):

```
<?xml version = "1.0" standalone="yes"?>
<!DOCTYPE document [
<!ELEMENT document (customer)*>
<!ELEMENT customer (name,date,orders)>
<!ELEMENT name (last_name,first_name)>
<!ELEMENT last_name (#PCDATA)>
<!ELEMENT first_name (#PCDATA)>
<!ELEMENT date (#PCDATA)>
<!ELEMENT orders (ITEM)*>
<!ELEMENT item (product,number,price)>
<!ELEMENT product (#PCDATA)>
<!ELEMENT number (#PCDATA)>
<!ELEMENT price (#PCDATA)>
]>
<document>
    <customer>
        <name>
            <last_name>Grant</last_name>
            <first_name>Cary</first_name>
        </name>
        <date>October 25, 2009</date>
            .
            .
            .
```

The full details on DTDs are coming up in the next chapter.

Okay, now we've taken a look at the items that can appear in a well-formed XML document's prolog—XML declarations, comments, processing instructions, and doctype declaration(s).

So how about the XML *elements*? That's coming up next.

Storing Your Data in XML Elements

Okay, now we get to the real meat of XML documents—the XML elements that actually contain the data. The W3C well-formedness rules say that if you have any elements in an XML document, they need to all be enclosed in a single *document element.*

In other words, if you look at an XML document as a tree of elements, the document element is the root of all the elements—and there can only be one root per document.

In our example, customers.xml, we'll call the document element <document> to emphasize that it is the document element, but you can use any legal XML element name. Here's what the document element looks like:

```
<?xml version = "1.0" standalone="yes"?>
<document>
        .
        .
        .
</document>
```

There are well-formedness rules for the names you can use in tag names. In fact, the XML specification is very specific about tag names; you can start a tag name with a letter, an underscore, or a colon. The next characters may be letters, digits, underscores, hyphens, periods, or colons (but no white space).

For example, here are some allowed XML tags:

```
<a64324>
<DOCUMENT>
<document>
<_Record>
<customer>
<PRODUCT>
```

Note that because XML processors are case sensitive, the <DOCUMENT> tag is not the same as a <document> tag.

Here are the corresponding closing tags:

```
</a64324>
</DOCUMENT>
</document>
</_Record>
</customer>
</PRODUCT>
```

Here are some tags that XML considers illegal:

```
<2009DOCUMENT>
<.document>
<Record Number>
<customer*name>
<PRODUCT(ID)>
```

To be well formed, a document must contain at least one element—that is, at least a document element.

Elements that can contain content—called non-empty elements—can contain either other elements or text. All non-empty elements must have an opening tag and a closing tag. That's different from HTML, where you can use elements without closing tags, such as the <img> tag, and browsers will know what you mean. In XML, it's important that if you have a non-empty element, you must have both an opening tag and a closing tag.

Armed with that knowledge, we can put together our customers.xml document to store data about customer purchases. We already have a document element, <document>, and now we can store data about an individual customer using a <customer> element:

```
<?xml version = "1.0" standalone="yes"?>
<document>
    <customer>
        .
        .
        .
    </customer>
</document>
```

There's an example of an element containing another element. We can also add a <name> element that has two child elements—<first_name> and <last_name>:

```
<?xml version = "1.0" standalone="yes"?>
<document>
    <customer>
        <name>
            <last_name>Grant</last_name>
            <first_name>Cary</first_name>
        </name>
            .
            .
            .
    </customer>
</document>
```

Note that here, we not only have an element (<name>) that contains other elements, but elements (**<last_name>** and **<first_name>**) that contain text. That's the two options for non-empty XML elements—they can contain text or other elements.

For each customer, we can also have a <date> element, indicating the date of the stored information, and an <orders> element that will contain the orders of the customer:

```
<?xml version = "1.0" standalone="yes"?>
<document>
    <customer>
        <name>
            <last_name>Grant</last_name>
            <first_name>Cary</first_name>
        </name>
        <date>October 25, 2009</date>
        <orders>
            .
            .
            .
        </orders>
    </customer>
</document>
```

Each customer may purchase several items, so inside the <orders> element, we can set up one <item> element for each purchased item:

```
<?xml version = "1.0" standalone="yes"?>
<document>
    <customer>
        <name>
            <last_name>Grant</last_name>
            <first_name>Cary</first_name>
        </name>
```

```
            <date>October 25, 2009</date>
            <orders>
                <item>
                      .
                      .
                      .
                </item>
                <item>
                      .
                      .
                      .
                </item>
            </orders>
        </customer>
</document>
```

Each item can have a <product> element indicating the product that was purchased:

```
<?xml version = "1.0" standalone="yes"?>
<document>
    <customer>
        <name>
            <last_name>Grant</last_name>
            <first_name>Cary</first_name>
        </name>
        <date>October 25, 2009</date>
        <orders>
            <item>
                <product>laser printer</product>
                     .
                     .
                     .
            </item>
            <item>
                <product>ink jet printer</product>
                     .
                     .
                     .
            </item>
        </orders>
    </customer>
</document>
```

And a <number> element to indicate the number of the item purchased:

```
<?xml version = "1.0" standalone="yes"?>
<document>
    <customer>
        <name>
```

```
            <last_name>Grant</last_name>
            <first_name>Cary</first_name>
        </name>
        <date>October 25, 2009</date>
        <orders>
            <item>
                <product>laser printer</product>
                <number>8</number>

                        .
                        .
                        .

            </item>
            <item>
                <product>ink jet printer</product>
                <number>24</number>

                        .
                        .
                        .

            </item>
        </orders>
    </customer>
</document>
```

And a <price> element, giving the price per item:

```
<?xml version = "1.0" standalone="yes"?>
document>
    <customer>
        <name>
            <last_name>Grant</last_name>
            <first_name>Cary</first_name>
        </name>
        <date>October 25, 2009</date>
        <orders>
            <item>
                <product>laser printer</product>
                <number>8</number>
                <price>$111.25</price>
            </item>
            <item>
                <product>ink jet printer</product>
                <number>24</number>
                <price>$44.98</price>
            </item>
        </orders>
    </customer>
</document>
```

That's it for one customer, but of course you can put as many as you want into customers.xml:

```
<?xml version = "1.0" standalone="yes"?>
<document>
    <customer>
        <name>
            <last_name>Grant</last_name>
            <first_name>Cary</first_name>
        </name>
        <date>October 25, 2009</date>
        <orders>
            <item>
                <product>laser printer</product>
                <number>8</number>
                <price>$111.25</price>
            </item>
            <item>
                <product>ink jet printer</product>
                <number>24</number>
                <price>$44.98</price>
            </item>
        </orders>
    </customer>
    <customer>
        <name>
            <last_name>Loy</last_name>
            <first_name>Myrna</first_name>
        </name>
        <date>October 25, 2009</date>
        <orders>
            <item>
                <product>flat screen</product>
                <number>12</number>
                <price>$344.95</price>
            </item>
            <item>
                <product>computer screen</product>
                <number>6</number>
                <price>$111.50</price>
            </item>
        </orders>
    </customer>
    <customer>
        <name>
            <last_name>Stewart</last_name>
            <first_name>Jimmy</first_name>
        </name>
        <date>October 25, 2009</date>
        <orders>
```

```
            <item>
                <product>CPU</product>
                <number>12</number>
                <price>$1452.95</price>
            </item>
            <item>
                <product>disk drive</product>
                <number>6</number>
                <price>$119.50</price>
            </item>
        </orders>
    </customer>
</document>
```

And that's a perfectly good well-formed XML document.

You can also have empty elements in XML—these elements don't have any content, and they're made up of a single tag. You can use empty elements whenever an element doesn't need any child elements or text in it. For example, for our best-paying customers, we might include an empty element named <pays_on_time/> like this:

```
<?xml version = "1.0" standalone="yes"?>
<document>
    <customer>
        <name>
            <last_name>Grant</last_name>
            <first_name>Cary</first_name>
        </name>
        <pays_on_time/>
        <date>October 25, 2009</date>
        <orders>
            <item>
                <product>laser printer</product>
                <number>8</number>
                <price>$111.25</price>
            </item>
            <item>
                <product>ink jet printer</product>
                <number>24</number>
                <price>$44.98</price>
            </item>
        </orders>
    </customer>
</document>
```

Note the final /> in <pays_on_time/>. That's the way you end an empty element in XML—with />. For an XML document to be well formed, all its empty elements must end with />.

In addition, elements can have attributes in XML.

Adding XML Attributes

Attributes in XML work much as they do in HTML—they're single words that appear in the opening tag of an element—or in an empty element—that you assign a value to with an equal sign. For example, we might add a gender attribute to each <customer> element, and ID and reference_number attributes to each <item> element like this:

```
<?xml version = "1.0" standalone="yes"?>
<document>
    <customer gender="male">
        <name>
            <last_name>Grant</last_name>
            <first_name>Cary</first_name>
        </name>
        <date>October 25, 2009</date>
        <orders>
            <item id="423" reference_number="943">
                <product>laser printer</product>
                <number>8</number>
                <price>$111.25</price>
            </item>
            <item id="483" reference_number="9876">
                <product>ink jet printer</product>
                <number>24</number>
                <price>$44.98</price>
            </item>
        </orders>
    </customer>
    <customer gender="female">
        <name>
            <last_name>Loy</last_name>
            <first_name>Myrna</first_name>
        </name>
        <date>October 25, 2009</date>
        <orders>
            <item id="477" reference_number="97654">
                <product>flat screen</product>
                <number>12</number>
                <price>$344.95</price>
            </item>
            <item id="464" reference_number="56544">
                <product>computer screen</product>
                <number>6</number>
                <price>$111.50</price>
            </item>
        </orders>
    </customer>
    <customer gender="male">
        <name>
            <last_name>Stewart</last_name>
```

```
            <first_name>Jimmy</first_name>
        </name>
        <date>October 25, 2009</date>
        <orders>
            <item id="421" reference_number="54334">
                <product>CPU</product>
                <number>12</number>
                <price>$1452.95</price>
            </item>
            <item id="411" reference_number="43432">
                <product>disk drive</product>
                <number>6</number>
                <price>$119.50</price>
            </item>
        </orders>
    </customer>
</document>
```

Want proof that this is a well-formed XML document? Open it in a browser, as shown in Figure 1-8. All browsers that can open XML documents have built-in XML processors, and if there are any well-formedness errors, the browser won't open the document but will display an error instead.

As you know, one of the well-formedness rules (in fact, the main one) is that there must be no nesting errors in the document. What would a browser say if we deliberately introduced a nesting error by swapping the end tags for the <customer> and <orders> elements, like this?

```
<?xml version = "1.0" standalone="yes"?>
<document>
    <customer gender="male">
        <name>
            <last_name>Grant</last_name>
            <first_name>Cary</first_name>
        </name>
        <date>October 25, 2009</date>
        <orders>
            <item id="423" reference_number="943">
                <product>laser printer</product>
                <number>8</number>
                <price>$111.25</price>
            </item>
            <item id="483" reference_number="9876">
                <product>ink jet printer</product>
                <number>24</number>
                <price>$44.98</price>
            </item>
        </customer>
    </orders>
        .
        .
        .
</document>
```

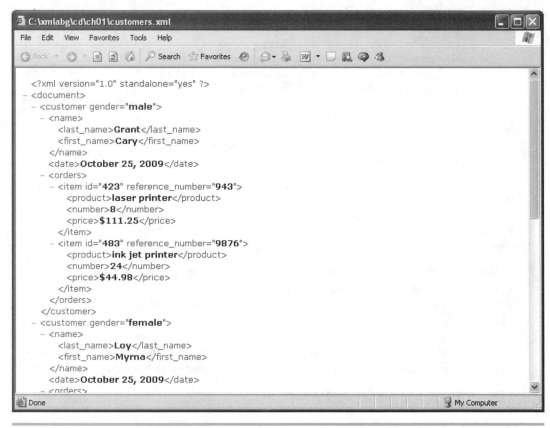

Figure 1-8 The customers.xml document in Internet Explorer

You can see the answer in Figure 1-9—Internet Explorer caught the error and is reporting it. Cool.

In well-formed XML documents, attribute names must follow the same rules as for tag names, which means that you can start an attribute name with a letter, an underscore, or a colon. The next characters may be letters, digits, underscores, hyphens, periods, and colons (but no whitespace, because you separate attribute name-value pairs with whitespace). Here are some examples showing legal attribute names:

```
<circle origin_x="10.0" origin_y="20.0" radius="10.0" />
<image src="image1.jpg">
<pen color="red" width="5">
<book pages="1231" >
```

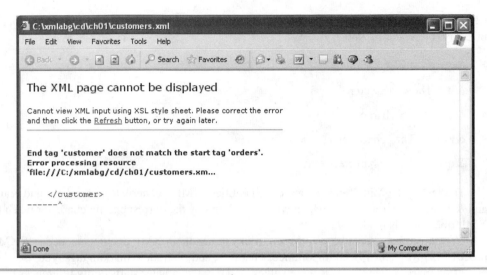

Figure 1-9   A nesting error in customers.xml

And here are some illegal attribute names:

```
<circle 1origin_x="10.0" 1origin_y="20.0" 1radius="10.0" />
<image src name="image1.jpg">
<pen color@="red" width@="5">
<book pages(exluding front matter)="1231" >
```

Here's another key well-formedness rule: every value you assign to an attribute in a well-formed XML document must be in quotes. You can use single quotes or double quotes, but you must enclose all attribute values in quotes.

That's unlike HTML, which doesn't require that you use quotation marks for attribute values. But believe it or not, if you don't enclose attribute values in quotation marks, it'll stop an XML processor cold.

Another well-formedness rule is that each element must have unique attributes—that is, you can't give two attributes in the same element the same name. So this is illegal:

```
<image src="image1.jpg" src="image2.jpg">
```

Use Only the Predefined Entity References

There's another form of markup besides the < and > used for elements in XML documents—you can also use & and ; just as you can in HTML—for example, the HTML © is replaced by the © symbol.

The items you set off with *&* and *;* are called *entity references,* and here are the five built-in entity references in XML:

- **&amp**   The & character

- **&lt**   The < character

- **&gt**   The > character

- **&apos**   The ' character

- **&quot**   The " character

The terms like "amp" and "lt" are called entities (XML's generic term for data) and & and < are entity references, which will be replaced by the corresponding character when the XML document is read.

Normally, characters like < and > are tricky to handle in XML documents, because XML processors give them special importance. That is, < and > straddle markup tags, you use quotation marks to surround attribute values, and the *&* character starts entity references. Replacing them with the preceding entity references makes them safe, because the XML processor will replace them with the appropriate character when processing the document.

Here's an example, entities.xml:

```
<?xml version = "1.0" standalone="yes"?>
<document>
   I like Ben &amp; Jerry&apos;s ice cream.
</document>
```

And you can see what entities.xml looks like in a browser in Figure 1-10.

Using these predefined entity references for sensitive characters like < and > is one way to tell the XML processor not to get confused by those characters. There's another way to do that as well—that is, turn off XML processing for a moment—and that's CDATA (character data) sections.

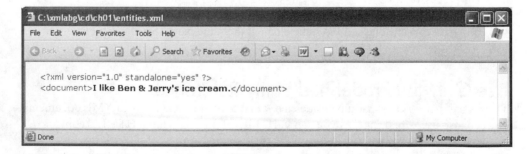

Figure 1-10   Using entity references

CDATA Sections

XML processors are very sensitive to characters like < and &. So what if you had a large section of text that contained a great many < and & characters that you didn't want to interpret as markup? You can use entity references like < and &, of course, but with many such characters, that's awkward and hard to read. Instead, you can use a CDATA section.

CDATA sections hold character data that is supposed to remain unparsed—that is, unread—by the XML processor. This is a useful thing in XML, because otherwise all the text in an XML document is parsed and searched for characters like < and &. You use CDATA section simply to tell the XML processor to leave the enclosed text alone, and pass it on unchanged to the underlying application.

You start a CDATA section with the markup <![CDATA[and end it with]]>. Here's an example, cdata.xml; in this case, we'll include the text of a <customer> element in a CDATA section as a text example of what a <customer> element should look like:

```
<?xml version = "1.0" standalone="yes"?>
<document>
  <example>
    <![CDATA[
    This is what a <customer> element looks like:
    <customer gender="male">
        <name>
            <last_name>Grant</last_name>
            <first_name>Cary</first_name>
        </name>
        <date>October 25, 2009</date>
        <orders>
            <item id="423" reference_number="943">
                <product>laser printer</product>
                <number>8</number>
                <price>$111.25</price>
            </item>
            <item id="483" reference_number="9876">
                <product>ink jet printer</product>
                <number>24</number>
                <price>$44.98</price>
            </item>
        </orders>
    </customer>
    ]]>
  </example>
</document>
```

You can see the results in Figure 1-11. There, the text in the CDATA section is just treated as a CDATA section—that is, the XML processor doesn't read it, but just passes it on, unread.

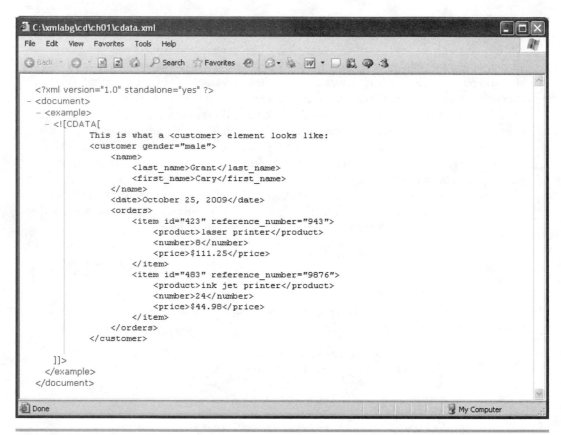

Figure 1-11   Using a CDATA section

And that is how CDATA sections work—they just tell the XML processor to stop processing for a moment. And that completes our coverage of well-formed XML documents. As already mentioned, we haven't covered all the well-formedness rules, but we've covered all the ones you're likely to run into. If you have a well-formedness issue that's giving you trouble, check with the XML 1.0 and 1.1 specifications themselves. All the well-formedness rules are in those documents.

Chapter 2

Creating Valid XML
Documents: Document
Type Definitions

Key Skills & Concepts

- Valid XML document

- Introducing DTDs

- Creating a DTD

- Declaring elements

- Declaring attributes

- Using an XML validator

This chapter starts to explore how to *validate* XML documents. When you validate an XML document, you check it against the grammar rules you've specified for it. For example—take a look at this XML:

```
<customer>
    <name>
        <last_name>Grant</last_name>
        <first_name>Cary</first_name>
    </name>
    <date>October 25, 2009</date>
    <orders>
        <item>
            <product>laser printer</product>
            <number>8</number>
            <price>$111.25</price>
        </item>
        <item>
            <product>ink jet printer</product>
            <number>24</number>
            <price>$44.98</price>
        </item>
    </orders>
</customer>
```

A validating XML processor can check to make sure this XML is structured the way you want to allow. Is a <last_name> element inside a <name> element legal? Should it come before or after the <first_name> element? Can an <orders> element contain multiple <item> elements? All these are things you can specify when you validate an XML document.

Remember, the emphasis in XML is data, and it's important that your data be transferred accurately. That means it's often advisable to set up the grammar rules for an XML document and let the XML processor validate your document—XML processors that can do that are called validating processors.

There are two ways to validate XML—with document type definitions (DTDs) and with XML schemas. This chapter is on DTDs, and the next is on XML schemas.

DTDs represent the original way to validate XML documents—in fact, DTDs are built into the XML 1.0 specification. You'll find all the rules for DTDs in that specification at www.w3.org/TR/xml/.

We'll get started with DTDs immediately.

Validating XML Documents

Want to see what a DTD looks like? Here's a DTD for our customers.xml document that we created in the preceding chapter in a new document, customersDTD.xml:

```
<?xml version = "1.0" standalone="yes"?>
<!DOCTYPE document [
<!ELEMENT document (customer)*>
<!ELEMENT customer (name,date,orders)>
<!ELEMENT name (last_name,first_name)>
<!ELEMENT last_name (#PCDATA)>
<!ELEMENT first_name (#PCDATA)>
<!ELEMENT date (#PCDATA)>
<!ELEMENT orders (item)*>
<!ELEMENT item (product,number,price)>
<!ELEMENT product (#PCDATA)>
<!ELEMENT number (#PCDATA)>
<!ELEMENT price (#PCDATA)>
]>
<document>
    <customer>
        <name>
            <last_name>Grant</last_name>
            <first_name>Cary</first_name>
        </name>
        <date>October 25, 2009</date>
        <orders>
            <item>
                <product>laser printer</product>
                <number>8</number>
                <price>$111.25</price>
            </item>
            <item>
                <product>ink jet printer</product>
                <number>24</number>
                <price>$44.98</price>
            </item>
        </orders>
    </customer>
```

```xml
<customer>
    <name>
        <last_name>Loy</last_name>
        <first_name>Myrna</first_name>
    </name>
    <date>October 25, 2009</date>
    <orders>
        <item>
            <product>flat screen</product>
            <number>12</number>
            <price>$344.95</price>
        </item>
        <item>
            <product>computer screen</product>
            <number>6</number>
            <price>$111.50</price>
        </item>
    </orders>
</customer>
<customer>
    <name>
        <last_name>Stewart</last_name>
        <first_name>Jimmy</first_name>
    </name>
    <date>October 25, 2009</date>
    <orders>
        <item>
            <product>CPU</product>
            <number>12</number>
            <price>$1452.95</price>
        </item>
        <item>
            <product>disk drive</product>
            <number>6</number>
            <price>$119.50</price>
        </item>
    </orders>
</customer>
</document>
```

This DTD might look a little odd, and we're going to decipher it in this chapter.

The idea is that you can use a DTD to validate your XML document, and you do that with an XML validator—that is, software. Here's a list of some available DTD validators:

- **W3C XML validator, validator.w3.org/** The official W3C HTML validator. Although it's officially for HTML, it also includes some XML support. Your XML document must be online to be checked with this validator.

- **Tidy www.w3.org/People/Raggett/tidy/**   Tidy is a beloved utility for cleaning up and repairing Web pages, and it includes limited support for XML. Your XML document must be online to be checked with this validator.

- **www.stg.brown.edu/service/xmlvalid/**   The excellent XML validator from the Scholarly Technology Group at Brown University. This is the only online XML validator that I know of that allows you to check XML documents that are not online—you can use the Web page's file upload control to specify the name of the file on your hard disk you want to have uploaded and checked.

In this chapter, we'll use the XML validator from the Scholarly Technology Group at Brown University, at www.stg.brown.edu/service/xmlvalid/. You can see that site in Figure 2-1, where I've clicked the Browse button and browsed to customersDTD.xml.

Clicking the Validate button in Figure 2-1 brings us to Figure 2-2, where the Scholarly Technology Group validator uploaded customersDTD.xml and validated the document.

If there had been any errors, the validator would have listed them. Cool—we've validated our first document.

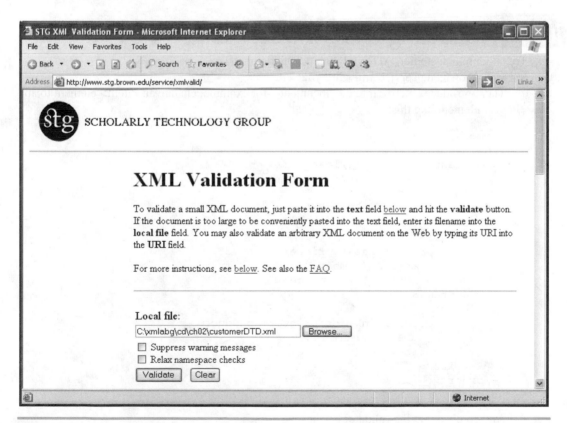

Figure 2-1   An online validator

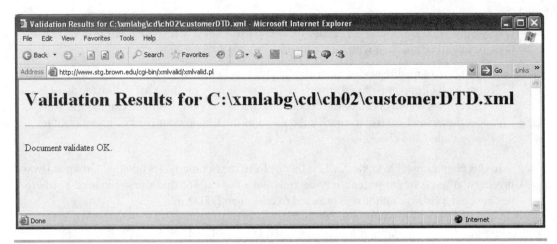

Figure 2-2 Validating an XML document

Try This Validating an XML Document

Try validating customersDTD.xml with the validator at
www.stg.brown.edu/service/xmlvalid/ yourself.

Then introduce an error into the document—for example, change an <item> element to an
<items> element like this:

```
<customer>
    <name>
        <last_name>Grant</last_name>
        <first_name>Cary</first_name>
    </name>
    <date>October 25, 2009</date>
    <orders>
        <items>
            <product>laser printer</product>
            <number>8</number>
            <price>$111.25</price>
        </items>
        <item>
            <product>ink jet printer</product>
            <number>24</number>
            <price>$44.98</price>
        </item>
    </orders>
</customer>
```

And confirm that the validator catches the error.

Now that we've validated our customersDTD.xml document, let's take it apart. We'll start by seeing how to set up a DTD.

Creating a DTD

To create a DTD, you use a <!DOCTYPE> element, as you see in customersDTD.xml:

```
<?xml version = "1.0" standalone="yes"?>
<!DOCTYPE document [
<!ELEMENT document (customer)*>
<!ELEMENT customer (name,date,orders)>
<!ELEMENT name (last_name,first_name)>
<!ELEMENT last_name (#PCDATA)>
<!ELEMENT first_name (#PCDATA)>
<!ELEMENT date (#PCDATA)>
<!ELEMENT orders (item)*>
<!ELEMENT item (product,number,price)>
<!ELEMENT product (#PCDATA)>
<!ELEMENT number (#PCDATA)>
<!ELEMENT price (#PCDATA)>
]>
<document>
    <customer>
        <name>
            <last_name>Grant</last_name>
            <first_name>Cary</first_name>
                .
                .
                .
```

The <!DOCTYPE> element encloses the actual DTD, which is placed between square brackets, [and]. If you've noticed that <!DOCTYPE> isn't exactly a proper XML element, you'd be right—it's not. Nor are the other elements you use inside a DTD to declare the XML elements and attributes in your document. In fact, that's one of the gripes that some people had with DTDs that led to the rise of XML schemas—every element you use in an XML schema is proper XML.

There are several ways to use the <!DOCTYPE> element, and we're using the first and most common way here:

```
<!DOCTYPE documentelement [DTD]>
```

That is, you have to give the document element name in the <!DOCTYPE> element before you actually add the DTD, which appears in brackets. In customersDTD.xml, the document element is just <document>, which means the <!DOCTYPE> element looks like this:

```
<?xml version = "1.0" standalone="yes"?>
<!DOCTYPE document [
```

```
      .
      .
  DTD goes here
      .
      .

]>
```

That's the usual way to create a DTD that's internal to an XML document. However, there are other ways to create DTDs—you can make them external to a document, which is very useful if the DTD is long and used by many documents. For example, your corporation might have a long DTD that you use for all your XML documents, and instead of including it in every document, you might just want to reference it in your XML documents so that the XML processor will know where to find it.

And it turns out that there are two types of external DTDs—those that are private (private to your group, for example) and those that are public (for public consumption). When you're referencing an external DTD, you use the keyword SYSTEM for a private DTD, and the keyword PUBLIC for a public DTD. And when you have an external DTD, you give the URL at which that DTD can be found in the <!DOCTYPE> element.

Here are the ways to use the <!DOCTYPE> element to create DTDs—we'll see how to create external DTDs (that's the last four variations on the <!DOCTYPE> element here) later in this chapter:

- <!DOCTYPE *documentelement* [*DTD*]>

- <!DOCTYPE *documentelement* SYSTEM *URL*>

- <!DOCTYPE *documentelement* SYSTEM *URL* [*DTD*]>

- <!DOCTYPE *documentelement* PUBLIC *identifier URL*>

- <!DOCTYPE *documentelement* PUBLIC *identifier URL* [*DTD*]>

Okay, now we've gotten our <!DOCTYPE> element for an internal DTD. The next step is to actually start declaring the grammar rules for the XML elements in customersDTD.xml in that DTD.

Declaring Elements in DTDs

Now we have to set up the grammar rules for the elements and attributes of our XML document, can an <orders> element contain <date> elements? Does a <last_name> element contain text or other elements? All these will be specified in our DTD.

To declare the syntax of an element in a DTD, you use the <!ELEMENT> element like this:

```
<!ELEMENT name content_model>
```

Here, *name* is the name of the element you're declaring and *content_model* is the content model of the element—that is, what the element can legally contain. The content model you use to declare elements can be set to

- ANY (any content at all is allowed)
- Child elements
- Text
- EMPTY (the element does not contain any content)

Let's take a look at these various possibilities.

Content Model: ANY

The first, and most lenient, content model you can specify for elements is ANY, which means that the element you're declaring may have any content at all. In practical terms, declaring an element with a content model of ANY just turns off validation for that element.

For example, in our customersDTD.xml document, here's how we could specify that the <document> element can contain any content, using a content model of ANY in the DTD:

```
<?xml version = "1.0" standalone="yes"?>
<!DOCTYPE document [
<!ELEMENT document ANY>
]>
<document>
</document>
```

This DTD means that you can use any content in the <document> element—text, other elements, or a mix of the two. Obviously, a content model of ANY just turns off validation for that element, and you'll see it used only very rarely.

Content Model: Child Elements

Take a look at a customer element in customersDTD.xml:

```
<customer>
    <name>
        <last_name>Grant</last_name>
        <first_name>Cary</first_name>
    </name>
    <date>October 25, 2009</date>
    <orders>
        <items>
            <product>laser printer</product>
            <number>8</number>
            <price>$111.25</price>
        </items>
        <item>
            <product>ink jet printer</product>
            <number>24</number>
            <price>$44.98</price>
        </item>
    </orders>
</customer>
```

Assuming we don't want to declare this element with a content model of ANY, how can we specify its possible content? That content is a <name> element, a <date> element, and an <orders> element in that order:

```
<customer>
    <name>
        .
        .
        .
    </name>
    <date>
        .
        .
        .
    </date>
    <orders>
        .
        .
        .
    </orders>
</customer>
```

You can list those child elements of the <customer> elements, in order, like this in the <!ELEMENT> element:

```
<?xml version = "1.0" standalone="yes"?>
<!DOCTYPE document [
<!ELEMENT customer (name,date,orders)>
    .
    .
    .

]>
```

That's the way you specify that an element can have various child elements, and in what order—the content model is given in parentheses, like (name,date,orders), which says that the <customer> element must have a <name> child element, followed by a <date> child element, followed by an <orders> child element.

And that's the way that you declare that an element has content that consists of child elements.

Content Model: Text

Take a look at the <date> element:

```
<customer>
    <name>
        <last_name>Grant</last_name>
        <first_name>Cary</first_name>
    </name>
```

```
    <date>October 25, 2009</date>
    <orders>
        <items>
            <product>laser printer</product>
            <number>8</number>
            <price>$111.25</price>
        </items>
        <item>
            <product>ink jet printer</product>
            <number>24</number>
            <price>$44.98</price>
        </item>
    </orders>
</customer>
```

This element doesn't contain child elements—it only contains text. How can you declare an element that contains text?

You use the #PCDATA content model. In DTDs, #PCDATA stands for parsed character data—that is, text that's already been parsed. Here's how you would declare the <date> element in the DTD so that it would have text content:

```
<?xml version = "1.0" standalone="yes"?>
<!DOCTYPE document [
<!ELEMENT date (#PCDATA)>
            .
            .
            .

]>
```

That's how you declare an element that has text content—by giving it a content model of #PCDATA. So now you know how to declare elements that contain child elements, and those that contain text.

Content Model: Multiple Children

Take a look at the <document> element in customersDTD.xml:

```
<?xml version = "1.0" standalone="yes"?>
<document>
    <customer>
            .
            .
            .

    </customer>
    <customer>
            .
            .
            .

    </customer>
```

```
    <customer>
        .
        .
        .
    </customer>
</document>
```

It's got three <customer> child elements—that is, three of the same type of elements. How do you handle that? You could do something like this:

```
<!DOCTYPE document [
<!ELEMENT document (customer, customer, customer)>
        .
        .
        .
]>
```

That specifies that the <document> element has three <customer> children alright, but what if there were four <customer> children? Or five?

You can specify that the <document> element has zero or more <customer> child elements using an asterisk (*) like this:

```
<!DOCTYPE document [
<!ELEMENT document (customer)*>
        .
        .
        .
]>
```

In a DTD, an asterisk is the sign for "zero or more." Here are the possible symbols:

- **a+** One or more occurrences of a
- **a*** Zero or more occurrences of a
- **a?** a or nothing
- **a, b** a followed by b
- **a | b** a or b but not both

For example, if you wanted to specify that a <document> element must contain one or more <customer> elements, you could do that this way in a DTD:

```
<!DOCTYPE document [
<!ELEMENT document (customer)+>
        .
        .
        .
]>
```

Try This   Be Your Own Validator

You now know everything you need to validate customersDTD.xml. Try working through the document and its entire DTD, validating the document as you go:

```
<?xml version = "1.0" standalone="yes"?>
<!DOCTYPE document [
<!ELEMENT document (customer)*>
<!ELEMENT customer (name,date,orders)>
<!ELEMENT name (last_name,first_name)>
<!ELEMENT last_name (#PCDATA)>
<!ELEMENT first_name (#PCDATA)>
<!ELEMENT date (#PCDATA)>
<!ELEMENT orders (item)*>
<!ELEMENT item (product,number,price)>
<!ELEMENT product (#PCDATA)>
<!ELEMENT number (#PCDATA)>
<!ELEMENT price (#PCDATA)>
]>
<document>
    <customer>
        <name>
            <last_name>Grant</last_name>
            <first_name>Cary</first_name>
        </name>
        <date>October 25, 2009</date>
        <orders>
            <item>
                <product>laser printer</product>
                <number>8</number>
                <price>$111.25</price>
            </item>
            <item>
                <product>ink jet printer</product>
                <number>24</number>
                <price>$44.98</price>
            </item>
        </orders>
    </customer>
    <customer>
        <name>
            <last_name>Loy</last_name>
            <first_name>Myrna</first_name>
        </name>
```

(continued)

```
        <date>October 25, 2009</date>
        <orders>
            <item>
                <product>flat screen</product>
                <number>12</number>
                <price>$344.95</price>
            </item>
            <item>
                <product>computer screen</product>
                <number>6</number>
                <price>$111.50</price>
            </item>
        </orders>
    </customer>
    <customer>
        <name>
            <last_name>Stewart</last_name>
            <first_name>Jimmy</first_name>
        </name>
        <date>October 25, 2009</date>
        <orders>
            <item>
                <product>CPU</product>
                <number>12</number>
                <price>$1452.95</price>
            </item>
            <item>
                <product>disk drive</product>
                <number>6</number>
                <price>$119.50</price>
            </item>
        </orders>
    </customer>
</document>
```

It's important to note that if you're validating an XML document using a DTD, every element must be declared in the DTD.

So far, we've just used the symbols +, *, and so on like this—to specify a number of <customer> elements:

```
<!ELEMENT document (customer)*>
```

But you can also create sequences using parentheses, like this:

```
<!ELEMENT document (customer, type, record)*>
```

In fact, it can get more complex than that—you can do things like this as well:

```
<!ELEMENT customer ((name,credit_rating?)+,date*,orders)>
```

So you can have multiple sequences using parentheses and *, +, ?, and so on. Note that you also have more precise control than just using *, +, ?, and so on—you can actually specify the number of specific elements at specific locations in your document like this:

```
<!ELEMENT document (customer, customer, customer)>
```

As you can see, DTDs give you fairly good control over what elements appear in what order in your document. However, DTDs don't give you any control over the content of those elements besides the various content models we're discussing—but with schemas, as we'll see, you can specify the legal content of elements with much more precision: instead of just text, you can also say that an element must contain a floating point number, a date, an integer, and so on.

Content Model: EMPTY

Your XML document may also include empty elements, like this empty element for customers who pay on time:

```
<customer>
    <name>
        <last_name>Grant</last_name>
        <first_name>Cary</first_name>
    </name>
    <date>October 25, 2009</date>
    <pays_on_time/>
    <orders>
        <item>
            <product>laser printer</product>
            <number>8</number>
            <price>$111.25</price>
        </item>
        <item>
            <product>ink jet printer</product>
            <number>24</number>
            <price>$44.98</price>
        </item>
    </orders>
</customer>
```

You can create empty elements with the content model EMPTY, which looks like this in a DTD:

```
<?xml version = "1.0" standalone="yes"?>
<!DOCTYPE document [
<!ELEMENT document (customer)*>
<!ELEMENT customer (name,date,orders)>
<!ELEMENT name (last_name,first_name)>
```

```
<!ELEMENT last_name (#PCDATA)>
<!ELEMENT first_name (#PCDATA)>
<!ELEMENT date (#PCDATA)>
<!ELEMENT pays_on_time EMPTY>
<!ELEMENT orders (item)*>
<!ELEMENT item (product,number,price)>
<!ELEMENT product (#PCDATA)>
<!ELEMENT number (#PCDATA)>
<!ELEMENT price (#PCDATA)>
]>
```

Note that we should make this element optional, which we can do with a *?* like this:

```
<?xml version = "1.0" standalone="yes"?>
<!DOCTYPE document [
<!ELEMENT document (customer)*>
<!ELEMENT customer (name,date,pays_on_time?,orders)>
<!ELEMENT name (last_name,first_name)>
<!ELEMENT last_name (#PCDATA)>
<!ELEMENT first_name (#PCDATA)>
<!ELEMENT date (#PCDATA)>
<!ELEMENT pays_on_time EMPTY>
<!ELEMENT orders (item)*>
<!ELEMENT item (product,number,price)>
<!ELEMENT product (#PCDATA)>
<!ELEMENT number (#PCDATA)>
<!ELEMENT price (#PCDATA)>
]>
```

Now we're free to use this new empty element in the XML document:

```
<?xml version = "1.0" standalone="yes"?>
<!DOCTYPE document [
<!ELEMENT document (customer)*>
<!ELEMENT customer (name,date,pays_on_time?,orders)>
<!ELEMENT name (last_name,first_name)>
<!ELEMENT last_name (#PCDATA)>
<!ELEMENT first_name (#PCDATA)>
<!ELEMENT date (#PCDATA)>
<!ELEMENT pays_on_time EMPTY>
<!ELEMENT orders (item)*>
<!ELEMENT item (product,number,price)>
<!ELEMENT product (#PCDATA)>
<!ELEMENT number (#PCDATA)>
<!ELEMENT price (#PCDATA)>
]>
<document>
    <customer>
```

```
            <name>
                <last_name>Grant</last_name>
                <first_name>Cary</first_name>
            </name>
            <date>October 25, 2009</date>
            <pays_on_time/>
            <orders>
                <item>
                    <product>laser printer</product>
                    <number>8</number>
                    <price>$111.25</price>
                </item>
                <item>
                    <product>ink jet printer</product>
                    <number>24</number>
                    <price>$44.98</price>
                </item>
            </orders>
        </customer>
            .
            .
            .
</document>
```

Cool.

Choices in DTDs

Let's say your business is growing and that in addition to customers, you want to handle corporate accounts. That means you might have <customer> elements *or* <account> elements at the same level in your document:

```
<document>
    <customer>
        .
        .
        .
    </customer>
    <account>
        .
        .
        .
    </account>
    <customer>
        .
        .
        .
    </customer>
</document>
```

How do you handle this kind of a situation with DTDs? You can use a DTD *choice*.
A choice means that either one element or another can appear at a specific location (choices
can also be among three items, or four, and so on). To create a choice, you use an upright bar
(|) like this:

```
<?xml version = "1.0" standalone="yes"?>
<!DOCTYPE document [
<!ELEMENT document (customer | account)*>
<!ELEMENT customer (name,date,orders)>
<!ELEMENT name (last_name,first_name)>
<!ELEMENT last_name (#PCDATA)>
<!ELEMENT first_name (#PCDATA)>
<!ELEMENT date (#PCDATA)>
<!ELEMENT orders (item)*>
<!ELEMENT item (product,number,price)>
<!ELEMENT product (#PCDATA)>
<!ELEMENT number (#PCDATA)>
<!ELEMENT price (#PCDATA)>
]>
```

Now a <document> element may contain both <customer> and <account> elements. Here's
what that looks like—note that you also have to declare the <account> element before using it:

```
<?xml version = "1.0" standalone="yes"?>
<!DOCTYPE document [
<!ELEMENT document (customer | account)*>
<!ELEMENT customer (name,date,orders)>
<!ELEMENT account (name,date,orders)>
<!ELEMENT name (last_name,first_name)>
<!ELEMENT last_name (#PCDATA)>
<!ELEMENT first_name (#PCDATA)>
<!ELEMENT date (#PCDATA)>
<!ELEMENT orders (item)*>
<!ELEMENT item (product,number,price)>
<!ELEMENT product (#PCDATA)>
<!ELEMENT number (#PCDATA)>
<!ELEMENT price (#PCDATA)>
]>
<document>
    <customer>
        <name>
            <last_name>Grant</last_name>
            <first_name>Cary</first_name>
        </name>
        <date>October 25, 2009</date>
        <orders>
            <item>
                <product>laser printer</product>
                <number>8</number>
```

```
                    <price>$111.25</price>
                </item>
                <item>
                    <product>ink jet printer</product>
                    <number>24</number>
                    <price>$44.98</price>
                </item>
            </orders>
        </customer>
        <account>
            <name>
                <last_name>Loy</last_name>
                <first_name>Myrna</first_name>
            </name>
            <date>October 25, 2009</date>
            <orders>
                <item>
                    <product>flat screen</product>
                    <number>12</number>
                    <price>$344.95</price>
                </item>
                <item>
                    <product>computer screen</product>
                    <number>6</number>
                    <price>$111.50</price>
                </item>
            </orders>
        </account>
        <customer>
            <name>
                <last_name>Stewart</last_name>
                <first_name>Jimmy</first_name>
            </name>
            <date>October 25, 2009</date>
            <orders>
                <item>
                    <product>CPU</product>
                    <number>12</number>
                    <price>$1452.95</price>
                </item>
                <item>
                    <product>disk drive</product>
                    <number>6</number>
                    <price>$119.50</price>
                </item>
            </orders>
        </customer>
</document>
```

Using choices like this in DTDs gives you even more flexibility in setting up the rules of your document's grammar.

Okay, we've seen a lot about working with XML elements in DTDs—now how about declaring XML *attributes*?

Handling Attributes in DTDs

Say that you wanted to add a type attribute to the <customer> element, indicating what type of customer someone has been (excellent, good, fair, and so on) like this:

```
<customer type="excellent">
    <name>
        <last_name>Grant</last_name>
        <first_name>Cary</first_name>
    </name>
    <date>October 25, 2009</date>
    <orders>
        <item>
            <product>laser printer</product>
            <number>8</number>
            <price>$111.25</price>
        </item>
        <item>
            <product>ink jet printer</product>
            <number>24</number>
            <price>$44.98</price>
        </item>
    </orders>
</customer>
```

That simple change has just broken your DTD, though—you can't use attributes in a DTD-validated XML document without declaring those attributes in the DTDs.

You declare attributes using an <!ATTLIST> element—the name means attribute list. Here's how to declare attributes using <!ATTLIST>:

```
<!ATTLIST element_name
    attribute_name type default_value
    attribute_name type default_value
    attribute_name type default_value
    .
    .
    .
    attribute_name type default_value>
```

In this case, *element_name* is the name of the element that you're declaring attributes for, *attribute_name* is the name of an attribute you're declaring, *type* is the attribute's type, and *default_value* represents its default value.

Here are the possible type values you can use:

- **CDATA**   Simple character data (that is, text that does not include any markup).

- **ENTITIES**   Multiple entity names (which must be declared in the DTD), separated by whitespace.

- **ENTITY**   Names an entity (which must be declared in the DTD).

- **Enumerated**   Represents a list of values; any one item from the list is an appropriate attribute value.

- **ID**   A proper XML name that must be unique (that is, not shared by any other attribute of the ID type).

- **IDREF**   Will hold the value of an id attribute of some element, usually another element that the current element is related to.

- **IDREFS**   Multiple IDs of elements, separated by whitespace.

- **NMTOKEN**   A name token, made up of one or more letters, digits, hyphens, underscores, colons, and periods.

- **NMTOKENS**   Multiple NMTOKENs in a list, separated by whitespace.

- **NOTATION**   A notation name (which must be declared in the DTD).

I'll take a look at the most common of these possibilities in this chapter.
Here are the possible default_value settings you can use:

- **VALUE**   A simple text value, enclosed in quotes.

- **#IMPLIED**   Indicates that there is no default value for this attribute, and this attribute need not be used.

- **#REQUIRED**   Indicates that there is no default value, but that a value must be assigned to this attribute.

- **#FIXED VALUE**   In this case, VALUE is the attribute's value, and the attribute must always have this value.

Here's a simple example, customersAttributes.xml, where we declare a type attribute of the CDATA type for the <customer> element and indicate that this attribute can be used or not as the author prefers:

```
<?xml version = "1.0" standalone="yes"?>
<!DOCTYPE document [
<!ELEMENT document (customer)*>
<!ELEMENT customer (name,date,orders)>
<!ELEMENT name (last_name,first_name)>
<!ELEMENT last_name (#PCDATA)>
<!ELEMENT first_name (#PCDATA)>
<!ELEMENT date (#PCDATA)>
```

```
<!ELEMENT orders (item)*>
<!ELEMENT item (product,number,price)>
<!ELEMENT product (#PCDATA)>
<!ELEMENT number (#PCDATA)>
<!ELEMENT price (#PCDATA)>
<!ATTLIST customer
    type CDATA #IMPLIED>
]>
<document>
    <customer type="excellent">
        <name>
            <last_name>Grant</last_name>
            <first_name>Cary</first_name>
        </name>
        <date>October 25, 2009</date>
        <orders>
            <item>
                <product>laser printer</product>
                <number>8</number>
                <price>$111.25</price>
            </item>
            <item>
                <product>ink jet printer</product>
                <number>24</number>
                <price>$44.98</price>
            </item>
        </orders>
    </customer>
    <customer type="fair">
        <name>
            <last_name>Loy</last_name>
            <first_name>Myrna</first_name>
        </name>
        <date>October 25, 2009</date>
        <orders>
            <item>
                <product>flat screen</product>
                <number>12</number>
                <price>$344.95</price>
            </item>
            <item>
                <product>computer screen</product>
                <number>6</number>
                <price>$111.50</price>
            </item>
        </orders>
    </customer>
    <customer type="poor">
        <name>
            <last_name>Stewart</last_name>
```

```
            <first_name>Jimmy</first_name>
        </name>
        <date>October 25, 2009</date>
        <orders>
            <item>
                <product>CPU</product>
                <number>12</number>
                <price>$1452.95</price>
            </item>
            <item>
                <product>disk drive</product>
                <number>6</number>
                <price>$119.50</price>
            </item>
        </orders>
    </customer>
</document>
```

Setting Default Values

Let's take a look at working with some default values. For example, you can set default values for attributes like this, where I'm setting the default value for the type attribute to be "fair"—and then omit that attribute in the middle customer in customersDefault.xml:

```
<?xml version = "1.0" standalone="yes"?>
<!DOCTYPE document [
<!ELEMENT document (customer)*>
<!ELEMENT customer (name,date,orders)>
<!ELEMENT name (last_name,first_name)>
<!ELEMENT last_name (#PCDATA)>
<!ELEMENT first_name (#PCDATA)>
<!ELEMENT date (#PCDATA)>
<!ELEMENT orders (item)*>
<!ELEMENT item (product,number,price)>
<!ELEMENT product (#PCDATA)>
<!ELEMENT number (#PCDATA)>
<!ELEMENT price (#PCDATA)>
<!ATTLIST customer
    type CDATA "fair">
]>
<document>
    <customer type="excellent">
        <name>
            <last_name>Grant</last_name>
            <first_name>Cary</first_name>
        </name>
        <date>October 25, 2009</date>
        <orders>
            <item>
                <product>laser printer</product>
```

```
                    <number>8</number>
                    <price>$111.25</price>
                </item>
                <item>
                    <product>ink jet printer</product>
                    <number>24</number>
                    <price>$44.98</price>
                </item>
            </orders>
        </customer>
        <customer>
            <name>
                <last_name>Loy</last_name>
                <first_name>Myrna</first_name>
            </name>
            <date>October 25, 2009</date>
            <orders>
                <item>
                    <product>flat screen</product>
                    <number>12</number>
                    <price>$344.95</price>
                </item>
                <item>
                    <product>computer screen</product>
                    <number>6</number>
                    <price>$111.50</price>
                </item>
            </orders>
        </customer>
        <customer type="poor">
            <name>
                <last_name>Stewart</last_name>
                <first_name>Jimmy</first_name>
            </name>
            <date>October 25, 2009</date>
            <orders>
                <item>
                    <product>CPU</product>
                    <number>12</number>
                    <price>$1452.95</price>
                </item>
                <item>
                    <product>disk drive</product>
                    <number>6</number>
                    <price>$119.50</price>
                </item>
            </orders>
        </customer>
    </document>
```

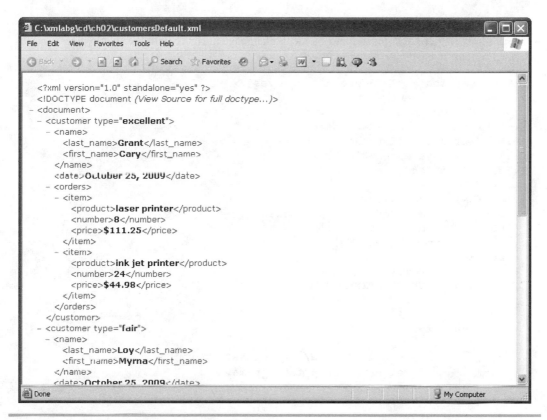

Figure 2-3 Setting default attribute values

You can see the results in Figure 2-3—note that Internet Explorer added a type attribute to the second customer and gave that attribute a value of "fair".

You can also make attributes *required* using the #REQUIRED default value. Here's how you would make the type attribute required:

```
<!ATTLIST customer
    type CDATA #REQUIRED>
]>
```

Try This Make an Attribute Required

Make the <customer> element's type attribute be required—and then omit that attribute in at least one <customer> element.

Next, open your XML document in Internet Explorer and verify that it catches the missing type attribute, which you've labeled required—and that Internet Explorer complains about it with an error message.

You can also make an attribute have a fixed value that you can't change. For example, here's how to give each <customer> element a language attribute with the fixed value "EN" (for English) in customersFixed.xml:

```
<?xml version = "1.0" standalone="yes"?>
<!DOCTYPE document [
<!ELEMENT document (customer)*>
<!ELEMENT customer (name,date,orders)>
<!ELEMENT name (last_name,first_name)>
<!ELEMENT last_name (#PCDATA)>
<!ELEMENT first_name (#PCDATA)>
<!ELEMENT date (#PCDATA)>
<!ELEMENT orders (item)*>
<!ELEMENT item (product,number,price)>
<!ELEMENT product (#PCDATA)>
<!ELEMENT number (#PCDATA)>
<!ELEMENT price (#PCDATA)>
<!ATTLIST customer
    language CDATA #FIXED "EN">
]>
<document>
    <customer>
        <name>
            <last_name>Grant</last_name>
            <first_name>Cary</first_name>
        </name>
        <date>October 25, 2009</date>
        <orders>
            <item>
                <product>laser printer</product>
                <number>8</number>
                <price>$111.25</price>
            </item>
            <item>
                <product>ink jet printer</product>
                <number>24</number>
                <price>$44.98</price>
            </item>
        </orders>
    </customer>
    <customer>
        <name>
            <last_name>Loy</last_name>
            <first_name>Myrna</first_name>
        </name>
        <date>October 25, 2009</date>
        <orders>
```

```
            <item>
                <product>flat screen</product>
                <number>12</number>
                <price>$344.95</price>
            </item>
            <item>
                <product>computer screen</product>
                <number>6</number>
                <price>$111.50</price>
            </item>
        </orders>
    </customer>
    <customer>
        <name>
            <last_name>Stewart</last_name>
            <first_name>Jimmy</first_name>
        </name>
        <date>October 25, 2009</date>
        <orders>
            <item>
                <product>CPU</product>
                <number>12</number>
                <price>$1452.95</price>
            </item>
            <item>
                <product>disk drive</product>
                <number>6</number>
                <price>$119.50</price>
            </item>
        </orders>
    </customer>
</document>
```

And you can see the results in Figure 2-4. As you see there, Internet Explorer added the language attribute to the <customer> elements and gave them a value of "EN".

Try This   Verifying That Fixed Attributes Are Really Fixed

Make the <customer> element's language attribute fixed to "EN"—and then try changing the attribute's value to "JP" (for Japanese) in one <customer> element.

Next, open your XML document in Internet Explorer and verify that it complains about the fixed attribute being changed.

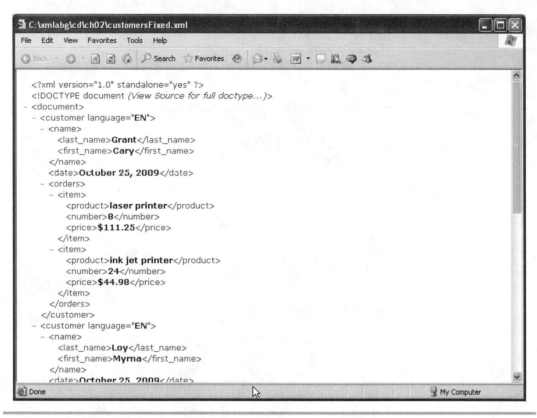

Figure 2-4 Setting fixed attribute values

Setting Attribute Types

Besides working with the default values of attributes, you can also set attribute *types*. The most popular attribute type is CDATA—character data, which is just text, but you can also restrict possible attribute values to a list of legal values. For example, here's how you restrict the possible values of an attribute named credit to "good" or "bad"—and give it a default value of "good":

```
<?xml version = "1.0" standalone="yes"?>
<!DOCTYPE document [
<!ELEMENT document (customer)*>
<!ELEMENT customer (name,date,orders)>
<!ELEMENT name (last_name,first_name)>
<!ELEMENT last_name (#PCDATA)>
<!ELEMENT first_name (#PCDATA)>
<!ELEMENT date (#PCDATA)>
<!ELEMENT orders (item)*>
<!ELEMENT item (product,number,price)>
<!ELEMENT product (#PCDATA)>
```

```
<!ELEMENT number (#PCDATA)>
<!ELEMENT price (#PCDATA)>
<!ATTLIST customer
    credit (good | bad) "good">
]>
<document>
    <customer credit="good">
        <name>
            <last_name>Grant</last_name>
            <first_name>Cary</first_name>
        </name>
        <date>October 25, 2009</date>
        <orders>
            <item>
                <product>laser printer</product>
                <number>8</number>
                <price>$111.25</price>
            </item>
            <item>
                <product>ink jet printer</product>
                <number>24</number>
                <price>$44.98</price>
            </item>
        </orders>
    </customer>
    <customer credit="bad">
        <name>
            <last_name>Loy</last_name>
            <first_name>Myrna</first_name>
        </name>
        <date>October 25, 2009</date>
        <orders>
            <item>
                <product>flat screen</product>
                <number>12</number>
                <price>$344.95</price>
            </item>
            <item>
                <product>computer screen</product>
                <number>6</number>
                <price>$111.50</price>
            </item>
        </orders>
    </customer>
    <customer credit="good">
        <name>
            <last_name>Stewart</last_name>
            <first_name>Jimmy</first_name>
        </name>
```

```
        <date>October 25, 2009</date>
        <orders>
            <item>
                <product>CPU</product>
                <number>12</number>
                <price>$1452.95</price>
            </item>
            <item>
                <product>disk drive</product>
                <number>6</number>
                <price>$119.50</price>
            </item>
        </orders>
    </customer>
</document>
```

External DTDs

You can also make DTDs external—which is a good idea if, for example, your whole site shares the same DTD (as in a corporate Web site)—or if you're using someone else's long DTD and don't want to reproduce it in every one of your XML documents.

So far, our DTDs have been built like this:

```
<!DOCTYPE documentelement [DTD] >
```

You can also use external private DTDs with the keyword SYSTEM and the URL of the DTD:

```
<!DOCTYPE documentelement SYSTEM URL>
```

Or, you can use an external private DTD—along with an internal DTD (for example, you might want to add some new elements not yet supported in the company's DTD), in which case you can add an internal DTD after the URL of the external DTD:

```
<!DOCTYPE documentelement SYSTEM URL [DTD] >
```

You can also use public DTDs that are not private, but intended for public consumption, with the PUBLIC keyword:

```
<!DOCTYPE documentelement PUBLIC identifier URL>
<!DOCTYPE documentelement PUBLIC identifier URL [DTD] >
```

Let's take a look at some examples. Here's how you can convert customers.xml to use an external DTD, external.dtd (note that the standalone attribute is now set to "no", since the document depends on another, external document):

```
<?xml version = "1.0" standalone="no"?>
<!DOCTYPE DOCUMENT SYSTEM "external.dtd">
```

```
<document>
    <customer>
        <name>
            <last_name>Grant</last_name>
            <first_name>Cary</first_name>
        </name>
        <date>October 25, 2009</date>
        <orders>
            <item>
                <product>laser printer</product>
                <number>8</number>
                <price>$111.25</price>
            </item>
            <item>
                <product>ink jet printer</product>
                <number>24</number>
                <price>$44.98</price>
            </item>
        </orders>
    </customer>
    <customer>
        <name>
            <last_name>Loy</last_name>
            <first_name>Myrna</first_name>
        </name>
        <date>October 25, 2009</date>
        <orders>
            <item>
                <product>flat screen</product>
                <number>12</number>
                <price>$344.95</price>
            </item>
            <item>
                <product>computer screen</product>
                <number>6</number>
                <price>$111.50</price>
            </item>
        </orders>
    </customer>
    <customer>
        <name>
            <last_name>Stewart</last_name>
            <first_name>Jimmy</first_name>
        </name>
        <date>October 25, 2009</date>
        <orders>
            <item>
                <product>CPU</product>
```

```
            <number>12</number>
            <price>$1452.95</price>
        </item>
        <item>
            <product>disk drive</product>
            <number>6</number>
            <price>$119.50</price>
        </item>
    </orders>
  </customer>
</document>
```

And here are the contents of external.dtd—just the normal DTD that goes between *[* and *]* in the <!DOCTYPE> element:

```
<!ELEMENT document (customer)*>
<!ELEMENT customer (name,date,orders)>
<!ELEMENT name (last_name,first_name)>
<!ELEMENT last_name (#PCDATA)>
<!ELEMENT first_name (#PCDATA)>
<!ELEMENT date (#PCDATA)>
<!ELEMENT orders (item)*>
<!ELEMENT item (product,number,price)>
<!ELEMENT product (#PCDATA)>
<!ELEMENT number (#PCDATA)>
<!ELEMENT price (#PCDATA)>
```

Note that this example assumes that external.dtd is in the same directory as the XML document—but that doesn't have to be the case. You can also have an external DTD at some URL, like this:

```
<!DOCTYPE document SYSTEM
    "http://www.starpowdernow.com/dtds/external.dtd">
```

It's almost as easy to use public external DTDs as private ones.

```
<!DOCTYPE documentelement PUBLIC identifier URL>
<!DOCTYPE documentelement PUBLIC identifier URL [DTD]>
```

Note the use of the keyword PUBLIC here instead of SYSTEM, indicating that the external DTD is for public use. Note in particular the identifier here—that's called a *formal public identifier,* or FPI. Here's an example that uses a PUBLIC external DTD, alone, and has an FPI (the part in the first set of quotation marks):

```
<!DOCTYPE document PUBLIC "-//starpowdernow//Custom XML Version 1.0//EN"
"http://www.starpowdernow.com/steve/external.dtd">
```

The FPI marks the DTD as yours and consists of four fields, separated by double slashes (*//*). Here are the fields:

- The first field in an FPI specifies the connection of the DTD to a formal standard. For DTDs you're defining yourself, this field should be "-". If a non-standards body has approved the DTD, use "+". For formal standards, this field is a reference to the standard itself (such as ISO/IEC 13449:2000).

- The second field must hold the name of the group or person that is going to maintain or be responsible for the DTD. In this case, you should use a name that is unique and identifies your group easily (for example, W3C simply uses W3C).

- The third field must indicate the type of document that is described, preferably followed by a unique identifier of some kind (such as Version 1.0). This part should include a version number that you'll update.

- The fourth field specifies the language your DTD uses (for example, for English you use EN. Note that two-letter language specifiers allow only a maximum of $24 \times 24 = 576$ possible languages; expect to see three-letter language specifiers in the near future).

Here's how you might specify an external public DTD in an example:

```
<!DOCTYPE documentelement PUBLIC identifier URL>
<!DOCTYPE documentelement PUBLIC identifier URL [DTD]>
```

Let's take a look at some examples. Here's how you can convert customers.xml to use an external DTD, external.dtd:

```
<?xml version = "1.0" standalone="no"?>
<!DOCTYPE document PUBLIC "-//starpowdernow//Custom XML Version 1.0//EN"
"http://www.starpowdernow.com/steve/external.dtd">
<document>
    <customer>
        <name>
            <last_name>Grant</last_name>
            <first_name>Cary</first_name>
        </name>
        <date>October 25, 2009</date>
        <orders>
            <item>
                <product>laser printer</product>
                <number>8</number>
                <price>$111.25</price>
            </item>
            <item>
                <product>ink jet printer</product>
                <number>24</number>
                <price>$44.98</price>
            </item>
        </orders>
    </customer>
    <customer>
```

```
<name>
     <last_name>Loy</last_name>
     <first_name>Myrna</first_name>
</name>
<date>October 25, 2009</date>
<orders>
     <item>
          <product>flat screen</product>
          <number>12</number>
          <price>$344.95</price>
     </item>
     <item>
          <product>computer screen</product>
          <number>6</number>
          <price>$111.50</price>
     </item>
</orders>
</customer>
<customer>
     <name>
          <last_name>Stewart</last_name>
          <first_name>Jimmy</first_name>
     </name>
     <date>October 25, 2009</date>
     <orders>
          <item>
               <product>CPU</product>
               <number>12</number>
               <price>$1452.95</price>
          </item>
          <item>
               <product>disk drive</product>
               <number>6</number>
               <price>$119.50</price>
          </item>
     </orders>
</customer>
</document>
```

Divide and Conquer: Namespaces

There's one last important topic for this chapter—XML namespaces. Let's say that you want to display some MathML—but that you also want to display some text and headers, perhaps even images, along with the MathML. How can you do that?

You could use XHTML, which is normal HTML written in XML. That is, there's a whole XML application named XHTML that has <html>, <head>, <body>, <h1>, and so on elements—but those elements are actually XML, not HTML. However, because they share the same names as HTML elements, you can display XHTML documents in browsers. And because XHTML is actually XML, you can validate those documents—something that's not so easy with pure HTML.

You can embed MathML into an XHTML document—after all, they're both XML—but that does give rise to one concern: element overlap. It turns out that XHTML and MathML have a few elements named the same, such as <var> and <select>. So how do you inform the browser which <var> or <select> element you mean—MathML's or XHTML's?

You can keep these XML dialects separate in the same document by using *namespaces.* Namespaces are like imaginary containers inside an XML document, and you can keep sections of XML separate with those containers (an example is coming up). By putting one XML dialect into one namespace and the other into another, the two won't conflict, even in the same document.

Because you make up your own element names in XML, this is a continual problem when you mix XML dialects in the same document—element conflict. Namespaces were created to keep the two dialects separate in the same document.

For example, say that you have this XML that stores a book title in this XML document you got from the library:

```
<?xml version = "1.0" standalone="yes"?>
<library>
    <book>
        <title>
            A Noisy Noise Annoys an Oyster.
        </title>
    </book>
</library>
```

Now say that you want to add your own review about the book to the library's document, but you don't want to make it look like it's their review. Instead, you can put the library's XML into its own namespace, and your XML into your own namespace. We start by declaring a *namespace prefix* that will be library here:

```
<?xml version = "1.0" standalone="yes"?>
<library
    xmlns:library="http://www.amazingterrificlibrary.com">
    <book>
        <title>
            A Noisy Noise Annoys an Oyster.
        </title>
    </book>
</library>
```

To define a namespace, you assign the xmlns:prefix attribute to a unique identifier, which in XML is usually a URL for the namespace (but doesn't have to be). After defining the library namespace, you can preface every tag and attribute name in this namespace with library: like this:

```
<?xml version = "1.0" standalone="yes"?>
<library:library
    xmlns:library="http://www.amazingterrificlibrary.com">
    <library:book>
        <library:title>
            A Noisy Noise Annoys an Oyster.
        </library:title>
    </library:book>
</library:library>
```

Now the tag and attribute names have actually been changed; for example, <book> is now <library:book> as far as the XML processor is concerned. And if you've defined tag and attribute names in a document's DTD, this means that you have to redefine the tags and attributes there as well to make the new names legal.

Because all tag and attribute names from the book namespace are now in their own namespace, I'm free to add my own namespace to the document now to allow me to add my own comments. I'll start by defining a new namespace named steve:

```
<?xml version = "1.0" standalone="yes"?>
<library:library
    xmlns:library="http://www.amazingterrificlibrary.com"
    xmlns:steve="http://www.starpowdernow.com/steve">
    <library:book>
        <library:title>
            A Noisy Noise Annoys an Oyster.
        </library:title>
    </library:book>
</library:library>
```

Now I can use the new steve namespace to add markup to the document like this, keeping it separate from the other markup:

```
<?xml version = "1.0" standalone="yes"?>
<library:library
    xmlns:library="http://www.amazingterrificlibrary.com"
    xmlns:steve="http://www.starpowdernow.com/steve">
    <library:book>
        <library:title>
            A Noisy Noise Annoys an Oyster.
        </library:title>
        <steve:review/>
            This book was OK, no great noises.
        </steve:review>
    </library:book>
</library:library>
```

And that's how namespaces work—as you can see, you can use them to separate tags, even tags with the same name, from each other. You can also use namespace prefixes on attributes.

As you can see, using multiple namespaces in the same document is no problem at all; just use the xmlns attribute in the enclosing element to define the appropriate namespaces.

In fact, you don't need to use the xmlns attribute in the root element; you can use this attribute in any element. Here's an example where I've moved the steve namespace definition to the element in which it's used:

```
<?xml version = "1.0" standalone="yes"?>
<library:library
    xmlns:library="http://www.amazingterrificlibrary.com">
    <library:book>
        <library:title>
            A Noisy Noise Annoys an Oyster.
        </library:title>
        <steve:review
        xmlns:steve="http://www.starpowdernow.com/steve"
        steve:ID="1000034"/>
            This book was OK, no great noises.
        </steve:review>
    </library:book>
</library:library>
```

You can also declare a namespace as the *default* namespace. Any elements and attributes without a namespace prefix are assumed to be in the default namespace. To create a default namespace, you just use the xmlns attribute—don't specify a prefix. Here's an example where all the library's XML is automatically in the default namespace:

```
<?xml version = "1.0" standalone="yes"?>
<library
    xmlns="http://www.amazingterrificlibrary.com"
    xmlns:steve="http://www.starpowdernow.com/steve">
    <book>
        <title>
            A Noisy Noise Annoys an Oyster.
        </title>
        <steve:review/>
            This book was OK, no great noises.
        </steve:review>
    </book>
</library>
```

Using default namespaces cleans up your XML, because you don't have to give every element and attribute a prefix.

Try This Mix XHTML and MathML

Here's your chance to put namespaces to work, mixing XHTML and MathML. This document,
xhtmlmathml.html, uses both XHTML and MathML in the same document, with namespaces
to keep them separate. It displays the equation $5x^2 - 2x + 8 = 0$ as well as some text. Work
through it—you should be able to understand what's going on here now (well, with the
exception of understanding the MathML!):

```
<?xml version="1.0" encoding="UTF-8"?>
<!DOCTYPE html PUBLIC "-//W3C//DTD XHTML 1.0 Transitional//EN"
"http://www.w3.org/tr/xhtml1/DTD/xhtml1-transitional.dtd">
<html xmlns="http://www.w3.org/1999/xhtml" xml:lang="en" lang="en"
    xmlns:m="http://www.w3.org/1998/Math/MathML">
    <head>
        <title>
            Using XHTML and MathML Together
        </title>
    </head>

    <body>
        <center>
            <h1>
                Using XHTML and MathML Together
            </h1>
        </center>
        <br/>
        Look at the equation
        <m:math>
            <m:mrow>
                <m:mrow>
                <m:mn>5</m:mn>
                    <m:mo>&InvisibleTimes;</m:mo>
                    <m:msup>
                        <m:mi>x</m:mi>
                        <m:mn>2</m:mn>
                    </m:msup>
                    <m:mo>-</m:mo>
                    <m:mrow>
                        <m:mn>2</m:mn>
                        <m:mo>&InvisibleTimes;</m:mo>
                        <m:mi>x</m:mi>
                    </m:mrow>
                    <m:mo>+</m:mo>
                    <m:mn>8</m:mn>
                </m:mrow>
```

```
            <m:mo>=</m:mo>
            <m:mn>0.</m:mn>
        </m:mrow>
    </m:math>
    <br/>
    What are the roots?
 </body>
</html>
```

You can see this document in the Amaya browser in Figure 2-5.

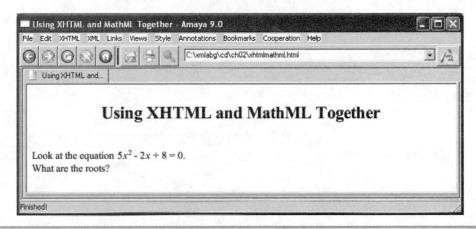

Figure 2-5   Using XHTML and MathML together

Chapter 3

Creating Valid
XML Documents:
XML Schemas

Key Skills & Concepts

- Introducing XML schemas

- Creating schemas

- Declaring elements

- Declaring elements by reference

- Using an XML schema validator

This chapter starts to explore validating XML documents using XML schemas. Schemas are the most recent way to validate XML documents, and as you're going to see, schemas offer a lot more validation power than DTDs do.

For example, DTDs don't let you specify the format of your data—except that it must be text—while schemas let you specify data types. For example, you can specify that the contents of an element be an integer, a floating point number, a date, and more (bear in mind that the actual data will be text, but schemas let you interpret that text as integers, floating point numbers, and so on).

Let's jump right in. Say that you're a famous art collector, with a collection worth millions. And that you're so good-hearted that you lend your paintings out to your fellow collectors— but only for a maximum of two weeks.

Being a careful XML author, you naturally want to store the details of each loan in an XML document. And being a careful art collector, you also naturally want to make sure that that XML document is valid, so you can use an XML schema to check it.

Here's what the XML document, document.xml, which records the loan of your paintings to other collectors, looks like:

```
<?xml version="1.0"?>
<transaction borrowDate="2009-10-15">
    <Lender phone="607.555.2222">
        <name>Doug Glass</name>
        <street>416 Disk Drive</street>
        <city>Medfield</city>
        <state>MA</state>
    </Lender>
    <Borrower phone="310.555.1111">
        <name>Britta Regensburg</name>
        <street>219 Union Drive</street>
        <city>Medfield</city>
        <state>CA</state>
    </Borrower>
```

```
<note>Lender wants these back in two weeks!</note>
<paintings>
    <painting paintingID="123-4567-890">
        <paintingTitle>The Castle</paintingTitle>
        <creationDate>1900-10-20</creationDate>
        <replacementValue>15000.95</replacementValue>
        <maxDaysOut>14</maxDaysOut>
    </painting>
    <painting paintingID="123-4567-891">
        <paintingTitle>The Cafe</paintingTitle>
        <creationDate>1901-10-21</creationDate>
        <replacementValue>19000.99</replacementValue>
        <maxDaysOut>14</maxDaysOut>
    </painting>
    <painting paintingID="123-4567-892">
        <paintingTitle>The Manor House</paintingTitle>
        <creationDate>1902-10-22</creationDate>
        <replacementValue>11000.95</replacementValue>
        <maxDaysOut>14</maxDaysOut>
    </painting>
    <painting paintingID="123-4567-893">
        <paintingTitle>The Condo</paintingTitle>
        <creationDate>1903-10-23</creationDate>
        <replacementValue>170000.99</replacementValue>
        <maxDaysOut>14</maxDaysOut>
    </painting>
</paintings>
</transaction>
```

Note that there's no XML schema in this document. When we created DTDs in the preceding chapter, we inserted those DTDs into their corresponding XML documents, or used a <!DOCTYPE> element in the document to link to an external DTD.

But the preceding XML document is just an XML document—no sign of an XML schema.

It turns out that the World Wide Web Consortium never specified any mechanism linking XML schemas with XML documents, so the two are separate documents. Microsoft and some other vendors have created non-standard XML processing instructions to connect XML documents and XML schemas together, but no industry standard has emerged, so we'll keep XML documents and the schemas used to validate them as separate documents (as is the norm).

The schema is written in an XML dialect named XML Schema Definition Language, often abbreviated as XSD. Here's what the actual schema, schema.xsd (.xsd is the usual extension for schema files), looks like—see if you can figure out what's going on here, at least partially:

```
<?xml version="1.0"?>
<xsd:schema xmlns:xsd="http://www.w3.org/2001/XMLSchema">

  <xsd:annotation>
    <xsd:documentation>
        Painting borrowing transaction schema.
```

```xml
      </xsd:documentation>
   </xsd:annotation>

   <xsd:element name="transaction" type="transactionType"/>

   <xsd:complexType name="transactionType">
     <xsd:sequence>
       <xsd:element name="Lender" type="address"/>
       <xsd:element name="Borrower" type="address"/>
       <xsd:element ref="note" minOccurs="0"/>
       <xsd:element name="paintings" type="paintings"/>
     </xsd:sequence>
     <xsd:attribute name="borrowDate" type="xsd:date"/>
   </xsd:complexType>

   <xsd:element name="note" type="xsd:string"/>

   <xsd:complexType name="address">
     <xsd:sequence>
       <xsd:element name="name" type="xsd:string"/>
       <xsd:element name="street" type="xsd:string"/>
       <xsd:element name="city" type="xsd:string"/>
       <xsd:element name="state" type="xsd:string"/>
     </xsd:sequence>
     <xsd:attribute name="phone" type="xsd:string"
       use="optional"/>
   </xsd:complexType>

   <xsd:complexType name="paintings">
     <xsd:sequence>
       <xsd:element name="painting" minOccurs="0" maxOccurs="10">
         <xsd:complexType>
           <xsd:sequence>
             <xsd:element name="paintingTitle" type="xsd:string"/>
             <xsd:element name="creationDate" type="xsd:date"
               minOccurs='0'/>
             <xsd:element name="replacementValue" type="xsd:decimal"/>
             <xsd:element name="maxDaysOut">
               <xsd:simpleType>
                 <xsd:restriction base="xsd:integer">
                   <xsd:maxInclusive value="14"/>
                 </xsd:restriction>
               </xsd:simpleType>
             </xsd:element>
           </xsd:sequence>
           <xsd:attribute name="paintingID" type="catalogID"/>
         </xsd:complexType>
       </xsd:element>
```

```
      </xsd:sequence>
    </xsd:complexType>

    <xsd:simpleType name="catalogID">
      <xsd:restriction base="xsd:string">
        <xsd:pattern value="\d{3}-\d{4}-\d{3}"/>
      </xsd:restriction>
    </xsd:simpleType>

  </xsd:schema>
```

There are a couple of things that we can note at the outset. First, note that schema.xsd is a well-formed XML document. That is, DTDs use non-XML elements like <!ELEMENT>, but XML schemas use only pure XML.

In other words, XML schemas use the XSD XML language, which is a prewritten XML application. The legal elements in the XSD language have already been decided on, and you can find them in Table 3-1. These are the XML elements that are legal to use in XML schemas.

Type	Description
all	Permits the elements in a group to appear in any order in the containing element.
annotation	Creates an annotation.
any	Permits any element from the given namespace(s) to appear in the containing sequence or choice element.
anyAttribute	Permits any attribute from the given namespace to appear in the containing complexType element or in the containing attributeGroup element.
appinfo	Specifies information to be used by applications within an annotation element.
attribute	Creates an attribute.
attributeGroup	Groups attribute declarations so that they can be used as a group for complex type definitions.
choice	Permits one, and only one, of the elements contained in the group to appear in the containing element.
complexContent	Contains extensions or restrictions on a complex type that contains mixed content or elements only.
complexType	Defines a complex type, which supports attributes and element content.
documentation	Holds text to be read or used by users within an annotation element.
element	Creates an element.
extension	Extends a simple type or a complex type that has simple content.
field	Indicates an XML Path Language (XPath) expression that gives the value to define a constraint (unique, key, and keyref elements).
group	Groups a set of element declarations so that they can be incorporated as a group into complex type definitions.

Table 3-1 The Legal Elements in the XSD Language

Type	Description
import	Imports a namespace whose schema components are referenced by the schema.
include	Includes the given schema document in the target namespace of the containing schema.
key	Indicates that an attribute or element value must be a key.
keyref	Indicates that an attribute or element value corresponds to those of the given key or unique element.
list	Defines a simpleType element as a list of values of a given data type.
notation	Contains the definition of a notation to describe the format of non-XML data within an XML document.
redefine	Permits simple and complex types as well as groups (and attribute groups from external schema files) to be redefined in the current schema.
restriction	Defines constraints, such as data types.
schema	Contains the definition of a schema.
selector	Indicates an XPath expression that selects a set of elements for an identity constraint for the unique, key, and keyref elements.
sequence	Requires the elements in the group to appear in the given sequence within the containing element.
simpleContent	Contains extensions or restrictions on a complexType element with character data or a simpleType element as content and contains no elements.
simpleType	Defines a simple type.
union	Defines a simpleType element as a collection of values from given simple data types.
unique	Indicates that an attribute or element value must be unique.

Table 3-1   The Legal Elements in the XSD Language *(continued)*

So now we have an example XML document and an example XML schema. The rest of this chapter will be dedicated to dissecting that schema.

How can we make sure the schema really validates the document? Just as with DTDs, there are online schema validators as well, such as the one at www.xmlme.com/validator.aspx, which you can see in Figure 3-1.

This validator expects to get the XML document and the XML schema as two separate documents, which you paste into text boxes in the validator's Web page. For example, you can see our XML document pasted into the box labeled "XML document".

The XML schema gets pasted into the box labeled "XML Schema" that you see in Figure 3-2.

To validate the document, click the Validate button you see in Figure 3-1. The results appear in Figure 3-3, where you can see the text "Validation Successful". Cool.

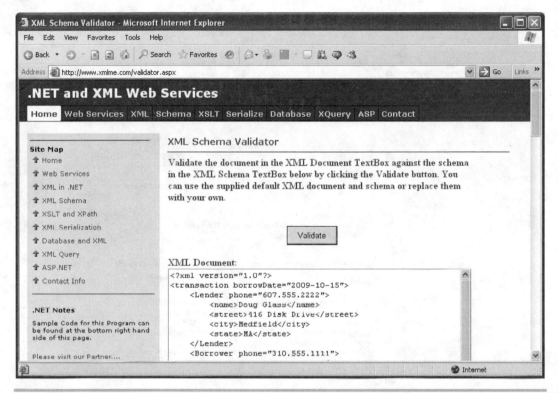

Figure 3-1 Validating an XML document: pasting in the document

Try This Validating an XML Document Using a Schema

Try validating document.xml with the validator at www.xmlme.com/validator.aspx yourself, using the XML schema you'll find in schema.xsd.

Now you're validating with an XML schema!

You can already start to see what's going on in our XML schema with lines like this:

```
<xsd:element name="note" type="xsd:string"/>
```

Here, we're declaring an element named <note> with the <xsd:element> element, and the type of the element is "xsd:string". Note the prefix xsd here—every element and attribute of the XSD language is in the XSD namespace, and schemas typically use the namespace prefix xsd for that namespace (although you don't have to—you can use any prefix you like).

Note also that the type of the <note> element is given as xsd:string. That's the way of saying that the element has text content (this would be CDATA in DTDs). Here's how the

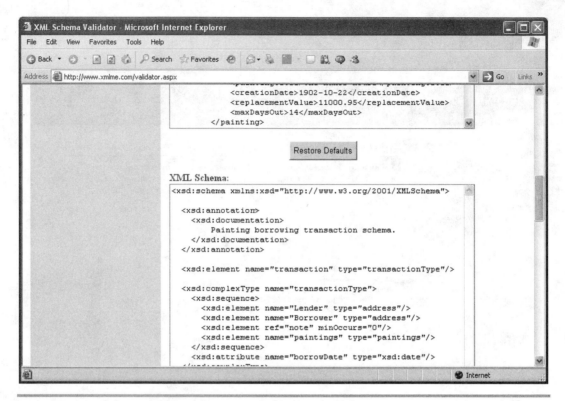

Figure 3-2 Validating an XML document: pasting in the schema

<note> element appears in our XML document—as you can see, its contents consist of just a text string:

```
<note>Lender wants these back in two weeks!</note>
```

The xsd:string type is one of the simple data types built into XML schemas—note that you use the same prefix for those data types as you use for schema elements, which is why the data type for simple text is xsd:string, not simply string.

You can see the XML schema built-in data types in Table 3-2. These are the data types that you can make your schema check—for example, if you declare the content of an XML element to be of type xsd:integer, then the element has to have text content that can be interpreted as an integer, such as <number>15</number> or <count>12</count>. Note also that if you don't want to enforce a particular data type for an XML element, you can always use the xsd:string type, which says the element content must be simple text.

Take a look at Table 3-2 to get familiar with the data types that are enforceable in an XML schema—and don't forget, when you use them in an actual schema, preface them with the xsd prefix (or other prefix you've connected to the XSD namespace, as we'll see in a minute).

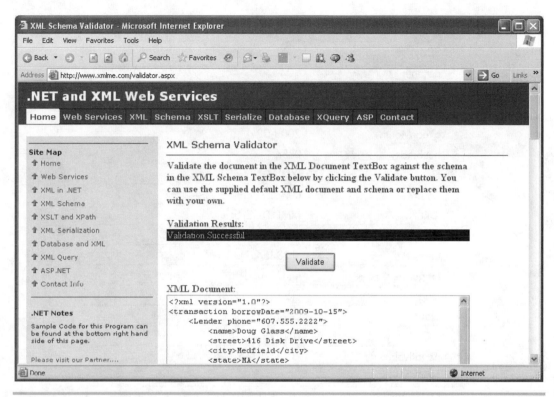

Figure 3-3 Validating an XML document

Type	Examples
anyURI	http://www.starpowdernow.com
base64Binary	GpM6
boolean	true, false, 1, 0
byte	-5, 116
date	2003-05-31
dateTime	2003-03-31T11:15:00.000-03:00
decimal	1.234, -1.234, 6000.00
double	12, 12.34E-5, 1.2222
duration	P1Y1M4DT10H50M11.7S
ENTITIES	(XML entities)
ENTITY	(XML entity)
float	12, 12.34E-5, 1.2222

Table 3-2 Simple Types Built Into an XML Schema

Type	Examples
gDay	---30
gMonth	--04--
gMonthDay	--03-30
gYear	2003
gYearMonth	2003-02
hexBinary	0BB6
ID	(XML ID)
IDREF	(XML ID REF)
IDREFS	(XML ID REFS)
int	10, 12345678
integer	-123456, -1, 10
language	en-US, fr, de
long	-1234, 12345678901234
Name	George
NCName	USData
negativeInteger	-123, -1345
NMTOKEN	US
NMTOKENS	US UK, DE UK FR
nonNegativeInteger	0, 1, 12345
nonPositiveInteger	-1234, -1, 0
normalizedString	Here is some text
NOTATION	(XML NOTATION)
positiveInteger	1, 12345
QName	doc:Data
short	-12, 1234
string	Here is some text
time	11:15:00.000
token	Here is some text
unsignedByte	0, 127
unsignedInt	0, 12345678
unsignedLong	0, 12678967543233
unsignedShort	0, 12678

Table 3-2 Simple Types Built Into an XML Schema *(continued)*

Okay, let's get started constructing our own XML schema, starting with seeing how to create XML schemas.

Creating an XML Schema

XML schemas are a creation of the World Wide Web consortium, and the W3C has published specifications that outline how schemas work. You'll find those specifications at

- www.w3.org/TR/xmlschema-0/

- www.w3.org/TR/xmlschema-1/

- www.w3.org/TR/xmlschema-2/

XML schemas are pretty complex beasts, and the W3C took the unusual step of making the first document listed, the XML Schema specification part 0 (www.w3.org/TR/xmlschema-0/), a tutorial that explains how schemas work. It's worth taking a look.

So how do you actually build an XML schema to match the W3C specifications? As you'd expect, you begin an XML schema with an XML declaration, since it's an XML document:

```
<?xml version="1.0"?>
        .
        .
        .
```

The document element for XML schemas is <xsd:schema>, like this:

```
<?xml version="1.0"?>
<xsd:schema>
        .
        .
        .
</xsd:schema>
```

Note that you also declare the namespace prefix you're going to use for the XSD schema language in the document element so that you can use that prefix throughout the schema. The official namespace for XML schemas is http://www.w3.org/2001/XMLSchema, so we'll use that (if you don't use this namespace, you'll get an error from XML schema validators):

```
<?xml version="1.0"?>
<xsd:schema xmlns:xsd="http://www.w3.org/2001/XMLSchema">
        .
        .
        .
</xsd:schema>
```

Okay, that creates the document element of our new schema. Now how about declaring some XML elements? There are many such elements in our sample XML document, and we've got to declare them all:

```xml
<?xml version="1.0"?>
<transaction borrowDate="2009-10-15">
    <Lender phone="607.555.2222">
        <name>Doug Glass</name>
        <street>416 Disk Drive</street>
        <city>Medfield</city>
        <state>MA</state>
    </Lender>
    <Borrower phone="310.555.1111">
        <name>Britta Regensburg</name>
        <street>219 Union Drive</street>
        <city>Medfield</city>
        <state>CA</state>
    </Borrower>
    <note>Lender wants these back in two weeks!</note>
        .
        .
        .
```

Declaring Elements

The whole point of XML schemas is to declare items in XML documents, like elements and attributes. We'll take a look at how to declare elements first, then attributes.

XML schemas make a difference between *simple* and *complex* elements, and you declare them differently.

- Simple elements are those that don't contain any child elements or attributes.

- Complex elements can contain both child elements and/or attributes.

That's the difference between simple and complex elements—bear it in mind, because we're going to need that.

Declaring Simple Elements

There is a simple element in the document.xml example—the <note> element, which just contains text, no child elements, no attributes:

```xml
<?xml version="1.0"?>
<transaction borrowDate="2009-10-15">
    <Lender phone="607.555.2222">
        <name>Doug Glass</name>
        <street>416 Disk Drive</street>
```

```
      <city>Medfield</city>
      <state>MA</state>
   </Lender>
   <Borrower phone="310.555.1111">
      <name>Britta Regensburg</name>
      <street>219 Union Drive</street>
      <city>Medfield</city>
      <state>CA</state>
   </Borrower>
   <note>Lender wants these back in two weeks!</note>
   <paintings>
      <painting paintingID="123-4567-890">
         <paintingTitle>The Castle</paintingTitle>
         <creationDate>1900-10-20</creationDate>
         <replacementValue>15000.95</replacementValue>
         <maxDaysOut>14</maxDaysOut>
      </painting>
         .
         .
         .
```

So how do you declare this element? It's a simple element, and its type (see Table 3-2) is xsd:string. You declare this element with the <xsd:element> element like this:

```
<?xml version="1.0"?>
<xsd:schema xmlns:xsd="http://www.w3.org/2001/XMLSchema">

  <xsd:element name="note" type="xsd:string"/>
         .
         .
         .
</xsd:schema>
```

Note two things here. First, you assign the name of the simple element you're declaring with the name attribute (name="note"). Second, the type of the element is given by the type attribute (type="xsd:string").

That's all it takes to declare a simple element—you just use a preexisting simple type from Table 3-2, and make that the type of the element. Easy.

In fact, XML schemas give you more power here—you can restrict the possible values that a simple element can take, as we're going to see soon. For example, you can specify that an element named <day_of_the_week> can only take integer values up to 7.

That declares the <note> element—it was as simple as that. Now let's go on to declaring complex elements.

Declaring Complex Elements

Declaring complex elements takes a little more thought than declaring simple ones. Complex elements can contain child elements and/or attributes, which simple elements cannot.

For an example of a complex element, take a look at the <transaction> element in our XML document:

```xml
<?xml version="1.0"?>
<transaction borrowDate="2009-10-15">
    <Lender phone="607.555.2222">
        <name>Doug Glass</name>
        <street>416 Disk Drive</street>
        <city>Medfield</city>
        <state>MA</state>
    </Lender>
    <Borrower phone="310.555.1111">
        <name>Britta Regensburg</name>
        <street>219 Union Drive</street>
        <city>Medfield</city>
        <state>CA</state>
    </Borrower>
    <note>Lender wants these back in two weeks!</note>
    <paintings>
        <painting paintingID="123-4567-890">
            <paintingTitle>The Castle</paintingTitle>
            <creationDate>1900-10-20</creationDate>
            <replacementValue>15000.95</replacementValue>
            <maxDaysOut>14</maxDaysOut>
        </painting>
        <painting paintingID="123-4567-891">
            <paintingTitle>The Cafe</paintingTitle>
            <creationDate>1901-10-21</creationDate>
            <replacementValue>19000.99</replacementValue>
            <maxDaysOut>14</maxDaysOut>
        </painting>
        <painting paintingID="123-4567-892">
            <paintingTitle>The Manor House</paintingTitle>
            <creationDate>1902-10-22</creationDate>
            <replacementValue>11000.95</replacementValue>
            <maxDaysOut>14</maxDaysOut>
        </painting>
        <painting paintingID="123-4567-893">
            <paintingTitle>The Condo</paintingTitle>
            <creationDate>1903-10-23</creationDate>
            <replacementValue>170000.99</replacementValue>
            <maxDaysOut>14</maxDaysOut>
        </painting>
    </paintings>
</transaction>
```

Here's what the <transaction> element looks like with its child elements made more explicit:

```
<?xml version="1.0"?>
<transaction borrowDate="2009-10-15">
    <Lender>
        .
        .
        .
    </Lender>
    <Borrower>
        .
        .
    </Borrower>
    <note>
        .
        .
        .
    </note>
    <paintings>
        .
        .
        .
    </paintings>
</transaction>
```

Okay, so a <transaction> element contains a <Lender> element, followed by a <Borrower> element, followed by a <note> element, followed by a <paintings> element. And the <transaction> element also has an attribute—borrowDate.

So how do we declare the <transaction> element? You have to create a complex type first, and then declare that element to be of that type. You didn't have to create your own type when you declared a simple element, because you used a built-in simple type (xsd:string). But with a complex element, which can have internal structure—child elements and attributes—you need to create your own complex type.

Say that the complex type you create for the <transaction> element is named transactionType. Then all you need to do is to declare the <transaction> element to be of that type (just as the <note> element was of the predefined type xsd:string):

```
<?xml version="1.0"?>
<xsd:schema xmlns:xsd="http://www.w3.org/2001/XMLSchema">

  <xsd:element name="note" type="xsd:string"/>

  <xsd:element name="transaction" type="transactionType"/>
        .
        .
        .
</xsd:schema>
```

That's the way it works with complex elements—you need to create a complex type, indicating what child elements and attributes you want the complex element to have.

So now we have to declare the complex type transactionType. You can do that with an <xsd:complexType> schema element. To declare the complex type transactionType, you assign "transactionType" to the <xsd:complexType> element's name attribute:

```
<?xml version="1.0"?>
<xsd:schema xmlns:xsd="http://www.w3.org/2001/XMLSchema">

  <xsd:element name="note" type="xsd:string"/>

  <xsd:element name="transaction" type="transactionType"/>

  <xsd:complexType name="transactionType">
          .
          .
          .
  </xsd:complexType>
          .
          .
          .
</xsd:schema>
```

Okay, that gets us started declaring the complex type transactionType. How do we give it a <Lender> child element, followed by a <Borrower> child element, followed by a <note> child element, followed by a <paintings> child element—in that order?

You can declare the child elements of a complex type with the <xsd:sequence> element, which lists the child elements in sequence (another option is to use the <xsd:all> element, which just lists the child elements in no special order):

```
<?xml version="1.0"?>
<xsd:schema xmlns:xsd="http://www.w3.org/2001/XMLSchema">

  <xsd:element name="note" type="xsd:string"/>

  <xsd:element name="transaction" type="transactionType"/>

  <xsd:complexType name="transactionType">
    <xsd:sequence>
          .
          .
          .
    </xsd:sequence>
  </xsd:complexType>
          .
          .
          .
</xsd:schema>
```

Okay, now we have to declare the child elements. The first child element is the <Lender> element—and that element itself is a complex element with its own child elements:

```
<Lender phone="607.555.2222">
    <name>Doug Glass</name>
    <street>416 Disk Drive</street>
    <city>Medfield</city>
    <state>MA</state>
</Lender>
```

The <Lender> element contains the lender's address, and we'll make the <Lender> element a complex element of the address type. Here's how we can add the <Lender> element to the <transaction> element's internal sequence of child elements:

```
<?xml version="1.0"?>
<xsd:schema xmlns:xsd="http://www.w3.org/2001/XMLSchema">

  <xsd:element name="note" type="xsd:string"/>

  <xsd:element name="transaction" type="transactionType"/>

  <xsd:complexType name="transactionType">
    <xsd:sequence>
      <xsd:element name="Lender" type="address"/>
          .

          .

          .

    </xsd:sequence>
  </xsd:complexType>
      .

      .

      .

</xsd:schema>
```

Here's how we add the other child elements to the <transaction> element's child element list (note that the <note> element is declared by reference, not by name, and we'll see how that works later in this chapter):

```
<?xml version="1.0"?>
<xsd:schema xmlns:xsd="http://www.w3.org/2001/XMLSchema">

  <xsd:element name="note" type="xsd:string"/>

  <xsd:element name="transaction" type="transactionType"/>

  <xsd:complexType name="transactionType">
    <xsd:sequence>
      <xsd:element name="Lender" type="address"/>
      <xsd:element name="Borrower" type="address"/>
```

```
      <xsd:element ref="note" minOccurs="0"/>
      <xsd:element name="paintings" type="paintings"/>
    </xsd:sequence>
  </xsd:complexType>
        .
        .
        .

</xsd:schema>
```

That's fine—that creates the sequence of child elements for the <transaction> element. The <transaction> element also has a borrowDate attribute, and here is a preview of how we're going to declare attributes in XML schemas—you use the <xsd:attribute> element:

```
<?xml version="1.0"?>
<xsd:schema xmlns:xsd="http://www.w3.org/2001/XMLSchema">

  <xsd:element name="note" type="xsd:string"/>

  <xsd:element name="transaction" type="transactionType"/>

  <xsd:complexType name="transactionType">
    <xsd:sequence>
      <xsd:element name="Lender" type="address"/>
      <xsd:element name="Borrower" type="address"/>
      <xsd:element ref="note" minOccurs="0"/>
      <xsd:element name="paintings" type="paintings"/>
    </xsd:sequence>
    <xsd:attribute name="borrowDate" type="xsd:date"/>
  </xsd:complexType>
        .
        .
        .

</xsd:schema>
```

Okay, that declares the <transaction> element, as well as its child elements and its attribute. Not bad.

However, we're not done. We've declared the <Lender> and <Borrower> child elements to be of the complex type address:

```
<?xml version="1.0"?>
<xsd:schema xmlns:xsd="http://www.w3.org/2001/XMLSchema">

  <xsd:element name="note" type="xsd:string"/>

  <xsd:element name="transaction" type="transactionType"/>

  <xsd:complexType name="transactionType">
    <xsd:sequence>
      <xsd:element name="Lender" type="address"/>
      <xsd:element name="Borrower" type="address"/>
```

```
    <xsd:element ref="note" minOccurs="0"/>
    <xsd:element name="paintings" type="paintings"/>
  </xsd:sequence>
  <xsd:attribute name="borrowDate" type="xsd:date"/>
 </xsd:complexType>
        .
        .
        .

</xsd:schema>
```

And now we've got to create the complex type address. In the <Lender> and <Borrower> elements, the address is stored with <name>, <street>, <city>, and <state> child elements:

```
<?xml version="1.0"?>
<transaction borrowDate="2009-10-15">
    <Lender phone="607.555.2222">
        <name>Doug Glass</name>
        <street>416 Disk Drive</street>
        <city>Medfield</city>
        <state>MA</state>
    </Lender>
    <Borrower phone="310.555.1111">
        <name>Britta Regensburg</name>
        <street>219 Union Drive</street>
        <city>Medfield</city>
        <state>CA</state>
    </Borrower>
        .
        .
        .
```

So we want to give the address complex type <name>, <street>, <city>, and <state> child elements, in that order:

```
<?xml version="1.0"?>
<xsd:schema xmlns:xsd="http://www.w3.org/2001/XMLSchema">

  <xsd:element name="note" type="xsd:string"/>

  <xsd:element name="transaction" type="transactionType"/>

  <xsd:complexType name="transactionType">
    <xsd:sequence>
      <xsd:element name="Lender" type="address"/>
      <xsd:element name="Borrower" type="address"/>
      <xsd:element ref="note" minOccurs="0"/>
      <xsd:element name="paintings" type="paintings"/>
    </xsd:sequence>
    <xsd:attribute name="borrowDate" type="xsd:date"/>
  </xsd:complexType>
```

```
<xsd:complexType name="address">
  <xsd:sequence>
    <xsd:element name="name" type="xsd:string"/>
    <xsd:element name="street" type="xsd:string"/>
    <xsd:element name="city" type="xsd:string"/>
    <xsd:element name="state" type="xsd:string"/>
  </xsd:sequence>
</xsd:complexType>
      .
      .
      .
</xsd:schema>
```

Note that all the child elements in the complex type address are themselves simple types—in this case, they're all of type xsd:string, which means we're done declaring those elements.

That's the way it works—you declare a complex element's complex type, and then declare the types of the child elements, all the way down until you get to simple, built-in types. When you come to simple, built-in types, you're done, because the XML schema validator knows how to deal with those.

So when you're declaring a complex element, you declare it and its child elements and keep going by declaring the types of those child elements all the way down to the simple built-in types.

The address complex type also has an attribute, phone, that we'll see how to create later:

```
<?xml version="1.0"?>
<xsd:schema xmlns:xsd="http://www.w3.org/2001/XMLSchema">

  <xsd:element name="note" type="xsd:string"/>

  <xsd:element name="transaction" type="transactionType"/>

  <xsd:complexType name="transactionType">
    <xsd:sequence>
      <xsd:element name="Lender" type="address"/>
      <xsd:element name="Borrower" type="address"/>
      <xsd:element ref="note" minOccurs="0"/>
      <xsd:element name="paintings" type="paintings"/>
    </xsd:sequence>
    <xsd:attribute name="borrowDate" type="xsd:date"/>
  </xsd:complexType>

  <xsd:complexType name="address">
    <xsd:sequence>
      <xsd:element name="name" type="xsd:string"/>
      <xsd:element name="street" type="xsd:string"/>
      <xsd:element name="city" type="xsd:string"/>
      <xsd:element name="state" type="xsd:string"/>
    </xsd:sequence>
```

```
  <xsd:attribute name="phone" type="xsd:string"
    use="optional"/>
  </xsd:complexType>

      .
      .
      .

  </xsd:complexType>
      .
      .
      .
</xsd:schema>
```

Okay, that creates the address type. But notice also that when declaring the <transaction> element's <paintings> child element, we gave that child element the type paintings:

```
<?xml version="1.0"?>
<xsd:schema xmlns:xsd="http://www.w3.org/2001/XMLSchema">

  <xsd:element name="note" type="xsd:string"/>

  <xsd:element name="transaction" type="transactionType"/>

  <xsd:complexType name="transactionType">
    <xsd:sequence>
      <xsd:element name="Lender" type="address"/>
      <xsd:element name="Borrower" type="address"/>
      <xsd:element ref="note" minOccurs="0"/>
      <xsd:element name="paintings" type="paintings"/>
    </xsd:sequence>
    <xsd:attribute name="borrowDate" type="xsd:date"/>
  </xsd:complexType>
      .
      .
      .
```

We have to declare the paintings type before the schema will be acceptable to a schema-based validator:

```
<?xml version="1.0"?>
<xsd:schema xmlns:xsd="http://www.w3.org/2001/XMLSchema">

  <xsd:element name="note" type="xsd:string"/>

  <xsd:element name="transaction" type="transactionType"/>

  <xsd:complexType name="transactionType">
    <xsd:sequence>
      <xsd:element name="Lender" type="address"/>
      <xsd:element name="Borrower" type="address"/>
```

```
        <xsd:element ref="note" minOccurs="0"/>
        <xsd:element name="paintings" type="paintings"/>
    </xsd:sequence>
    <xsd:attribute name="borrowDate" type="xsd:date"/>
  </xsd:complexType>

  <xsd:complexType name="address">
    <xsd:sequence>
      <xsd:element name="name" type="xsd:string"/>
      <xsd:element name="street" type="xsd:string"/>
      <xsd:element name="city" type="xsd:string"/>
      <xsd:element name="state" type="xsd:string"/>
    </xsd:sequence>
    <xsd:attribute name="phone" type="xsd:string"
      use="optional"/>
  </xsd:complexType>

  <xsd:complexType name="paintings">
        .
        .
        .
  </xsd:complexType>
        .
        .
        .
</xsd:schema>
```

The <paintings> element contains these child elements:

```
<?xml version="1.0"?>
<transaction borrowDate="2009-10-15">
    <Lender phone="607.555.2222">
        <name>Doug Glass</name>
        <street>416 Disk Drive</street>
        <city>Medfield</city>
        <state>MA</state>
    </Lender>
    <Borrower phone="310.555.1111">
        <name>Britta Regensburg</name>
        <street>219 Union Drive</street>
        <city>Medfield</city>
        <state>CA</state>
    </Borrower>
    <note>Lender wants these back in two weeks!</note>
    <paintings>
        <painting paintingID="123-4567-890">
            <paintingTitle>The Castle</paintingTitle>
            <creationDate>1900-10-20</creationDate>
            <replacementValue>15000.95</replacementValue>
```

```
            <maxDaysOut>14</maxDaysOut>
        </painting>
        <painting paintingID="123-4567-891">
            <paintingTitle>The Cafe</paintingTitle>
            <creationDate>1901-10-21</creationDate>
            <replacementValue>19000.99</replacementValue>
            <maxDaysOut>14</maxDaysOut>
        </painting>
        <painting paintingID="123-4567-892">
            <paintingTitle>The Manor House</paintingTitle>
            <creationDate>1902-10-22</creationDate>
            <replacementValue>11000.95</replacementValue>
            <maxDaysOut>14</maxDaysOut>
        </painting>
        <painting paintingID="123-4567-893">
            <paintingTitle>The Condo</paintingTitle>
            <creationDate>1903-10-23</creationDate>
            <replacementValue>170000.99</replacementValue>
            <maxDaysOut>14</maxDaysOut>
        </painting>
    </paintings>
</transaction>
```

Note that what we've got here are four <painting> child elements. That's the first time we've encountered multiple elements of the same kind. What if we wanted to allow, say, up to ten <painting> elements inside a <paintings> element?

XML schemas are up to the task.

Specifying the Minimum and Maximum Number of Times an Element Can Occur

When you declare an element with the <xsd:element> element, you can specify how many times the element you're declaring can occur at that spot. To say that the maximum number of occurrences of the element is ten, you set the <xsd:element> element's maxOccurs attribute equal to 10:

```
<?xml version="1.0"?>
<xsd:schema xmlns:xsd="http://www.w3.org/2001/XMLSchema">

  <xsd:element name="note" type="xsd:string"/>

  <xsd:element name="transaction" type="transactionType"/>

  <xsd:complexType name="transactionType">
    <xsd:sequence>
      <xsd:element name="Lender" type="address"/>
      <xsd:element name="Borrower" type="address"/>
      <xsd:element ref="note" minOccurs="0"/>
```

```
      <xsd:element name="paintings" type="paintings"/>
    </xsd:sequence>
    <xsd:attribute name="borrowDate" type="xsd:date"/>
  </xsd:complexType>

  <xsd:complexType name="address">
    <xsd:sequence>
      <xsd:element name="name" type="xsd:string"/>
      <xsd:element name="street" type="xsd:string"/>
      <xsd:element name="city" type="xsd:string"/>
      <xsd:element name="state" type="xsd:string"/>
    </xsd:sequence>
    <xsd:attribute name="phone" type="xsd:string"
      use="optional"/>
  </xsd:complexType>

  <xsd:complexType name="paintings">
    <xsd:sequence>
      <xsd:element name="painting" maxOccurs="10">
        .
        .
        .
    </xsd:sequence>
  </xsd:complexType>

</xsd:schema>
```

And to specify the minimum number of occurrences of the element, you use the minOccurs attribute. The default value for minOccurs is 1, and the default value for maxOccurs is the same as the value of minOccurs.

Setting a value of minOccurs to 1 means the element is required to be at that location, and setting a value of 0 for minOccurs means that the element is optional. For example, we can make the <note> element optional, as well as the <painting> element, like this, by setting minOccurs to 0:

```
<?xml version="1.0"?>
<xsd:schema xmlns:xsd="http://www.w3.org/2001/XMLSchema">

  <xsd:element name="note" type="xsd:string"/>

  <xsd:element name="transaction" type="transactionType"/>

  <xsd:complexType name="transactionType">
    <xsd:sequence>
      <xsd:element name="Lender" type="address"/>
      <xsd:element name="Borrower" type="address"/>
      <xsd:element ref="note" minOccurs="0"/>
      <xsd:element name="paintings" type="paintings"/>
    </xsd:sequence>
```

```
      <xsd:attribute name="borrowDate" type="xsd:date"/>
    </xsd:complexType>

    <xsd:complexType name="address">
      <xsd:sequence>
        <xsd:element name="name" type="xsd:string"/>
        <xsd:element name="street" type="xsd:string"/>
        <xsd:element name="city" type="xsd:string"/>
        <xsd:element name="state" type="xsd:string"/>
      </xsd:sequence>
      <xsd:attribute name="phone" type="xsd:string"
        use="optional"/>
    </xsd:complexType>

    <xsd:complexType name="paintings">
      <xsd:sequence>
        <xsd:element name="painting" minOccurs="0" maxOccurs="10">
             .
             .
             .
      </xsd:sequence>
    </xsd:complexType>

</xsd:schema>
```

To indicate that there is no upper bound to the maxOccurs attribute, set it to the value "unbounded".

We still have to declare the type of the <painting> element. Are we going to do that with a complex type? Yes, but we're not going to use an <xsd:complexType> element to do it—we're going to use an anonymous complex type.

Declaring Anonymous Types

When you declare a complex type using <xsd:complexType>, you give that complex type a name, such as "address":

```
<?xml version="1.0"?>
<xsd:schema xmlns:xsd="http://www.w3.org/2001/XMLSchema">
         .
         .
         .
  <xsd:complexType name="address">
    <xsd:sequence>
      <xsd:element name="name" type="xsd:string"/>
      <xsd:element name="street" type="xsd:string"/>
      <xsd:element name="city" type="xsd:string"/>
      <xsd:element name="state" type="xsd:string"/>
    </xsd:sequence>
    <xsd:attribute name="phone" type="xsd:string"
```

```
          use="optional"/>
      </xsd:complexType>
            .
            .
            .
```

However, there's another way to declare complex types without giving the new type a
name at all—you can declare the new type anonymously, without a name.

That works just fine if you only plan to use the new complex type once in your schema—if
so, there's no reason to give the new type a name, because you're not going to refer to it
throughout your schema.

Here's how to do it—you just use the <xsd:complexType> element—without a name
attribute—inside an <xsd:element> element:

```
<?xml version="1.0"?>
<xsd:schema xmlns:xsd="http://www.w3.org/2001/XMLSchema">

  <xsd:element name="transaction" type="transactionType"/>

  <xsd:element name="note" type="xsd:string"/>

  <xsd:complexType name="transactionType">
    <xsd:sequence>
      <xsd:element name="Lender" type="address"/>
      <xsd:element name="Borrower" type="address"/>
      <xsd:element ref="note" minOccurs="0"/>
      <xsd:element name="paintings" type="paintings"/>
    </xsd:sequence>
    <xsd:attribute name="borrowDate" type="xsd:date"/>
  </xsd:complexType>

  <xsd:complexType name="address">
    <xsd:sequence>
      <xsd:element name="name" type="xsd:string"/>
      <xsd:element name="street" type="xsd:string"/>
      <xsd:element name="city" type="xsd:string"/>
      <xsd:element name="state" type="xsd:string"/>
    </xsd:sequence>
    <xsd:attribute name="phone" type="xsd:string"
      use="optional"/>
  </xsd:complexType>

  <xsd:complexType name="paintings">
    <xsd:sequence>
      <xsd:element name="painting" minOccurs="0" maxOccurs="10">
        <xsd:complexType>
          .
          .
          .
        </xsd:complexType>
```

```
        </xsd:element>
      </xsd:sequence>
    </xsd:complexType>

</xsd:schema>
```

Now you're free to declare the type of the <painting> element inside the nested <xsd:complexType> element—no name needed for that type.

Okay, so what's in a <painting> element? Here's what one looks like:

```
<painting paintingID-"123-4567-890">
    <paintingTitle>The Castle</paintingTitle>
    <creationDate>1900-10-20</creationDate>
    <replacementValue>15000.95</replacementValue>
    <maxDaysOut>14</maxDaysOut>
</painting>
```

So there's a <paintingTitle> child element, followed by a <creationDate> child element, followed by a <replacementValue> child element, followed by a <maxDaysOut> child element. That means we should start this anonymous type with a sequence:

```
<?xml version="1.0"?>
<xsd:schema xmlns:xsd="http://www.w3.org/2001/XMLSchema">

  <xsd:element name="transaction" type="transactionType"/>

  <xsd:complexType name="transactionType">
    <xsd:sequence>
      <xsd:element name="Lender" type="address"/>
      <xsd:element name="Borrower" type="address"/>
      <xsd:element ref="note" minOccurs="0"/>
      <xsd:element name="paintings" type="paintings"/>
    </xsd:sequence>
    <xsd:attribute name="borrowDate" type="xsd:date"/>
  </xsd:complexType>

  <xsd:element name="note" type="xsd:string"/>

  <xsd:complexType name="address">
    <xsd:sequence>
      <xsd:element name="name" type="xsd:string"/>
      <xsd:element name="street" type="xsd:string"/>
      <xsd:element name="city" type="xsd:string"/>
      <xsd:element name="state" type="xsd:string"/>
    </xsd:sequence>
    <xsd:attribute name="phone" type="xsd:string"
      use="optional"/>
  </xsd:complexType>

  <xsd:complexType name="paintings">
    <xsd:sequence>
```

```
        <xsd:element name="painting" minOccurs="0" maxOccurs="10">
          <xsd:complexType>
            <xsd:sequence>

                .
                .
                .

            </xsd:sequence>
          </xsd:complexType>
        </xsd:element>
       </xsd:sequence>
     </xsd:complexType>

</xsd:schema>
```

And here's what goes into the sequence—note that the <creationDate> child element is of type xsd:date, the <replacementValue> child element is of type xsd:decimal (to allow numbers like 17009.99), and the <maxDaysOut> element is declared to be of a simple type whose values we restrict—we'll see how that works in the next chapter:

```
<?xml version="1.0"?>
<xsd:schema xmlns:xsd="http://www.w3.org/2001/XMLSchema">

  <xsd:element name="transaction" type="transactionType"/>

  <xsd:complexType name="transactionType">
    <xsd:sequence>
      <xsd:element name="Lender" type="address"/>
      <xsd:element name="Borrower" type="address"/>
      <xsd:element ref="note" minOccurs="0"/>
      <xsd:element name="paintings" type="paintings"/>
    </xsd:sequence>
    <xsd:attribute name="borrowDate" type="xsd:date"/>
  </xsd:complexType>

  <xsd:element name="note" type="xsd:string"/>

  <xsd:complexType name="address">
    <xsd:sequence>
      <xsd:element name="name" type="xsd:string"/>
      <xsd:element name="street" type="xsd:string"/>
      <xsd:element name="city" type="xsd:string"/>
      <xsd:element name="state" type="xsd:string"/>
    </xsd:sequence>
    <xsd:attribute name="phone" type="xsd:string"
      use="optional"/>
  </xsd:complexType>

  <xsd:complexType name="paintings">
    <xsd:sequence>
```

```
<xsd:element name="painting" minOccurs="0" maxOccurs="10">
  <xsd:complexType>
    <xsd:sequence>
     <xsd:element name="paintingTitle" type="xsd:string"/>
     <xsd:element name="creationDate" type="xsd:date"
       minOccurs='0'/>
     <xsd:element name="replacementValue" type="xsd:decimal"/>
     <xsd:element name="maxDaysOut">
       <xsd:simpleType>
         <xsd:restriction base="xsd:integer">
           <xsd:maxInclusive value="14"/>
         </xsd:restriction>
       </xsd:simpleType>
     </xsd:element>
    </xsd:sequence>
  </xsd:complexType>
 </xsd:element>
 </xsd:sequence>
</xsd:complexType>

</xsd:schema>
```

And that's how you declare elements using anonymous types. Note that if you want to declare a number of elements to be of the same type, you should create a named type that you can use to declare a number of elements—anonymous types are only useful to declare single elements.

What if you have a situation where you want to use the *same* element in a number of places in your document? For example, we have a <note> element that's handy for adding comments to our XML document, and you could see how you might want to add a <note> child element to several other elements. How do you handle this one? You declare the <note> element by *reference*.

Declaring Elements by Reference

To use an element such as <note> in a number of different places in the same document, you can start by declaring it at the top level—that is, outside any other declaration, like this:

```
<?xml version="1.0"?>
<xsd:schema xmlns:xsd="http://www.w3.org/2001/XMLSchema">

  <xsd:element name="note" type="xsd:string"/>

  <xsd:element name="transaction" type="transactionType"/>

  <xsd:complexType name="transactionType">
    <xsd:sequence>
      <xsd:element name="Lender" type="address"/>
      <xsd:element name="Borrower" type="address"/>
      <xsd:element ref="note" minOccurs="0"/>
```

```
        <xsd:element name="paintings" type="paintings"/>
      </xsd:sequence>
      <xsd:attribute name="borrowDate" type="xsd:date"/>
    </xsd:complexType>

    <xsd:complexType name="address">
      <xsd:sequence>
        <xsd:element name="name" type="xsd:string"/>
        <xsd:element name="street" type="xsd:string"/>
        <xsd:element name="city" type="xsd:string"/>
        <xsd:element name="state" type="xsd:string"/>
      </xsd:sequence>
      <xsd:attribute name="phone" type="xsd:string"
        use="optional"/>
      </xsd:complexType>

        .
        .
        .

</xsd:schema>
```

Now you can add a <note> child element to any other element you're declaring. To do that, you use the <xsd:element> element's ref attribute, not its name attribute, to declare the <note> element. That looks like this, where we're adding the <note> element as a child element of the <transaction> element:

```
<?xml version="1.0"?>
<xsd:schema xmlns:xsd="http://www.w3.org/2001/XMLSchema">

  <xsd:element name="note" type="xsd:string"/>

  <xsd:element name="transaction" type="transactionType"/>

  <xsd:complexType name="transactionType">
    <xsd:sequence>
      <xsd:element name="Lender" type="address"/>
      <xsd:element name="Borrower" type="address"/>
      <xsd:element ref="note" minOccurs="0"/>
      <xsd:element name="paintings" type="paintings"/>
    </xsd:sequence>
    <xsd:attribute name="borrowDate" type="xsd:date"/>
  </xsd:complexType>

  <xsd:complexType name="address">
    <xsd:sequence>
      <xsd:element name="name" type="xsd:string"/>
      <xsd:element name="street" type="xsd:string"/>
      <xsd:element name="city" type="xsd:string"/>
      <xsd:element name="state" type="xsd:string"/>
```

```
  </xsd:sequence>
  <xsd:attribute name="phone" type="xsd:string"
    use="optional"/>
  </xsd:complexType>
        .
        .
        .

</xsd:schema>
```

As things stand, we only use <note> once in our sample document to show how it's done, but you could add <note> child elements to other elements as well—for example, here's how you can add a <note> child element to the address type as well:

```
<?xml version="1.0"?>
<xsd:schema xmlns:xsd="http://www.w3.org/2001/XMLSchema">

  <xsd:element name="note" type="xsd:string"/>

  <xsd:element name="transaction" type="transactionType"/>

  <xsd:complexType name="transactionType">
    <xsd:sequence>
      <xsd:element name="Lender" type="address"/>
      <xsd:element name="Borrower" type="address"/>
      <xsd:element ref="note" minOccurs="0"/>
      <xsd:element name="paintings" type="paintings"/>
    </xsd:sequence>
    <xsd:attribute name="borrowDate" type="xsd:date"/>
  </xsd:complexType>

  <xsd:complexType name="address">
    <xsd:sequence>
      <xsd:element name="name" type="xsd:string"/>
      <xsd:element ref="note" minOccurs="0"/>
      <xsd:element name="street" type="xsd:string"/>
      <xsd:element name="city" type="xsd:string"/>
      <xsd:element name="state" type="xsd:string"/>
    </xsd:sequence>
    <xsd:attribute name="phone" type="xsd:string"
      use="optional"/>
  </xsd:complexType>
        .
        .
        .

</xsd:schema>
```

When you declare an element at the top level, there's no limit to the number of times you can declare that element by reference as a child element of other elements.

Chapter 4

XML Schemas: Creating Your Own Types

Key Skills & Concepts

- Declaring attributes
- Restricting attribute values
- Using XML facets
- Creating XML schema choices
- Annotating XML schemas

This chapter tops off our coverage on XML schemas. Here, we're going to see how to declare attributes, give attributes default values, create our own simple types (you saw how to create your own complex types in the preceding chapter), declare empty elements, create elements and attributes groups, and more.

We'll begin by picking up where we left off in the preceding chapter—with declaring attributes in an XML schema.

Declaring Attributes

Our example XML document, Document.xml, has a number of XML attributes in use:

```xml
<?xml version="1.0"?>
<transaction borrowDate="2009-10-15">
    <Lender phone="607.555.2222">
        <name>Doug Glass</name>
        <street>416 Disk Drive</street>
        <city>Medfield</city>
        <state>MA</state>
    </Lender>
    <Borrower phone="310.555.1111">
        <name>Britta Regensburg</name>
        <street>219 Union Drive</street>
        <city>Medfield</city>
        <state>CA</state>
    </Borrower>
    <note>Lender wants these back in two weeks!</note>
    <paintings>
        <painting paintingID="123-4567-890">
            <paintingTitle>The Castle</paintingTitle>
            <creationDate>1900-10-20</creationDate>
            <replacementValue>15000.95</replacementValue>
            <maxDaysOut>14</maxDaysOut>
        </painting>
```

```
    <painting paintingID="123-4567-891">
        <paintingTitle>The Cafe</paintingTitle>
        <creationDate>1901-10-21</creationDate>
        <replacementValue>19000.99</replacementValue>
        <maxDaysOut>14</maxDaysOut>
    </painting>
    <painting paintingID="123-4567-892">
        <paintingTitle>The Manor House</paintingTitle>
        <creationDate>1902-10-22</creationDate>
        <replacementValue>11000.95</replacementValue>
        <maxDaysOut>14</maxDaysOut>
    </painting>
    <painting paintingID="123-4567-893">
        <paintingTitle>The Condo</paintingTitle>
        <creationDate>1903-10-23</creationDate>
        <replacementValue>170000.99</replacementValue>
        <maxDaysOut>14</maxDaysOut>
    </painting>
  </paintings>
</transaction>
```

Since an XML schema processor has to check everything about an XML document, attributes also need to be declared. And you declare attributes with the <xsdd:attribute> element.

Here, for example, is how you declare the <transaction> element's borrowDate attribute—we'll make this attribute of the xsd:date simple, built-in type:

```
<xsd:attribute name="borrowDate" type="xsd:date"/>
```

Where do you declare this attribute? You declare it when you declare the type of the element that uses the attribute. We made the <transaction> element of the type we named "transactionType" like this:

```
<xsd:complexType name="transactionType">
  <xsd:sequence>
    <xsd:element name="Lender" type="address"/>
    <xsd:element name="Borrower" type="address"/>
    <xsd:element ref="note" minOccurs="0"/>
    <xsd:element name="paintings" type="paintings"/>
  </xsd:sequence>
</xsd:complexType>
```

You add the <xsd:attribute> element when declaring this type, and put it in after the sequence of child elements:

```
<xsd:complexType name="transactionType">
  <xsd:sequence>
    <xsd:element name="Lender" type="address"/>
    <xsd:element name="Borrower" type="address"/>
    <xsd:element ref="note" minOccurs="0"/>
```

```
    <xsd:element name="paintings" type="paintings"/>
  </xsd:sequence>
  <xsd:attribute name="borrowDate" type="xsd:date"/>
</xsd:complexType>
```

And that declares the borrowDate attribute of the <transaction> element.

If you have multiple attributes, you can list them one right after the other. Say, for example, that you wanted to add a language attribute to the transactionType type that you can assign strings to—you could declare that like this:

```
<xsd:complexType name="transactionType">
  <xsd:sequence>
    <xsd:element name="Lender" type="address"/>
    <xsd:element name="Borrower" type="address"/>
    <xsd:element ref="note" minOccurs="0"/>
    <xsd:element name="paintings" type="paintings"/>
  </xsd:sequence>
  <xsd:attribute name="borrowDate" type="xsd:date"/>
  <xsd:attribute name="language" type="xsd:string"/>
</xsd:complexType>
```

There are other possibilities as well. For example, the <Lender> and <Borrower> elements have an attribute named phone:

```
<Lender phone="607.555.2222">
    <name>Doug Glass</name>
    <street>416 Disk Drive</street>
    <city>Medfield</city>
    <state>MA</state>
</Lender>
<Borrower phone="310.555.1111">
    <name>Britta Regensburg</name>
    <street>219 Union Drive</street>
    <city>Medfield</city>
    <state>CA</state>
</Borrower>
```

And the <Lender> and <Borrower> elements are declared to be of type "address":

```
<xsd:complexType name="transactionType">
  <xsd:sequence>
    <xsd:element name="Lender" type="address"/>
    <xsd:element name="Borrower" type="address"/>
    <xsd:element ref="note" minOccurs="0"/>
    <xsd:element name="paintings" type="paintings"/>
  </xsd:sequence>
  <xsd:attribute name="borrowDate" type="xsd:date"/>
</xsd:complexType>
```

In the address type, then, we can declare the phone attribute this way, making it of type xsd:string—that is, simple text:

```
<xsd:complexType name="address">
  <xsd:sequence>
    <xsd:element name="name" type="xsd:string"/>
    <xsd:element name="street" type="xsd:string"/>
    <xsd:element name="city" type="xsd:string"/>
    <xsd:element name="state" type="xsd:string"/>
  </xsd:sequence>
  <xsd:attribute name="phone" type="xsd:string"/>
</xsd:complexType>
```

But now we can do more with the phone attribute—we can make its use optional with the <xsd:attribute> element's use attribute like this:

```
<xsd:complexType name="address">
  <xsd:sequence>
    <xsd:element name="name" type="xsd:string"/>
    <xsd:element name="street" type="xsd:string"/>
    <xsd:element name="city" type="xsd:string"/>
    <xsd:element name="state" type="xsd:string"/>
  </xsd:sequence>
  <xsd:attribute name="phone" type="xsd:string"
    use="optional"/>
</xsd:complexType>
```

And that makes the phone attribute optional (the default for attributes, if you don't use the use attribute, is to make them required). What possibilities are there for the use attribute? We'll take a look at that in a couple of pages.

There are other possibilities for declaring attributes as well—you can restrict the possible values that an attribute can take. You do that by creating your own simple type—that is, you don't actually create a new type like xsd:integer or xsd:string, but you put restrictions on an existing simple type.

Here's an example. The <painting> elements in our sample XML document have an attribute named paintingID that's set to a string consisting of three digits, a dash, four digits, another dash, and three more digits:

```
<paintings>
    <painting paintingID="123-4567-890">
        <paintingTitle>The Castle</paintingTitle>
        <creationDate>1900-10-20</creationDate>
        <replacementValue>15000.95</replacementValue>
        <maxDaysOut>14</maxDaysOut>
    </painting>
    <painting paintingID="123-4567-891">
        <paintingTitle>The Cafe</paintingTitle>
        <creationDate>1901-10-21</creationDate>
        <replacementValue>19000.99</replacementValue>
        <maxDaysOut>14</maxDaysOut>
    </painting>
```

```
    <painting paintingID="123-4567-892">
        <paintingTitle>The Manor House</paintingTitle>
        <creationDate>1902-10-22</creationDate>
        <replacementValue>11000.95</replacementValue>
        <maxDaysOut>14</maxDaysOut>
    </painting>
    <painting paintingID="123-4567-893">
        <paintingTitle>The Condo</paintingTitle>
        <creationDate>1903-10-23</creationDate>
        <replacementValue>170000.99</replacementValue>
        <maxDaysOut>14</maxDaysOut>
    </painting>
</paintings>
```

Can you actually restrict the values the paintingID can take to have that format—a string consisting of three digits, a dash, four digits, another dash, and three more digits? Yes, you can. There are several ways to restrict the values that attributes can take, and one is to restrict strings to match *regular expressions*. Regular expressions are beyond the scope of this book—and you won't have to know them to read this book—but using them, you can set up a template that strings must match. For example, the regular expression that matches the legal attribute values we want is "\d{3}-\d{4}-\d{3}" (\d stands for "digit"), and, as we're going to see later in this chapter, you can create a simple type named, say, catalogID, consisting of a string consisting of three digits, a dash, four digits, another dash, and three more digits like this:

```
<xsd:simpleType name="catalogID">
  <xsd:restriction base="xsd:string">
    <xsd:pattern value="\d{3}-\d{4}-\d{3}"/>
  </xsd:restriction>
</xsd:simpleType>
```

Then all you have to do is to declare the paintingID attribute to be of that type when you declare that attribute:

```
<xsd:complexType name="paintings">
  <xsd:sequence>
    <xsd:element name="painting" minOccurs="0" maxOccurs="10">
      <xsd:complexType>
        <xsd:sequence>
          <xsd:element name="paintingTitle" type="xsd:string"/>
          <xsd:element name="creationDate" type="xsd:date"
            minOccurs='0'/>
          <xsd:element name="replacementValue" type="xsd:decimal"/>
          <xsd:element name="maxDaysOut">
            <xsd:simpleType>
              <xsd:restriction base="xsd:integer">
                <xsd:maxInclusive value="14"/>
              </xsd:restriction>
```

```
          </xsd:simpleType>
        </xsd:element>
      </xsd:sequence>
      <xsd:attribute name="paintingID" type="catalogID"/>
    </xsd:complexType>
  </xsd:element>
  </xsd:sequence>
</xsd:complexType>
```

So we've seen that you can declare elements and give their simple type (attributes can't be of a complex type) with the <xsd:attribute> element. And we've seen that you can set an attribute's use (for example, optional or not) with the use attribute. And you can restrict the possible values attributes can take as well. Here's how the attributes are declared in our XML schema, schema.xsd:

```
<?xml version="1.0"?>
<xsd:schema xmlns:xsd="http://www.w3.org/2001/XMLSchema">

  <xsd:annotation>
    <xsd:documentation>
        Painting borrowing transaction schema.
    </xsd:documentation>
  </xsd:annotation>

  <xsd:element name="transaction" type="transactionType"/>

  <xsd:complexType name="transactionType">
    <xsd:sequence>
      <xsd:element name="Lender" type="address"/>
      <xsd:element name="Borrower" type="address"/>
      <xsd:element ref="note" minOccurs="0"/>
      <xsd:element name="paintings" type="paintings"/>
    </xsd:sequence>
    <xsd:attribute name="borrowDate" type="xsd:date"/>
  </xsd:complexType>

  <xsd:element name="note" type="xsd:string"/>

  <xsd:complexType name="address">
    <xsd:sequence>
      <xsd:element name="name" type="xsd:string"/>
      <xsd:element name="street" type="xsd:string"/>
      <xsd:element name="city" type="xsd:string"/>
      <xsd:element name="state" type="xsd:string"/>
    </xsd:sequence>
    <xsd:attribute name="phone" type="xsd:string"
      use="optional"/>
  </xsd:complexType>
```

```
<xsd:complexType name="paintings">
  <xsd:sequence>
    <xsd:element name="painting" minOccurs="0" maxOccurs="10">
      <xsd:complexType>
        <xsd:sequence>
         <xsd:element name="paintingTitle" type="xsd:string"/>
         <xsd:element name="creationDate" type="xsd:date"
           minOccurs='0'/>
         <xsd:element name="replacementValue" type="xsd:decimal"/>
         <xsd:element name="maxDaysOut">
            <xsd:simpleType>
              <xsd:restriction base="xsd:integer">
                <xsd:maxInclusive value="14"/>
              </xsd:restriction>
            </xsd:simpleType>
         </xsd:element>
        </xsd:sequence>
        <xsd:attribute name="paintingID" type="catalogID"/>
      </xsd:complexType>
    </xsd:element>
  </xsd:sequence>
</xsd:complexType>

<xsd:simpleType name="catalogID">
  <xsd:restriction base="xsd:string">
    <xsd:pattern value="\d{3}-\d{4}-\d{3}"/>
  </xsd:restriction>
</xsd:simpleType>

</xsd:schema>
```

Okay—now we're going to take a look at the possibilities for the <xsd:attribute> element's use attribute to see how to make attributes optional or not, and then we'll take a look at creating our own simple types, and making attributes of those types.

Try This Adding an Attribute

Try adding another attribute, nationality, to the <Lender> and <Borrower> elements, and assign a string to that attribute:

```
<?xml version="1.0"?>
<transaction borrowDate="2009-10-15">
    <Lender phone="607.555.2222" nationality="US">
        <name>Doug Glass</name>
        <street>416 Disk Drive</street>
        <city>Medfield</city>
        <state>MA</state>
    </Lender>
```

```
<Borrower phone="310.555.1111" nationality="US">
    <name>Britta Regensburg</name>
    <street>219 Union Drive</street>
    <city>Medfield</city>
    <state>CA</state>
</Borrower>
<note>Lender wants these back in two weeks!</note>
<paintings>
    .
    .
    .
```

Note that adding this new attribute will mean editing the address type in our sample XML schema.

When you're done, make sure your XML document and schema validate at www.xmlme .com/validator.aspx.

Specifying Attribute Use

You can specify what the legal uses for attributes are with the use attribute of the <xsd: attribute> element. Here are the possible values for the use attribute:

- **required**   The attribute is required, and it may have any value. (This is the default.)

- **optional**   The attribute is optional, and it may have any value.

- **prohibited**   The attribute must not appear.

For example, this attribute declaration makes the phone attribute in the address type optional:

```
<xsd:complexType name="address">
  <xsd:sequence>
    <xsd:element name="name" type="xsd:string"/>
    <xsd:element name="street" type="xsd:string"/>
    <xsd:element name="city" type="xsd:string"/>
    <xsd:element name="state" type="xsd:string"/>
  </xsd:sequence>
  <xsd:attribute name="phone" type="xsd:string"
    use="optional"/>
</xsd:complexType>
```

And this makes the phone attribute required (which is also the default if you omit the use attribute):

```
<xsd:complexType name="address">
  <xsd:sequence>
    <xsd:element name="name" type="xsd:string"/>
```

```
   <xsd:element name="street" type="xsd:string"/>
   <xsd:element name="city" type="xsd:string"/>
   <xsd:element name="state" type="xsd:string"/>
 </xsd:sequence>
 <xsd:attribute name="phone" type="xsd:string"
   use="required"/>
 </xsd:complexType>
```

Besides the use attribute, there are two more attributes of the <xsd:attribute> element that are worth noting—fixed and default.

You can set a default value for attributes in XML schemas, just as you can in DTDs. In XML schemas, you use the default attribute in the <xsd:attribute> element. For example, say that you added a language attribute to the address type and wanted to give it the default value "EN" (for English) if no other value is assigned to the attribute in the element in which it appears. You could give the language attribute this default value like this in the address type:

```
<xsd:complexType name="address">
  <xsd:sequence>
    <xsd:element name="name" type="xsd:string"/>
    <xsd:element name="street" type="xsd:string"/>
    <xsd:element name="city" type="xsd:string"/>
    <xsd:element name="state" type="xsd:string"/>
  </xsd:sequence>
  <xsd:attribute name="phone" type="xsd:string"
    use="required"/>
  <xsd:attribute name="language" type="xsd:string"
    default="EN"/>
</xsd:complexType>
```

What if you wanted to insist that the language attribute be set to "EN", so that it would be an error if it wasn't set to "EN"? You could do that with the fixed attribute:

```
<xsd:complexType name="address">
  <xsd:sequence>
    <xsd:element name="name" type="xsd:string"/>
    <xsd:element name="street" type="xsd:string"/>
    <xsd:element name="city" type="xsd:string"/>
    <xsd:element name="state" type="xsd:string"/>
  </xsd:sequence>
  <xsd:attribute name="phone" type="xsd:string"
    use="required"/>
  <xsd:attribute name="language" type="xsd:string"
    fixed="EN"/>
</xsd:complexType>
```

And you can also use the fixed and default attributes when declaring elements. For example, say that you have an element named <term> that can contain an integer value:

```
<term>600</term>
```

Now say that you want to make the default contents of this element a value of 800 if you don't specify anything else—here's what that would look like when you declared the <term> element using the default attribute:

```
<xsd:element name="term" type="xsd:integer" default="800"/>
```

And you could also specify that you wanted to fix the <term> element's content to always be 800 like this, using the fixed attribute:

```
<xsd:element name="term" type="xsd:integer" fixed="800"/>
```

Try This   Fixing an Attribute

Try fixing the nationality attribute that you added to the <Lender> and <Borrower> elements to "US":

```
<?xml version="1.0"?>
<transaction borrowDate="2009-10-15">
    <Lender phone="607.555.2222" nationality="US">
        <name>Doug Glass</name>
        <street>416 Disk Drive</street>
        <city>Medfield</city>
        <state>MA</state>
    </Lender>
    <Borrower phone="310.555.1111" nationality="US">
        <name>Britta Regensburg</name>
        <street>219 Union Drive</street>
        <city>Medfield</city>
        <state>CA</state>
    </Borrower>
    <note>Lender wants these back in two weeks!</note>
    <paintings>
        .
        .
        .
```

Note that, as before, altering this new attribute will mean editing the address type in our sample XML schemas.

When you're done, make sure your XML document and schema validate at www.xmlme .com/validator.aspx.

Restricting Simple Types

Now let's talk about restricting the values that simple types can have. For example, you saw the paintingID attribute is assigned strings of a certain format:

```
<paintings>
    <painting paintingID="123-4567-890">
        <paintingTitle>The Castle</paintingTitle>
        <creationDate>1900-10-20</creationDate>
        <replacementValue>15000.95</replacementValue>
        <maxDaysOut>14</maxDaysOut>
    </painting>
    <painting paintingID="123-4567-891">
        <paintingTitle>The Cafe</paintingTitle>
        <creationDate>1901-10-21</creationDate>
        <replacementValue>19000.99</replacementValue>
        <maxDaysOut>14</maxDaysOut>
    </painting>
    <painting paintingID="123-4567-892">
        <paintingTitle>The Manor House</paintingTitle>
        <creationDate>1902-10-22</creationDate>
        <replacementValue>11000.95</replacementValue>
        <maxDaysOut>14</maxDaysOut>
    </painting>
    <painting paintingID="123-4567-893">
        <paintingTitle>The Condo</paintingTitle>
        <creationDate>1903-10-23</creationDate>
        <replacementValue>170000.99</replacementValue>
        <maxDaysOut>14</maxDaysOut>
    </painting>
</paintings>
```

Since we're restricting the possible values the paintingID attribute can take, we can't just make paintingID an attribute of an existing simple type, like xsd:string. Instead, we'll create our own simple type and call it catalogID, making paintingID an attribute of the catalogID type:

```
<xsd:complexType name="paintings">
  <xsd:sequence>
    <xsd:element name="painting" minOccurs="0" maxOccurs="10">
      <xsd:complexType>
        <xsd:sequence>
          <xsd:element name="paintingTitle" type="xsd:string"/>
          <xsd:element name="creationDate" type="xsd:date"
            minOccurs='0'/>
          <xsd:element name="replacementValue" type="xsd:decimal"/>
          <xsd:element name="maxDaysOut">
            <xsd:simpleType>
              <xsd:restriction base="xsd:integer">
                <xsd:maxInclusive value="14"/>
```

```
        </xsd:restriction>
      </xsd:simpleType>
    </xsd:element>
  </xsd:sequence>
  <xsd:attribute name="paintingID" type="catalogID"/>
  </xsd:complexType>
 </xsd:element>
 </xsd:sequence>
</xsd:complexType>
```

Here's how we create the catalogID simple type (note that this is the <xsd:simpleType> element, not the <xsd:complexType> element):

```
<xsd:simpleType name="catalogID">
    .
    .
    .
</xsd:simpleType>
```

To restrict the possible values this new simple type can contain, you use an <xsd:restriction> element. In that element, you specify the base type you're restricting with the base attribute—in this case, we're making the paintingID attribute be of type xsd:string, but restricting it to strings of a certain format. That means the base type we're restring is xsd:string:

```
<xsd:simpleType name="catalogID">
  <xsd:restriction base="xsd:string">
    .
    .
    .
  </xsd:restriction>
</xsd:simpleType>
```

Okay, but how do we restrict the string type? We want the simple type we're creating to match the regular expression "\d{3}-\d{4}-\d{3}", and you can enforce that constraint with the XML schema *facet* <xsd:pattern>. A facet is an element that lets you construct a constraint—and the <xsd:pattern> facet lets you constrain strings based on how well they match a regular expression. Here's how we complete the catalogID simple type:

```
<xsd:simpleType name="catalogID">
  <xsd:restriction base="xsd:string">
    <xsd:pattern value="\d{3}-\d{4}-\d{3}"/>
  </xsd:restriction>
</xsd:simpleType>
```

Okay, that's one example of creating a simple type, which we accomplished by restricting the values a string can take. But as mentioned earlier, you won't have to know about regular expressions to read this book, so let's take a look at some other examples of creating simple types.

For example, let's say we wanted to create a new simple type (which you can use to create attributes or elements) named dayOfMonth that can only take values from 1 to 31:

```
<xsd:simpleType name="dayOfMonth">
        .
        .
        .
</xsd:simpleType>
```

Since this simple type can only take values from 1 to 31, let's base it on the xsd:integer type with an <xsd:restriction> element:

```
<xsd:simpleType name="dayOfMonth">
    <xsd:restriction base="xsd:integer">
        .
        .
        .
    </xsd:restriction>
</xsd:simpleType>
```

Now we need to use a facet to restrict the possible values this simple type can take. Or rather, we'll need two facets—one to make the lower limit 1 and one to make the upper limit 31. To set the lower limit, you can use the <xsd:minInclusive> schema facet like this:

```
<xsd:simpleType name="dayOfMonth">
    <xsd:restriction base="xsd:integer">
        <xsd:minInclusive value="1"/>
        .
        .
    </xsd:restriction>
</xsd:simpleType>
```

And to make the upper limit of legal values 31, you can use the <xsd:maxInclusive> facet like this:

```
<xsd:simpleType name="dayOfMonth">
    <xsd:restriction base="xsd:integer">
        <xsd:minInclusive value="1"/>
        <xsd:maxInclusive value="31"/>
    </xsd:restriction>
</xsd:simpleType>
```

As you can see, in addition to the <xsd:facet>, XML schemas support the <xsd:maxInclusive> and <xsd:minInclusive> facets.

Here's another popular facet—the <xsd:enumeration> facet, which allows you to list the possible values a simple type can take. For example, say you want to create a simple type named weekday based on xsd:string that can only take the values "Sunday", "Monday", "Tuesday", and so on:

```
<xsd:simpleType name="weekday">
         .
         .
         .
</xsd:simpleType>
```

We'll base this new simple type on the existing xsd:string type:

```
<xsd:simpleType name="weekday">
   <xsd:restriction base="xsd:string">
         .
         .
         .
   </xsd:restriction>
</xsd:simpleType>
```

Now we'll use the <xsd:enumeration> facet to list the actual values this new simple type can take. For example, "Sunday" is a legal value:

```
<xsd:simpleType name="weekday">
    <xsd:restriction base="xsd:string">
        <xsd:enumeration value="Sunday"/>
         .
         .
         .
    </xsd:restriction>
</xsd:simpleType>
```

And so is "Monday":

```
<xsd:simpleType name="weekday">
    <xsd:restriction base="xsd:string">
        <xsd:enumeration value="Sunday"/>
        <xsd:enumeration value="Monday"/>
         .
         .
         .
    </xsd:restriction>
</xsd:simpleType>
```

Here are all the days of the week:

```
<xsd:simpleType name="weekday">
    <xsd:restriction base="xsd:string">
        <xsd:enumeration value="Sunday"/>
        <xsd:enumeration value="Monday"/>
        <xsd:enumeration value="Tuesday"/>
        <xsd:enumeration value="Wednesday"/>
```

```
            <xsd:enumeration value="Thursday"/>
            <xsd:enumeration value="Friday"/>
            <xsd:enumeration value="Saturday"/>
        </xsd:restriction>
    </xsd:simpleType>
```

That restricts this new simple type to the days of the week. Cool.

Try This Using the <xsd:enumeration> facet

Try creating an attribute for the <transaction> element of the weekday simple type:

```
<xsd:simpleType name="weekday">
    <xsd:restriction base="xsd:string">
        <xsd:enumeration value="Sunday"/>
        <xsd:enumeration value="Monday"/>
        <xsd:enumeration value="Tuesday"/>
        <xsd:enumeration value="Wednesday"/>
        <xsd:enumeration value="Thursday"/>
        <xsd:enumeration value="Friday"/>
        <xsd:enumeration value="Saturday"/>
    </xsd:restriction>
</xsd:simpleType>
```

When you're done, make sure your XML document and schema validate at www.xmlme.com/validator.aspx.

What facets are there, and what built-in types can you use them with? You'll find the answer in Table 4-1.

Type	length	minLength	maxLength	pattern	enumeration	whiteSpace
anyURI	x	x	x	x	x	x
base64Binary	x	x	x	x	x	x
boolean				x		x
byte				x	x	x
date				x	x	x
dateTime				x	x	x
decimal				x	x	x
double				x	x	x
duration				x	x	x
ENTITIES	x	x	x	x	x	x
ENTITY	x	x	x	x	x	x

Table 4-1 Simple Types and Applicable Facets

Type	length	minLength	maxLength	pattern	enumeration	whiteSpace
float				x	x	x
gDay				x	x	x
gMonth				x	x	x
gMonthDay				x	x	x
gYear				x	x	x
gYearMonth				x	x	x
hexBinary	x	x	x	x	x	x
ID	x	x	x	x	x	x
IDREF	x	x	x	x	x	x
IDREFS	x	x	x		x	x
int				x	x	x
integer				x	x	x
language	x	x	x	x	x	x
long				x	x	x
Name	x	x	x	x	x	x
NCName	x	x	x	x	x	x
negativeInteger				x	x	x
NMTOKEN	x	x	x	x	x	x
NMTOKENS	x	x	x		x	x
nonNegativeInteger				x	x	x
nonPositiveInteger				x	x	x
normalizedString	x	x	x	x	x	x
NOTATION	x	x	x	x	x	x
positiveInteger				x	x	x
QName	x	x	x	x	x	x
short				x	x	x
string	x	x	x	x	x	x
time				x	x	x
token	x	x	x	x	x	x
unsignedByte				x	x	x
unsignedInt				x	x	x
unsignedLong				x	x	x
unsignedShort				x	x	x

Table 4-1   Simple Types and Applicable Facets *(continued)*

The numeric simple types, and those simple types that can be ordered, also have some additional facets, which you see in Table 4-2.

Facets like the ones in Tables 4-1 and 4-2 give you great power in XML schemas: not only can you check the format of your data, you can check its content as well. That's a heck of a lot more than you could do with DTDs.

Type	max Inclusive	max Exclusive	min Inclusive	min Exclusive	totalDigits	fractionDigits
byte	y	y	y	y	y	y
unsignedByte	y	y	y	y	y	y
integer	y	y	y	y	y	y
positiveInteger	y	y	y	y	y	y
negativeInteger	y	y	y	y	y	y
nonNegativeInteger	y	y	y	y	y	y
nonPositiveInteger	y	y	y	y	y	y
int	y	y	y	y	y	y
unsignedInt	y	y	y	y	y	y
long	y	y	y	y	y	y
unsignedLong	y	y	y	y	y	y
short	y	y	y	y	y	y
unsignedShort	y	y	y	y	y	y
decimal	y	y	y	y	y	y
float	y	y	y	y		
double	y	y	y	y		
time	y	y	y	y		
dateTime	y	y	y	y		
duration	y	y	y	y		
date	y	y	y	y		
gMonth	y	y	y	y		
gYear	y	y	y	y		
gYearMonth	y	y	y	y		
gDay	y	y	y	y		
gMonthDay	y	y	y	y		

Table 4-2 Ordered Simple Types and Applicable Facets

Making Selections with XML Schema Choices

Here's more schema power—you can also allow multiple choices for which element appears at a specific location. Let's see an example to make this clear. Here's what our sample XML document looks like now—note that the borrower and the lender both have <name> elements:

```
<?xml version="1.0"?>
<transaction borrowDate="2009-10-15">
    <Lender phone="607.555.2222">
        <name>Doug Glass</name>
        <street>416 Disk Drive</street>
        <city>Medfield</city>
        <state>MA</state>
    </Lender>
    <Borrower phone="310.555.1111">
        <name>Britta Regensburg</name>
        <street>219 Union Drive</street>
        <city>Medfield</city>
        <state>CA</state>
    </Borrower>
    <note>Lender wants these back in two weeks!</note>
    <paintings>
        <painting paintingID="123-4567-890">
            <paintingTitle>The Castle</paintingTitle>
            <creationDate>1900-10-20</creationDate>
            <replacementValue>15000.95</replacementValue>
            <maxDaysOut>14</maxDaysOut>
        </painting>
        <painting paintingID="123-4567-891">
            <paintingTitle>The Cafe</paintingTitle>
            <creationDate>1901-10-21</creationDate>
            <replacementValue>19000.99</replacementValue>
            <maxDaysOut>14</maxDaysOut>
        </painting>
        <painting paintingID="123-4567-892">
            <paintingTitle>The Manor House</paintingTitle>
            <creationDate>1902-10-22</creationDate>
            <replacementValue>11000.95</replacementValue>
            <maxDaysOut>14</maxDaysOut>
        </painting>
        <painting paintingID="123-4567-893">
            <paintingTitle>The Condo</paintingTitle>
            <creationDate>1903-10-23</creationDate>
            <replacementValue>170000.99</replacementValue>
            <maxDaysOut>14</maxDaysOut>
        </painting>
    </paintings>
</transaction>
```

Now let's say that we wanted to start lending paintings to big underworld figures (on the assumption that the mob can pay more for a painting loan than a legitimate museum), so we need to allow for the possibility that instead of a <name> element, we might have an <alias> element in the same location, like this for Big Louie:

```
<?xml version="1.0"?>
<transaction borrowDate="2009-10-15">
    <Lender phone="607.555.2222">
        <name>Doug Glass</name>
        <street>416 Disk Drive</street>
        <city>Medfield</city>
        <state>MA</state>
    </Lender>
    <Borrower phone="310.555.1111">
        <alias>Big Louie</alias>
        <street>219 Union Drive</street>
        <city>Medfield</city>
        <state>CA</state>
    </Borrower>
    <note>Lender wants these back in two weeks!</note>
    <paintings>
        .
        .
        .
```

Obviously, our XML schema, as it stands, won't allow an <alias> element to appear where it's expecting a <name> element. But Big Louie always gets his way, so we'll use an XML schema <xsd:choice> element to specify that either a <name> element or an <alias> element can appear at the same location in the document. Here's what that <xsd:choice> element looks like:

```
<?xml version="1.0"?>
<xsd:schema xmlns:xsd="http://www.w3.org/2001/XMLSchema">

  <xsd:annotation>
    <xsd:documentation>
        Painting borrowing transaction schema.
    </xsd:documentation>
  </xsd:annotation>

  <xsd:element name="transaction" type="transactionType"/>

  <xsd:complexType name="transactionType">
    <xsd:sequence>
      <xsd:element name="Lender" type="address"/>
      <xsd:element name="Borrower" type="address"/>
      <xsd:element ref="note" minOccurs="0"/>
      <xsd:element name="paintings" type="paintings"/>
    </xsd:sequence>
```

```
      <xsd:attribute name="borrowDate" type="xsd:date"/>
   </xsd:complexType>

   <xsd:element name="note" type="xsd:string"/>

   <xsd:complexType name="address">
     <xsd:sequence>
       <xsd:choice>
         <xsd:element name="name" type="xsd:string"/>
         <xsd:element name="alias" type="xsd:string"/>
       </xsd:choice>
       <xsd:element name="street" type="xsd:string"/>
       <xsd:element name="city" type="xsd:string"/>
       <xsd:element name="state" type="xsd:string"/>
     </xsd:sequence>
     <xsd:attribute name="phone" type="xsd:string"
       use="optional"/>
   </xsd:complexType>

   <xsd:complexType name="paintings">
     <xsd:sequence>
       <xsd:element name="painting" minOccurs="0" maxOccurs="10">
         <xsd:complexType>
           <xsd:sequence>
             <xsd:element name="paintingTitle" type="xsd:string"/>
             <xsd:element name="creationDate" type="xsd:date"
               minOccurs='0'/>
             <xsd:element name="replacementValue" type="xsd:decimal"/>
             <xsd:element name="maxDaysOut">
               <xsd:simpleType>
                 <xsd:restriction base="xsd:integer">
                   <xsd:maxInclusive value="14"/>
                 </xsd:restriction>
               </xsd:simpleType>
             </xsd:element>
           </xsd:sequence>
           <xsd:attribute name="paintingID" type="catalogID"/>
         </xsd:complexType>
       </xsd:element>
     </xsd:sequence>
   </xsd:complexType>

   <xsd:simpleType name="catalogID">
     <xsd:restriction base="xsd:string">
       <xsd:pattern value="\d{3}-\d{4}-\d{3}"/>
     </xsd:restriction>
   </xsd:simpleType>

</xsd:schema>
```

That's how an XML schema <xsd:choice> element works—it says that, at the current point in the XML document, you can use any of the elements listed in the <xsd:choice> element. So our <xsd:choice> element says that at the current location in the XML document, you can use *either* a <name> element or an <alias> element:

```
<xsd:choice>
  <xsd:element name="name" type="xsd:string"/>
  <xsd:element name="alias" type="xsd:string"/>
</xsd:choice>
```

Try This Creating a Choice in an XML Schema

Try adding a third option to this <xsd:choice> element besides <name> and <alias>: <nickname>. Your choice element should look something like this:

```
<xsd:choice>
  <xsd:element name="name" type="xsd:string"/>
  <xsd:element name="alias" type="xsd:string"/>
  <xsd:element name="nickname" type="xsd:string"/>
</xsd:choice>
```

Next, put a few <nickname> elements into your XML document. When you're done, make sure your XML document and schema validate at www.xmlme.com/validator.aspx.

Creating Empty Elements

As you know, empty elements can contain attributes—but no other content. They can't contain text, and they can't have child elements. So how do you declare them in an XML schema?

You simply declare empty elements to contain no content other than attributes. That's all you need to do. Here's an example—let's say we wanted to declare an XML <img> element that paralleled the HTML <img> element, which is also an empty element. We can give our <img> element src, width, and height attributes, just like the HTML <img> element supports.

We create the <img> element like this in a schema, using <xsd:element>:

```
<xsd:element name="img">
      .
      .
      .
</xsd:element>
```

And we'll declare this new element with an anonymous complex type like this:

```
<xsd:element name="img">
  <xsd:complexType>
        .
        .
        .
  </xsd:complexType>
</xsd:element>
```

The anonymous complex type will only have attributes, so we start by adding the src attribute:

```
<xsd:element name="img">
  <xsd:complexType>
    <xsd:attribute name="src" type="xsd:string" />
        .
        .
        .
  </xsd:complexType>
</xsd:element>
```

Here's what the whole declaration looks like:

```
<xsd:element name="img">
  <xsd:complexType>
    <xsd:attribute name="src" type="xsd:string" />
    <xsd:attribute name="width" type="xsd:decimal" />
    <xsd:attribute name="height" type="xsd:decimal" />
  </xsd:complexType>
</xsd:element>
```

Voila! There's a new empty element with three attributes. Not bad.

Creating Element Groups

Note that our address type has three elements you'll often find together: <street>, <city>, and <state>:

```
<xsd:complexType name="address">
  <xsd:sequence>
    <xsd:element name="name" type="xsd:string"/>
    <xsd:element name="street" type="xsd:string"/>
    <xsd:element name="city" type="xsd:string"/>
    <xsd:element name="state" type="xsd:string"/>
  </xsd:sequence>
  <xsd:attribute name="phone" type="xsd:string"
    use="optional"/>
</xsd:complexType>
```

Using an XML schema, you can collect elements together into an *element group,* and then refer to that group by name. That's often useful if you use the same elements, in the same order, in a number of places in a schema. For example, in addition to the address type, you might have a businessAddress type, which includes the same three elements in the same order:

```xsd
<xsd:complexType name="address">
  <xsd:sequence>
    <xsd:element name="name" type="xsd:string"/>
    <xsd:element name="street" type="xsd:string"/>
    <xsd:element name="city" type="xsd:string"/>
    <xsd:element name="state" type="xsd:string"/>
  </xsd:sequence>
  <xsd:attribute name="phone" type="xsd:string"
    use="optional"/>
</xsd:complexType>

<xsd:complexType name="businessAddress">
  <xsd:sequence>
    <xsd:element name="name" type="xsd:string"/>
    <xsd:element name="street" type="xsd:string"/>
    <xsd:element name="city" type="xsd:string"/>
    <xsd:element name="state" type="xsd:string"/>
  </xsd:sequence>
  <xsd:attribute name="phone" type="xsd:string"
    use="optional"/>
</xsd:complexType>
```

In situations like this, it can make sense to declare an element group, and to reference that group in the address and businessAddress types.

Here's how to declare the element group, which we'll call addressData—you use an <xsd:group> element:

```xsd
<xsd:group name="addressData">
    .
    .
    .
</xsd:group>
```

You can treat an <xsd:group> element much like an <xsd:complexType> element, setting up, for example, a sequence of child elements like this:

```xsd
<xsd:group name="addressData">
    <xsd:sequence>
    .
    .
    .
    </xsd:sequence>
</xsd:group>
```

And all that remains is to add the actual child elements:

```
<xsd:group name="addressData">
  <xsd:sequence>
    <xsd:element name="street" type="xsd:string"/>
    <xsd:element name="city" type="xsd:string"/>
    <xsd:element name="state" type="xsd:string"/>
  </xsd:sequence>
</xsd:group>
```

Now the new addressData group is ready to go. You can refer to that group in other types, like the address and businessAddress types, like this, using the <xsd:group> element:

```
<xsd:complexType name="address">
  <xsd:sequence>
    <xsd:element name="name" type="xsd:string"/>
    <xsd:group ref="addressData"/>
  </xsd:sequence>
  <xsd:attribute name="phone" type="xsd:string"
    use="optional"/>
</xsd:complexType>

<xsd:complexType name="businessAddress">
  <xsd:sequence>
    <xsd:element name="name" type="xsd:string"/>
    <xsd:group ref="addressData"/>
  </xsd:sequence>
  <xsd:attribute name="phone" type="xsd:string"
    use="optional"/>
</xsd:complexType>
```

And there you go—you've created a new element group and put it to work.

In addition to element groups, you can also create attribute groups, coming up next.

Creating Attribute Groups

Many XML elements share the same set of attributes, and that's also common in HTML, where there are a common set of attributes (style, lang, and so on) that all elements share. In XML schemas, you can avoid duplicating <xsd:attribute> elements in such cases by declaring *attribute groups*.

Here's an example—say that our address and businessAddress types both share phone, cell, and email attributes:

```
<xsd:complexType name="address">
  <xsd:sequence>
    <xsd:element name="name" type="xsd:string"/>
    <xsd:group ref="addressData"/>
  </xsd:sequence>
```

```
  <xsd:attribute name="phone" type="xsd:string" use="optional"/>
  <xsd:attribute name="cell" type="xsd:string"/>
  <xsd:attribute name="email" type="xsd:string"/>
</xsd:complexType>

<xsd:complexType name="businessAddress">
  <xsd:sequence>
    <xsd:element name="name" type="xsd:string"/>
    <xsd:group ref="addressData"/>
  </xsd:sequence>
  <xsd:attribute name="phone" type="xsd:string" use="optional"/>
  <xsd:attribute name="cell" type="xsd:string"/>
  <xsd:attribute name="email" type="xsd:string"/>
</xsd:complexType>
```

You can make this shorter by putting the phone, cell, and email attributes into an attribute group named, say, addressAttributes. Here's how to create that group, using the <xsd:attributeGroup> element:

```
<xsd:attributeGroup name="addressAttributes">
      .
      .
      .
</xsd:attributeGroup>
```

Then you can add the attributes to this group, starting with the phone attribute:

```
<xsd:attributeGroup name="addressAttributes">
    <xsd:attribute name="phone" type="xsd:string" use="optional"/>
      .
      .
      .
</xsd:attributeGroup>
```

Here's the whole group:

```
<xsd:attributeGroup name="addressAttributes">
    <xsd:attribute name="phone" type="xsd:string" use="optional"/>
    <xsd:attribute name="cell" type="xsd:string"/>
    <xsd:attribute name="email" type="xsd:string"/>
</xsd:attributeGroup>
```

Now you can refer to the new attribute group using the <xsd:attributeGroup> element throughout your schema. Here's how we add that attribute group to the address and businessAddress complex types:

```
<xsd:complexType name="address">
  <xsd:sequence>
    <xsd:element name="name" type="xsd:string"/>
    <xsd:group ref="addressData"/>
  </xsd:sequence>
```

```
    <xsd:attributeGroup ref="addressAttributes"/>
  </xsd:complexType>

  <xsd:complexType name="businessAddress">
    <xsd:sequence>
      <xsd:element name="name" type="xsd:string"/>
      <xsd:group ref="addressData"/>
    </xsd:sequence>
    <xsd:attributeGroup ref="addressAttributes"/>
  </xsd:complexType>
```

And that gives both the address and businessAddress complex type the attributes phone, cell, and e-mail all at once. Nice.

Creating All Groups

Is there an alternative to listing child elements in sequence, where they must appear in that sequence, or it's an error? Yes, there is—you can use *all groups,* declared with <xsd:all>.

All you've got to do is to replace <xsd:sequence> with <xsd:all>. Note that any element in an all group can appear no more than once (which means that the allowed values of minOccurs and maxOccurs are 0 and 1 only).

Here's an example—currently, our transactionType complex type uses <xsd:sequence> to declare a sequence of child elements:

```
<xsd:complexType name="transactionType">
  <xsd:sequence>
    <xsd:element name="Lender" type="address"/>
    <xsd:element name="Borrower" type="address"/>
    <xsd:element ref="note" minOccurs="0"/>
    <xsd:element name="paintings" type="paintings"/>
  </xsd:sequence>
  <xsd:attribute name="borrowDate" type="xsd:date"/>
</xsd:complexType>
```

You can change that to an all group with <xsd:all> instead:

```
<xsd:complexType name="transactionType">
  <xsd:all>
    <xsd:element name="Lender" type="address"/>
    <xsd:element name="Borrower" type="address"/>
    <xsd:element ref="note" minOccurs="0"/>
    <xsd:element name="paintings" type="paintings"/>
  </xsd:all>
  <xsd:attribute name="borrowDate" type="xsd:date"/>
</xsd:complexType>
```

Now the <Lender>, <Borrower>, <note>, and <painting> elements can appear in any order in elements of the transactionType type. Very nice.

Schemas and Namespaces

One of the big ideas behind schemas was to allow XML processors to validate documents that use namespaces (which DTDs have a problem with). To allow that, the <xsd:schema> element has a new attribute: *targetNamespace*.

The targetNamespace attribute specifies just what it sounds like—the namespace the schema is targeted to. That is, you might have multiple namespaces in an XML document for multiple XML dialects in use in the document (as in our example at the end of Chapter 2 where we mixed XHTML and MathML) and want to use a different schema to validate the XML data in each different dialect (e.g., XHTML and MathML).

The way to do that is to give each schema you use its own targetNamespace attribute. That way, the XML processor will know what XML dialect that schema is targeted to.

Here's an example showing how to use the targetNamespace attribute. Say that you placed our sample XML document into the namespace "http://www.starpowdernow.com/steve":

```
<?xml version="1.0"?>
<transaction borrowDate="2009-10-15" xmlns="http://www.starpowdernow.com/steve">
    <Lender phone="607.555.2222">
        <name>Doug Glass</name>
        <street>416 Disk Drive</street>
        <city>Medfield</city>
        <state>MA</state>
    </Lender>
    <Borrower phone="310.555.1111">
        <name>Britta Regensburg</name>
        <street>219 Union Drive</street>
        <city>Medfield</city>
        <state>CA</state>
    </Borrower>
    <note>Lender wants these back in two weeks!</note>
    <paintings>
        <painting paintingID="123-4567-890">
            <paintingTitle>The Castle</paintingTitle>
            <creationDate>1900-10-20</creationDate>
            <replacementValue>15000.95</replacementValue>
            <maxDaysOut>14</maxDaysOut>
        </painting>
        <painting paintingID="123-4567-891">
            <paintingTitle>The Cafe</paintingTitle>
            <creationDate>1901-10-21</creationDate>
            <replacementValue>19000.99</replacementValue>
            <maxDaysOut>14</maxDaysOut>
        </painting>
        <painting paintingID="123-4567-892">
            <paintingTitle>The Manor House</paintingTitle>
            <creationDate>1902-10-22</creationDate>
            <replacementValue>11000.95</replacementValue>
            <maxDaysOut>14</maxDaysOut>
        </painting>
        <painting paintingID="123-4567-893">
            <paintingTitle>The Condo</paintingTitle>
            <creationDate>1903-10-23</creationDate>
            <replacementValue>170000.99</replacementValue>
            <maxDaysOut>14</maxDaysOut>
```

```
      </painting>
    </paintings>
</transaction>
```

Then you could indicate that our XML schema was targeted to the XML document's namespace by using the <xsd:schema> element's targetNamespace attribute:

```
<?xml version="1.0"?>
<xsd:schema xmlns:xsd="http://www.w3.org/2001/XMLSchema"
targetNamespace="http://www.starpowdernow.com/steve">

  <xsd:element name="transaction" type="transactionType"/>

  <xsd:complexType name="transactionType">
    <xsd:sequence>
      <xsd:element name="Lender" type="address"/>
      <xsd:element name="Borrower" type="address"/>
      <xsd:element ref="note" minOccurs="0"/>
      <xsd:element name="paintings" type="paintings"/>
    </xsd:sequence>
    <xsd:attribute name="borrowDate" type="xsd:date"/>
  </xsd:complexType>
          .
          .
          .
</xsd:schema>
```

And that's all you need. Now if you add other XML dialects to the sample XML document—a little MathML, perhaps—you can use a different schema for the MathML portion of the XML document, and your XML processor will be able to keep the two schemas straight and use them for the appropriate parts of that document.

Annotating Schemas

XML schemas are themselves well-formed and valid XML documents, so you can use standard XML comments in them. However, you can also use the <xsd:annotation> element to annotate an XML schema.

There are good reasons to annotate a schema using <xsd:annotation> rather than simple XML comments. The XML processor will simply strip out the XML comments and discard them, but an XML processor can be written to make use of the annotations in <xsd:annotation> elements. For example, notations that are marked as documentation can be copied by the XML processor and placed in a separate document to be read as instructions by people using the XML document. Or you can place instructions to the XML processor itself in an annotation.

Here's how you create an annotation—using the <xsd:annotation> element:

```
<xsd:annotation>
      .
      .
      .
</xsd:annotation>
```

There are two possible child elements of the <xsd:annotation> element, and the first is <xsd:documentation>, which indicates that this annotation should be treated as documentation:

```
<?xml version="1.0"?>
<xsd:schema xmlns:xsd="http://www.w3.org/2001/XMLSchema">

  <xsd:annotation>
    <xsd:documentation>
        Painting borrowing transaction schema.
    </xsd:documentation>
  </xsd:annotation>

  <xsd:element name="transaction" type="transactionType"/>

  <xsd:complexType name="transactionType">
    <xsd:sequence>
      <xsd:element name="Lender" type="address"/>
      <xsd:element name="Borrower" type="address"/>
      <xsd:element ref="note" minOccurs="0"/>
      <xsd:element name="paintings" type="paintings"/>
    </xsd:sequence>
    <xsd:attribute name="borrowDate" type="xsd:date"/>
  </xsd:complexType>
        .
        .
        .
</xsd:schema>
```

The other possible child element of an <xsd:annotation> element is <xsd:appInfo>, which means that the annotation should be interpreted as instructions or other information directed to the XML processor itself. Here's an example, where we're turning spell checking on (assuming that the XML processor has been written to understand instructions like this):

```
<?xml version="1.0"?>
<xsd:schema xmlns:xsd="http://www.w3.org/2001/XMLSchema">

  <xsd:annotation>
    <xsd:appInfo>
        spellChecking=on
    </xsd:appInfo>
  </xsd:annotation>

  <xsd:element name="transaction" type="transactionType"/>

  <xsd:complexType name="transactionType">
    <xsd:sequence>
      <xsd:element name="Lender" type="address"/>
      <xsd:element name="Borrower" type="address"/>
```

```
        <xsd:element ref="note" minOccurs="0"/>
        <xsd:element name="paintings" type="paintings"/>
      </xsd:sequence>
      <xsd:attribute name="borrowDate" type="xsd:date"/>
    </xsd:complexType>
            .
            .
            .

</xsd:schema>
```

And that's it for our coverage of XML schemas. As you can see, they're particularly powerful, allowing you to specify everything down to the actual content in XML elements. They're extremely useful to XML authors, and you should get to know them well.

Chapter 5

Formatting XML with Cascading Style Sheets

Key Skills & Concepts

- Introducing CSS

- Connecting CSS to XML documents

- Formatting XML

- Creating style rules

In this chapter, we're going to take a look at formatting XML documents using Cascading Style Sheets—CSS. This begins our survey of working with the data in XML documents, which is going to continue through extracting data with Extensible Stylesheet Language Transformations (XSLT) and using some simple programming in the coming chapters.

This chapter starts us off working with the data in XML documents; we'll use CSS here to format that data for display. You'll often find CSS used to format XML—for example, some online Web server may generate its reports on user activity in XML format—and that report might be hard to read in XML. Using CSS, you can pick out just the data you want to display and format it nicely so that it appears, for example, in large fonts, without any XML tags.

We'll start this chapter off with an example, showing how to format Rudyard Kipling's *The Jungle Book*.

Using *The Jungle Book*

Here's Rudyard Kipling's *The Jungle Book*—the beginning of it, anyway—formatted as an XML document:

```
<?xml version="1.0" standalone="yes"?>
<document>
  <title>The Jungle Book</title>
  <author>By Rudyard Kipling</author>
  <section>Mowgli's Brothers</section>
  <p>
    It was seven o'clock of a very warm evening in the Seeonee
    hills when Father Wolf woke up from his day's rest, scratched
    himself, yawned, and spread out his paws one after the other
    to get rid of the sleepy feeling in their tips.
  </p>
  <p>
    Mother Wolf lay with her big gray nose dropped across her four
    tumbling, squealing cubs, and the moon shone into the mouth of
    the cave where they all lived.
  </p>
```

```
<p>
   "Augrh!" said Father Wolf. "It is time to hunt again." He was
   going to spring down hill when a little shadow with a bushy
   tail crossed the threshold and whined: "Good luck go with you,
   O Chief of the Wolves. And good luck and strong white teeth go
   with noble children that they may never forget the hungry in
   this world."
</p>
<p>
   It was the jackal Tabaqui, the Dish licker and the wolves of India
   despise Tabaqui because he runs about making mischief, and telling
   tales, and eating rags and pieces of leather from the village
   rubbish-heaps.
</p>
</document>
```

Note that we've added XML elements like <title>, <author>, and <p> (for paragraph) elements to give this document some XML structure. Here's what the document looks like from an XML processor's point of view:

```
<?xml version="1.0" standalone="yes"?>
<document>
   <title>...</title>
   <author>...</author>
   <section>...</section>
   <p>...</p>
   <p>...</p>
   <p>...</p>
   <p>...</p>
</document>
```

You can open this XML document, which we'll call junglebook.xml, in a browser that displays XML like the Internet Explorer, as shown in Figure 5-1.

As you can see, the raw XML appears in Figure 5-1—and nothing more than the raw XML. There's no formatting there at all.

Try This Creating a Sample XML Document

To follow along in this chapter, start by creating your own XML document (in a pinch, you can use the sample for this chapter, junglebook.xml). Use the same structure as junglebook.xml:

```
<?xml version="1.0" standalone="yes"?>
<document>
   <title>...</title>
   <author>...</author>
   <section>...</section>
   <p>...</p>
```

(continued)

```
<p>...</p>
<p>...</p>
<p>...</p>
</document>
```

But use your own text in your sample document.

When you're done, open the document in a browser that can display XML to confirm that your document is well formed. In this chapter, we'll work on adding formatting to your document.

Introducing CSS

We're going to format our junglebook.xml document using Cascading Style Sheets, CSS. Browsers like Internet Explorer that can display XML can also often format XML documents like junglebook.xml using CSS.

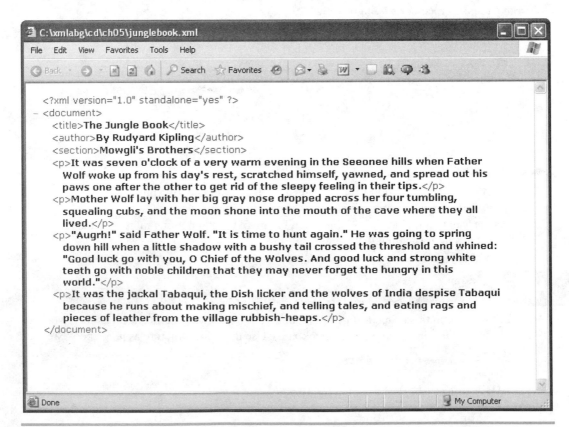

Figure 5-1 Our sample XML document

That's a good thing, because simply trying to read a straight XML document can be a little difficult—take a look at Figure 5-1, for example. You see all the actual XML markup there— that is, the XML declaration and the XML tags—that make reading the actual text a little difficult. And all the text is formatted the same way—there's no text that's especially treated as larger title text, for example.

Using CSS, you can specify how to format the text data inside each XML element. That is, you can format the text in the <title> element differently from the text in the <author> element, for example.

Even though CSS was developed for use with HTML, it works just fine with XML too, if your browser supports it.

There are two levels of CSS today, and they're both W3C specifications—CSS1 and CSS2. You'll find these specifications at www.w3.org/TR/REC-CSS1 and www.w3.org/TR/REC-CSS2. CSS2 includes all of CSS1 and adds some additional features like aural style sheets, support for various media types, and other advanced features. In fact, CSS3 is under development, and you can read all about it at www.w3.org/Style/CSS/current-work.

Here are a few additional online CSS resources:

- The W3C CSS validator is at http://jigsaw.w3.org/css-validator/, and it'll check the CSS in your pages for you.

- The W3C TIDY program can convert styles in HTML documents to CSS for you. You can find TIDY at http://tidy.sourceforge.net/.

- There are many CSS resources available at the W3C CSS page, www.w3.org/Style/CSS/, including CSS tutorials and links to free tools. If you are going to be using a lot of CSS, take a look at this page first.

So what does a cascading style sheet actually look like? Here's an example style sheet, format.css (the .css is the usual file extension you give to Cascading Style Sheet files), which we'll dissect in a few pages, that we can use to format junglebook.xml:

```
title {display: block; font-size: 24pt; font-weight: bold;
    text-align: center; text-decoration: underline}
author {display: block; font-size: 18pt; font-weight: bold;
    text-align: center}
section {display: block; font-size: 16pt; font-weight: bold;
    text-align: center; font-style: italic}
p {display: block; margin-top: 10}
```

We're going to take this style sheet apart soon, but you can already get an idea how it works—you specify the XML element you want to format (title, author, etc.) and then follow that with the actual formatting you want to use in curly braces.

Okay, we've got a style sheet, format.css, How do we use it to format junglebook.xml?

Connecting a Style Sheet to an XML Document

As you might recall from Chapter 1, you use an XML processing instruction, <?xml-stylesheet?>, to connect CSS style sheets to XML documents. And, as you might recall from Chapter 2, XML doesn't come with any processing instructions built in—any processing instructions you use are up to the XML processor you're using.

The <?xml-stylesheet?> processing instruction is understood by all browsers that can use CSS to format XML. You start this processing instruction this way:

```
<?xml-stylesheet...?>
```

Then you can add the type attribute, which specifies the type of the style sheet, which is CSS here:

```
<?xml-stylesheet type="text/css"...?>
```

Finally, you have to give the location of the style sheet, using the href attribute. We'll place the style sheet, format.css, in the same directory as junglebook.xml, so here's what the whole processing instruction looks like:

```
<?xml-stylesheet type="text/css" href="format.css"?>
```

Note that you can give the URL of the CSS file, and as long as the browser can access that URL, you'll be fine. For example:

```
<?xml-stylesheet type="text/css"
  href="http://www.starpowdernow.com/steve/format.css"?>
```

Okay, now we have the processing instruction that we'll use to connect format.css with junglebook.xml. We can add that processing instruction to the prolog of junglebook.xml, calling the result junglebook2.xml:

```
<?xml version="1.0" standalone="yes"?>
<?xml-stylesheet type="text/css" href="format.css"?>
<document>
  <title>The Jungle Book</title>
  <author>By Rudyard Kipling</author>
  <section>Mowgli's Brothers</section>
  <p>
    It was seven o'clock of a very warm evening in the Seeonee
    hills when Father Wolf woke up from his day's rest, scratched
    himself, yawned, and spread out his paws one after the other
    to get rid of the sleepy feeling in their tips.
  </p>
  <p>
    Mother Wolf lay with her big gray nose dropped across her four
    tumbling, squealing cubs, and the moon shone into the mouth of
    the cave where they all lived.
  </p>
```

```
<p>
    "Augrh!" said Father Wolf. "It is time to hunt again." He was
    going to spring down hill when a little shadow with a bushy
    tail crossed the threshold and whined: "Good luck go with you,
    O Chief of the Wolves. And good luck and strong white teeth go
    with noble children that they may never forget the hungry in
    this world."
</p>
<p>
    It was the jackal Tabaqui, the Dish licker and the wolves of India
    despise Tabaqui because he runs about making mischief, and telling
    tales, and eating rags and pieces of leather from the village
    rubbish-heaps.
</p>
</document>
```

And you can see the results in Figure 5-2—voila, junglebook.xml has been formatted!

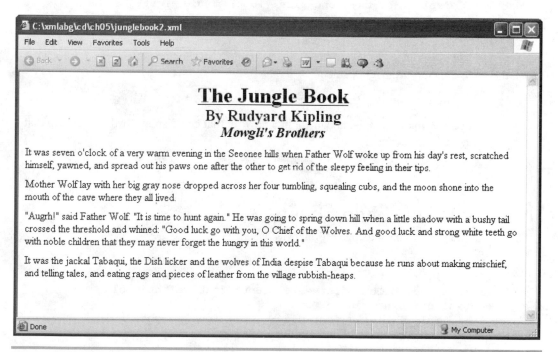

Figure 5-2 Formatting our sample XML document

Try This Formatting Your Sample XML Document

Try applying format.css to your sample XML document. Here's what format.css looks like:

```
title {display: block; font-size: 24pt; font-weight: bold;
    text-align: center; text-decoration: underline}
author {display: block; font-size: 18pt; font-weight: bold;
    text-align: center}
section {display: block; font-size: 16pt; font-weight: bold;
    text-align: center; font-style: italic}
p {display: block; margin-top: 10}
```

Assuming you've formatted your XML document using the same XML elements as we have in the sample XML document in this chapter, junglebook.xml, you'll be able to use format.css:

```
title {display: block; font-size: 24pt; font-weight: bold;
    text-align: center; text-decoration: underline}
author {display: block; font-size: 18pt; font-weight: bold;
    text-align: center}
section {display: block; font-size: 16pt; font-weight: bold;
    text-align: center; font-style: italic}
p {display: block; margin-top: 10}
```

Now add this processing instruction to your sample XML document, and place format.css in the same directory as that document:

```
<?xml-stylesheet type="text/css" href="format.css"?>
```

When you're done, open the document in a browser that can display XML to confirm that the styles are applied correctly.

Understanding Style Sheets

The style sheet we've been using is format.css:

```
title {display: block; font-size: 24pt; font-weight: bold;
    text-align: center; text-decoration: underline}
author {display: block; font-size: 18pt; font-weight: bold;
    text-align: center}
section {display: block; font-size: 16pt; font-weight: bold;
    text-align: center; font-style: italic}
p {display: block; margin-top: 10}
```

Note the structure of format.css—you select the element you want to format, and follow that with the actual style specification in curly braces.

The way you specify an element to format is to use a *selector*. Element names, such as the ones you see in format.css, are one such type of selector, but there are others, as we're going to see. The part in the curly braces that specifies the formatting is called the *style*. So the general form of style sheets is this:

```
selector {style}
selector {style}
selector {style}
selector {style}
        .
        .
        .
```

Put together, a selector and a style form, a *style rule*, in CSS. That is, a style rule consists of a selector and a style. So you can also look at CSS style sheets this way:

```
style rule
style rule
style rule
style rule
        .
        .
        .
```

That is, the process of creating CSS style sheets is really the process of creating style rules. For that reason, we'll take a look at how to create selectors first, followed by a discussion of how to create styles.

Creating Style Sheet Selectors

Style rules are made up of selectors and styles, and we're going to go through how to create selectors first. As its name implies, a selector lets you select some item in your XML document, such as the contents of an element. But selectors can also select other things, such as just the first letter of the text in an XML element.

As it stands, the format.css file uses the simplest form of selectors—element selectors.

Selecting by Element

In format.css, you specify what item you want to select by giving element names like this:

```
title {display: block; font-size: 24pt; font-weight: bold;
    text-align: center; text-decoration: underline}
author {display: block; font-size: 18pt; font-weight: bold;
    text-align: center}
section {display: block; font-size: 16pt; font-weight: bold;
    text-align: center; font-style: italic}
p {display: block; margin-top: 10}
```

Those are called *element selectors,* and they're the simplest form of selectors. To format the contents of an XML element, you can just use element selectors. Want to format the contents of the <author> element? Just use "author" as a selector.

You can also *group* elements together in selectors.

Grouping Elements

If a number of elements share the same styles, you can group element selectors onto the same line. For example, say that you wanted to format the <title>, <author>, and <section> elements the same way. You could put them into the same style rule like this, where you separate them with commas:

```
title, author, section {display: block; font-size: 24pt; font-weight:
    bold; text-align: center; text-decoration: underline}
p {display: block; margin-top: 10}
```

And you can see the results in Figure 5-3, where the contents of the <title>, <author>, and <section> elements have all been formatted the same way.

You can also use *pseudo-elements* as selectors.

Selecting by Pseudo-Element

Besides using elements as selectors for rules, you can also use *pseudo-elements.* A pseudo-element lets you do such things as select the first letter of an element's content, or the first line.

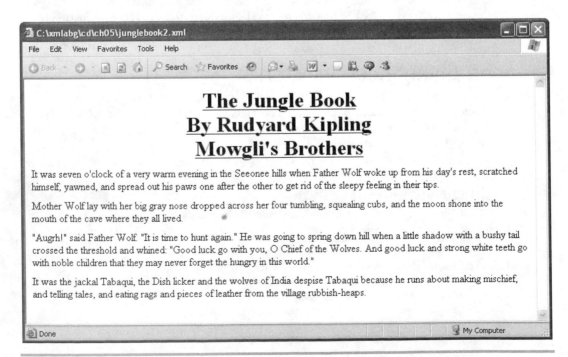

Figure 5-3   Formatting our sample XML document with element groups

There are two pseudo-elements in CSS1: *first-letter,* which refers to the first letter of a block of text, and *first-line,* which refers to the block's first line. Two more pseudo-elements were introduced in CSS2—*before* and *after,* which let you specify what should go immediately before and after elements.

You use these pseudo-elements like this: *p:first-letter* to refer to the first letter of a <p> element. Here's what that looks like in a new CSS style sheet, format2.css:

```
title {display: block; font-size: 24pt; font-weight: bold;
    text-align: center; text-decoration: underline}
author {display: block; font-size: 10pt, font-weight: bold;
    text-align: center}
section {display: block; font-size: 16pt; font-weight: bold;
    text-align: center; font-style: italic}
p {display: block; margin-top: 10}
p:first-letter {font-size: 18pt; float: left; vertical-align:
    text-top}
```

Note that format2.css includes both a style rule for the selector p as well as the selector p:first-letter. You can see the results in Figure 5-4—as you can see in the figure, the first letter of each <p> element has been styled to be larger than the standard text in <p> elements. Cool.

You can also create selectors that select based on the value of an element's id attribute.

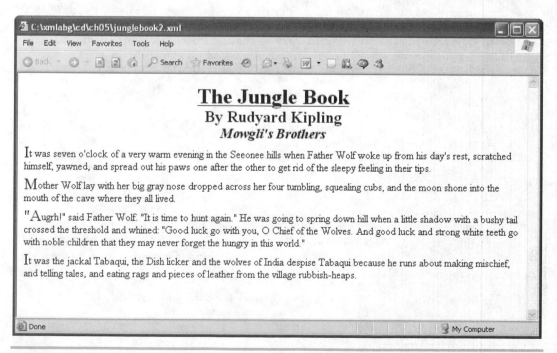

Figure 5-4   Formatting our sample XML document with pseudo-elements

Selecting by ID

Let's say that you want to format the first paragraph of text in our sample XML document in bold. How could you pick out just the first paragraph?

You might do that by giving it an id attribute, which you might set to, say, "first", indicating that this is the first paragraph like this in junglebook3.xml:

```
<?xml version="1.0" standalone="yes"?>
<document>
  <title>The Jungle Book</title>
  <author>By Rudyard Kipling</author>
  <section>Mowgli's Brothers</section>
  <p id="first">
    It was seven o'clock of a very warm evening in the Seeonee
    hills when Father Wolf woke up from his day's rest, scratched
    himself, yawned, and spread out his paws one after the other
    to get rid of the sleepy feeling in their tips.
  </p>
  <p>
    Mother Wolf lay with her big gray nose dropped across her four
    tumbling, squealing cubs, and the moon shone into the mouth of
    the cave where they all lived.
  </p>
  <p>
    "Augrh!" said Father Wolf. "It is time to hunt again." He was
    going to spring down hill when a little shadow with a bushy
    tail crossed the threshold and whined: "Good luck go with you,
    O Chief of the Wolves. And good luck and strong white teeth go
    with noble children that they may never forget the hungry in
    this world."
  </p>
  <p>
    It was the jackal Tabaqui, the Dish licker and the wolves of India
    despise Tabaqui because he runs about making mischief, and telling
    tales, and eating rags and pieces of leather from the village
    rubbish-heaps.
  </p>
</document>
```

Can you style that paragraph separately from the other paragraphs? Yes, you can, using CSS. To select an element with an id attribute, just follow the element name with a sharp symbol (#) and the id value. That looks like this in format3.css, where we're making the first paragraph appear in bold:

```
title {display: block; font-size: 24pt; font-weight: bold;
    text-align: center; text-decoration: underline}
author {display: block; font-size: 18pt; font-weight: bold;
    text-align: center}
```

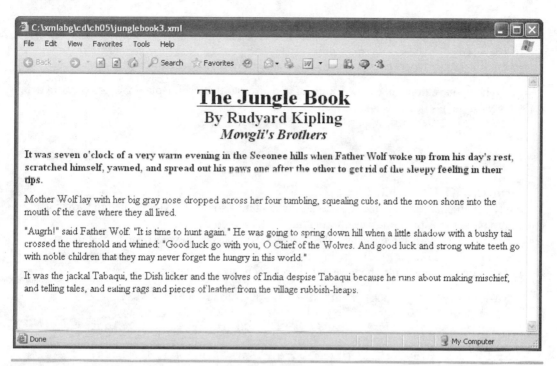

Figure 5-5   Formatting our sample XML document by ID

```
section {display: block; font-size: 16pt; font-weight: bold;
    text-align: center; font-style: italic}
p {display: block; margin-top: 10}
p#first {display: block; margin-top: 10; font-weight: bold}
```

You can see junglebook3.xml and format3.css at work in Figure 5-5—where the first paragraph, and only the first paragraph, is in bold. Nice.

Note that formatting by ID, like some other topics in this chapter, may only work in certain browsers!

Try This   Formatting Your Sample XML Document by ID

Try adding formatting by ID to you sample XML document. In this case, make your first paragraph appear larger by giving it the ID "first" and formatting it this way:

```
title {display: block; font-size: 24pt; font-weight: bold;
    text-align: center; text-decoration: underline}
author {display: block; font-size: 18pt; font-weight: bold;
    text-align: center}
```

(continued)

```
section {display: block; font-size: 16pt; font-weight: bold;
    text-align: center; font-style: italic}
p {display: block; margin-top: 10}
p#first {display: block; margin-top: 10; font-size: 24pt}
```

When you're done, open the document in a browser that can display XML to confirm that the new style has been applied correctly.

And you can also apply styles by *class*.

Selecting by Class

No two elements can have the same id attribute value—so what if you wanted to format a dozen paragraphs the same way? Formatting by ID would be out.

In this case, you can format by class instead. You can create your own classes in a style sheet by naming the class and creating a selector that is the name of the class, preceded by a dot (.). For example, here's how we might create a new class named "blue":

```
title {display: block; font-size: 24pt; font-weight: bold;
    text-align: center; text-decoration: underline}
author {display: block; font-size: 18pt; font-weight: bold;
    text-align: center}
section {display: block; font-size: 16pt; font-weight: bold;
    text-align: center; font-style: italic}
p {display: block; margin-top: 10}
.blue ...
```

Now we've got to add a style for the blue class—we can make that class's text appear in blue and its background in cyan like this in format4.css:

```
title {display: block; font-size: 24pt; font-weight: bold;
    text-align: center; text-decoration: underline}
author {display: block; font-size: 18pt; font-weight: bold;
    text-align: center}
section {display: block; font-size: 16pt; font-weight: bold;
    text-align: center; font-style: italic}
p {display: block; margin-top: 10}
.blue {color:blue; background-color: cyan}
```

Now you can make any number of XML elements members of blue class, which means they'll be formatted using that class. You specify formatting by class with the class attribute (this attribute is not built into XML—it's supported by browsers that support formatting by class), assigning that attribute a value of "blue". For example, here's how you can format the second and fourth paragraphs using the blue class in junglebook4.xml:

```
<?xml version="1.0" standalone="yes"?>
<?xml-stylesheet type="text/css" href="format4.css"?>
```

```
<document>
  <title>The Jungle Book</title>
  <author>By Rudyard Kipling</author>
  <section>Mowgli's Brothers</section>
  <p>
    It was seven o'clock of a very warm evening in the Seeonee
    hills when Father Wolf woke up from his day's rest, scratched
    himself, yawned, and spread out his paws one after the other
    to get rid of the sleepy feeling in their tips.
  </p>
  <p class="blue">
    Mother Wolf lay with her big gray nose dropped across her four
    tumbling, squealing cubs, and the moon shone into the mouth of
    the cave where they all lived.
  </p>
  <p>
    "Augrh!" said Father Wolf. "It is time to hunt again." He was
    going to spring down hill when a little shadow with a bushy
    tail crossed the threshold and whined: "Good luck go with you,
    O Chief of the Wolves. And good luck and strong white teeth go
    with noble children that they may never forget the hungry in
    this world."
  </p>
  <p class="blue">
    It was the jackal Tabaqui, the Dish licker and the wolves of India
    despise Tabaqui because he runs about making mischief, and telling
    tales, and eating rags and pieces of leather from the village
    rubbish-heaps.
  </p>
</document>
```

And you can see the results in Figure 5-6—although you can't see it in the black-and-white figure, the text in the second and fourth paragraphs is indeed blue.

Try This Formatting Your Sample XML Document by Class

Try adding formatting using style classes to your sample XML document. In this case, create a new style class named "bold" that is just like normal paragraph text—but in bold:

```
title {display: block; font-size: 24pt; font-weight: bold;
    text-align: center; text-decoration: underline}
author {display: block; font-size: 18pt; font-weight: bold;
    text-align: center}
section {display: block; font-size: 16pt; font-weight: bold;
    text-align: center; font-style: italic}
```

(continued)

```
p {display: block; margin-top: 10}
.bold {display: block; margin-top: 10; font-weight: bold}
```

Now use your new class to format the second and fourth paragraphs of your sample XML document in bold. When you're done, open the document in a browser that can display XML to confirm that the new bold class has been applied correctly.

In fact, you can even create styles that apply only to specific types of elements. For example, you might want to create a class that applies only to <p> elements named "green", where the text is in green and the background is in light green:

```
title {display: block; font-size: 24pt; font-weight: bold;
    text-align: center; text-decoration: underline}
author {display: block; font-size: 18pt; font-weight: bold;
    text-align: center}
section {display: block; font-size: 16pt; font-weight: bold;
    text-align: center; font-style: italic}
p {display: block; margin-top: 10}
p.green {color:green; background-color: lightgreen}
```

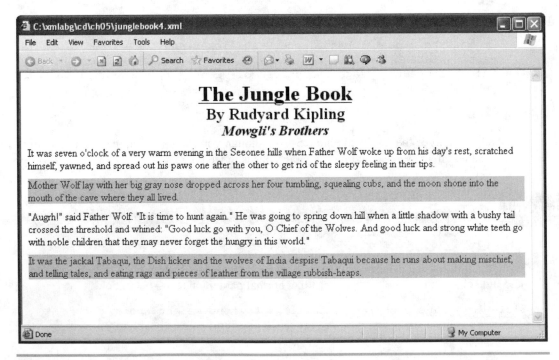

Figure 5-6   Formatting our sample XML document by class

Now you can use the green class with your <p> elements like this, where I'm styling the first and third paragraphs using this class in junglebook5.xml:

```
<?xml version="1.0" standalone="yes"?>
<?xml-stylesheet type="text/css" href="format5.css"?>
<document>
   <title>The Jungle Book</title>
   <author>By Rudyard Kipling</author>
   <section>Mowgli's Brothers</section>
   <p class="green">
      It was seven o'clock of a very warm evening in the Seeonee
      hills when Father Wolf woke up from his day's rest, scratched
      himself, yawned, and spread out his paws one after the other
      to get rid of the sleepy feeling in their tips.
   </p>
   <p>
      Mother Wolf lay with her big gray nose dropped across her four
      tumbling, squealing cubs, and the moon shone into the mouth of
      the cave where they all lived.
   </p>
   <p class="green">
      "Augrh!" said Father Wolf. "It is time to hunt again." He was
      going to spring down hill when a little shadow with a bushy
      tail crossed the threshold and whined: "Good luck go with you,
      O Chief of the Wolves. And good luck and strong white teeth go
      with noble children that they may never forget the hungry in
      this world."
   </p>
   <p>
      It was the jackal Tabaqui, the Dish licker and the wolves of India
      despise Tabaqui because he runs about making mischief, and telling
      tales, and eating rags and pieces of leather from the village
      rubbish-heaps.
   </p>
</document>
```

And the results appear in Figure 5-7—as you can see (or could if the figure was in color!), the first and third paragraphs are indeed formatted differently.

This new green class really is specific to <p> elements—if you try to use it with, say, the <section> elements:

```
<?xml version="1.0" standalone="yes"?>
<?xml-stylesheet type="text/css" href="format5.css"?>
<document>
   <title>The Jungle Book</title>
   <author>By Rudyard Kipling</author>
   <section  class="green">Mowgli's Brothers</section>
   <p class="green">
      It was seven o'clock of a very warm evening in the Seeonee
      hills when Father Wolf woke up from his day's rest, scratched
```

```
        himself, yawned, and spread out his paws one after the other
        to get rid of the sleepy feeling in their tips.
    </p>
    <p>
        Mother Wolf lay with her big gray nose dropped across her four
        tumbling, squealing cubs, and the moon shone into the mouth of
        the cave where they all lived.
    </p>
    <p class="green">
        "Augrh!" said Father Wolf. "It is time to hunt again." He was
        going to spring down hill when a little shadow with a bushy
        tail crossed the threshold and whined: "Good luck go with you,
        O Chief of the Wolves. And good luck and strong white teeth go
        with noble children that they may never forget the hungry in
        this world."
    </p>
    <p>
        It was the jackal Tabaqui, the Dish licker and the wolves of India
        despise Tabaqui because he runs about making mischief, and telling
        tales, and eating rags and pieces of leather from the village
        rubbish-heaps.
    </p>
</document>
```

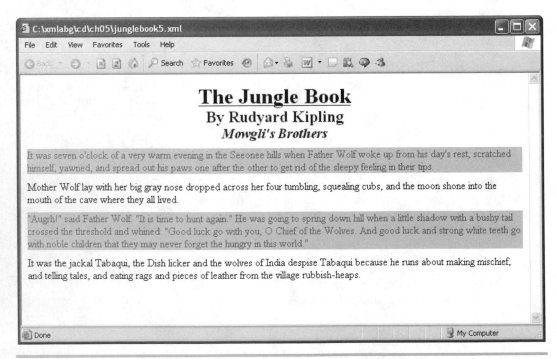

Figure 5-7   Formatting our sample XML document with the green class

then the result is that the class attribute is simply ignored in the <section> element—and the result is the same as in Figure 5-7.

There are already a number of "pseudo-classes" available in browsers that support style classes for XML; here's a sample of these classes:

- **:focus**   Refers to the element with the focus (the item that is the target of keystrokes). For example, p:focus selects the <p> element with the focus.

- **:first-child**   Refers to the first child of the indicated element. For example, p:first-child selects the first child of the <p> element.

- **:link, :visited, :active, :hover**   Refer to hyperlink-like elements. The :link pseudo-class refers to elements that have been designated as links, :visited specifies the style of visited links, :active specifies the style of links as they're being activated, and :hover specifies the style as the mouse hovers over them.

Okay, we're almost ready to turn to discussing how to create styles in CSS (like underlining, bold, colors, and so on). But before we do, there's one more topic we should take a look at when it comes to applying styles—using *inline styles*.

Using Inline Styles

Browsers that let you format XML using CSS also support inline styles, where you can use the style attribute in XML elements to apply styles.

When you use the style attribute, you simply assign the style you want to any XML element right there in the element—no style sheet needed. For example, take a look at junglebookinline.xml, where I'm using the text-decoration style to underline only the text in the last paragraph:

```
<?xml version="1.0" standalone="yes"?>
<?xml-stylesheet type="text/css" href="format5.css"?>
<document>
  <title>The Jungle Book</title>
  <author>By Rudyard Kipling</author>
  <section>Mowgli's Brothers</section>
  <p class="green">
    It was seven o'clock of a very warm evening in the Seeonee
    hills when Father Wolf woke up from his day's rest, scratched
    himself, yawned, and spread out his paws one after the other
    to get rid of the sleepy feeling in their tips.
  </p>
  <p>
    Mother Wolf lay with her big gray nose dropped across her four
    tumbling, squealing cubs, and the moon shone into the mouth of
    the cave where they all lived.
  </p>
```

```
<p class="green">
  "Augrh!" said Father Wolf. "It is time to hunt again." He was
  going to spring down hill when a little shadow with a bushy
  tail crossed the threshold and whined: "Good luck go with you,
  O Chief of the Wolves. And good luck and strong white teeth go
  with noble children that they may never forget the hungry in
  this world."
</p>
<p style="text-decoration: underline">
  It was the jackal Tabaqui, the Dish licker and the wolves of India
  despise Tabaqui because he runs about making mischief, and telling
  tales, and eating rags and pieces of leather from the village
  rubbish-heaps.
</p>
</document>
```

And you can see the result in Figure 5-8, where, as you can see, the last paragraph is indeed underlined.

That finishes our coverage of creating selectors—now it's time to take a look at the real meat of working with CSS—using the styles themselves.

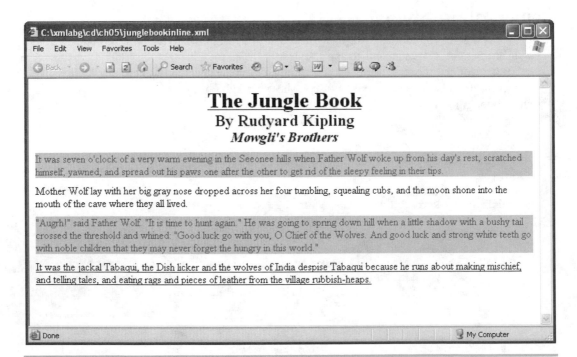

Figure 5-8 Formatting our sample XML document with inline styles

Using CSS Styles

The format.css file looks like this:

```
title {display: block; font-size: 24pt; font-weight: bold;
    text-align: center; text-decoration: underline}
author {display: block; font-size: 18pt; font-weight: bold;
    text-align: center}
section {display: block; font-size: 16pt; font-weight: bold;
    text-align: center; font-style: italic}
p {display: block; margin-top: 10}
```

Each line here is a style rule, made up of a selector followed by the styles you want to apply in curly braces.

Each style, such as "font-size: 16pt" is made up of a style *property,* which is font-size here, and a *setting or value,* which is 16pt (16 points) here.

We've taken a look at how selectors work, and now it's time to get familiar with the available styles. We'll start by creating *block elements.*

Creating Block Elements

Note the display: block pairs in format.css:

```
title {display: block; font-size: 24pt; font-weight: bold;
    text-align: center; text-decoration: underline}
author {display: block; font-size: 18pt; font-weight: bold;
    text-align: center}
section {display: block; font-size: 16pt; font-weight: bold;
    text-align: center; font-style: italic}
p {display: block; margin-top: 10}
```

What's that all about? This sets the display style to "block", which means that each such styled element is set off from the other elements vertically. For example, <h1> headers in HTML documents get their own line in the browser window, because they're formatted as block elements.

That means that if you want to set off a style element's content vertically from the other elements in the document, set the display style to "block".

Formatting Text

As you might expect, there are many ways to format text in CSS. Here's an overview of the text styles you can use:

- **float**   Indicates how text should flow around this element. Set to left to move the element to the left of the display area and have text flow around it to the right, right to move the element to the right and have text flow around the element to the left, or none.

- **font-family**   To set the font face (note that you can specify a number of options here, separated by commas, and the first face supported by the browser will be used).

- **font-size** The size of the text's font.

- **font-stretch** Indicates the desired amount of condensing or expansion in the letters used to draw the text.

- **font-style** Specifies whether the text is to be rendered using a normal, italic, or oblique face.

- **font-variant** Indicates if the text is to be rendered using the normal letters for lowercase characters or rendered using small-cap letters for lowercase characters.

- **font-weight** Refers to the boldness or lightness of the glyphs used to render the text, relative to other fonts in the same font family.

- **line-height** Indicates the height given to each line. Set to an absolute measurement or a percentage value like 200% to create double spacing.

- **text-align** Sets the alignment of text; set to left, right, center, or justify.

- **text-decoration** To underline the text, set to underline, overline, line-through, or blink; to remove inherited decorations, set to none.

- **text-indent** Sets the indentation of the first line of block-level elements. Set to an absolute value like 10px for 10 pixels, or 4pt for four points.

- **text-transform** Indicates if you want to display text in all uppercase, all lowercase, or with initial letters capitalized. Set to capitalize, uppercase, lowercase, or none.

- **vertical-align** Sets the vertical alignment of text; set to baseline, sub, super, top, text-top, middle, bottom, or text-bottom.

There's a lot of styles here, so let's take a look at some of these styles in more detail. Here's a new CSS file, format6.css, which we'll use to format the Jungle Book document. We start off by setting the size of the font used for each element with the font-size style—the most common way of setting this style is to assign it a font size in points (a point is 1/72 of an inch):

```
title {display: block; font-size: 24pt}
author {display: block; font-size: 18pt}
section {display: block; font-size: 16pt}
p {display: block; font-size: 18pt}
```

Okay, that sets the font size of each element—<title>, <author>, and so on.

Next, we'll format some of the elements in bold. You might think there's a style such as "font-bold" that you can use for this purpose, but the actual font style you use is font-weight, which you can use to set bold text. Here are the most common settings for the font-weight style:

- normal (this is the default)

- bold

- bolder

- lighter

Here's how we format several elements' text in bold—simply by setting the font-weight property to "bold":

```
title {display: block; font-size: 24pt; font-weight: bold}
author {display: block; font-size: 18pt; font-weight: bold}
section {display: block; font-size: 16pt; font-weight: bold}
p {display: block; font-size: 18pt}
```

Now how about setting some of the text to italic? Do you do that with the font-weight style? Nope, you use the font-style style, which takes these values most commonly:

- normal

- italic

- oblique

Let's make the <section> and <p> elements' text appear in italics, like this in format6.css:

```
title {display: block; font-size: 24pt; font-weight: bold}
author {display: block; font-size: 18pt; font-weight: bold}
section {display: block; font-size: 16pt; font-weight: bold; font-style: italic}
p {display: block; font-size: 18pt; font-style: italic}
```

How about setting the alignment of the text in an element? For example, you could center the text, or left-align it, and so on. For that, you use the aptly named text-alignment property, which commonly takes these values:

- left

- right

- center

- justify

Here's how we center the text in all the elements in the Jungle Book document:

```
title {display: block; font-size: 24pt; font-weight: bold;
text-align: center}
author {display: block; font-size: 18pt; font-weight: bold;
text-align: center}
section {display: block; font-size: 16pt; font-weight: bold;
text-align: center}
p {display: block; font-size: 18pt; font-style: italic; font-family:
Arial, Helvetica; text-align: center}
```

Okay—now how about underlining some text? Is there a text-underline property? Nope—in fact, it would take you some time to guess what the correct property is here unless you already know it—it's text-decoration. The text-decoration property commonly takes these values:

- none
- underline
- overline
- line-through

Here's how we underline the title in format6.css using the text-decoration property:

```
title {display: block; font-size: 24pt; font-weight: bold;
text-align: center; text-decoration: underline}
author {display: block; font-size: 18pt; font-weight: bold;
text-align: center}
section {display: block; font-size: 16pt; font-weight: bold;
text-align: center; font-style: italic}
p {display: block; font-size: 18pt; font-style: italic}
```

You can also set the actual font used with the font-family property. For example, you can set the font used to format <p> elements to Arial like this:

```
title {display: block; font-size: 24pt; font-weight: bold;
text-align: center; text-decoration: underline}
author {display: block; font-size: 18pt; font-weight: bold;
text-align: center}
section {display: block; font-size: 16pt; font-weight: bold;
text-align: center; font-style: italic}
p {display: block; font-size: 18pt; font-style: italic; font-family:
Arial}
```

What if the computer your page is displayed on doesn't have Arial font installed? It turns out that you can assign a list of fonts to the font-family property—for example, if the browser couldn't find the Arial font, here's how you specify it should search for Helvetica instead:

```
title {display: block; font-size: 24pt; font-weight: bold;
text-align: center; text-decoration: underline}
author {display: block; font-size: 18pt; font-weight: bold;
text-align: center}
section {display: block; font-size: 16pt; font-weight: bold;
text-align: center; font-style: italic}
p {display: block; font-size: 18pt; font-style: italic; font-family:
Arial, Helvetica}
```

You can list as many fonts as you like, in a comma-separated list.

You can also format the vertical spacing between paragraphs with the margin-top property, which works like this:

```
title {display: block; font-size: 24pt; font-weight: bold;
text-align: center; text-decoration: underline}
author {display: block; font-size: 18pt; font-weight: bold;
text-align: center}
section {display: block; font-size: 16pt; font-weight: bold;
text-align: center; font-style: italic}
p {display: block; font-size: 18pt; font-style: italic; font-family:
Arial, Helvetica; text-align: center; margin-top: 10}
```

You can see what this looks like, complete with Arial font, in Figure 5-9.

As a last resort, you can assign a *generic* font family to the font-family property to use if the user's computer doesn't have the one you specified. The browser will select a font family that's similar. Generic font families include serif, sans serif, cursive, and monospace.

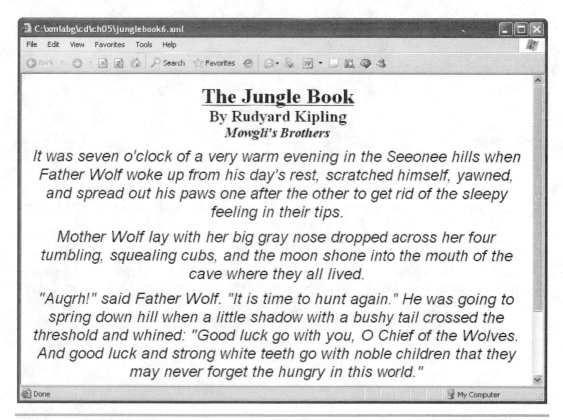

Figure 5-9   Formatting our sample XML document with text styles

Styling with Colors

As you might imagine, CSS has a number of ways of styling colors and backgrounds, and here are the appropriate properties:

- **color** Sets the foreground (text) color.

- **background-color** Sets the background color.

- **background-image** Sets the background image.

- **background-repeat** Specifies if the background image should be tiled; set to repeat, repeat-x, repeat-y, no-repeat.

- **background-attachment** Specifies if the background scrolls with the rest of the document.

- **background-position** Sets the initial position of the background.

What colors can you use? There are only 16 standard colors built into CSS, and here they are:

Aqua	Gray	Navy	Silver
Black	Green	Olive	Teal
Blue	Lime	Purple	White
Fuchsia	Maroon	Red	Yellow

That means that you can assign any of these values to color properties. In fact, modern browsers support many more colors by name than these 16. For example, Internet Explorer can support all the color names you see in Table 5-1, which means you can use any of those names in CSS style sheets you use to format XML in Internet Explorer.

If you're unsure about color names, you can always refer to colors with HTML color values, such as #ff7f50 where the # means the following numbers are in hexadecimal. Color values are really color triplets in the format $rrggbb, where rr is the red color value, gg the green, and bb the blue. All color values are in the hexadecimal range 00 to ff (in decimal, that's 0 to 255).

Here's an example, format7.css, that uses the background-color property to set background colors:

```
document {background-color: #ff7f50}
title {display: block; font-size: 24pt; font-weight: bold;
text-align: center; text-decoration: underline}
```

```
author {display: block; font-size: 18pt; font-weight: bold;
text-align: center}
section {display: block; font-size: 16pt; font-weight: bold;
text-align: center; font-style: italic}
p {display: block}
```

AliceBlue	AntiqueWhite	Aqua	Aquamarine	Azure
Beige	Bisque	Black	BlanchedAlmond	Blue
BlueViolet	Brown	BurlyWood	CadetBlue	Chartreuse
Chocolate	Coral	CornflowerBlue	Cornsilk Crimson	Cyan
DarkBlue	DarkCyan	DarkGoldenrod	DarkGray	DarkGreen
DarkKhaki	DarkMagenta	DarkOliveGreen	DarkOrange	DarkOrchid
DarkRed	DarkSalmon	DarkSeaGreen	DarkSlateBlue	DarkSlateGray
DarkTurquoise	DarkViolet	DeepPink	DeepSkyBlue	DimGray
DodgerBlue	FireBrick	FloralWhite	ForestGreen	Fuchsia
Gainsboro	GhostWhite	Gold	Goldenrod	Gray
Green	GreenYellow	Honeydew	HotPink	IndianRed
Indigo	Ivory	Khaki	Lavender	LavenderBlush
LawnGreen	LemonChiffon	LightBlue	LightCoral	LightCyan
LightGoldenrodYellow	LightGreen	LightGrey	LightPink	LightSalmon
LightSeaGreen	LightSkyBlue	LightSlateGray	LightSteelBlue	LightYellow
Lime	LimeGreen	Linen	Magenta	Maroon
MediumAquamarine	MediumBlue	MediumOrchid	MediumPurple	MediumSeaGreen
MediumSlateBlue	MediumSpringGreen	MediumTurquoise	MediumVioletRed	MidnightBlue
MintCream	MistyRose	Moccasin	NavajoWhite	Navy
OldLace	Olive	OliveDrab	Orange	OrangeRed
Orchid	PaleGoldenrod	PaleGreen	PaleTurquoise	PaleVioletRed
PapayaWhip	PeachPuff	Peru	Pink	Plum
PowderBlue	Purple	Red	RosyBrown	RoyalBlue
SaddleBrown	Salmon	SandyBrown	SeaGreen	Seashell
Sienna	Silver	SkyBlue	SlateBlue	SlateGray
Snow	SpringGreen	SteelBlue	Tan	Teal
Thistle	Tomato	Turquoise	Violet	Wheat
White	WhiteSmoke	Yellow	YellowGreen	

Table 5-1   Internet Explorer Supported Colors

We can also use the color property to set the text of the foreground text, like this, where I'm using the color name blue:

```
document {background-color: #ff7f50}
title {display: block; font-size: 24pt; font-weight: bold;
text-align: center; text-decoration: underline}
author {display: block; font-size: 18pt; font-weight: bold;
text-align: center; color: blue}
section {display: block; font-size: 16pt; font-weight: bold;
text-align: center; font-style: italic}
p {display: block}
```

Note that because we formatted the <document> element, all contained elements will also be formatted—which means the whole document:

```
<?xml version="1.0" standalone="yes"?>
<?xml-stylesheet type="text/css" href="format7.css"?>
<document>
  <title>The Jungle Book</title>
  <author>By Rudyard Kipling</author>
  <section>Mowgli's Brothers</section>
  <p>
    It was seven o'clock of a very warm evening in the Seeonee
    hills when Father Wolf woke up from his day's rest, scratched
    himself, yawned, and spread out his paws one after the other
    to get rid of the sleepy feeling in their tips.
  </p>
  <p>
    Mother Wolf lay with her big gray nose dropped across her four
    tumbling, squealing cubs, and the moon shone into the mouth of
    the cave where they all lived.
  </p>
  <p>
    "Augrh!" said Father Wolf. "It is time to hunt again." He was
    going to spring down hill when a little shadow with a bushy
    tail crossed the threshold and whined: "Good luck go with you,
    O Chief of the Wolves. And good luck and strong white teeth go
    with noble children that they may never forget the hungry in
    this world."
  </p>
  <p>
    It was the jackal Tabaqui, the Dish licker and the wolves of India
    despise Tabaqui because he runs about making mischief, and telling
    tales, and eating rags and pieces of leather from the village
    rubbish-heaps.
  </p>
</document>
```

You can see the results in Figure 5-10, where the new colors appear (in glorious black and white in the book, of course).

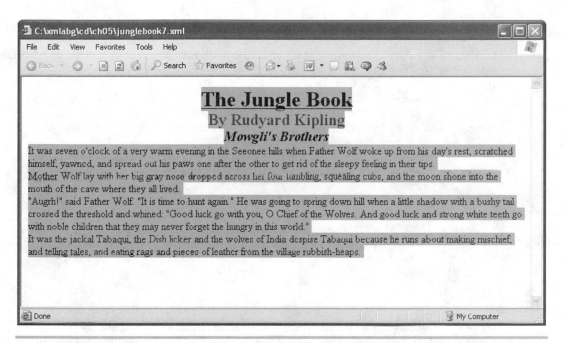

Figure 5-10 Formatting our sample XML document with colors

We saw another example earlier in the chapter with format5.css and junglebook5.xml, where we defined a color class named green and applied it:

```
title {display: block; font-size: 24pt; font-weight: bold;
    text-align: center; text-decoration: underline}
author {display: block; font-size: 18pt; font-weight: bold;
    text-align: center}
section {display: block; font-size: 16pt; font-weight: bold;
    text-align: center; font-style: italic}
p {display: block; margin-top: 10}
p.green {color:green; background-color: lightgreen}
```

Here's how we used the green style class:

```
<?xml version="1.0" standalone="yes"?>
<?xml-stylesheet type="text/css" href="format5.css"?>
<document>
   <title>The Jungle Book</title>
   <author>By Rudyard Kipling</author>
   <section>Mowgli's Brothers</section>
   <p class="green">
   It was seven o'clock of a very warm evening in the Seeonee
   hills when Father Wolf woke up from his day's rest, scratched
   himself, yawned, and spread out his paws one after the other
   to get rid of the sleepy feeling in their tips.
   </p>
```

```
<p>
    Mother Wolf lay with her big gray nose dropped across her four
    tumbling, squealing cubs, and the moon shone into the mouth of
    the cave where they all lived.
</p>
<p class="green">
    "Augrh!" said Father Wolf. "It is time to hunt again." He was
    going to spring down hill when a little shadow with a bushy
    tail crossed the threshold and whined: "Good luck go with you,
    O Chief of the Wolves. And good luck and strong white teeth go
    with noble children that they may never forget the hungry in
    this world."
</p>
<p>
    It was the jackal Tabaqui, the Dish licker and the wolves of India
    despise Tabaqui because he runs about making mischief, and telling
    tales, and eating rags and pieces of leather from the village
    rubbish-heaps.
</p>
</document>
```

You can also add background images to your formatted XML documents to dazzle users. For example, say you had the image you see in Figure 5-11 and wanted to use it as the background image for your document.

You can specify that you want to use the image in Figure 5-11, image.jpg, with the background-image property if you use the CSS url function like this in format8.css:

```
document {background-image: url(image.jpg)}
title {display: block; font-size: 24pt; font-weight: bold;
text-align: center; text-decoration: underline}
author {display: block; font-size: 18pt; font-weight: bold;
text-align: center}
section {display: block; font-size: 16pt; font-weight: bold;
text-align: center; font-style: italic}
p {display: block}
```

Figure 5-11   A background image

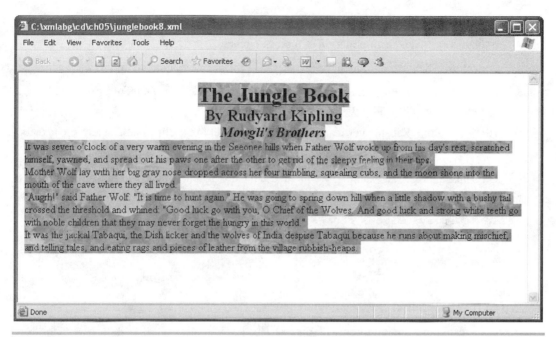

Figure 5-12 Formatting our sample XML document with background image

You can also indicate that the background image should be repeated, tiling the document, with the background-repeat property:

```
document {background-image: url(image.jpg); background-repeat: repeat}
title {display: block; font-size: 24pt; font-weight: bold;
text-align: center; text-decoration: underline}
author {display: block; font-size: 18pt; font-weight: bold;
text-align: center}
section {display: block; font-size: 16pt; font-weight: bold;
text-align: center; font-style: italic}
p {display: block}
```

You can see the results in Figure 5-12, where the background image is displayed.

Styling with Margins, Indentations, and Alignments

You can also format text with margins, indentations, and text alignments as well. Here are the relevant properties:

- **line-height**   Indicates the height given to each line. Set to an absolute measurement or a percentage value like 200% to create double spacing.

- **margin-left**   Sets the left margin of a block element.

- **margin-right** Sets the right margin of a block element.

- **margin-top** Sets the top margin of a block element.

- **text-align** Sets the alignment of text; set to left, right, center, or justify.

- **text-indent** Sets the indentation of the first line of block-level elements. Set to an absolute value like 10px for 10 pixels, or 4pt for four points.

- **vertical-align** Sets the vertical alignment of text; set to baseline, sub, super, top, text-top, middle, bottom, or text-bottom.

Let's take a look at an example. We might use the text-indent property to indent the text in <p> elements by 40 pixels, which you indicate with the expression 40px this way in format9.css:

```
title {display: block; font-size: 24pt; font-weight: bold;
text-align: center; text-decoration: underline}
author {display: block; font-size: 18pt; font-weight: bold;
text-align: center}
section {display: block; font-size: 16pt; font-weight: bold;
text-align: center; font-style: italic}
p {display: block; text-indent: 40px}
```

Let's also move the left margin 20 pixels to the left like this:

```
title {display: block; font-size: 24pt; font-weight: bold;
text-align: center; text-decoration: underline}
author {display: block; font-size: 18pt; font-weight: bold;
text-align: center}
section {display: block; font-size: 16pt; font-weight: bold;
text-align: center; font-style: italic}
p {display: block; text-indent: 40px; margin-left: 20px}
```

And you can see the results in Figure 5-13. Cool.

You can also format your XML in list format for clarity.

Styling into Lists

Oftentimes there's plenty of data in an XML document that you want to display, and formatting that data into lists can make the data display clearer. Here are the style properties you use to format data into lists:

- **list-item** Sets the display property to this value to create a list.

- **list-style-image** Sets the image that will be used as the list item marker. Internet Explorer only.

- **list-style-type** Sets the appearance of the list item marker, such as disc, circle, square, decimal, lowercase Roman, uppercase Roman, and others.

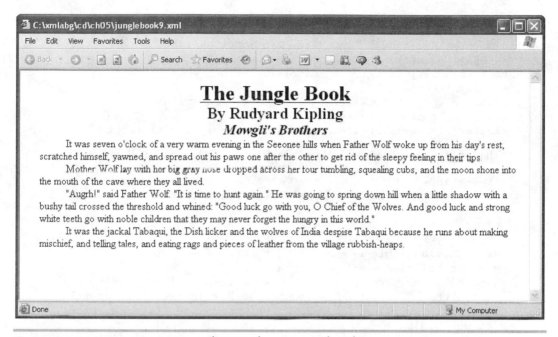

Figure 5-13 Formatting our sample XML document with indents

Let's give this a shot, formatting our <p> elements into a bulleted list. You can start by creating a new style class, circle, that uses circles as bullets. You start by setting the display property to "list-item" in format10.css:

```
title {display: block; font-size: 24pt; font-weight: bold;
text-align: center; text-decoration: underline}
author {display: block; font-size: 18pt; font-weight: bold;
text-align: center}
section {display: block; font-size: 16pt; font-weight: bold;
text-align: center; font-style: italic}
p.circle {display:list-item}
```

We'll use hollow circles as the list bullets in this example, so set the list-style-type to "circle":

```
title {display: block; font-size: 24pt; font-weight: bold;
text-align: center; text-decoration: underline}
author {display: block; font-size: 18pt; font-weight: bold;
text-align: center}
section {display: block; font-size: 16pt; font-weight: bold;
text-align: center; font-style: italic}
p.circle {display:list-item; list-style-type: circle}
```

To make the bullets visible, we'll indent the left margin by 20 pixels like this:

```
title {display: block; font-size: 24pt; font-weight: bold;
text-align: center; text-decoration: underline}
author {display: block; font-size: 18pt; font-weight: bold;
text-align: center}
section {display: block; font-size: 16pt; font-weight: bold;
text-align: center; font-style: italic}
p.circle {display:list-item; list-style-type: circle; margin-left: 20px}
```

That's fine; now in junglebook10.xml, we'll use the circle class for all <p> elements:

```
<?xml version="1.0" standalone="yes"?>
<?xml-stylesheet type="text/css" href="format10.css"?>
<document>
    <title>The Jungle Book</title>
    <author>By Rudyard Kipling</author>
    <section class="green">Mowgli's Brothers</section>
    <p class="circle">
        It was seven o'clock of a very warm evening in the Seeonee
        hills when Father Wolf woke up from his day's rest, scratched
        himself, yawned, and spread out his paws one after the other
        to get rid of the sleepy feeling in their tips.
    </p>
    <p class="circle">
        Mother Wolf lay with her big gray nose dropped across her four
        tumbling, squealing cubs, and the moon shone into the mouth of
        the cave where they all lived.
    </p>
    <p class="circle">
        "Augrh!" said Father Wolf. "It is time to hunt again." He was
        going to spring down hill when a little shadow with a bushy
        tail crossed the threshold and whined: "Good luck go with you,
        O Chief of the Wolves. And good luck and strong white teeth go
        with noble children that they may never forget the hungry in
        this world."
    </p>
    <p class="circle">
        It was the jackal Tabaqui, the Dish licker and the wolves of India
        despise Tabaqui because he runs about making mischief, and telling
        tales, and eating rags and pieces of leather from the village
        rubbish-heaps.
    </p>
</document>
```

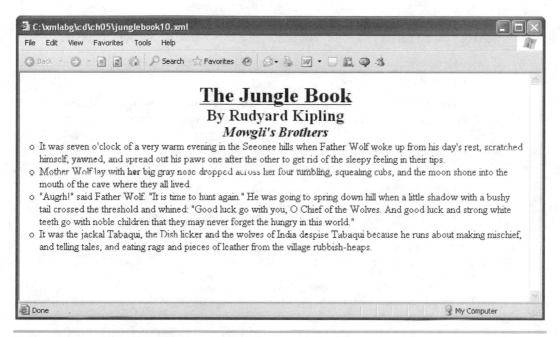

Figure 5-14   Formatting our sample XML document into lists

Great—you can see the results in Figure 5-14, where you see the circle bullets. Very nice. The last topic we'll take a look at in this chapter is how to format your XML data with borders, which can make your display clearer.

Styling with Borders

There are a number of border styles in CSS:

- **border-bottom-width**   Width of the bottom of the border; set to an absolute measurement like 10px for 10 pixels, or 4pt for four points, or a keyword: thin, medium, or thick.

- **border-color**   The color you want the border to be displayed in (use a predefined color or a color triplet). Setting this property to one value sets the color of the whole border; two values set the top and bottom borders to the first value and the right and left borders to the second; four values set the color of all border parts in order: top, right, bottom, and left.

- **border-left-width**   Width of the left edge of the border; set to an absolute measurement like 10px for 10 pixels, or 4pt for four points, or a keyword: thin, medium, or thick.

- **border-right-width**   Width of the right edge of the border; set to an absolute measurement like 10px for 10 pixels, or 4pt for four points, or a keyword: thin, medium, or thick.

- **border-style**   Sets the border style. Possible values: dotted, dashed, solid, double, groove, ridge, inset, and outset.

- **border-top-width**   Width of the top of the border; set to an absolute measurement like 10px for 10 pixels, or 4pt for four points, or a keyword: thin, medium, or thick.

Let's put this to work in format11.css, where we can draw a border around the <section> element:

```
title {display: block; font-size: 24pt; font-weight: bold;
text-align: center; text-decoration: underline}
author {display: block; font-size: 18pt; font-weight: bold;
text-align: center}
section {display: block; font-size: 16pt; font-weight: bold;
text-align: center; font-style: italic; border-style: solid}
p {display:block}
```

And the results appear in Figure 5-15. Nice.

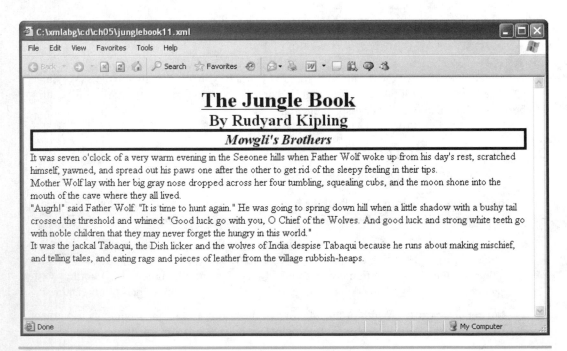

Figure 5-15   Formatting our sample XML document with borders

You can even make the border dotted if you like:

```
title {display: block; font-size: 24pt; font-weight: bold;
text-align: center; text-decoration: underline}
author {display: block; font-size: 18pt; font-weight: bold;
text-align: center}
section {display: block; font-size: 16pt; font-weight: bold;
text-align: center; font-style: italic; border-style: dotted}
p {display:block}
```

And you can see the dotted border in Figure 5-16.

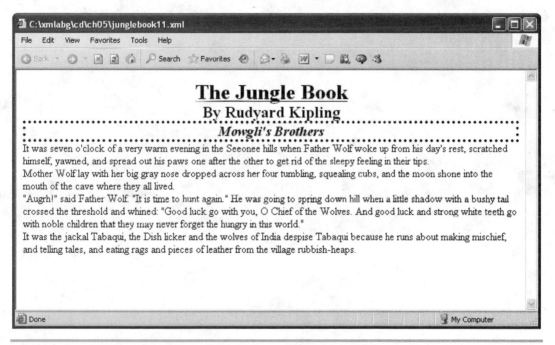

Figure 5-16 Formatting our sample XML document with dotted borders

Chapter 6

Finding Your Way with XSLT and XPath

Key Skills & Concepts

- Introducing XSLT

- Introducing XPath

- Extracting data from XML documents

- Reading element values

- Finding attribute values

This chapter starts us off using Extensible Stylesheet Language Transformations (XSLT) to extract data from XML documents—without any programming. Using XSLT is the easiest way to read data from XML documents and work with that data, and we're going to see how that works in this chapter and the next. Along the way, we'll also see an allied specification at work—XPath, which is part of XSLT and which lets you address the specific data in an XML document. For example, you can use XPath to target the contents of a particular element in an XML document, or a particular attribute value.

XSLT is a specification of the World Wide Web Consortium, the W3C. There are two versions that you'll find in common use—version 1.0 and version 2.0. You can find the corresponding specifications at these sites:

- The XSLT 1.0 recommendation is at www.w3.org/TR/xslt/.

- The XSLT 2.0 recommendation is at www.w3.org/TR/xslt20/.

Version 2.0 is the latest version, but a great deal of software still only supports version 1.0. We'll be using version 2.0 in this chapter.

XSLT is a lot of fun, so let's get started immediately. We'll begin by creating a sample XML document—and then see how to create XSLT style sheets to extract data from that document—for example, if your sample document records data about a set of friends, you can use XSLT to extract the names of all your friends and format the result into an HTML page that you can view in a standard browser.

Creating a Sample XML Document

Let's create a sample XML document that does just that—contains data on your friends. We can start this document, friends.xml, with—as you'd expect—an XML declaration:

```
<?xml version="1.0"?>
        .
        .
        .
```

We can make the document element <friends>:

```
<?xml version="1.0"?>
<friends>
        .
        .
        .
</friends>
```

And we can create a <friend> element to store our first friend in:

```
<?xml version="1.0"?>
<friends>
    <friend>
        .
        .
        .
    </friend>
</friends>
```

Okay, what comes first in the <friend> element? The friend's name, naturally, like this:

```
<?xml version="1.0"?>
<friends>
    <friend>
        <name>Sam Snead</name>
        .
        .
        .
    </friend>
</friends>
```

Next, we can store our friend's age:

```
<?xml version="1.0"?>
<friends>
    <friend>
        <name>Sam Snead</name>
        <age>19</age>
        .
        .
        .
    </friend>
</friends>
```

In fact, we can do better than that—let's also add a units attribute to the <age> element, indicating that ages are measured in years:

```
<?xml version="1.0"?>
<friends>
    <friend>
```

```
      <name>Sam Snead</name>
      <age units="years">19</age>
      .
      .
      .
   </friend>
</friends>
```

Okay, what's next? We can add the friend's height:

```
<?xml version="1.0"?>
<friends>
   <friend>
      <name>Sam Snead</name>
      <age units="years">19</age>
      <height>70</height>
      .
      .
      .
   </friend>
</friends>
```

And let's make the units of height inches:

```
<?xml version="1.0"?>
<friends>
   <friend>
      <name>Sam Snead</name>
      <age units="years">19</age>
      <height units="inches">70</height>
      .
      .
      .
   </friend>
</friends>
```

Okay so far. Now we can add the friend's weight this way:

```
<?xml version="1.0"?>
<friends>
   <friend>
      <name>Sam Snead</name>
      <age units="years">19</age>
      <height units="inches">70</height>
      <weight>160</weight>
      .
      .
      .
   </friend>
</friends>
```

And we can make the units of the <weight> element pounds:

```
<?xml version="1.0"?>
<friends>
    <friend>
        <name>Sam Snead</name>
        <age units="years">19</age>
        <height units="inches">70</height>
        <weight units="pounds">160</weight>
              .
              .
              .
    </friend>
</friends>
```

That's looking good so far. How about eye color? Here we go:

```
<?xml version="1.0"?>
<friends>
    <friend>
        <name>Sam Snead</name>
        <age units="years">19</age>
        <height units="inches">70</height>
        <weight units="pounds">160</weight>
        <eyecolor units="color">blue</eyecolor>
              .
              .
              .
    </friend>
</friends>
```

We can also store the distance the friend lives from us like this:

```
<?xml version="1.0"?>
<friends>
    <friend>
        <name>Sam Snead</name>
        <age units="years">19</age>
        <height units="inches">70</height>
        <weight units="pounds">160</weight>
        <eyecolor units="color">blue</eyecolor>
        <distance units="miles">43.4</distance>
    </friend>
</friends>
```

Let's add a little more here—an XML comment, indicating that the distance is measured to the friend's home:

```
<?xml version="1.0"?>
<friends>
```

```
    <friend>
        <name>Sam Snead</name>
        <age units="years">19</age>
        <height units="inches">70</height>
        <weight units="pounds">160</weight>
        <eyecolor units="color">blue</eyecolor>
        <distance units="miles">43.4</distance><!--To friend's home-->
    </friend>
</friends>
```

Great, that records our first friend, Sam Snead. How about a few others? We can add them like this:

```
<?xml version="1.0"?>
<friends>
    <friend>
        <name>Sam Snead</name>
        <age units="years">19</age>
        <height units="inches">70</height>
        <weight units="pounds">160</weight>
        <eyecolor units="color">blue</eyecolor>
        <distance units="miles">43.4</distance><!--To friend's home-->
    </friend>

    <friend>
        <name>Paige Turner</name>
        <age units="years">23</age>
        <height units="inches">67</height>
        <weight units="pounds">110</weight>
        <eyecolor units="color">brown</eyecolor>
        <distance units="miles">66.8</distance><!--To friend's home-->
    </friend>

    <friend>
        <name>Ralph Kramden</name>
        <age units="years">32</age>
        <height units="inches">71</height>
        <weight units="pounds">182</weight>
        <eyecolor units="color">hazel</eyecolor>
        <distance units="miles">28.4</distance><!--To friend's home-->
    </friend>

</friends>
```

That's fine—now we have three friends, Sam Snead, Paige Turner, and Ralph Kramden. You can see this XML document, friends.xml, in Figure 6-1 in Internet Explorer.

As you can see, the raw XML appears in Figure 6-1—and nothing more than the raw XML. There's no formatting there at all. We're about to change all that.

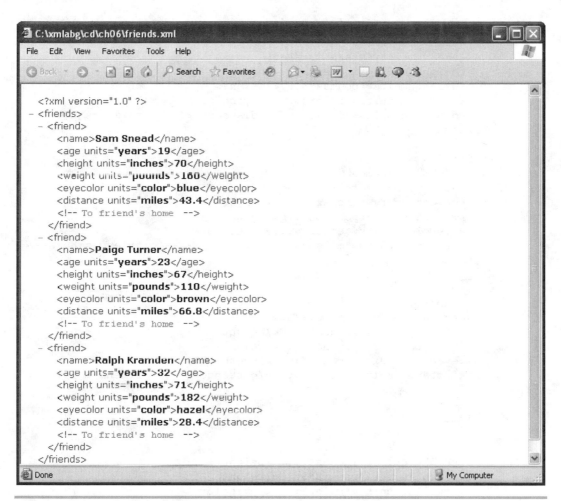

```
C:\xmlabg\cd\ch06\friends.xml
File   Edit   View   Favorites   Tools   Help

Back   ▾   ○   ▾   ✕   ▣   ⌂   ▫ Search   ☆ Favorites   ✉   ▦ ▾   ▧   ▦   ▾   ▢   ▧   ▣   ▨

   <?xml version="1.0" ?>
 - <friends>
   - <friend>
       <name>Sam Snead</name>
       <age units="years">19</age>
       <height units="inches">70</height>
       <weight units="pounds">160</weight>
       <eyecolor units="color">blue</eyecolor>
       <distance units="miles">43.4</distance>
       <!-- To friend's home -->
     </friend>
   - <friend>
       <name>Paige Turner</name>
       <age units="years">23</age>
       <height units="inches">67</height>
       <weight units="pounds">110</weight>
       <eyecolor units="color">brown</eyecolor>
       <distance units="miles">66.8</distance>
       <!-- To friend's home -->
     </friend>
   - <friend>
       <name>Ralph Kramden</name>
       <age units="years">32</age>
       <height units="inches">71</height>
       <weight units="pounds">182</weight>
       <eyecolor units="color">hazel</eyecolor>
       <distance units="miles">28.4</distance>
       <!-- To friend's home -->
     </friend>
   </friends>

 Done                                              My Computer
```

Figure 6-1 Our sample XML document

Try This Creating a Sample XML Document

To follow along in this chapter, start by creating your own XML document (in a pinch, you can use the sample for this chapter, friends.xml). Use the same structure as friends.xml, putting in as many of your friends as you like:

```
<?xml version="1.0"?>
<friends>
```

(continued)

```
<friend>
    <name>...</name>
    <age units="years">...</age>
    <height units="inches">...</height>
    <weight units="pounds">...</weight>
    <eyecolor units="color">...</eyecolor>
    <distance units="miles">...</distance><!--To friend's home-->
</friend>

<friend>
    <name>...</name>
    <age units="years">...</age>
    <height units="inches">...</height>
    <weight units="pounds">...</weight>
    <eyecolor units="color">...</eyecolor>
    <distance units="miles">...</distance><!--To friend's home-->
</friend>

<friend>
    <name>...</name>
    <age units="years">...</age>
    <height units="inches">...</height>
    <weight units="pounds">...</weight>
    <eyecolor units="color">...</eyecolor>
    <distance units="miles">...</distance><!--To friend's home-->
</friend>

<friend>
    <name>...</name>
    <age units="years">...</age>
    <height units="inches">...</height>
    <weight units="pounds">...</weight>
    <eyecolor units="color">...</eyecolor>
    <distance units="miles">...</distance><!--To friend's home-->
</friend>

</friends>
```

Using the same elements and attributes—but adding your own friends—will allow you to follow along in this chapter as we extract data from this document using XSLT.

When you're done, open the document in Internet Explorer to check that your document is well formed . . . .

First Formatting of the Sample XML Document

Formatting XML documents using XSLT is something like formatting them with CSS, which you saw in the preceding chapter. You create a style sheet, separate from the XML document itself, and use software to process the XML document with the style sheet.

Say that, for example, you wanted to strip out and display the names of your friends from the sample XML document. Here's an XSLT style sheet, format.xsl (.xsl is the usual file extension you give to XSLT style sheets) that will do exactly that:

```
<?xml version="1.0"?>
<xsl:stylesheet version="2.0" xmlns:xsl="http://www.w3.org/1999/XSL/Transform">

    <xsl:template match="friends">
        <html>
            <xsl:apply-templates/>
        </html>
    </xsl:template>

    <xsl:template match="friend">
        <p>
            <xsl:value-of select="name"/>
        </p>
    </xsl:template>

</xsl:stylesheet>
```

Okay, that looks a little strange, but we'll give it a try. You connect XSLT style sheets, like CSS style sheets, to XML documents with the <?xml-stylesheet?> element. Here's what that looks like—note that here, the type attribute is set to "text/xsl", not "text/css", and the href attribute points to the XSLT style sheet, format.xsl:

```
<?xml version="1.0"?>
<?xml-stylesheet type="text/xsl" href="format.xsl"?>
<friends>

    <friend>
        <name>Sam Snead</name>
        <age units="years">19</age>
        <height units="inches">70</height>
        <weight units="pounds">160</weight>
        <eyecolor units="color">blue</eyecolor>
        <distance units="miles">43.4</distance><!--To friend's home-->
    </friend>
```

```
<friend>
    <name>Paige Turner</name>
    <age units="years">23</age>
    <height units="inches">67</height>
    <weight units="pounds">110</weight>
    <eyecolor units="color">brown</eyecolor>
    <distance units="miles">66.8</distance><!--To friend's home-->
</friend>

<friend>
    <name>Ralph Kramden</name>
    <age units="years">32</age>
    <height units="inches">71</height>
    <weight units="pounds">182</weight>
    <eyecolor units="color">hazel</eyecolor>
    <distance units="miles">28.4</distance><!--To friend's home-->
</friend>

</friends>
```

Okay, that connects format.xsl to friends.xml. To make sure the XSLT processor can find format.xsl, put the two files, friends.xml and format.xsl, into the same directory.

Now friends.xml and format.xsl are connected. How do you actually make the XSLT transformation happen? There are three ways that you can transform documents using XSLT:

- **On a Web server**   A server program, such as a Java servlet or a JavaServer Page (JSP), can use a style sheet to transform a document automatically and serve it to the client browser.

- **In the client**   A client program, such as a browser, can perform the transformation, reading in the style sheet you specify with the <?xml-stylesheet?> processing instruction. Internet Explorer can handle transformations this way.

- **With a separate program**   There are several standalone programs, often based on the Java programming language (which has support for XSLT built in), that will perform XSLT transformations.

To make this easy to follow along, we'll use a browser—Internet Explorer—to make the XSLT transformation happen. Now that the two documents are connected with the <?xml-stylesheet?> processing instruction, you can simply open friends.xml in Internet Explorer—and you can see the result in Figure 6-2.

As you can see in the figure, the XSLT style sheet has stripped out the names of the friends in friends.xml and formatted them for the display you see in Figure 6-2. Very cool!

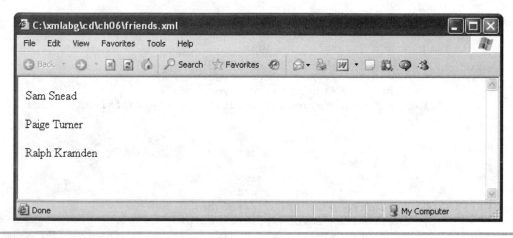

Figure 6-2 Our sample XML document formatted

Try This Extracting the Names from Your Sample XML Document

Try using format.xsl to extract the names of your friends from your XML document:

```
<?xml version="1.0"?>
<xsl:stylesheet version="2.0" xmlns:xsl="http://www.w3.org/1999/XSL/Transform">

    <xsl:template match="friends">
        <html>
            <xsl:apply-templates/>
        </html>
    </xsl:template>

    <xsl:template match="friend">
        <p>
            <xsl:value-of select="name"/>
        </p>
    </xsl:template>

</xsl:stylesheet>
```

Put format.xsl to work by adding this <?xml-stylesheet?> processing instruction to your sample XML document:

```
<?xml version="1.0"?>
<?xml-stylesheet type="text/xsl" href="format.xsl"?>
<friends>
```

(continued)

```
<friend>
    <name>...</name>
    <age units="years">...</age>
    <height units="inches">...</height>
    <weight units="pounds">...</weight>
    <eyecolor units="color">...</eyecolor>
    <distance units="miles">...</distance><!--To friend's home-->
</friend>

<friend>
    <name>...</name>
    <age units="years">...</age>
    <height units="inches">...</height>
    <weight units="pounds">...</weight>
    <eyecolor units="color">...</eyecolor>
    <distance units="miles">...</distance><!--To friend's home-->
</friend>

<friend>
    <name>...</name>
    <age units="years">...</age>
    <height units="inches">...</height>
    <weight units="pounds">...</weight>
    <eyecolor units="color">...</eyecolor>
    <distance units="miles">...</distance><!--To friend's home-->
</friend>

<friend>
    <name>...</name>
    <age units="years">...</age>
    <height units="inches">...</height>
    <weight units="pounds">...</weight>
    <eyecolor units="color">...</eyecolor>
    <distance units="miles">...</distance><!--To friend's home-->
</friend>

</friends>
```

When you're done, open the document in Internet Explorer to check that the names from your document appear.

Alright, we're in business—now let's start creating XSLT style sheets from scratch.

Creating Our First XSLT Style Sheet: Replacing the Entire Document

Let's start the process of understanding XSLT style sheets by creating a new style sheet, format1.xsl. The goal of this style sheet will be to replace our whole XML document with the text "Friend data will go here."

This new style sheet, format1.xsl, is a real XSL document, so it starts with an XML declaration:

```
<?xml version="1.0"?>
```

Next comes the style sheet's document element, which is always <xsl:stylesheet>. (Do not confuse the <xsl:stylesheet> document element in the style sheet with the <?xml-stylesheet?> processing instruction in the XML document.) The xsl namespace prefix is connected to the URL http://www.w3.org/1999/XSL/Transform (the same namespace URL as XSLT 1.0 uses):

```
<?xml version="1.0"?>
<xsl:stylesheet xmlns:xsl="http://www.w3.org/1999/XSL/Transform">
        .
        .
        .
</xsl:stylesheet>
```

You must also indicate the version of XSLT you're using in the style sheet's document element, and that's 2.0 for us:

```
<?xml version="1.0"?>
<xsl:stylesheet version="2.0" xmlns:xsl="http://www.w3.org/1999/XSL/Transform">
        .
        .
        .
</xsl:stylesheet>
```

Okay, now it's time to work with the XML document itself. We want to replace the data in the document with the message "Friend data will go here." The data in our XML document is all stored in the <friends> document element:

```
<?xml version="1.0"?>
<?xml-stylesheet type="text/xsl" href="format1.xsl"?>
<friends>
        .
        .
        .
</friends>
```

So if you think about it, we want to replace the <friends> element with our "Friend data will go here." message. How do we do that?

We have to create an XSLT *template.*

Applying XSLT Templates

XSLT works by applying templates to your XML document—that's how it extracts data from your XML without actually writing any programming. A template matches a node—such as an element—in your XML document, and inside the template you tell XSLT what to do with the node's data.

In this first example, we want to replace the <friends> element in our XML document, and we'll use an XSLT template to do that, because you use templates to match XML nodes and tell XSLT what to do with the node's data.

You create a new XSLT template with the XSLT <template> element. Because all XSLT elements are in the xsl namespace, that's actually <xsl:template>:

```
<?xml version="1.0"?>
<xsl:stylesheet version="2.0" xmlns:xsl="http://www.w3.org/1999/XSL/Transform">

    <xsl:template>
         .
         .
         .
    </xsl:template>

</xsl:stylesheet>
```

How do you match this template to the <friends> element? You use the <xsl:template> element's match attribute, setting that attribute equal to the name of the element node it's to match, which is "friends":

```
<?xml version="1.0"?>
<xsl:stylesheet version="2.0" xmlns:xsl="http://www.w3.org/1999/XSL/Transform">

    <xsl:template match="friends">
         .
         .
         .
    </xsl:template>

</xsl:stylesheet>
```

Okay, now we've got an XSLT template that matches the <friends> document element in our XML document. Here's the key: *what you put into the template replaces the node it matches.*

In this case, we want to replace the data in the <friends> element—and all contained elements—with the message "Friend data will go here." So we could just do this:

```
<?xml version="1.0"?>
<xsl:stylesheet version="2.0" xmlns:xsl="http://www.w3.org/1999/XSL/Transform">

    <xsl:template match="friends">
        Friend data will go here.
    </xsl:template>

</xsl:stylesheet>
```

Will that work? Yes, it will, but since this result will be displayed in a browser, let's actually create a small Web page to be displayed in place of the XML data. We start with an HTML <html> element:

```
<?xml version="1.0"?>
<xsl:stylesheet version="2.0" xmlns:xsl="http://www.w3.org/1999/XSL/Transform">

    <xsl:template match="friends">
        <html>
            .
            .
            .
        </html>
    </xsl:template>

</xsl:stylesheet>
```

Then let's add a <head> element to our new Web page:

```
<?xml version="1.0"?>
<xsl:stylesheet version="2.0" xmlns:xsl="http://www.w3.org/1999/XSL/Transform">

    <xsl:template match="friends">
        <html>
            <head>
                <title>
                    Friend data will go here.
                </title>
            </head>
            .
            .
            .
        </html>
    </xsl:template>

</xsl:stylesheet>
```

Then, finally, let's add our "Friend data will go here." message in the Web page's <body> element:

```
<?xml version="1.0"?>
<xsl:stylesheet version="2.0" xmlns:xsl="http://www.w3.org/1999/XSL/Transform">

    <xsl:template match="friends">
        <html>
            <head>
                <title>
                    Friend data will go here.
                </title>
            </head>
            <body>
                Friend data will go here.
            </body>
        </html>
    </xsl:template>

</xsl:stylesheet>
```

So what have we done? We've instructed XSLT to read in the XML document and replace its document element—and therefore all its contained data—with this Web page:

```
<html>
    <head>
        <title>
            Friend data will go here.
        </title>
    </head>
    <body>
        Friend data will go here.
    </body>
</html>
```

That completes format1.xsl. Now we can use it in a new version of our XML document, friends1.xml:

```
<?xml version="1.0"?>
<?xml-stylesheet type="text/xsl" href="format1.xsl"?>
<friends>
    <friend>
        <name>...</name>
        <age units="years">...</age>
        <height units="inches">...</height>
        <weight units="pounds">...</weight>
        <eyecolor units="color">...</eyecolor>
        <distance units="miles">...</distance><!--To friend's home-->
    </friend>
```

```
<friend>
    <name>...</name>
    <age units="years">...</age>
    <height units="inches">...</height>
    <weight units="pounds">...</weight>
    <eyecolor units="color">...</eyecolor>
    <distance units="miles">...</distance><!--To friend's home-->
</friend>

<friend>
    <name>...</name>
    <age units="years">...</age>
    <height units="inches">...</height>
    <weight units="pounds">...</weight>
    <eyecolor units="color">...</eyecolor>
    <distance units="miles">...</distance><!--To friend's home-->
</friend>

<friend>
    <name>...</name>
    <age units="years">...</age>
    <height units="inches">...</height>
    <weight units="pounds">...</weight>
    <eyecolor units="color">...</eyecolor>
    <distance units="miles">...</distance><!--To friend's home-->
</friend>

</friends>
```

Okay, were we successful? Will all the XML data in friends1.xml be replaced with our Web page? Open friends1.xml in Internet Explorer, as shown in Figure 6-3, to get your answer—the Web page does indeed appear, having replaced all XML data in friends1.xml. Very nice.

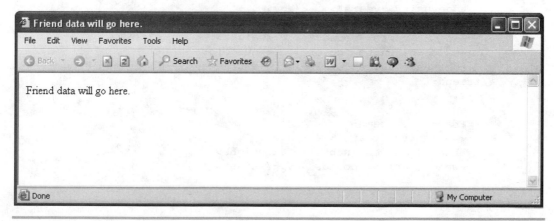

Figure 6-3   Our sample XML document replaced with a Web page

Try This   Replacing the Data in Your Sample XML Document

Try using format1.xsl to replace all the XML data in your XML document:

```
<?xml version="1.0"?>
<xsl:stylesheet version="2.0" xmlns:xsl="http://www.w3.org/1999/XSL/Transform">

    <xsl:template match="friends">
        <html>
            <head>
                <title>
                    Friend data will go here.
                </title>
            </head>
            <body>
                Friend data will go here.
            </body>
        </html>
    </xsl:template>

</xsl:stylesheet>
```

Except in this case, replace the message "Friend data will go here." with your own message, such as "XSLT really works!"

Put format1.xsl to work by adding this <?xml-stylesheet?> processing instruction to your sample XML document:

```
<?xml version="1.0"?>
<?xml-stylesheet type="text/xsl" href="format1.xsl"?>
<friends>
    <friend>
        <name>...</name>
        <age units="years">...</age>
        <height units="inches">...</height>
        <weight units="pounds">...</weight>
        <eyecolor units="color">...</eyecolor>
        <distance units="miles">...</distance><!--To friend's home-->
    </friend>

    <friend>
        <name>...</name>
        <age units="years">...</age>
        <height units="inches">...</height>
        <weight units="pounds">...</weight>
```

```
      <eyecolor units="color">...</eyecolor>
      <distance units="miles">...</distance><!--To friend's home-->
   </friend>

   <friend>
      <name>...</name>
      <age units="years">...</age>
      <height units="inches">...</height>
      <weight units="pounds">...</weight>
      <eyecolor units="color">...</eyecolor>
      <distance units="miles">...</distance><!--To friend's home-->
   </friend>

   <friend>
      <name>...</name>
      <age units="years">...</age>
      <height units="inches">...</height>
      <weight units="pounds">...</weight>
      <eyecolor units="color">...</eyecolor>
      <distance units="miles">...</distance><!--To friend's home-->
   </friend>

</friends>
```

When you're done, open the document in Internet Explorer to check that all the XML data in your document has been replaced with your new message.

Okay, we've been successful in creating our first XSLT template. But all it did was to replace all the data in our XML document with a Web page. What if we start working with the individual elements, like <friend> elements, in the XML document? That's coming up next.

Replacing <friend> Elements

So far, we've been able to match the <friends> document element of our sample XML document. Now we're going to try to replace the three <friend> elements with a new message, say, "Friend data.":

```
<?xml version="1.0"?>
<?xml-stylesheet type="text/xsl" href="format1.xsl"?>
<friends>
    <friend>
        .
        .
        .
    </friend>
```

```
    <friend>
        .
        .
        .
    </friend>

    <friend>
        .
        .
        .
    </friend>

</friends>
```

Here's how we matched the <friends> document element:

```
<?xml version="1.0"?>
<xsl:stylesheet version="2.0" xmlns:xsl="http://www.w3.org/1999/XSL/Transform">

    <xsl:template match="friends">
        .
        .
        .
    </xsl:template>

</xsl:stylesheet>
```

To match the three <friend> elements contained in the <friends> element, can you just create a template like this?

```
<?xml version="1.0"?>
<xsl:stylesheet version="2.0" xmlns:xsl="http://www.w3.org/1999/XSL/Transform">

    <xsl:template match="friend">
        .
        .
        .
    </xsl:template>

</xsl:stylesheet>
```

No, you can't, because of the way XSLT works. When you apply an XSLT style sheet to an XML document, XSLT only checks to see if any template matches the document element—no contained elements. In other words, the default behavior is to search for templates that match the document element only—if you want to match any other nodes, you have to apply the templates *yourself*.

So we'll start by matching the document element <friends> in format2.xsl:

```
<?xml version="1.0"?>
<xsl:stylesheet version="2.0" xmlns:xsl="http://www.w3.org/1999/XSL/Transform">
```

```
    <xsl:template match="friends">
        .
        .
        .
    </xsl:template>

</xsl:stylesheet>
```

Okay, at this point, we've matched the <friends> element. Now we've got to construct the Web page where each <friend> element will be replaced by the phrase "Friend data." We start by adding an <html> element for our new Web page:

```
<?xml version="1.0"?>
<xsl:stylesheet version="2.0" xmlns:xsl="http://www.w3.org/1999/XSL/Transform">

    <xsl:template match="friends">
        <html>
        .
        .
        .
        </html>
    </xsl:template>

</xsl:stylesheet>
```

Now we've got to create a new template for <friend> elements—and make XSLT find that new template. You can do that by applying new templates yourself.

Applying New Templates

So far, we've replaced the <friends> element with an <html> element. Now we want to find and replace the contained <friend> elements with a new template that we'll write. To apply the new <friend> template, you use the <xsl:apply-templates/> element like this:

```
<?xml version="1.0"?>
<xsl:stylesheet version="2.0" xmlns:xsl="http://www.w3.org/1999/XSL/Transform">

    <xsl:template match="friends">
        <html>
            <xsl:apply-templates/>
        </html>
    </xsl:template>

</xsl:stylesheet>
```

This element says: "Stop right here and search for other templates that might match at this stage." When searching for child elements, XSLT only goes down one step at a time by

default, so now that we're in the template for the <friends> element, you can go down one
level to find child elements, which means the three <friend> elements are visible to XSLT:

```
<?xml version="1.0"?>
<?xml-stylesheet type="text/xsl" href="format1.xsl"?>
<friends>
    <friend>
        .
        .
        .
    </friend>

    <friend>
        .
        .
        .
    </friend>

    <friend>
        .
        .
        .
    </friend>

</friends>
```

Great—at this point, we can create a new template to match <friend> elements:

```
<?xml version="1.0"?>
<xsl:stylesheet version="2.0" xmlns:xsl="http://www.w3.org/1999/XSL/Transform">

    <xsl:template match="friends">
        <html>
            <xsl:apply-templates/>
        </html>
    </xsl:template>

    <xsl:template match="friend">
        .
        .
        .
    </xsl:template>

</xsl:stylesheet>
```

This new template will be applied when XSLT encounters the <xsl:apply-templates/> element
in the friends template.

In the new template, we match the three <friend> elements, one after the other. We'll replace each <friend> element with this HTML:

```
<p>
    Friend data.
</p>
```

Here's what it looks like in our style sheet:

```
<?xml version="1.0"?>
<xsl:stylesheet version="2.0" xmlns:xsl="http://www.w3.org/1999/XSL/Transform">

    <xsl:template match="friends">
        <html>
            <xsl:apply-templates/>
        </html>
    </xsl:template>

    <xsl:template match="friend">
        <p>
            Friend data.
        </p>
    </xsl:template>

</xsl:stylesheet>
```

Did it work? You can see the results in Figure 6-4, where each of the three <friend> elements has been replaced by the text "Friend data." Cool.

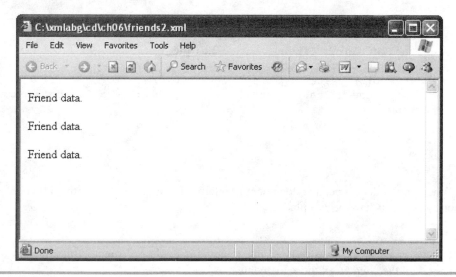

Figure 6-4 Our sample XML document with the <friend> elements replaced

Try This Replacing the <friend> Elements in Your Sample XML Document

Try using format2.xsl to replace all the <friend> elements in your XML document:

```
<?xml version="1.0"?>
<xsl:stylesheet version="2.0" xmlns:xsl="http://www.w3.org/1999/XSL/Transform">

    <xsl:template match="friends">
        <html>
            <xsl:apply-templates/>
        </html>
   </xsl:template>

    <xsl:template match="friend">
        <p>
            Friend data.
        </p>
    </xsl:template>

</xsl:stylesheet>
```

However, change "Friend data." to a message of your own choosing. Then connect format2.xsl to your sample XML document:

```
<?xml version="1.0"?>
<?xml-stylesheet type="text/xsl" href="format2.xsl"?>
<friends>
    <friend>
        <name>...</name>
        <age units="years">...</age>
        <height units="inches">...</height>
        <weight units="pounds">...</weight>
        <eyecolor units="color">...</eyecolor>
        <distance units="miles">...</distance><!--To friend's home-->
    </friend>
        .
        .
        .
</friends>
```

When you're done, open the document in Internet Explorer and verify that all your <friend> elements have been replaced.

Okay, so far so good—we've been able to target individual elements. But now how about working with the *contents* of those elements?

Extracting the Value of <name> Elements

Let's focus on the <name> elements for a minute in our sample XML document:

```
<?xml version="1.0"?>
<friends>
    <friend>
        <name>Sam Snead</name>
        <age units="years">19</age>
        <height units="inches">70</height>
        <weight units="pounds">160</weight>
        <eyecolor units="color">blue</eyecolor>
        <distance units="miles">43.4</distance><!--To friend's home-->
    </friend>

    <friend>
        <name>Paige Turner</name>
        <age units="years">23</age>
        <height units="inches">67</height>
        <weight units="pounds">110</weight>
        <eyecolor units="color">brown</eyecolor>
        <distance units="miles">66.8</distance><!--To friend's home-->
    </friend>

    <friend>
        <name>Ralph Kramden</name>
        <age units="years">32</age>
        <height units="inches">71</height>
        <weight units="pounds">182</weight>
        <eyecolor units="color">hazel</eyecolor>
        <distance units="miles">28.4</distance><!--To friend's home-->
    </friend>

</friends>
```

So how do we access the contents of each <name> element and display each friend's name? After all, that's usually the name of the game in XSLT—data access. Let's put together a new style sheet, format2.xsl, that does just that—extracts the name of any friends in the document.

We'll start format3.xsl as usual for an XSLT style sheet:

```
<?xml version="1.0"?>
<xsl:stylesheet version="2.0" xmlns:xsl="http://www.w3.org/1999/XSL/Transform">
        .
        .
        .
</xsl:stylesheet>
```

Next, we'll match the document element, which is automatically searched for like this:

```
<?xml version="1.0"?>
<xsl:stylesheet version="2.0" xmlns:xsl="http://www.w3.org/1999/XSL/Transform">

    <xsl:template match="friends">
        .
        .
        .
    </xsl:template>

</xsl:stylesheet>
```

We want to work with the <name> elements, which are child elements of the <friend> elements, not with the <friends> element directly, so we want to create a new template that matches the <friend> elements. In the friends template, we can add <html> tags like this:

```
<?xml version="1.0"?>
<xsl:stylesheet version="2.0" xmlns:xsl="http://www.w3.org/1999/XSL/Transform">

    <xsl:template match="friends">
        <html>
        .
        .
        .
        </html>
    </xsl:template>

</xsl:stylesheet>
```

And to get to the <friend> elements, we use an <xsl:apply-templates/> element this way:

```
<?xml version="1.0"?>
<xsl:stylesheet version="2.0" xmlns:xsl="http://www.w3.org/1999/XSL/Transform">

    <xsl:template match="friends">
        <html>
            <xsl:apply-templates/>
        </html>
    </xsl:template>

</xsl:stylesheet>
```

And we can add the new template to match <friend> elements this way in the style sheet:

```
<?xml version="1.0"?>
<xsl:stylesheet version="2.0" xmlns:xsl="http://www.w3.org/1999/XSL/Transform">

    <xsl:template match="friends">
        <html>
            <xsl:apply-templates/>
        </html>
```

```
    </xsl:template>

    <xsl:template match="friend">
        .
        .
        .
    </xsl:template>

</xsl:stylesheet>
```

Let's give each friend's name its own HTML <p> element:

```
<?xml version="1.0"?>
<xsl:stylesheet version="2.0" xmlns:xsl="http://www.w3.org/1999/XSL/Transform">

    <xsl:template match="friends">
        <html>
            <xsl:apply-templates/>
        </html>
    </xsl:template>

    <xsl:template match="friend">
        <p>
        .
        .
        .
        </p>
    </xsl:template>

</xsl:stylesheet>
```

That's fine. But now we've got to see how to extract the contents of the <name> element inside each <friend> element.

Using <xsl:value-of>

We've been able to create a template that matches and is called for every <friend> element in our sample document:

```
<?xml version="1.0"?>
<friends>
    <friend>
        .
        .
        .
    </friend>

    <friend>
        .
        .
        .
    </friend>
```

```
    <friend>
        .
        .
        .
    </friend>

</friends>
```

What we actually want to do is to extract the name from the <name> child element in each <friend> element:

```
<?xml version="1.0"?>
<friends>
    <friend>
        <name>Sam Snead</name>
        .
        .
        .
    </friend>

    <friend>
        <name>Paige Turner</name>
        .
        .
        .
    </friend>

    <friend>
        <name>Ralph Kramden</name>
        .
        .
        .
    </friend>

</friends>
```

Here's the key: *In each template, you're automatically working with the child elements of the element the template matches.* That means that in our template that matches the <friend> elements, we have automatic access to the child elements of the <friend> elements.

Okay, so we have access to the child elements of the <friend> elements in the friend template. To actually extract the value of an element—that is, the text in it—you use the <xsl: value-of/> element:

```
<?xml version="1.0"?>
<xsl:stylesheet version="2.0" xmlns:xsl="http://www.w3.org/1999/XSL/Transform">

    <xsl:template match="friends">
        <html>
            <xsl:apply-templates/>
        </html>
```

```
    </xsl:template>

    <xsl:template match="friend">
        <p>
            <xsl:value-of/>
        </p>
    </xsl:template>

</xsl:stylesheet>
```

We have to indicate which child element we want to extract the value of using the <xsl: value of> element's select attribute. We want to extract the value of the <name> child element, so we use the select attribute like this:

```
<?xml version="1.0"?>
<xsl:stylesheet version="2.0" xmlns:xsl="http://www.w3.org/1999/XSL/Transform">

    <xsl:template match="friends">
        <html>
            <xsl:apply-templates/>
        </html>
    </xsl:template>

    <xsl:template match="friend">
        <p>
            <xsl:value-of select="name"/>
        </p>
    </xsl:template>

</xsl:stylesheet>
```

Great—and there you have it, format3.xsl. Does it work? Take a look at Figure 6-5, where you see the names from the sample XML document. Nice.

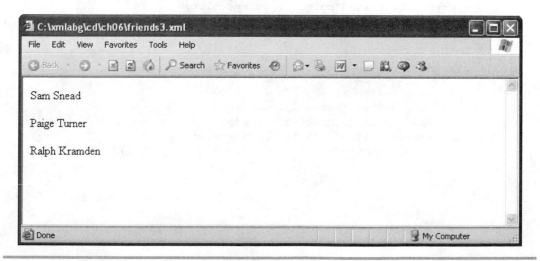

Figure 6-5   Our sample XML document's names

Try This Extracting the Eye Color from Your Sample XML Document

Try modifying format3.xsl:

```
<?xml version="1.0"?>
<xsl:stylesheet version="2.0" xmlns:xsl="http://www.w3.org/1999/XSL/Transform">

    <xsl:template match="friends">
        <html>
            <xsl:apply-templates/>
        </html>
    </xsl:template>

    <xsl:template match="friend">
        <p>
            <xsl:value-of select="name"/>
        </p>
    </xsl:template>

</xsl:stylesheet>
```

so that you can extract each friend's eye color instead of name:

```
<?xml version="1.0"?>
<?xml-stylesheet type="text/xsl" href="format3.xsl"?>
<friends>
    <friend>
        <name>...</name>
        <age units="years">...</age>
        <height units="inches">...</height>
        <weight units="pounds">...</weight>
        <eyecolor units="color">...</eyecolor>
        <distance units="miles">...</distance><!--To friend's home-->
    </friend>

    <friend>
        <name>...</name>
        <age units="years">...</age>
        <height units="inches">...</height>
        <weight units="pounds">...</weight>
        <eyecolor units="color">...</eyecolor>
        <distance units="miles">...</distance><!--To friend's home-->
    </friend>
```

```
<friend>
    <name>...</name>
    <age units="years">...</age>
    <height units="inches">...</height>
    <weight units="pounds">...</weight>
    <eyecolor units="color">...</eyecolor>
    <distance units="miles">...</distance><!--To friend's home-->
</friend>

<friend>
    <name>...</name>
    <age units="years">...</age>
    <height units="inches">...</height>
    <weight units="pounds">...</weight>
    <eyecolor units="color">...</eyecolor>
    <distance units-"miles">...</distance><!--To friend's home-->
</friend>

</friends>
```

When you're done, open the document in Internet Explorer to check your friends' eye colors. (If you haven't used an <eyecolor> element in your sample document, extract the values of friends' ages.)

Okay, we've made considerable progress.

Extracting Multiple Elements Values

We've been able to extract the value of the <name> elements in the friends document, but what if you also wanted to store your friends' nicknames? There's nothing in XML that says you can't have multiple elements with the same name, even at the same level. For example, here's how you might store your friends' nicknames in friends4.xml:

```
<?xml version="1.0"?>
<?xml-stylesheet type="text/xsl" href="format4.xsl"?>
<friends>
    <friend>
        <name>Sam Snead</name>
        <name>Ace</name>
        <age units="years">19</age>
        <height units="inches">70</height>
        <weight units="pounds">160</weight>
        <eyecolor units="color">blue</eyecolor>
        <distance units="miles">43.4</distance><!--To friend's home-->
    </friend>
```

```
<friend>
    <name>Paige Turner</name>
    <name>Bookie</name>
    <age units="years">23</age>
    <height units="inches">67</height>
    <weight units="pounds">110</weight>
    <eyecolor units="color">brown</eyecolor>
    <distance units="miles">66.8</distance><!--To friend's home-->
</friend>

<friend>
    <name>Ralph Kramden</name>
    <name>Ralphie Boy</name>
    <age units="years">32</age>
    <height units="inches">71</height>
    <weight units="pounds">182</weight>
    <eyecolor units="color">hazel</eyecolor>
    <distance units="miles">28.4</distance><!--To friend's home-->
</friend>

</friends>
```

Alright, now we've got two names to extract for each friend. How do we do that? So far, our style sheet looks like this:

```
<?xml version="1.0"?>
<xsl:stylesheet version="2.0" xmlns:xsl="http://www.w3.org/1999/XSL/Transform">

    <xsl:template match="friends">
        <html>
            <xsl:apply-templates/>
        </html>
    </xsl:template>

<xsl:template match="friend">
    <p>
        <xsl:value-of select="name"/>
    </p>
</xsl:template>

</xsl:stylesheet>
```

But this style sheet can only handle a single <name> child element. Now that there are two <name> child elements, how do we extract both of them in the same template?

It turns out that you can loop over multiple elements in the same template with the <xsl: for-each> element. For example, to loop over all child name elements of the current <friend> element, you can use <xsl:for-each> this way:

```
<?xml version="1.0"?>
<xsl:stylesheet version="2.0" xmlns:xsl="http://www.w3.org/1999/XSL/Transform">

    <xsl:template match="friends">
        <html>
            <xsl:apply-templates/>
        </html>
    </xsl:template>

<xsl:template match="friend">
    <xsl:for-each select="name">
        <p>
            <xsl:value-of/>
        </p>
    </xsl:for-each>
</xsl:template>

</xsl:stylesheet>
```

Inside the <xsl:for-each> loop, the element you're working with is the current <name> element. That means we can't use this <xsl:value-of> element as it stands anymore:

```
<xsl:value-of select="name"/>
```

because it refers to a <name> *child* element—but <name> is the *current* element, not a child. So how do you use the select element to refer to the current element? It turns out that you can use a dot (.) to stand for the current element, so here's the way the <xsl:value-of> element looks:

```
<?xml version="1.0"?>
<xsl:stylesheet version="2.0" xmlns:xsl="http://www.w3.org/1999/XSL/Transform">

    <xsl:template match="friends">
        <html>
            <xsl:apply-templates/>
        </html>
    </xsl:template>

<xsl:template match="friend">
    <xsl:for-each select="name">
        <p>
            <xsl:value-of select="."/>
        </p>
    </xsl:for-each>
</xsl:template>

</xsl:stylesheet>
```

And there we have it—now we're able to pick out the values of multiple <name> elements, as you can see in Figure 6-6. Excellent.

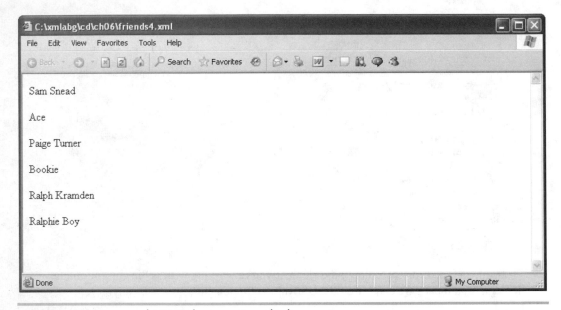

Figure 6-6 Our sample XML document's multiple names

Try This Extracting Multiple Items from Your Sample XML Document

Assume that all your friends now have vacation houses, so there are now two <distance> elements for each friend—one to their home, one to their vacation house:

```
<?xml version="1.0"?>
<?xml-stylesheet type="text/xsl" href="format4.xsl"?>
<friends>
    <friend>
        <name>...</name>
        <age units="years">...</age>
        <height units="inches">...</height>
        <weight units="pounds">...</weight>
        <eyecolor units="color">...</eyecolor>
        <distance units="miles">...</distance><!--To friend's home-->
        <distance units="miles">...</distance><!--To vacation home-->
    </friend>

    <friend>
        <name>...</name>
        <age units="years">...</age>
        <height units="inches">...</height>
        <weight units="pounds">...</weight>
```

```
    <eyecolor units="color">...</eyecolor>
    <distance units="miles">...</distance><!--To friend's home-->
    <distance units="miles">...</distance><!--To vacation home-->
</friend>

<friend>
    <name>...</name>
    <age units="years">...</age>
    <height units="inches">...</height>
    <weight units="pounds">...</weight>
    <eyecolor units="color">...</eyecolor>
    <distance units="miles">...</distance><!--To friend's home-->
    <distance units="miles">...</distance><!--To vacation home-->
</friend>

<friend>
    <name>...</name>
    <age units="years">...</age>
    <height units="inches">...</height>
    <weight units="pounds">...</weight>
    <eyecolor units="color">...</eyecolor>
    <distance units="miles">...</distance><!--To friend's home-->
    <distance units="miles">...</distance><!--To vacation home-->
</friend>

</friends>
```

Try modifying format4.xsl:

```
<?xml version="1.0"?>
<xsl:stylesheet version="2.0" xmlns:xsl="http://www.w3.org/1999/XSL/Transform">

    <xsl:template match="friends">
        <html>
            <xsl:apply-templates/>
        </html>
    </xsl:template>

    <xsl:template match="friend">
        <p>
            <xsl:value-of select="name"/>
        </p>
    </xsl:template>

</xsl:stylesheet>
```

so that you can extract each friend's two distances.

When you're done, open the document in Internet Explorer to check that your friend's distances appear.

Chapter 7

Formatting XML with XSL Transformations

Key Skills & Concepts

- Matching the root node
- Matching elements
- Matching element descendants
- Matching attributes
- Matching comments

In the preceding chapter, we got our start with XSLT, but there's lots more to come. The XPath part of XSLT—that is, the way you match nodes in an XML document—is a very deep topic, and we'll take a better look at it in this chapter. Knowing how to select elements, attributes, and even comments in XML documents is crucial to mastering XSLT.

We'll get started with a discussion of the match attribute in the <xsl:template> element, which is the basis of selecting nodes in XSLT.

Working with the Match Attribute

You use the match attribute of the <xsl:template> element to match nodes, like this:

```
<xsl:template match="friends">
    <html>
        <xsl:apply-templates/>
    </html>
</xsl:template>
```

It turns out that you can use the match attribute to match more than just element names—you can also use it to match comments, child elements, attributes, and more. We'll take a look at what you can do with the match attribute—and therefore, what nodes you can match with XSLT templates—here.

The other way of selecting nodes using XSLT is with the select attribute:

```
<xsl:template match="friend">
    <p>
        <xsl:value-of select="name"/>
    </p>
</xsl:template>
```

which is an attribute of the XSLT elements <xsl:apply-templates>, <xsl:value-of>, <xsl:for-each>, <xsl:copy-of>, and <xsl:sort>.

It turns out that you can assign XPath expressions to both the match and select attributes—but that the select attribute can take more advanced XPath expressions. We'll see what the difference is in this chapter. First, we'll start with the match attribute, seeing what kind of XPath expressions you can assign to it.

We'll start by finding out how to work with an XML document's root node.

Matching the Root Node

Technically, an XML document's root node is the node that comes before everything in an XML document—and I mean *everything*. Here, I'll represent the root node with an asterisk (*):

```
*<?xml version="1.0"?>
<friends>
    <friend>
        <name>Sam Snead</name>
        <age units="years">19</age>
        <height units="inches">70</height>
        <weight units="pounds">160</weight>
        <eyecolor units="color">blue</eyecolor>
        <distance units="miles">43.4</distance><!--To friend's home-->
    </friend>
        .
        .
        .
```

XPath gives you access to the root node, if you want it, with the expression "/", which matches the root node. For example, this template matches the root node and applies any matching templates to the children of the root node:

```
<xsl:template match="/">
    <html>
        <xsl:apply-templates/>
    </html>
</xsl:template>
```

Note that this template is already a default template in XSLT—it says to start by applying any templates XSLT finds that match the children of the root node—and, of course, the document element is a child of the root node. So this template really just makes the rule explicit in XSLT—XSLT will automatically search for templates that match the document element.

And besides the root node, you can also match element nodes.

Matching Element Nodes

As you already know, you can also match element nodes in XSLT templates. You do that simply by using the element name as an XPath expression—that's how to match an element node.

For example, you can match the <friends> element this way:

```
<xsl:template match="friends">
  <html>
    <xsl:apply-templates/>
  </html>
</xsl:template>
```

This template matches the <friends> element node (which is also the document node) in our sample XML document:

```
<?xml version="1.0"?>
<friends>
    <friend>
        <name>Sam Snead</name>
        <age units="years">19</age>
        <height units="inches">70</height>
        <weight units="pounds">160</weight>
        <eyecolor units="color">blue</eyecolor>
        <distance units="miles">43.4</distance><!--To friend's home-->
    </friend>
        .
        .
        .
</friends>
```

Good, you can match the document element with no trouble. But can you match the child elements inside the document element?

Matching Child Element Nodes

Okay, you've been able to match the document element, <friends>, but what if you wanted to match the child elements of the <friends> element—that is, the <friend> elements?

```
<?xml version="1.0"?>
<friends>
    <friend>
        <name>Sam Snead</name>
        <age units="years">19</age>
        <height units="inches">70</height>
        <weight units="pounds">160</weight>
        <eyecolor units="color">blue</eyecolor>
        <distance units="miles">43.4</distance><!--To friend's home-->
    </friend>

    <friend>
        <name>Paige Turner</name>
        <age units="years">23</age>
        <height units="inches">67</height>
        <weight units="pounds">110</weight>
```

```
        <eyecolor units="color">brown</eyecolor>
        <distance units="miles">66.8</distance><!--To friend's home-->
    </friend>

    <friend>
        <name>Ralph Kramden</name>
        <age units="years">32</age>
        <height units="inches">71</height>
        <weight units="pounds">182</weight>
        <eyecolor units="color">hazel</eyecolor>
        <distance units="miles">28.4</distance><!--To friend's home-->
    </friend>

</friends>
```

We saw in this preceding chapter that you could match <friend> elements by first matching the enclosing <friends> elements and then adding a new template for <friend> elements:

```
<?xml version="1.0"?>
<xsl:stylesheet version="2.0" xmlns:xsl="http://www.w3.org/1999/XSL/Transform">

    <xsl:template match="friends">
        <html>
            <xsl:apply-templates/>
        </html>
    </xsl:template>

    <xsl:template match="friend">
        <p>
            <xsl:value-of select="."/>
        </p>
    </xsl:template>

</xsl:stylesheet>
```

It turns out that you can do the same thing—match <friend> elements when you start with the <friend> element—by using the XPath expression "friend/friends". Here's how that would look—this style sheet does the same as the previous one:

```
<?xml version="1.0"?>
<xsl:stylesheet version="2.0" xmlns:xsl="http://www.w3.org/1999/XSL/Transform">

  <xsl:template match="friends/friend">
    <p>
      <xsl:value-of select="."/>
    </p>
  </xsl:template>

</xsl:stylesheet>
```

The match="friends/friend" attribute says to start at <friends> elements and then match all <friend> elements that are children of the <friends> element.

Let's say you actually wanted the contents of the <name> element inside each <friend> element. You could create multiple templates to match each <name> element, going from the <friends> elements to the <friend> elements, to the <name> element inside each <friend> element:

```
<?xml version="1.0"?>
<xsl:stylesheet version="2.0" xmlns:xsl="http://www.w3.org/1999/XSL/Transform">

    <xsl:template match="friends">
        <html>
            <xsl:apply-templates/>
        </html>
    </xsl:template>

    <xsl:template match="friend">
        <p>
            <xsl:apply-templates/>
        </p>
    </xsl:template>

    <xsl:template match="name">
        <p>
            <xsl:value-of select="."/>
        </p>
    </xsl:template>

</xsl:stylesheet>
```

Or you could do the same thing using the XPath expression "friends/friend/name" like this:

```
<?xml version="1.0"?>
<xsl:stylesheet version="2.0" xmlns:xsl="http://www.w3.org/1999/XSL/Transform">

  <xsl:template match="friends/friend/name">
    <p>
      <xsl:value-of select="."/>
    </p>
  </xsl:template>

</xsl:stylesheet>
```

Cool.

You can use the expression "friend/name" to match all <name> elements that are direct children of <friend> elements. And you can use an asterisk (*) as a wildcard matching any element—for example, you can use the expression "friend/*/name" to match all <name> elements that are *grandchildren* of <friend> elements.

There's even an easier way to perform both matches—just use the expression "friend// name", which matches all <name> elements that are inside <friend> elements, no matter how many levels deep (the matched elements are called *descendants* of the <friend> element). In other words, "friend//name" matches "friend/name", "friend/*/name", "friend/*/*/name", and so on.

So now you're getting familiar with XPath expressions—not only can you use "name" as an XPath expression, but also "friend/name", "friend//name", "friend/*/name", "friend/*/*/name", and so on.

Okay—now let's take a look at something we've never seen before: matching XML attributes.

Matching Attributes

Note that many of the elements in our sample XML document have attributes named units:

```
<?xml version="1.0"?>
<friends>
    <friend>
        <name>Sam Snead</name>
        <age units="years">19</age>
        <height units="inches">70</height>
        <weight units="pounds">160</weight>
        <eyecolor units="color">blue</eyecolor>
        <distance units="miles">43.4</distance><!--To friend's home-->
    </friend>

    <friend>
        <name>Paige Turner</name>
        <age units="years">23</age>
        <height units="inches">67</height>
        <weight units="pounds">110</weight>
        <eyecolor units="color">brown</eyecolor>
        <distance units="miles">66.8</distance><!--To friend's home-->
    </friend>

    <friend>
        <name>Ralph Kramden</name>
        <age units="years">32</age>
        <height units="inches">71</height>
        <weight units="pounds">182</weight>
        <eyecolor units="color">hazel</eyecolor>
        <distance units="miles">28.4</distance><!--To friend's home-->
    </friend>

</friends>
```

How can you recover the value of those attributes? What XPath expression can you use to match an attribute?

It turns out that the answer is simple—you just prefix the attribute name with an at sign (@). So to access the value of the units attribute, you can match such an attribute as @units. In XSLT, attributes are nodes, and you can use them with the match or select attribute.

Let's take a look at a fancy-pants example. In this example, we'll format our friends into a table—a column for their name, a column for their age, and so on. We start out by creating the

HTML table with the <table> element, and putting in headers for each column ("Name", "Age", and so on):

```
<?xml version="1.0"?>
<xsl:stylesheet version="2.0"
xmlns:xsl="http://www.w3.org/1999/XSL/Transform">

    <xsl:template match="friends">
        <html>
            <head>
                <title>
                    My Friends
                </title>
            </head>
            <body>
                <h1>
                    My Friends
                </h1>
                <table border="1">
                    <td>Name</td>
                    <td>Age</td>
                    <td>Weight</td>
                    <td>Height</td>
                    <xsl:apply-templates/>
                </table>
            </body>
        </html>
    </xsl:template>
        .
        .
        .
```

Notice that we use <xsl:apply-templates/> here to apply some templates to get the actual friend data. We can create a new template to match the <friend> element, and then apply new templates for the elements whose data we want (we're going to skip eye color)—note that you can use the select attribute with <xsl:apply-templates> to indicate exactly what element you want to find matching templates for:

```
<?xml version="1.0"?>
<xsl:stylesheet version="2.0"
xmlns:xsl="http://www.w3.org/1999/XSL/Transform">

    <xsl:template match="friends">
        <html>
            <head>
                <title>
                    My Friends
                </title>
            </head>
```

```
        <body>
            <h1>
                My Friends
            </h1>
            <table border="1">
                <td>Name</td>
                <td>Age</td>
                <td>Weight</td>
                <td>Height</td>
                <xsl:apply-templates/>
            </table>
        </body>
    </html>
  </xsl:template>

<xsl:template match="friend">
    <tr>
        <td><xsl:value-of select="name"/></td>
        <td><xsl:apply-templates select="age"/></td>
        <td><xsl:apply-templates select="weight"/></td>
        <td><xsl:apply-templates select="height"/></td>
    </tr>
</xsl:template>
            .
    .
    .
```

And then for each <age>, <weight>, and <height> element, we'll extract the value of the element and place it into the HTML table like this:

```
<?xml version="1.0"?>
<xsl:stylesheet version="2.0"
xmlns:xsl="http://www.w3.org/1999/XSL/Transform">

    <xsl:template match="friends">
        <html>
            <head>
                <title>
                    My Friends
                </title>
            </head>
            <body>
                <h1>
                    My Friends
                </h1>
                <table border="1">
                    <td>Name</td>
                    <td>Age</td>
                    <td>Weight</td>
                    <td>Height</td>
```

```
                  <xsl:apply-templates/>
              </table>
          </body>
      </html>
  </xsl:template>

  <xsl:template match="friend">
      <tr>
          <td><xsl:value-of select="name"/></td>
          <td><xsl:apply-templates select="age"/></td>
          <td><xsl:apply-templates select="weight"/></td>
          <td><xsl:apply-templates select="height"/></td>
      </tr>
  </xsl:template>

  <xsl:template match="age">
      <xsl:value-of select="."/>
  </xsl:template>

  <xsl:template match="weight">
      <xsl:value-of select="."/>
  </xsl:template>

  <xsl:template match="height">
      <xsl:value-of select="."/>
  </xsl:template>
</xsl:stylesheet>
```

Okay, swell—that gives us the table you see in Figure 7-1. However, notice a problem with that table—the columns just hold strings of numbers—19, 23, 32, and so on. What are the units of those numbers?

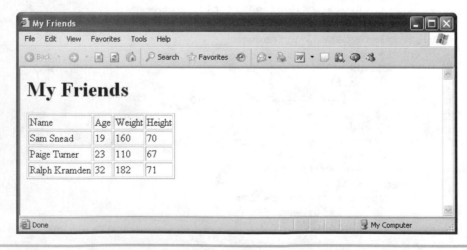

Figure 7-1   First attempt at formatting our sample document

To get the units of the number you see in Figure 7-1, you can extract the value of the units attribute from the <age>, <weight>, and <height> elements by referring to that value as @units.

Let's put this to work. We'll insert the units, like "years" after the values like 19. But note that we don't just want "19years"—we have to put a space between the 19 and the "years". To insert direct text into an XSLT style sheet's output, you can use the <xsl:text> element—to insert a space, for example, you could use <xsl:text> </xsl:text>.

That means that to insert a space and the value of the units attribute for every numerical value, we add this to our style sheet, format1.xsl:

```
<?xml version="1.0"?>
<xsl:stylesheet version="2.0"
xmlns:xsl="http://www.w3.org/1999/XSL/Transform">

    <xsl:template match="friends">
        <html>
            <head>
                <title>
                    My Friends
                </title>
            </head>
            <body>
                <h1>
                    My Friends
                </h1>
                <table border="1">
                    <td>Name</td>
                    <td>Age</td>
                    <td>Weight</td>
                    <td>Height</td>
                    <xsl:apply-templates/>
                </table>
            </body>
        </html>
    </xsl:template>

    <xsl:template match="friend">
        <tr>
            <td><xsl:value-of select="name"/></td>
            <td><xsl:apply-templates select="age"/></td>
            <td><xsl:apply-templates select="weight"/></td>
            <td><xsl:apply-templates select="height"/></td>
        </tr>
    </xsl:template>

    <xsl:template match="age">
        <xsl:value-of select="."/>
        <xsl:text> </xsl:text>
        <xsl:value-of select="@units"/>
    </xsl:template>
```

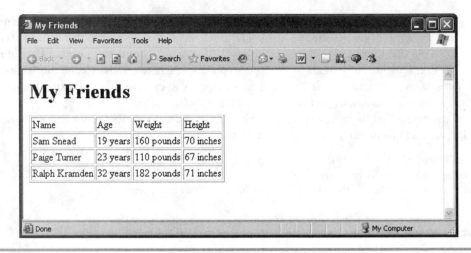

Figure 7-2 Adding attribute values to a table

```
<xsl:template match="weight">
    <xsl:value-of select="."/>
    <xsl:text> </xsl:text>
    <xsl:value-of select="@units"/>
</xsl:template>

<xsl:template match="height">
    <xsl:value-of select="."/>
    <xsl:text> </xsl:text>
    <xsl:value-of select="@units"/>
</xsl:template>
</xsl:stylesheet>
```

And that's all we need—you can see the new results in Figure 7-2, where the value of the attributes has indeed been read and displayed. Very cool indeed!

Try This Working with Attribute Values

Try changing the units attribute to the measure attribute in your sample XML document:

```
<?xml version="1.0"?>
<friends>
    <friend>
        <name>...</name>
        <age measure="years">...</age>
        <height measure="inches">...</height>
        <weight measure="pounds">...</weight>
        <eyecolor measure="color">...</eyecolor>
        <distance measure="miles">...</distance>
    </friend>
```

```
<friend>
    <name>...</name>
    <age measure="years">...</age>
    <height measure="inches">...</height>
    <weight measure="pounds">...</weight>
    <eyecolor measure="color">...</eyecolor>
    <distance measure="miles">...</distance>
</friend>

<friend>
    <name>...</name>
    <age measure="years">...</age>
    <height measure="inches">...</height>
    <weight measure="pounds">...</weight>
    <eyecolor measure="color">...</eyecolor>
    <distance measure="miles">...</distance>
</friend>

<friend>
    <name>...</name>
    <age measure="years">...</age>
    <height measure="inches">...</height>
    <weight measure="pounds">...</weight>
    <eyecolor measure="color">...</eyecolor>
    <distance measure="miles">...</distance>
</friend>

</friends>
```

Now modify format1.xsl so that it picks up the values of the measure attributes and displays them, formatting the results in a table. When you're done, open the document in Internet Explorer to check it, as usual.

Just as you can use * for element wildcards, so you can use @* as a wildcard for attributes. For example, "friend/@*" would match any attribute of a <friend> element.

Matching by ID

You can also match elements by id attribute. For example, say you give your first friend, Sam Snead, the id attribute "Sam":

```
<?xml version="1.0"?>
<friends>
    <friend id="Sam">
        <name>Sam Snead</name>
        <age units="years">19</age>
        <height units="inches">70</height>
        <weight units="pounds">160</weight>
```

```
        <eyecolor units="color">blue</eyecolor>
        <distance units="miles">43.4</distance><!--To friend's home-->
    </friend>
         .
         .
         .
```

Then you could match any element that has an id value of "Sam" by assigning the expression "id('Sam')" to the match attribute like this:

```
<xsl:template match = "id('Sam')">
    <h2><xsl:value-of select="."/></h2>
</xsl:template>
```

But there's a catch—to match by ID, the XSLT processor has to know what attribute you're treating as the id attribute (it doesn't have to be named "ID" or "id"), and you have to tell it that with a DTD or an XML schema.

Matching XML Comments

Using XSLT, you can even match and extract XML comments. We happen to have XML comments built into our sample XML document for this very purpose like this:

```
<?xml version="1.0"?>
<friends>
    <friend>
        <name>Sam Snead</name>
        <age units="years">19</age>
        <height units="inches">70</height>
        <weight units="pounds">160</weight>
        <eyecolor units="color">blue</eyecolor>
        <distance units="miles">43.4</distance><!--To friend's home-->
    </friend>
         .
         .
         .
```

You match comments by assigning comment() to the match attribute, something like this in format2.xsl:

```
<?xml version="1.0"?>
<xsl:stylesheet version="2.0" xmlns:xsl="http://www.w3.org/1999/XSL/Transform">

    <xsl:template match="friends">
        <html>
            <xsl:apply-templates/>
        </html>
    </xsl:template>
```

```
<xsl:template match="friend">
    <html>
        <xsl:apply-templates/>
    </html>
</xsl:template>

<xsl:template match="comment()">
  <xsl:text>The comment is: "</xsl:text>
    <xsl:value-of select="."/>
  <xsl:text>".</xsl:text>
  <br/>
</xsl:template>

</xsl:stylesheet>
```

But look at what we get, as you can see in Figure 7-3.

It looks like all of each friend's data has been stripped out and simply plunked into the output document. Here's what that data looks like for Sam Snead:

```
<?xml version="1.0"?>
<friends>
    <friend>
        <name>Sam Snead</name>
        <age units="years">19</age>
        <height units="inches">70</height>
        <weight units="pounds">160</weight>
        <eyecolor units="color">blue</eyecolor>
        <distance units="miles">43.4</distance><!--To friend's home-->
    </friend>
        .
        .
        .
```

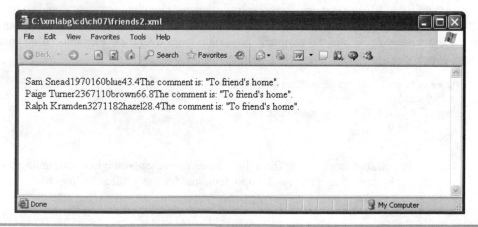

Figure 7-3 First attempt at extracting comments

Why did that happen? It happened because XSLT has a very bad habit—if you don't supply a match for all data in an XML document, it simply places that data into the output document. It's as though this template were added to your style sheet by default to match any element (as represented by the wildcard *):

```
<xsl:template match="*">
  <xsl:value-of select="."/>
</xsl:template>
```

So how do you cure XSLT of this bad habit? The only way is to provide a match for all the data in your XML document. For example, if you wanted to create an output document with only your friends' ages, you might think you could do that like this:

```
<?xml version="1.0"?>
<xsl:stylesheet version="2.0" xmlns:xsl="http://www.w3.org/1999/XSL/Transform">

    <xsl:template match="friends">
        <html>
            <xsl:apply-templates/>
        </html>
    </xsl:template>

    <xsl:template match="friend">
        <html>
            <xsl:apply-templates/>
        </html>
    </xsl:template>

    <xsl:template match="age">
      <xsl:value-of select="."/>
    </xsl:template>
</xsl:stylesheet>
```

But since you haven't matched the elements <name>, <height>, <weight>, and so on, all the data in those elements will be stripped out and dumped as plain text into the output document when you execute this template, because it loops over these elements (if no template loops over specific elements, they will not appear in the output):

```
<xsl:template match="friend">
    <html>
        <xsl:apply-templates/>
    </html>
</xsl:template>
```

So how do you suppress the data from the elements <name>, <height>, <weight> and so on? You do that by providing a catch-all empty template for the wildcard * like this:

```
<?xml version="1.0"?>
<xsl:stylesheet version="2.0" xmlns:xsl="http://www.w3.org/1999/XSL/Transform">
```

```
<xsl:template match="friends">
    <html>
        <xsl:apply-templates/>
    </html>
</xsl:template>

<xsl:template match="friend">
    <html>
        <xsl:apply-templates/>
    </html>
</xsl:template>

<xsl:template match="age">
  <xsl:value-of select="."/>
</xsl:template>

<xsl:template match="*">
</xsl:template>

</xsl:stylesheet>
```

Now these elements do not go unmatched—they are matched by the catch-all template, which is empty, so nothing goes into the output document from those elements.

In general, when you use XSLT and see data from your XML elements simply stripped out of your XML document and placed into the output document in plain text, it's because they were looped over but went unmatched—and so, by default, their data was simply placed in the output document. Why XSLT has this very bad habit is a mystery—it really seems that the much more logical behavior would be to only place data in the output document if you explicitly ask for it.

Okay, so how do we fix format2.xsl to only pick out the comments in our document? You can do that by suppressing the elements with a catch-all empty template to match them like this one:

```
<?xml version="1.0"?>
<xsl:stylesheet version="2.0" xmlns:xsl="http://www.w3.org/1999/XSL/Transform">

    <xsl:template match="friends">
        <html>
            <xsl:apply-templates/>
        </html>
    </xsl:template>

    <xsl:template match="friend">
        <html>
            <xsl:apply-templates/>
        </html>
    </xsl:template>

    <xsl:template match="comment()">
      <xsl:text>The comment is: "</xsl:text>
```

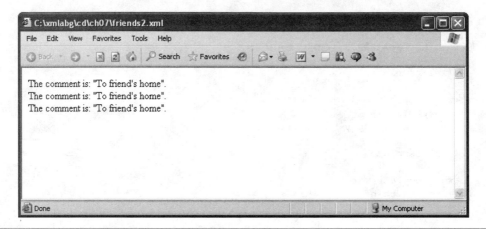

Figure 7-4 Corrected attempt at extracting comments

```
    <xsl:value-of select="."/>
   <xsl:text>".</xsl:text>
   <br/>
 </xsl:template>

 <xsl:template match="*">
 </xsl:template>

</xsl:stylesheet>
```

And that corrects the problem, as you see in Figure 7-4.

And that's how you match comments in XSLT—and more important, how you match unmatched elements so that their data doesn't end up in the output document by default.

Try This Using Empty Catch-All Templates

Try modifying the style sheet you just saw so that it picks out and displays only <weight> elements instead of <age> elements:

```
<?xml version="1.0"?>
<xsl:stylesheet version="2.0" xmlns:xsl="http://www.w3.org/1999/XSL/Transform">

    <xsl:template match="friends">
        <html>
            <xsl:apply-templates/>
        </html>
    </xsl:template>
```

```
    <xsl:template match="friend">
        <html>
            <xsl:apply-templates/>
        </html>
    </xsl:template>

    <xsl:template match="weight">
      <xsl:value-of select="."/>
    </xsl:template>

</xsl:stylesheet>
```

Confirm that as it stands, all the data from the other elements in your sample document is stripped out and placed into the output document by default. Next, add an empty catch-all template to this style sheet to suppress the other elements, and confirm that that works.

Matching XML Processing Instructions

You can also match XML processing instructions like the <?xml-stylesheet?> processing instruction:

```
<?xml version="1.0"?>
<?xml-stylesheet type="text/xsl" href="format2.xsl"?>
<friends>
    <friend>
        <name>Sam Snead</name>
        <age units="years">19</age>
        <height units="inches">70</height>
        <weight units="pounds">160</weight>
        <eyecolor units="color">blue</eyecolor>
        <distance units="miles">43.4</distance><!--To friend's home-->
    </friend>
        .
        .
        .
</friends>
```

You match processing instructions with the expression processing-instruction() like this:

```
<xsl:template match="processing-instruction()">
    <i>
        Found a processing instruction!
    </i>
</xsl:template>
```

Matching Either/Or Expressions

Say you wanted to match both <age> elements and <name> elements. You could do that with two different templates:

```
<xsl:template match="name">
    <B>
        <xsl:apply-templates/>
    </B>
</xsl:template>

<xsl:template match="age">
    <B>
        <xsl:apply-templates/>
    </B>
</xsl:template>
```

Or you could use only *one* template if you match "age" *or* "name" like this: "age | name":

```
<?xml version="1.0"?>
<xsl:stylesheet version="2.0" xmlns:xsl="http://www.w3.org/1999/XSL/Transform">

    <xsl:template match="friends">
        <html>
            <xsl:apply-templates/>
        </html>
    </xsl:template>

    <xsl:template match="friend">
        <p>
            <xsl:apply-templates/>
        </p>
    </xsl:template>

    <xsl:template match="name | age">
        <B>
            <xsl:apply-templates/>
        </B>
    </xsl:template>

    <xsl:template match="*">
    </xsl:template>

</xsl:stylesheet>
```

Using the Or operator, |, you can condense two or more templates together.

Matching with [ ]

You can also enclose what's called a predicate inside square brackets, [and], to further qualify your matches. For example, using predicates, you can match

- If the value of an attribute is a given string

- The value of an element

- If an element encloses a particular child, attribute, or other element

- The position of a node in the node tree

Here's an example, format3.xls and friends3.xml. Say that you added a gender attribute to each <friend> element like this in friends3.xml:

```
<?xml version="1.0"?>
<?xml-stylesheet type="text/xsl" href="format3.xsl"?>
<friends>
    <friend gender="male">
        <name>Sam Snead</name>
        <age units="years">19</age>
        <height units="inches">70</height>
        <weight units="pounds">160</weight>
        <eyecolor units="color">blue</eyecolor>
        <distance units="miles">43.4</distance><!--To friend's home-->
    </friend>

    <friend gender="female">
        <name>Paige Turner</name>
        <age units="years">23</age>
        <height units="inches">67</height>
        <weight units="pounds">110</weight>
        <eyecolor units="color">brown</eyecolor>
        <distance units="miles">66.8</distance><!--To friend's home-->
    </friend>

    <friend gender="male">
        <name>Ralph Kramden</name>
        <age units="years">32</age>
        <height units="inches">71</height>
        <weight units="pounds">182</weight>
        <eyecolor units="color">hazel</eyecolor>
        <distance units="miles">28.4</distance><!--To friend's home-->
    </friend>

</friends>
```

Now say that you only wanted to list your male friends. You could pick them out in format3.xsl like this, using the predicate @gender = 'male':

```
<?xml version="1.0"?>
<xsl:stylesheet version="2.0" xmlns:xsl="http://www.w3.org/1999/XSL/Transform">
```

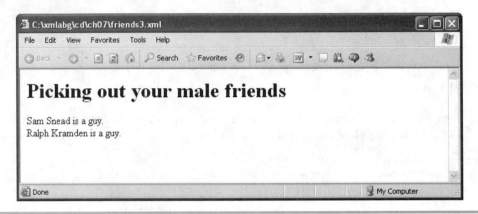

Figure 7-5 Picking out your male friends with XSLT

```
<xsl:template match="friends">
    <html>
        <h1>Picking out your male friends</h1>
        <xsl:apply-templates/>
    </html>
</xsl:template>

<xsl:template match="friend[@gender = 'male']">
        <xsl:value-of select="name"/> is a guy.
        <br/>
</xsl:template>

<xsl:template match="*">
</xsl:template>

</xsl:stylesheet>
```

You can see the results in Figure 7-5, where we've been successful in picking out the male friends.

Try This   Matching Attribute Values

Add a language attribute to each <name> element something like this in your sample XML document:

```
<?xml version="1.0"?>
<friends>
    <friend>
        <name language="French">...</name>
        <age measure="years">...</age>
```

```
        <height measure="inches">...</height>
        <weight measure="pounds">...</weight>
        <eyecolor measure="color">...</eyecolor>
        <distance measure="miles">...</distance>
    </friend>

    <friend>
        <name language="English">...</name>
        <age measure="years">...</age>
        <height measure="inches">...</height>
        <weight measure="pounds">...</weight>
        <eyecolor measure="color">...</eyecolor>
        <distance measure="miles">...</distance>
    </friend>

    <friend>
        <name language="German">...</name>
        <age measure="years">...</age>
        <height measure="inches">...</height>
        <weight measure="pounds">...</weight>
        <eyecolor measure="color">...</eyecolor>
        <distance measure="miles">...</distance>
    </friend>

    <friend>
        <name language="English">...</name>
        <age measure="years">...</age>
        <height measure="inches">...</height>
        <weight measure="pounds">...</weight>
        <eyecolor measure="color">...</eyecolor>
        <distance measure="miles">...</distance>
    </friend>


</friends>
```

Then write an XSLT style sheet to pick out and list your friends whose language is English. Confirm your results in Internet Explorer.

Here are some more examples; this expression matches <friend> elements that have child <name> elements:

```
<xsl:template match = "friend[name]">
```

This expression matches any element that has a <name> child element:

```
<xsl:template match = "*[name]">
```

This expression matches any <friend> element that has either a <name> or <age> child element:

```
<xsl:template match="friend[name | age]">
```

Expressions like "friend[name | age]" are really XPath expressions, and we'll wind up this chapter, and our coverage of XSLT, with a discussion of XPath and some examples showing how to use it with XSLT.

Using XPath

You assign XPath expressions to the match (used in the <xsl:template> element) and select (used in the <xsl:apply-templates>, <xsl:value-of>, <xsl:for-each>, <xsl:copy-of>, and <xsl:sort> elements) attributes in XSLT, and we've been dealing with XPath since the beginning of the preceding chapter. Now it's time to dig a little deeper. You use XPath to specify exactly what node or nodes you want to work with in an XML document, passing that node or those nodes to XSLT via the match or select attribute.

To specify a node or set of nodes in XPath, you use a *location path.* A location path, in turn, consists of one or more *location steps,* separated by / or //. If you start the location path with /, the location path is called an *absolute location path,* since you're specifying the path from the root node of the document; otherwise, the location path is *relative,* starting with the current node, which is called the *context node.*

A location step is made up of an *axis,* a *node test,* and zero or more *predicates.* For example, in the expression child::friend[position() = 5], which picks out the fifth child <friend> element, *child* is the name of the axis, *friend* is the node test, and *[position() = 5]* is a predicate. You can create location paths with one or more location steps, such as /descendant:: friend/child::name, which selects all the <name> elements that have a <friend> parent. The best way to understand all this is by example, and we'll see plenty of them in a few pages. In the meantime, I'll take a look at what kind of axes, node tests, and predicates XPath supports.

XPath Axes

There are 13 axes available in XPath, and here they are:

- The ancestor axis holds the ancestors of the context node; the ancestors of the context node are the parent of context node and the parent's parent and so forth, back to and including the root node.

- The ancestor-or-self axis holds the context node and the ancestors of the context node.

- The attribute axis holds the attributes of the context node.

- The child axis holds the children of the context node.

- The descendant axis holds the descendants of the context node. A descendant is a child or a child of a child and so on.

- The descendant-or-self axis contains the context node and the descendants of the context node.

- The following axis holds all nodes in the same document as the context node that come after the context node.

- The following-sibling axis holds all the following siblings of the context node. A sibling is a node on the same level as the context node.

- The namespace axis holds the namespace nodes of the context node.

- The parent axis holds the parent of the context node.

- The preceding axis contains all nodes that come before the context node.

- The preceding-sibling axis contains all the preceding siblings of the context node. A sibling is a node on the same level as the context node.

- The self axis contains the context node.

For example, say you have a template that matches <friend> elements, and want to put the value of the <name>, <age>, and <height> child elements into the output document. You could do that this way:

```
<xsl:template match="friend">
    <html>
        <center>
            <xsl:value-of select="child::name"/>
        </center>
        <center>
            <xsl:value-of select="child::age"/>
        </center>
        <center>
            <xsl:value-of select="child::height"/>
        </center>
    </html>
</xsl:template>
```

Hey, wait a minute, you say—you already know this can be done like this—with no child:: term at all:

```
<xsl:template match="friend">
    <html>
        <center>
            <xsl:value-of select="name"/>
        </center>
        <center>
            <xsl:value-of select="age"/>
        </center>
        <center>
            <xsl:value-of select="height"/>
        </center>
    </html>
</xsl:template>
```

And you're right—it turns out that you can abbreviate child::childname as just childname in XPath. So whenever we've been using an expression like <xsl:value-of select="height"/>, technically, that's really been <xsl:value-of select="child::height"/>. Here are the abbreviations you can use in XPath:

- self::node() can be abbreviated as .
- parent::node() can be abbreviated as ..
- child::*childname* can be abbreviated as *childname*
- attribute::*childname* can be abbreviated as @*childname*
- /descendant-or-self::node()/ can be abbreviated as //

So what's the difference between the match attribute and the select attribute in XSLT? It turns out that the match element only supports the use of the child, descendant, and attribute axes, while you can use all thirteen axes in expressions you assign to the select attribute.

Okay, that's an overview of the XPath axes. Now how about the XPath node tests?

XPath Node Tests

You can use names of nodes as node tests (such as the names of elements), or the wildcard * to select element nodes. For example, the expression */name selects all <name> elements that are grandchildren of the context node.

Besides nodes and the wildcard character, you can also use these node tests:

- The comment() node test selects comment nodes.
- The node() node test selects any type of node.
- The processing-instruction() node test selects a processing instruction node. You can specify the name of the processing instruction to select in the parentheses.
- The text() node test selects a text node.

We'll mostly use element names as node tests in our coverage of XSLT.

XPath Predicates

The XPath predicate is the part that goes into the square brackets, [and], at the end of the expression, and it's here you have the most power. XPath predicates can be broken up into four types, depending on the value they evaluate to:

- Node-set
- True/false
- Numerical
- String

That is, some predicates return node-sets (containing one or more XML nodes), some return true or false values, some return numbers, and so on. We'll take a quick look at each type—with plenty of examples.

Node-Set Predicates

As you can tell from its name, a node-set predicate is simply a set of nodes. An expression like child::friend returns a node set of all <friend> elements. The expression child::friend/child:: name returns a node list of all <name> elements that are children of <friend> elements.

Note that to select a node or nodes from a node set, you can use various XPath functions that work on node sets in predicates. Here are those functions:

- **count(*node-set*)**   Returns the number of nodes in *node-set*. Omitting *node-set* makes this function use the context node.

- **id(*string ID*)**   Returns a node set containing the element whose ID matches the string passed to the function, or an empty node set if no element has the specified ID. In fact, you can list multiple IDs separated by whitespace, and this function will return a node set of the elements with those IDs.

- **last()**   Returns the number of nodes in a node set.

- **local-name(*node-set*)**   Returns the local name of the first node in the node set. Omitting *node-set* makes this function use the context node.

- **name(*node-set*)**   Returns the full, qualified name of the first node in the node set. Omitting *node-set* makes this function use the context node.

- **namespace-uri(*node-set*)**   Returns the namespace of the first node in the node set. Omitting *node-set* makes this function use the context node.

- **position()**   Returns the position of the context node in the context node set (starting with 1).

Let's take a look at an example before this all becomes to steep to handle. For example, the position() function, which returns the position of the context node among its siblings, is a good one. For example, here's how you can number your friends in order in format4.xsl:

```xml
<?xml version="1.0"?>
<xsl:stylesheet version="2.0" xmlns:xsl="http://www.w3.org/1999/XSL/Transform">

    <xsl:template match="friends">
        <html>
            <head>
                <title>
                    My Friends
                </title>
            </head>
            <body>
                <h1>
                    My Friends
                </h1>
```

```
                <xsl:apply-templates select="friend"/>
            </body>
        </html>
    </xsl:template>

    <xsl:template match="friend">
        <p>
            <xsl:value-of select="position()"/>.
            <xsl:value-of select="name"/>
        </p>
    </xsl:template>

</xsl:stylesheet>
```

And you can see the results in Figure 7-6, where your friends have been numbered in order.

True/False Predicates

There are a number of XPath operators that you can use to form true/false results, and here they are:

- != means "is not equal to"

- < means "is less-than" (use < in XML documents)

- <= means "is less-than or equal to" (use <= in XML documents)

- = means "is equal to"

- > means "is greater-than"

- >= means "is greater-than or equal to"

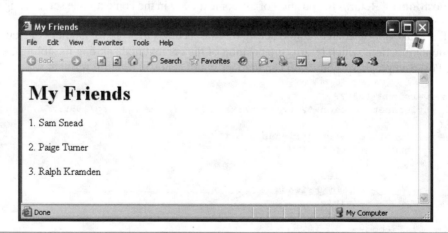

Figure 7-6 Numbering your friends with XSLT

Let's see an example, format5.xsl. To find the last friend in your list, the third friend, you can use the predicate [position = 3], which makes the XPath expression friend[position = 3]. So here's how you can display just your third friend with format5.xsl:

```
<?xml version="1.0"?>
<xsl:stylesheet version="2.0" xmlns:xsl="http://www.w3.org/1999/XSL/Transform">

    <xsl:template match="friends">
        <html>
            <head>
                <title>
                    My Last Friend
                </title>
            </head>
            <body>
                <h1>
                    My Last Friend
                </h1>
                <xsl:apply-templates select="friend"/>
            </body>
        </html>
    </xsl:template>

    <xsl:template match="friend[position() = 3]">
        <p>
            <xsl:value-of select="name"/>
        </p>
    </xsl:template>

    <xsl:template match="*">
    </xsl:template>

</xsl:stylesheet>
```

But what if you add a fourth friend? That friend would then be the last one. So instead of placing the actual number (3) of the last friend in, you could use the XPath last() function, which returns the number of the last node in the current node set, like this in format5.xsl:

```
<?xml version="1.0"?>
<xsl:stylesheet version="2.0" xmlns:xsl="http://www.w3.org/1999/XSL/Transform">

    <xsl:template match="friends">
        <html>
            <head>
                <title>
                    My Last Friend
                </title>
            </head>
            <body>
                <h1>
                    My Last Friend
                </h1>
```

```
                    <xsl:apply-templates select="friend"/>
             </body>
        </html>
    </xsl:template>

    <xsl:template match="friend[position() = last()]">
        <p>
            <xsl:value-of select="name"/>
        </p>
    </xsl:template>

    <xsl:template match="*">
    </xsl:template>

</xsl:stylesheet>
```

And you can see the results in Figure 7-7, where you have indeed picked out your last friend from friends5/xml.

Numerical Predicates

You can also work with numbers in predicates, using these operators:

- **+** Addition

- **–** Subtraction

- ***** Multiplication

- **div** Division (the / character which stands for division in other languages is already used in XML and XPath)

- **mod** Returns the modulus of two numbers (the remainder after dividing the first by the second)

For example, the element <xsl:value-of select="2 + 3"/> inserts the string "5" into the output document.

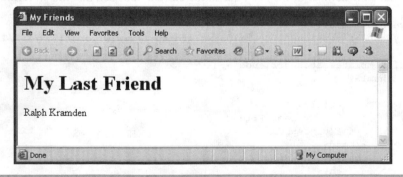

Figure 7-7 Selecting your last friend with XSLT

Here's an example that selects all friends whose weight divided by their height is greater than 2:

```
<xsl:template match="friends">

   <html>
     <body>
       <xsl:apply-templates select="friend[weight div height > 2]"/>
     </body>
   </html>
</xsl:template>
```

Cool, eh?

You can also use these XPath functions that work on numbers:

- **ceiling()**   Returns the smallest integer larger than the number you pass it.

- **floor()**   Returns the largest integer smaller than the number you pass it.

- **round()**   Rounds the number you pass it to the nearest integer.

- **sum()**   Returns the sum of the numbers you pass it.

- **count()**   Returns the nodes in the node set.

Want to find the average age of your friends? You could do that like this:

```
<xsl:template match="friends">
    <html>
        <body>
            The average age of your friends is:
            <xsl:value-of select="sum(age) div count(age)"/>
        </body>
    </html>
</xsl:template>
```

As you can see, you can work in depth with the data you extract from XML documents.

String Predicates

Finally, you can also handle strings in predicates. Here are the XPath functions that let you work with strings:

- **starts-with(*string1*, *string2*)**   Returns true if the first string starts with the second one.

- **contains(*string1*, *string2*)**   Returns true if the first string contains the second one.

- **substring(*string1*, *offset*, *length*)**   Returns *length* characters from the string, starting at *offset*.

- **substring-before(*string1*, *string2*)**   Returns the part of *string1* up to the first occurrence of *string2*.

- **substring-after(*string1*, *string2*)**   Returns the part of *string1* after the first occurrence of *string2*.

- **string-length(*string1*)**   Returns the number of characters in *string1*.

- **normalize-space(*string1*)**   Returns *string1* after leading and trailing whitespace is stripped and multiple consecutive whitespace is replaced with a single space.

- **translate(*string1*, *string2*, *string3*)**   Returns *string1* with all occurrences of the characters in *string2* replaced by the matching characters in *string3*.

- **concat(*string1*, *string2*, …)**   Returns all strings concatenated (that is, joined) together.

- **format-number(*number1*, *string2*, *string3*)**   Returns a string holding the formatted string version of *number1*, using *string2* as a formatting string (create the formatting strings as you would for the Java language's java.text.DecimalFormat method), and *string3* as the optional locale string.

Here's an example that selects all your friends whose name includes the word "Sam":

```
<?xml version="1.0"?>
<xsl:stylesheet version="2.0" xmlns:xsl="http://www.w3.org/1999/XSL/Transform">

    <xsl:template match="friends">
        <html>
            <head>
                <title>
                    My Friends Named Sam
                </title>
            </head>
            <body>
                <h1>
                    My Friends Named Sam
                </h1>
                <xsl:apply-templates select="friend"/>
            </body>
        </html>
    </xsl:template>

    <xsl:template match="friend[contains(name, 'Sam')]">
        <p>
            <xsl:value-of select="name"/>
        </p>
    </xsl:template>

    <xsl:template match="*">
    </xsl:template>

</xsl:stylesheet>
```

And you can see the results in Figure 7-8. Very nice.
We'll finish the chapter with some XPath examples.

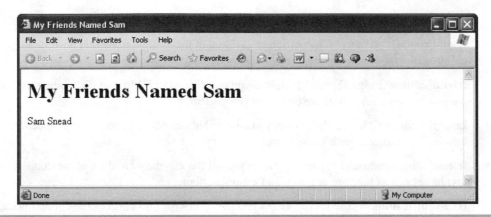

Figure 7-8 Selecting Sam with XSLT

Some XPath Examples

There's no question about it—XPath can get confusing. It's best understood in terms of examples, so here's a bunch of them:

- **friend**   Gives you the <friend> element children of the context node.
- *****   Gives you all element children of the context node.
- **text()**   Gives you all text node children of the context node.
- **@units**   Gives you the units attribute of the context node.
- **@***   Gives you all the attributes of the context node.
- **friend[3]**   Gives you the third <friend> child of the context node.
- **friend[first()]**   Gives you the first <friend> child of the context node.
- ***/friend**   Gives you all <friend> grandchildren of the context node.
- **/friends/friend[3]/name[2]**   Gives you the second <name> element of the third <friend> element of the <friends> element.
- **//friend**   Gives you all the <friend> descendants of the document root.
- **friends//friend**   Gives you the <friend> element descendants of the <friends> element children of the context node.
- **//friend/name**   Gives you all the <name> elements that have a <friend> parent.
- **.**   Gives you the context node itself.
- **.//friend**   Gives you the <friend> element descendants of the context node.
- **..**   Gives you the parent of the context node.

- **../@units**   Gives you the units attribute of the parent of the context node.

- **friend[name]**   Gives you the <friend> children of the context node that have <name> children.

- **friend[name="Paige Turner"]**   Gives you the <friend> children of the context node that have <name> children with text equal to "Paige Turner".

- **height[@units = "inches"]**   Gives you all <height> children of the context node that have a units attribute with value "inches".

- **friend[@language and @units]**   Gives you all the <friend> children of the context node that have both a language attribute and a units attribute.

- **friend[6][@units = "inches"]**   Gives you the sixth <friend> child of the context node, only if that child has a units attribute with value "inches".

Whew. As you can see, there's tremendous power built into XSLT and XPath, ready for you to use—but it can take a little effort to figure it out.

Chapter 8

Extending XML
with XHTML

Key Skills & Concepts

- Introducing XHTML
- Creating XHTML documents
- Using text, images, and more
- Validating your XHTML document

Welcome to the world of Extensible Hypertext Markup Language, or XHTML. XHTML is just HTML—but it's written using XML! That is, XHTML is actually a dialect of XML, with predefined elements built in. But those predefined XML elements have the same names as HTML elements. There's an XHTML element named <html>, for example, and another one named <body>, and another one named <head>, and so on. So to a browser, an XHTML document looks just like an HTML document—which means that XHTML will work with modern-day HTML browsers.

So if it looks just like HTML and acts just like HTML, what's the point? The point is that HTML can be sloppy, and with XHTML documents—which are in fact XML documents—you can make sure they're well formed, and even valid. That's behind the popularity of XHTML—making sure a Web document is correct before putting in on the Web. Up to half the software in a browser is there to correct the mistakes people make in creating Web pages, which means that much of what you see in a Web browser may be the Web browser trying to guess what the HTML author meant. That's not a good situation for corporations, which may be involved in legal tangles as a result.

With XHTML, that problem is alleviated. XHTML is a product of the World Wide Web Consortium (W3C), just as HTML is (and in fact, according to W3C, XHTML is designed to replace HTML). You can check an XHTML document for validity, and if the browser then displays the page in a manner you didn't intend, it's the browser's fault. There's a logo you can place in your Web pages to indicate that they're valid XHTML—and you've probably come across many such pages, whether you noticed it or not. XHTML is becoming popular because you can validate it rigorously.

In addition, XHTML is extensible—that is, you can add your own elements to it. When you include a DTD or XML schema, the result can still be checked for validity. And, using a combination of JavaScript (to handle events such as mouse clicks) and CSS (to format the appearance of the new element), you can actually create your own XHTML elements, and have them appear as you like in a standard Web browsers. That's why XHTML is called *Extensible* Hypertext Markup Language.

Since XHTML is actually XML, it's a fit topic for our study, so let's start digging into the topic.

Getting Started with XHTML

Take a look at this very exciting HTML document, html.html:

```
<html>
    <head>
        <title>
            Welcome to my page
        </title>
    </head>

    <body>
        <h1>
            Welcome to HTML!
        </h1>
        Here's my page.
        <br>
        Do you like it?
    </body>
</html>
```

It's just a simple Web page with a little text, and you can see it in a browser in Figure 8-1. Not bad.

Now let's write the same page in XHTML, xhtml.html (you use the extension .html for XHTML so that Web browsers won't be confused).

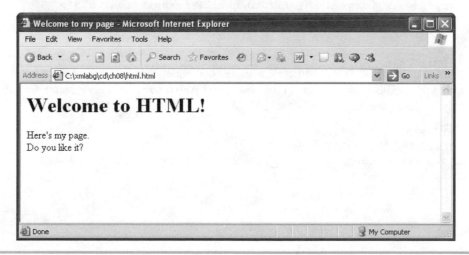

Figure 8-1 A cool HTML document

Since XHTML is a standard XML, you might think that our XHTML document should start with an XML declaration—and you'd be right. All XML documents must start with an XML declaration:

```
<?xml version="1.0"?>
    .
    .
    .
```

Why does this work with HTML browsers? It works because Web browsers ignore all markup they don't understand—that's the fact that will help XHTML work just as well as HTML in browsers.

You can validate XHTML documents, and the W3C provides DTDs (not XML schemas) for that purpose. As we're going to see, there are several varieties of XHTML, depending on how rigorous you want to be. The most commonly used version of XHTML today is XHTML 1.0 Transitional, and you can find its DTD at http://www.w3.org/TR/xhtml1/DTD/xhtml1-transitional. dtd (Internet Explorer actually downloads this DTD to check your XHTML document, although you have to expressly check—using JavaScript—if there were any validation errors).

To write a valid XHTML document, you have to refer to an XHTML DTD like the DTD for XHTML 1.0 Transitional, treating that DTD as an external DTD. You've seen how to do that in Chapter 2, so you shouldn't be surprised to see that our XHTML document has a <!DOCTYPE> element, complete with a Formal Public Identifier and the URL of the DTD:

```
<?xml version="1.0"?>
<!DOCTYPE html PUBLIC "-//W3C//DTD XHTML 1.0 Transitional//EN"
"http://www.w3.org/TR/xhtml1/DTD/xhtml1-transitional.dtd">
    .
    .
    .
```

Note that in this <!DOCTYPE> element, the document element is given as <html>, which is what you'd expect for a document that a standard Web browser can understand. So let's add the document element, which all other XHTML elements will be enclosed by:

```
<?xml version="1.0"?>
<!DOCTYPE html PUBLIC "-//W3C//DTD XHTML 1.0 Transitional//EN"
"http://www.w3.org/TR/xhtml1/DTD/xhtml1-transitional.dtd">
<html>
    .
    .
    .
</html>
```

Like any good XML dialect, XHTML has its own namespace (so you can add elements from other XML dialects to the document without worrying about overlapping with XHTML). That namespace is given by the URL string "http://www.w3.org/1999/xhtml", so we can create that namespace here with the xmlns attribute in the document element, <html> (bear in mind that the browser, treating this document as HTML, will ignore this attribute):

```
<?xml version="1.0"?>
<!DOCTYPE html PUBLIC "-//W3C//DTD XHTML 1.0 Transitional//EN"
"http://www.w3.org/TR/xhtml1/DTD/xhtml1-transitional.dtd">
<html xmlns="http://www.w3.org/1999/xhtml">
    .
    .
    .
</html>
```

We're not done yet with the document element. In XHTML, you also usually include the xml:lang attribute and the lang attribute, set to the language you're using, which is English here, so we'll use the standard value "en":

```
<?xml version="1.0"?>
<!DOCTYPE html PUBLIC "-//W3C//DTD XHTML 1.0 Transitional//EN"
"http://www.w3.org/TR/xhtml1/DTD/xhtml1-transitional.dtd">
<html xmlns="http://www.w3.org/1999/xhtml" xml:lang="en" lang="en">
    .
    .
    .
</html>
```

Fine, that completes the document element. You might think that after all the rigmarole up to this point that the rest of the XHTML will be similarly complex, but if so, you're in for a pleasant surprise. From now on, the XHTML looks just like HTML, although there are a few rules to follow (such as that every opening tag must have a corresponding closing tag—this is XML, after all) that we'll see more about in a few pages. So we can create the <head> section of the document just like the <head> section of the HTML page:

```
<?xml version="1.0"?>
<!DOCTYPE html PUBLIC "-//W3C//DTD XHTML 1.0 Transitional//EN"
"http://www.w3.org/TR/xhtml1/DTD/xhtml1-transitional.dtd">
<html xmlns="http://www.w3.org/1999/xhtml" xml:lang="en" lang="en">
    <head>
        <title>
            Welcome to my page
        </title>
    </head>
    .
    .
    .
</html>
```

And then you can add the <body> section, changing the text "Welcome to HTML!" to "Welcome to XHTML!":

```
<?xml version="1.0"?>
<!DOCTYPE html PUBLIC "-//W3C//DTD XHTML 1.0 Transitional//EN"
"http://www.w3.org/TR/xhtml1/DTD/xhtml1-transitional.dtd">
<html xmlns="http://www.w3.org/1999/xhtml" xml:lang="en" lang="en">
```

```
    <head>
        <title>
            Welcome to my page
        </title>
    </head>

    <body>
        <h1>
            Welcome to XHTML!
        </h1>
        Here's my page.
        <br>
        Do you like it?
    </body>
</html>
```

In fact, there's a small problem here that stops this document from being a well-formed XML. Can you spot what it is?

The issue is that the <br> element doesn't have a closing tag, </br>, because it's an empty element in HTML. And you write empty elements with a closing slash (/) in XML, like this:

```
<?xml version="1.0"?>
<!DOCTYPE html PUBLIC "-//W3C//DTD XHTML 1.0 Transitional//EN"
"http://www.w3.org/TR/xhtml1/DTD/xhtml1-transitional.dtd">
<html xmlns="http://www.w3.org/1999/xhtml" xml:lang="en" lang="en">
    <head>
        <title>
            Welcome to my page
        </title>
    </head>

    <body>
        <h1>
            Welcome to XHTML!
        </h1>
        Here's my page.
        <br/>
        Do you like it?
    </body>
</html>
```

Fortunately, Web browsers have no problem with closing an element this way, so the resulting Web page, xhtml.html, works just as it should, as you can see in Figure 8-2. Nice.

That gives us an introduction to XHTML—now let's look behind the scenes.

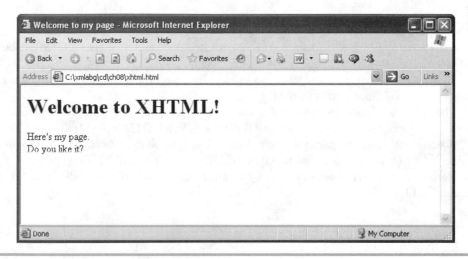

Figure 8-2 A super-cool XHTML document

Try This   Creating an XHTML Document

Try modifying our XHTML document to personalize it. For example, if your name is Steve, change the page to something like this:

```
<?xml version="1.0"?>
<!DOCTYPE html PUBLIC "-//W3C//DTD XHTML 1.0 Transitional//EN"
"http://www.w3.org/TR/xhtml1/DTD/xhtml1-transitional.dtd">
<html xmlns="http://www.w3.org/1999/xhtml" xml:lang="en" lang="en">
    <head>
        <title>
            Welcome to Steve's XHTML page!
        </title>
    </head>

    <body>
        <h1>
            Welcome to Steve's XHTML page!
        </h1>
        Here's Steve's page.
        <br/>
        Pretty good, huh?
    </body>
</html>
```

When you're done modifying it, save the page with the .html extension and open it in a Web browser to confirm that your page works.

Validating XHTML

It turns out that W3C has a validator you can use to check the validity of your XHTML document, and you can find this validator at http://validator.w3.org.

To use the XHTML validator, click the Validate By Direct Input tab, as shown in Figure 8-3, paste in the XHTML of your document, and click Check.

The W3C validator does its work and you can see the results in Figure 8-4—our document passed, as you can see with the message "This Page Is Valid XHTML 1.0 Transitional!"

If you scroll down the page you see in Figure 8-4, you see the official XHTML logo in Figure 8-5 that you can place in your pages to indicate that it's valid XHTML 1.0.

Here's the XHTML you can add to your page to display the official valid XHTML 1.0 Transitional logo:

```
<p>
  <a href="http://validator.w3.org/check?uri=referer"><img
      src="http://www.w3.org/Icons/valid-xhtml10"
      alt="Valid XHTML 1.0 Transitional" height="31" width="88"/>
  </a>
</p>
```

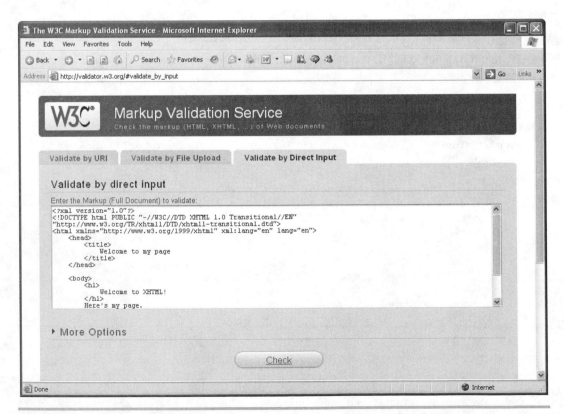

Figure 8-3 Validating an XHTML document

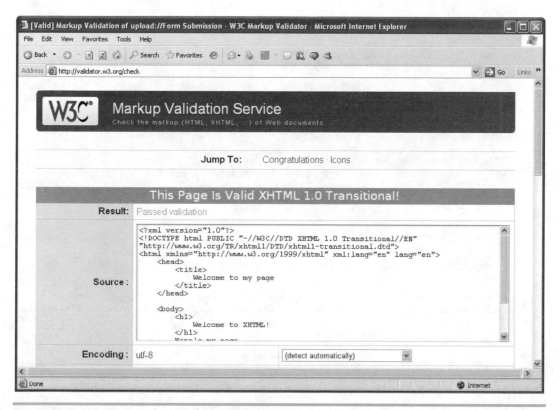

Figure 8-4   An XHTML document that validated

Try This   Validating an XHTML Document

Try validating your sample XHTML document at the W3C site, http://validator.w3.org.

See if you can get the XHTML 1.0 Transitional logo, and if so, add the preceding XHTML to your document to display the validation logo.

Great—now we've taken an XHTML document from scratch all the way up to validating it. Now let's take a deeper look at XHTML.

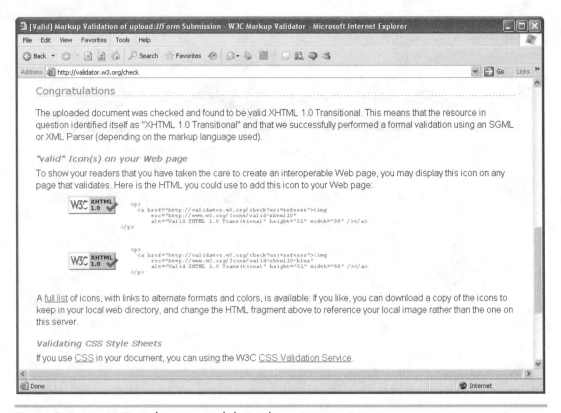

Figure 8-5   An XHTML document validation logo

Understanding XHTML

The standard version of XHTML these days, version 1.0, is just a rewrite of HTML 4.0 in XML. You can find the W3C recommendation for XHTML 1.0 at www.w3.org/TR/xhtml1. That recommendation is really just a set of DTDs that provide validity checks for documents that are supposed to mimic HTML 4.0 (actually HTML 4.01).

There are actually three versions of XHTML 1.0, as given by three DTDs, and here they are—XHTML 1.0 Transitional, the loosest in terms of rigorousness, is by far the most popular (and the one we'll use in this chapter)—note that "deprecated" means considered obsolete:

● **The strict XHTML 1.0 DTD**   The strict DTD is based on straight HTML 4.0 and does not include support for elements and attributes that W3C considers deprecated. This is the version of XHTML 1.0 that W3C hopes people will migrate to in time.

● **The transitional XHTML 1.0 DTD**   The transitional DTD is based on the transitional HTML 4 DTD. This DTD has support for the many elements and attributes that were deprecated in HTML 4.0 but are still popular, like the <center> and <font> elements. This DTD is also named the "loose" DTD. It is the most popular version of XHTML at the moment.

- **The frameset XHTML 1.0 DTD**   The frameset DTD is based on the frameset HTML 4.0 DTD. This is the DTD you should work with when you're creating pages based on frames, because in that case, you replace the <body> element with a <frameset> element. The DTD has to reflect that, so you use the frameset DTD when working with frames; that's the difference between the XHTML 1.0 transitional and frameset DTDs—the frameset DTD replaces the <body> element with the <frameset> element.

Here are the <!DOCTYPE> elements you use for the three versions of XHTML 1.0—first, the strict version:

```
<!DOCTYPE html
    PUBLIC "-//W3C//DTD XHTML 1.0 Strict//EN"
    "http://www.w3.org/TR/xhtml1/DTD/xhtml1-strict.dtd">
```

then, the transitional version:

```
<!DOCTYPE html
    PUBLIC "-//W3C//DTD XHTML 1.0 Transitional//EN"
    "http://www.w3.org/TR/xhtml1/DTD/xhtml1-transitional.dtd">
```

and finally, the frameset version, which you use for documents that have frames:

```
<!DOCTYPE html
    PUBLIC "-//W3C//DTD XHTML 1.0 Frameset//EN"
    "http://www.w3.org/TR/xhtml1/DTD/xhtml1-frameset.dtd">
```

In addition to XHTML 1.0, there's also XHTML 1.1, but the feeling is that the W3C may have overreached itself with this version, and it's been only a working draft for years. You can find it at www.w3.org/TR/xhtml11.

However, XHTML 1.1 is stricter than strict. It removes all the display elements from XHTML—you're supposed to use CSS to display your text instead. As of this writing, XHTML 1.1 has only been adopted by a very few sites, and we're going to stick with XHTML 1.0 Transitional in this chapter.

One good thing about XHTML 1.1 is that its DTD is *modular.* That is, it consists of modules that can be added or omitted from the complete DTD. That can be useful if, for example, you're a cell phone manufacturer who wants to display XHTML documents as far as text goes, but not as far as XHTML tables go—you can just omit the tables module from the DTD.

Now let's take a look at the differences between HTML and XHTML as we begin ramping up the creation of our own XHTML pages.

The Differences Between HTML and XHTML

It turns out that the W3C has a number of requirements for documents before they can be called true XHTML documents. Here's the list of requirements documents must meet:

- The document must successfully validate against one of the W3C XHTML DTDs.

- The document element must be <html>.

- The document element, <html>, must set an XML namespace for the document, using the xmlns attribute. This namespace must be "http://www.w3.org/1999/xhtml".

- There must be a <!DOCTYPE> element, and it must appear before the document element.

These are all issues we've taken care of already in our sample document, and they're part of making sure your XHTML is valid XML.

As an XHTML author, you must bear in mind several differences between HTML and XHTML—again, mostly having to do with the difference between XML and HTML. Here's a list of the major differences:

- XHTML documents must be well-formed XML documents.

- Element and attribute names must be in lowercase.

- Nonempty elements need end tags; end tags can't be omitted as they can sometimes in HTML.

- Attribute values must always be quoted.

- You cannot use "standalone" attributes that are not assigned values. If need be, assign a dummy value to an attribute, like action = "action".

- Empty elements need to be ended with the /> characters. In practice, this does not seem to be a problem for the major browsers, which is a lucky thing for XHTML, because it's definitely not standard HTML.

- The <a> element cannot contain other <a> elements.

- The <pre> element cannot contain the <img>, <object>, <big>, <small>, <sub>, or <sup> elements.

- The <button> element cannot contain the <input>, <select>, <textarea>, <label>, <button>, <form>, <fieldset>, <iframe>, or <isindex> elements.

- The <label> element cannot contain other <label> elements.

- The <form> element cannot contain other <form> elements.

- You must use the id attribute and not the name attribute, even on elements that have also had a name attribute. In XHTML 1.0, the name attribute of the <a>, <applet>, <form>, <frame>, <iframe>, <img>, and <map> elements is formally deprecated. In practice, this is a little difficult in browsers like Netscape Navigator that support name and not id; in that case, you should use both attributes in the same element, even though it's not legal XHTML.

- You must escape sensitive characters. For example, when an attribute value contains an ampersand (&), the ampersand must be expressed as &.

Okay, let's take a look at the specific XHTML elements, and what's considered legal.

Using <html>, the Document Element

The document element in XHTML is <html>, and these attributes are legal in this element:

- **dir** Sets the direction of text that doesn't have an inherent direction in which you should read it, called directionally neutral text. You can set this attribute to LTR, left-to-right text, or RTL, right-to-left text. (XHTML 1.0 Strict, XHTML 1.0 Transitional, XHTML 1.0 Frameset, XHTML 1.1)

- **lang** Specifies the base language used in the element. Only applies when the document is interpreted as HTML. (XHTML 1.0 Strict, XHTML 1.0 Transitional, XHTML 1.0 Frameset, XHTML 1.1)

- **xml:lang** Specifies the base language for the element when the document is interpreted as XML. (XHTML 1.0 Strict, XHTML 1.0 Transitional, XHTML 1.0 Frameset, XHTML 1.1)

- **xmlns** Required. Set this attribute to "http://www.w3.org/1999/xhtml". (XHTML 1.0 Strict, XHTML 1.0 Transitional, XHTML 1.0 Frameset, XHTML 1.1)

We've seen <html> at work as shown here, where we also use it to declare the XHTML namespace:

```
<?xml version="1.0"?>
<!DOCTYPE html PUBLIC "-//W3C//DTD XHTML 1.0 Transitional//EN"
"http://www.w3.org/TR/xhtml1/DTD/xhtml1-transitional.dtd">
<html xmlns="http://www.w3.org/1999/xhtml" xml:lang="en" lang="en">
    <head>
        <title>
            Welcome to my page
        </title>
    </head>

    <body>
        <h1>
            Welcome to XHTML!
        </h1>
        Here's my page.
        <br/>
        Do you like it?
    </body>
</html>
```

In XHTML, the <html> element can contain a <head> element and a <body> element (or a <head> element and a <frameset> element in the XHTML 1.0 frameset document).

Using <head> to Create Head Sections

The <head> section is a child of the <html> element and contains elements like <title>, which contains the title of the document you want displayed in the browser's title bar. Here are the legal attributes of the <head> element:

- **dir**   Sets the direction of text that doesn't have an inherent direction in which you should read it, called directionally neutral text. You can set this attribute to LTR, left-to-right text, or RTL, right-to-left text. (XHTML 1.0 Strict, XHTML 1.0 Transitional, XHTML 1.0 Frameset, XHTML 1.1)

- **lang**   Specifies the base language used in the element. Only applies when the document is interpreted as HTML. (XHTML 1.0 Strict, XHTML 1.0 Transitional, XHTML 1.0 Frameset, XHTML 1.1)

- **profile**   Specifies the location of one or more whitespace-separated metadata profile URLs. (XHTML 1.0 Strict, XHTML 1.0 Transitional, XHTML 1.0 Frameset, XHTML 1.1)

- **xml:lang**   Specifies the base language for the element when the document is interpreted as an XML document. (XHTML 1.0 Strict, XHTML 1.0 Transitional, XHTML 1.0 Frameset, XHTML 1.1)

We've seen the <head> element at work like this:

```
<?xml version="1.0"?>
<!DOCTYPE html PUBLIC "-//W3C//DTD XHTML 1.0 Transitional//EN"
"http://www.w3.org/TR/xhtml1/DTD/xhtml1-transitional.dtd">
<html xmlns="http://www.w3.org/1999/xhtml" xml:lang="en" lang="en">
    <head>
        <title>
            Welcome to my page
        </title>
    </head>

    <body>
        <h1>
            Welcome to XHTML!
        </h1>
        Here's my page.
        <br/>
        Do you like it?
    </body>
</html>
```

Here are the elements that can legally appear in the document's head:

- **<base>**   Specifies the base URI for the document.

- **<isindex>**   Supports rudimentary input control.

- **<link>** Specifies the relationship between the document and an external object.

- **<meta>** Contains information about the document.

- **<noscript>** Contains text that appears only if the browser does not support the <script> tag.

- **<object>** Embeds an object.

- **<script>** Contains programming scripts, such as JavaScript code.

- **<style>** Contains style information used for rendering elements.

- **<title>** The document's title, which appears in the browser.

The head of every XHTML document is supposed to contain a <title> element, which holds the title of the document, and that's coming up next.

Using <title> to Hold the Document's Title

The <title> element holds the title of the document, which appears in the browser's title bar. Here are the legal attributes of the <title> element:

- **dir** Sets the direction of text that doesn't have an inherent direction in which you should read it, called directionally neutral text. You can set this attribute to LTR, left-to-right text, or RTL, right-to-left text. (XHTML 1.0 Strict, XHTML 1.0 Transitional, XHTML 1.0 Frameset, XHTML 1.1)

- **lang** Specifies the base language used in the element. Only applies when the document is interpreted as HTML. (XHTML 1.0 Strict, XHTML 1.0 Transitional, XHTML 1.0 Frameset, XHTML 1.1)

- **xml:lang** Specifies the base language for the element when the document is interpreted as an XML document. (XHTML 1.0 Strict, XHTML 1.0 Transitional, XHTML 1.0 Frameset, XHTML 1.1)

The contents of the <title> element are text, and we've already seen the <title> element in action:

```
<?xml version="1.0"?>
<!DOCTYPE html PUBLIC "-//W3C//DTD XHTML 1.0 Transitional//EN"
"http://www.w3.org/TR/xhtml1/DTD/xhtml1-transitional.dtd">
<html xmlns="http://www.w3.org/1999/xhtml" xml:lang="en" lang="en">
    <head>
        <title>
            Welcome to my page
        </title>
    </head>
```

```
<body>
    <h1>
        Welcome to XHTML!
    </h1>
    Here's my page.
    <br/>
    Do you like it?
</body>
</html>
```

Using <body> to Hold the Document's Body

The <body> element is a big one—it's where the main part of the Web page, including all the elements you want to display, goes. Here are the legal attributes for this element:

- **alink** Deprecated in HTML 4.0. Sets the color of hyperlinks when they're being activated. (XHTML 1.0 Transitional, XHTML 1.0 Frameset)

- **background** Deprecated in HTML 4.0. Holds the URI of an image to be used in tiling the browser's background. (XHTML 1.0 Transitional, XHTML 1.0 Frameset)

- **bgcolor** Deprecated in HTML 4.0. Sets the color of the browser's background. (XHTML 1.0 Transitional, XHTML 1.0 Frameset)

- **class** Style class of the element. (XHTML 1.0 Strict, XHTML 1.0 Transitional, XHTML 1.0 Frameset, XHTML 1.1)

- **dir** Sets the direction of text that doesn't have an inherent direction in which you should read it, called directionally neutral text. You can set this attribute to LTR, left-to-right text, or RTL, right-to-left text. (XHTML 1.0 Strict, XHTML 1.0 Transitional, XHTML 1.0 Frameset, XHTML 1.1)

- **id** You use the ID to refer to the element; set this attribute to a unique identifier. (XHTML 1.0 Strict, XHTML 1.0 Transitional, XHTML 1.0 Frameset, XHTML 1.1)

- **lang** Specifies the base language used in the element. Only applies when the document is interpreted as HTML. (XHTML 1.0 Strict, XHTML 1.0 Transitional, XHTML 1.0 Frameset, XHTML 1.1)

- **link** Deprecated in HTML 4.0. Sets the color of hyperlinks that have not yet been visited. (XHTML 1.0 Transitional, XHTML 1.0 Frameset)

- **style** Set to an inline style to specify how the browser should display the element. (XHTML 1.0 Strict, XHTML 1.0 Transitional, XHTML 1.0 Frameset, XHTML 1.1)

- **text** Deprecated in HTML 4.0. Sets the color of the text in the document. (XHTML 1.0 Transitional, XHTML 1.0 Frameset)

- **title**   Contains the title of the body (which might be displayed in tool tips). (XHTML 1.0 Strict, XHTML 1.0 Transitional, XHTML 1.0 Frameset, XHTML 1.1)

- **vlink**   Deprecated in HTML 4.0. Sets the color of hyperlinks that have been visited already. (XHTML 1.0 Transitional, XHTML 1.0 Frameset)

- **xml:lang**   Specifies the base language for the element when the document is interpreted as an XML document. (XHTML 1.0 Strict, XHTML 1.0 Transitional, XHTML 1.0 Frameset, XHTML 1.1)

And we've already used the <body> element, of course:

```
<?xml version="1.0"?>
<!DOCTYPE html PUBLIC "-//W3C//DTD XHTML 1.0 Transitional//EN"
"http://www.w3.org/TR/xhtml1/DTD/xhtml1-transitional.dtd">
<html xmlns="http://www.w3.org/1999/xhtml" xml:lang="en" lang="en">
    <head>
        <title>
            Welcome to my page
        </title>
    </head>

    <body>
        <h1>
            Welcome to XHTML!
        </h1>
        Here's my page.
        <br/>
        Do you like it?
    </body>
</html>
```

Here's a shocker—the following cherished <body> elements have been deprecated in HTML 4.01—and therefore, they're not available in XHTML Strict 1.0 or XHTML 1.1 (they are still available in XHTML 1.0 Transitional—giving you an idea why the Transitional form of XHTML is the most popular):

- alink

- background

- bgcolor

- link

- text

- vlink

So if you can't use these formatting attributes anymore, how do you specify, say, the color or visited links in an XHTML 1.0 Strict page? You're supposed to use CSS to do that—here's an example:

```
<?xml version="1.0"?>
<!DOCTYPE html PUBLIC "-//W3C//DTD XHTML 1.0 Transitional//EN"
"http://www.w3.org/TR/xhtml1/DTD/xhtml1-transitional.dtd">
<html xmlns="http://www.w3.org/1999/xhtml" xml:lang="en" lang="en">
    <head>
        <title>
            Welcome to my page
        </title>
        <style type="text/css">
            body {background: white; color: black}
            a:link {color: red}
            a:visited {color: green}
            a:active {color: blue}
        </style>
    </head>

    <body>
        <h1>
            Welcome to XHTML!
        </h1>
        Here's my page.
        <br/>
        Do you like it?
        Want to check out more about XHTML?
        Take a look at:
        <a href="http://www.w3.org">W3C</a>.
    </body>
</html>
```

If you don't like the look of this, stick with XHTML 1.0 Transitional.

Try This ## Styling an XHTML Document

Try styling your sample XHTML document the way Strict XHTML 1.0 or XHTML 1.1 does, using a <style> element instead of using <body> attributes like color or bgcolor. Start with the <style> element you just saw:

```
<style type="text/css">
    body {background: white; color: black}
    a:link {color: red}
```

```
         a:visited {color: green}
         a:active {color: blue}
   </style>
```

Give your sample XHTML element red text and a cyan background. Also, set the colors of hyperlinks, visited hyperlinks, and active hyperlinks (those with the mouse cursor directly over them) to red, white, and blue respectively.

Great—now we've taken an XHTML document from scratch all the way up to validating it. Now let's take a deeper look at XHTML.

Using Headings: <h1> Through <h6>

The headings <h1> to <h6> are always popular, and here are the legal attributes for those headings in XHTML:

- **align**   Gives the alignment of text in the heading. The possible values are left (the default), center, right, or justify. (XHTML 1.0 Transitional, XHTML 1.0 Frameset)

- **class**   Style class of the element. (XHTML 1.0 Strict, XHTML 1.0 Transitional, XHTML 1.0 Frameset, XHTML 1.1)

- **dir**   Sets the direction of text that doesn't have an inherent direction in which you should read it, called directionally neutral text. You can set this attribute to LTR, left-to-right text, or RTL, right-to-left text. (XHTML 1.0 Strict, XHTML 1.0 Transitional, XHTML 1.0 Frameset, XHTML 1.1)

- **id**   You use the ID to refer to the element; set this attribute to a unique identifier. (XHTML 1.0 Strict, XHTML 1.0 Transitional, XHTML 1.0 Frameset, XHTML 1.1)

- **lang**   Specifies the base language used in the element. Only applies when the document is interpreted as HTML. (XHTML 1.0 Strict, XHTML 1.0 Transitional, XHTML 1.0 Frameset, XHTML 1.1)

- **style**   Set to an inline style to specify how the browser should display the element. (XHTML 1.0 Strict, XHTML 1.0 Transitional, XHTML 1.0 Frameset, XHTML 1.1)

- **title**   Contains the title of the element (which might be displayed in tool tips). (XHTML 1.0 Strict, XHTML 1.0 Transitional, XHTML 1.0 Frameset, XHTML 1.1)

- **xml:lang**   Specifies the base language for the element when the document is interpreted as an XML document. (XHTML 1.0 Strict, XHTML 1.0 Transitional, XHTML 1.0 Frameset, XHTML 1.1)

We've already put headings to work like this:

```
<?xml version="1.0"?>
<!DOCTYPE html PUBLIC "-//W3C//DTD XHTML 1.0 Transitional//EN"
"http://www.w3.org/TR/xhtml1/DTD/xhtml1-transitional.dtd">
<html xmlns="http://www.w3.org/1999/xhtml" xml:lang="en" lang="en">
    <head>
        <title>
            Welcome to my page
        </title>
    </head>

    <body>
        <h1>
            Welcome to XHTML!
        </h1>
        Here's my page.
        <br/>
        Do you like it?
    </body>
</html>
```

Here's an example XHTML page, headings.html, using all the available headings:

```
<?xml version="1.0"?>
<!DOCTYPE html PUBLIC "-//W3C//DTD XHTML 1.0 Transitional//EN"
"http://www.w3.org/TR/xhtml1/DTD/xhtml1-transitional.dtd">
<html xmlns="http://www.w3.org/1999/xhtml" xml:lang="en" lang="en">
    <head>
        <title>
            The &lt;h1&gt; - &lt;h6&gt; Headings
        </title>
    </head>

    <body>
        <center>
            <h1>Here is an &lt;h1&gt; heading</h1>
            <h2>Here is an &lt;h2&gt; heading</h2>
            <h3>Here is an &lt;h3&gt; heading</h3>
            <h4>Here is an &lt;h4&gt; heading</h4>
            <h5>Here is an &lt;h5&gt; heading</h5>
            <h6>Here is an &lt;h6&gt; heading</h6>
        </center>
    </body>
</html>
```

And you can see this page in Figure 8-6.

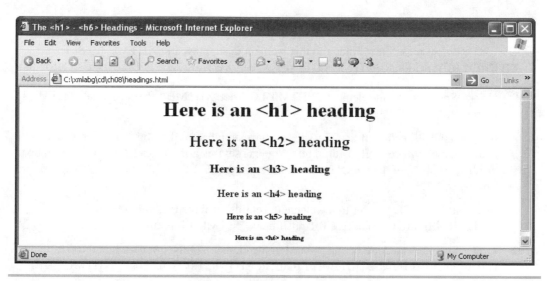

Figure 8-6   An XHTML document showing the available headings

Using Plain Text

Using plain text in XHTML is just the same as using plain text in HTML—you just put it into a page and the browser displays it. We've already seen plain text in action in our sample XHTML document:

```
<?xml version="1.0"?>
<!DOCTYPE html PUBLIC "-//W3C//DTD XHTML 1.0 Transitional//EN"
"http://www.w3.org/TR/xhtml1/DTD/xhtml1-transitional.dtd">
<html xmlns="http://www.w3.org/1999/xhtml" xml:lang="en" lang="en">
    <head>
        <title>
            Welcome to my page
        </title>
    </head>

    <body>
        <h1>
            Welcome to XHTML!
        </h1>
        Here's my page.
        <br/>
        Do you like it?
    </body>
</html>
```

Plain text is okay, but it can also be a little boring. Let's start taking a look at some formatting options.

Using <b> to Make Text Bold

The <b> element makes text bold, and this element is supported in XHTML 1.0 Strict, XHTML 1.0 Transitional, XHTML 1.0 Frameset, and XHTML 1.1. Here are its legal attributes:

- **class**   Style class of the element. (XHTML 1.0 Strict, XHTML 1.0 Transitional, XHTML 1.0 Frameset, XHTML 1.1)

- **dir**   Sets the direction of text that doesn't have an inherent direction in which you should read it, called directionally neutral text. You can set this attribute to LTR, left-to-right text, or RTL, right-to-left text. (XHTML 1.0 Strict, XHTML 1.0 Transitional, XHTML 1.0 Frameset, XHTML 1.1)

- **id**   You use the ID to refer to the element; set this attribute to a unique identifier. (XHTML 1.0 Strict, XHTML 1.0 Transitional, XHTML 1.0 Frameset, XHTML 1.1)

- **lang**   Specifies the base language used in the element. Only applies when the document is interpreted as HTML. (XHTML 1.0 Strict, XHTML 1.0 Transitional, XHTML 1.0 Frameset, XHTML 1.1)

- **style**   Set to an inline style to specify how the browser should display the element. (XHTML 1.0 Strict, XHTML 1.0 Transitional, XHTML 1.0 Frameset, XHTML 1.1)

- **title**   Contains the title of the element (which might be displayed in tool tips). (XHTML 1.0 Strict, XHTML 1.0 Transitional, XHTML 1.0 Frameset, XHTML 1.1)

- **xml:lang**   Specifies the base language for the element when the document is interpreted as an XML document. (XHTML 1.0 Strict, XHTML 1.0 Transitional, XHTML 1.0 Frameset, XHTML 1.1)

Plenty of style purists would prefer that you use CSS styling to style elements for all display aspects, but the good old <b> element remains a great and convenient way to format your text. Here's an example, bold.html, putting the <b> element to work, making a line of text bold:

```
<?xml version="1.0"?>
<!DOCTYPE html PUBLIC "-//W3C//DTD XHTML 1.0 Transitional//EN"
"http://www.w3.org/TR/xhtml1/DTD/xhtml1-transitional.dtd">
<html xmlns="http://www.w3.org/1999/xhtml" xml:lang="en" lang="en">
    <head>
        <title>
            Welcome to my page
        </title>
    </head>

    <body>
        <h1>
            Welcome to XHTML!
        </h1>
```

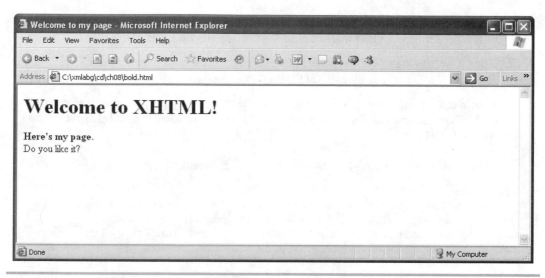

Figure 8-7   An XHTML document showing some bold text

```
        <b>Here's my page.</b>
        <br/>
        Do you like it?
    </body>
</html>
```

You can see this page in Figure 8-7.

Using <i> to Make Text Italic

Here's another easy formatting XHTML element: <i>, to make text italic. Here are the <i> element's legal attributes:

- **class**   Style class of the element. (XHTML 1.0 Strict, XHTML 1.0 Transitional, XHTML 1.0 Frameset, XHTML 1.1)

- **dir**   Sets the direction of text that doesn't have an inherent direction in which you should read it, called directionally neutral text. You can set this attribute to LTR, left-to-right text, or RTL, right-to-left text. (XHTML 1.0 Strict, XHTML 1.0 Transitional, XHTML 1.0 Frameset, XHTML 1.1)

- **id**   You use the ID to refer to the element; set this attribute to a unique identifier. (XHTML 1.0 Strict, XHTML 1.0 Transitional, XHTML 1.0 Frameset, XHTML 1.1)

- **lang**   Specifies the base language used in the element. Only applies when the document is interpreted as HTML. (XHTML 1.0 Strict, XHTML 1.0 Transitional, XHTML 1.0 Frameset, XHTML 1.1)

- **style**   Set to an inline style to specify how the browser should display the element. (XHTML 1.0 Strict, XHTML 1.0 Transitional, XHTML 1.0 Frameset, XHTML 1.1)

- **title**   Contains the title of the element (which might be displayed in tool tips). (XHTML 1.0 Strict, XHTML 1.0 Transitional, XHTML 1.0 Frameset, XHTML 1.1)

- **xml:lang**   Specifies the base language for the element when the document is interpreted as an XML document. (XHTML 1.0 Strict, XHTML 1.0 Transitional, XHTML 1.0 Frameset, XHTML 1.1)

Making text italic couldn't be simpler—here's an example:

```
<?xml version="1.0"?>
<!DOCTYPE html PUBLIC "-//W3C//DTD XHTML 1.0 Transitional//EN"
"http://www.w3.org/TR/xhtml1/DTD/xhtml1-transitional.dtd">
<html xmlns="http://www.w3.org/1999/xhtml" xml:lang="en" lang="en">
    <head>
        <title>
            Welcome to my page
        </title>
    </head>

    <body>
        <h1>
            Welcome to XHTML!
        </h1>
        <i>Here's my page.</i>
        <br/>
        Do you like it?
    </body>
</html>
```

Using <font> to Specify Text Font

The <font> element is the big one for formatting text, and here are its attributes in XHTML:

- **class**   Style class of the element. (XHTML 1.0 Transitional, XHTML 1.0 Frameset)

- **color**   Deprecated. Sets the color of the text. (XHTML 1.0 Transitional, XHTML 1.0 Frameset)

- **dir**   Sets the direction of text that doesn't have an inherent direction in which you should read it, called directionally neutral text. You can set this attribute to LTR, left-to-right text, or RTL, right-to-left text. (XHTML 1.0 Transitional, XHTML 1.0 Frameset)

- **face**   Deprecated. You can set this attribute to a single font name or a list of names separated by commas. The browser will select the first font face from the list it can find. (XHTML 1.0 Transitional, XHTML 1.0 Frameset)

- **id** You use the ID to refer to the element; set this attribute to a unique identifier. (XHTML 1.0 Transitional, XHTML 1.0 Frameset)

- **lang** Specifies the base language used in the element. Only applies when the document is interpreted as HTML. (XHTML 1.0 Transitional, XHTML 1.0 Frameset)

- **size** Deprecated. Size of the text. Possible values range from 1 through 7. (XHTML 1.0 Transitional, XHTML 1.0 Frameset)

- **style** Set to an inline style to specify how the browser should display the element. (XHTML 1.0 Transitional, XHTML 1.0 Frameset)

- **title** Contains the title of the element (which might be displayed in tool tips). (XHTML 1.0 Transitional, XHTML 1.0 Frameset)

- **xml:lang** Specifies the base language for the element when the document is interpreted as an XML document. (XHTML 1.0 Transitional, XHTML 1.0 Frameset)

This element has always been very popular, but with the new emphasis on using styles in style sheets, you can imagine that it was headed out the door. And it has indeed been deprecated in HTML 4.0, which means you'll only find <font> in the XHTML 1.0 transitional and frameset DTDs. However, due to the popularity of the <font> element, it's still very much in use, despite the efforts to get rid of it. In fact, on a sheer numbers basis, it's probably more popular than using CSS styles to format text these days (and if you want to, you can also use CSS styles with the <font> element by using the style attribute).

Here's an example, font.html, putting the <font> element to work:

```
<?xml version="1.0"?>
<!DOCTYPE html PUBLIC "-//W3C//DTD XHTML 1.0 Transitional//EN"
"http://www.w3.org/TR/xhtml1/DTD/xhtml1-transitional.dtd">
<html xmlns="http://www.w3.org/1999/xhtml" xml:lang="en" lang="en">
    <head>
        <title>
            Using the &lt;font&gt; Element
        </title>
    </head>

    <body>
        <font size="6" color="#ff0000" face="Arial">
        Using the &lt;font&gt; element.
        </font>
    </body>
</html>
```

You can see this page in a browser in Figure 8-8 (where the text appears in red in real life).

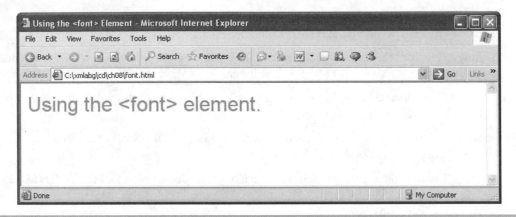

Figure 8-8 An XHTML document showing how to use the <font> element

Try This Using the <font> Element

Although deprecated in HTML 4.0, the <font> element is still supported in XHTML 1.0 Transitional. Modify our example to display blue text in the Courier font:

```
<?xml version="1.0"?>
<!DOCTYPE html PUBLIC "-//W3C//DTD XHTML 1.0 Transitional//EN"
"http://www.w3.org/TR/xhtml1/DTD/xhtml1-transitional.dtd">
<html xmlns="http://www.w3.org/1999/xhtml" xml:lang="en" lang="en">
    <head>
        <title>
            Using the &lt;font&gt; Element
        </title>
    </head>

    <body>
        <font size="6" color="#ff0000" face="Arial">
        Using the &lt;font&gt; element.
        </font>
    </body>
</html>
```

Then check your results in a browser to make sure it's okay.

Using <img> to Display Images

You use the <img> element to display images in XHTML. Here are its legal attributes:

- **align**   Sets the alignment of text relative to the image on the screen. Possible settings are: left, right, top, texttop, middle, absmiddle, baseline, bottom, and absbottom. (XHTML 1.0 Transitional, XHTML 1.0 Frameset)

- **alt**   Required. This attribute holds the text that should be displayed instead of an image for browsers that cannot handle graphics or have graphics disabled. (XHTML 1.0 Strict, XHTML 1.0 Transitional, XHTML 1.0 Frameset, XHTML 1.1)

- **border**   Specifies whether or not the image has a border, and if so, how thick the border is. Set to 0 for no border, or a positive integer pixel value. (XHTML 1.0 Transitional, XHTML 1.0 Frameset)

- **class**   Style class of the element. (XHTML 1.0 Strict, XHTML 1.0 Transitional, XHTML 1.0 Frameset, XHTML 1.1)

- **height**   Specifies the height of the image, in pixels. (XHTML 1.0 Strict, XHTML 1.0 Transitional, XHTML 1.0 Frameset, XHTML 1.1)

- **hspace**   Sets the horizontal spacing (both left and right sides) around the image. Set to pixel measurements. (XHTML 1.0 Transitional, XHTML 1.0 Frameset)

- **id**   You use the ID to refer to the element; set this attribute to a unique identifier. (XHTML 1.0 Strict, XHTML 1.0 Transitional, XHTML 1.0 Frameset, XHTML 1.1)

- **ismap**   Specifies that this image is to be used as an image map along with a map file. (XHTML 1.0 Strict, XHTML 1.0 Transitional, XHTML 1.0 Frameset, XHTML 1.1)

- **lang**   Specifies the base language used in the element. Only applies when the document is interpreted as HTML. (XHTML 1.0 Strict, XHTML 1.0 Transitional, XHTML 1.0 Frameset, XHTML 1.1)

- **longdesc**   Contains a longer description of the image. Allows descriptions to contain markup. Set to a URI. (XHTML 1.0 Strict, XHTML 1.0 Transitional, XHTML 1.0 Frameset, XHTML 1.1)

- **src**   Required. Specifies the URI of the image to display. (XHTML 1.0 Strict, XHTML 1.0 Transitional, XHTML 1.0 Frameset, XHTML 1.1)

- **style**   Inline style indicating how to render the element. (XHTML 1.0 Strict, XHTML 1.0 Transitional, XHTML 1.0 Frameset, XHTML 1.1)

- **title**   Contains the title of the body (which might be displayed in tool tips). (XHTML 1.0 Strict, XHTML 1.0 Transitional, XHTML 1.0 Frameset, XHTML 1.1)

- **usemap** Specifies the URI—usually inside the current document—of a client-side image map. (XHTML 1.0 Strict, XHTML 1.0 Transitional, XHTML 1.0 Frameset, XHTML 1.1)

- **vspace** Sets the vertical spacing around the image. Set to pixel measurements. (XHTML 1.0 Transitional, XHTML 1.0 Frameset)

- **width** Indicates the width of the image. Set to pixel measurements. (XHTML 1.0 Strict, XHTML 1.0 Transitional, XHTML 1.0 Frameset, XHTML 1.1)

- **xml:lang** Specifies the base language for the element when the document is interpreted as an XML document. (XHTML 1.0 Strict, XHTML 1.0 Transitional, XHTML 1.0 Frameset, XHTML 1.1)

Here's an example showing how the <img> element works, assuming we have an image named image.jpg:

```
<?xml version="1.0"?>
<!DOCTYPE html PUBLIC "-//W3C//DTD XHTML 1.0 Transitional//EN"
"http://www.w3.org/TR/xhtml1/DTD/xhtml1-transitional.dtd">
<html xmlns="http://www.w3.org/1999/xhtml" xml:lang="en" lang="en">
    <head>
        <title>
            Using the &lt;img&gt; Element
        </title>
    </head>

    <body>
        <center>
            <h1>
                Using the &lt;img&gt; Element
            </h1>
            <img src="image.jpg"
                width="200" height="200" alt="An image" />
        </center>
    </body>
</html>
```

You can see the results in Figure 8-9.

Let's finish up by taking a look at creating tables using XHTML.

Creating Tables

You create tables in XHTML with the <table>, <tr> (table row), and <td> (table data) elements. Here are the legal attributes of the <table> element in XHTML:

- **align** Deprecated in HTML 4.0. Sets the horizontal alignment of the table in the browser window. Set to left, center, or right. (XHTML 1.0 Transitional, XHTML 1.0 Frameset)

- **bgcolor** Deprecated in HTML 4.0. Sets the background color of table cells. Even though this attribute is deprecated, style sheet support for tables is still limited and inconsistent between browsers today. (XHTML 1.0 Transitional, XHTML 1.0 Frameset)

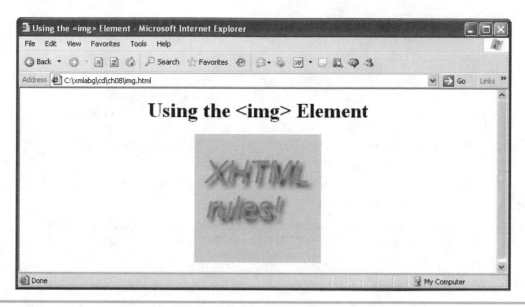

Figure 8-9   An XHTML document showing how to use the <img> element

- **border**   Sets the border width as measured in pixels. If you set this attribute to 0, the border is invisible. (XHTML 1.0 Transitional, XHTML 1.0 Frameset)

- **cellpadding**   Specifies the spacing between cell walls and cell contents in pixels. (XHTML 1.0 Strict, XHTML 1.0 Transitional, XHTML 1.0 Frameset, XHTML 1.1)

- **cellspacing**   Specifies the distance between cells. Set to a value in pixels. (XHTML 1.0 Strict, XHTML 1.0 Transitional, XHTML 1.0 Frameset, XHTML 1.1)

- **class**   Style class of the element. (XHTML 1.0 Strict, XHTML 1.0 Transitional, XHTML 1.0 Frameset, XHTML 1.1)

- **dir**   Sets the direction of text that doesn't have an inherent direction in which you should read it, called directionally neutral text. You can set this attribute to LTR, left-to-right text, or RTL, right-to-left text. (XHTML 1.0 Strict, XHTML 1.0 Transitional, XHTML 1.0 Frameset, XHTML 1.1)

- **frame**   Determines the outer border display of the table using the Complex Table Model. You use this attribute with the rules attribute. Possible values: void (no borders), above (border on top side only), below (border on bottom side only), hsides (horizontal borders only), vsides (vertical borders only), lhs (border on left side only), rhs (border on right side only), box (border on all four sides), border (the default, the same as box). (XHTML 1.0 Strict, XHTML 1.0 Transitional, XHTML 1.0 Frameset, XHTML 1.1)

- **id**   You use the ID to refer to the element; set this attribute to a unique identifier. (XHTML 1.0 Strict, XHTML 1.0 Transitional, XHTML 1.0 Frameset, XHTML 1.1)

● **lang** Specifies the base language used in the element. Only applies when the document is interpreted as HTML. (XHTML 1.0 Strict, XHTML 1.0 Transitional, XHTML 1.0 Frameset, XHTML 1.1)

● **rules** Specifies the interior struts in a table using the Complex Table Model. Set to: none (no interior struts), groups (horizontal struts are displayed between table groups created with the thead, tbody, tfoot, and colgroup tags), rows (horizontal struts are displayed between all table rows), cols (vertical struts are displayed between all table columns), and all (struts are displayed between all table cells). (XHTML 1.0 Strict, XHTML 1.0 Transitional, XHTML 1.0 Frameset, XHTML 1.1)

● **style** Inline style indicating how to render the element. (XHTML 1.0 Strict, XHTML 1.0 Transitional, XHTML 1.0 Frameset, XHTML 1.1)

● **summary** Gives summary information for nonvisual browsers. (XHTML 1.0 Strict, XHTML 1.0 Transitional, XHTML 1.0 Frameset, XHTML 1.1)

● **title** Contains the title of the element. (XHTML 1.0 Strict, XHTML 1.0 Transitional, XHTML 1.0 Frameset, XHTML 1.1)

● **width** Sets the width of the table; set to a pixel value or a percentage of the display area (add a percent sign [%] to such values). (XHTML 1.0 Strict, XHTML 1.0 Transitional, XHTML 1.0 Frameset, XHTML 1.1)

● **xml:lang** Specifies the base language for the element when the document is interpreted as an XML document. (XHTML 1.0 Strict, XHTML 1.0 Transitional, XHTML 1.0 Frameset, XHTML 1.1)

Let's create an example, table.html, that will display a tic tac toe board. Here's how we start, with the <table> element:

```
<?xml version="1.0"?>
<!DOCTYPE html PUBLIC "-//W3C//DTD XHTML 1.0 Transitional//EN"
"http://www.w3.org/tr/xhtml1/DTD/xhtml1-transitional.dtd">
<html xmlns="http://www.w3.org/1999/xhtml" xml:lang="en" lang="en">
    <head>
        <title>
            Creating XHTML Tables
        </title>
    </head>

    <body>
        <center>
            <h1>
                Creating XHTML Tables
            </h1>
            <table border="1">
                .
                .
                .
```

```
        </table>
      </center>
    </body>
</html>
```

To create the rows of the table, you use the XHTML <tr> element, which has the following legal attributes:

- **align** Specifies the horizontal alignment of the text in this table row. Set to left, center, right, justify, or char. Unlike other align attributes, this one is not deprecated. (XHTML 1.0 Strict, XHTML 1.0 Transitional, XHTML 1.0 Frameset, XHTML 1.1)

- **bgcolor** Deprecated in HTML 4.0. Specifies the background color of the table cells. (XHTML 1.0 Transitional, XHTML 1.0 Frameset)

- **char** Specifies a character to align text on. (XHTML 1.0 Strict, XHTML 1.0 Transitional, XHTML 1.0 Frameset, XHTML 1.1)

- **charoff** Sets the alignment offset to the first character to align on. (XHTML 1.0 Strict, XHTML 1.0 Transitional, XHTML 1.0 Frameset, XHTML 1.1)

- **class** Style class of the element. (XHTML 1.0 Strict, XHTML 1.0 Transitional, XHTML 1.0 Frameset, XHTML 1.1)

- **dir** Sets the direction of text that doesn't have an inherent direction in which you should read it, called directionally neutral text. You can set this attribute to LTR, left-to-right text, or RTL, right-to-left text. (XHTML 1.0 Strict, XHTML 1.0 Transitional, XHTML 1.0 Frameset, XHTML 1.1)

- **id** You use the ID to refer to the element; set this attribute to a unique identifier. (XHTML 1.0 Strict, XHTML 1.0 Transitional, XHTML 1.0 Frameset, XHTML 1.1)

- **lang** Specifies the base language used in the element. Only applies when the document is interpreted as HTML. (XHTML 1.0 Strict, XHTML 1.0 Transitional, XHTML 1.0 Frameset, XHTML 1.1)

- **style** Inline style indicating how to render the element. (XHTML 1.0 Strict, XHTML 1.0 Transitional, XHTML 1.0 Frameset, XHTML 1.1)

- **title** Contains the title of the element. (XHTML 1.0 Strict, XHTML 1.0 Transitional, XHTML 1.0 Frameset, XHTML 1.1)

- **valign** Sets the vertical alignment of the data in this row. Possible values: top, middle, bottom, or baseline. (XHTML 1.0 Strict, XHTML 1.0 Transitional, XHTML 1.0 Frameset, XHTML 1.1)

- **xml:lang** Specifies the base language for the element when the document is interpreted as an XML document. (XHTML 1.0 Strict, XHTML 1.0 Transitional, XHTML 1.0 Frameset, XHTML 1.1)

We'll create four rows in the table—three rows of tic tac toe, and one row of headers (with the text "Tic", "Tac", "Toe"). Here's how to create the four rows:

```
<?xml version="1.0"?>
<!DOCTYPE html PUBLIC "-//W3C//DTD XHTML 1.0 Transitional//EN"
"http://www.w3.org/tr/xhtml1/DTD/xhtml1-transitional.dtd">
<html xmlns="http://www.w3.org/1999/xhtml" xml:lang="en" lang="en">
    <head>
        <title>
            Creating XHTML Tables
        </title>
    </head>

    <body>
        <center>
            <h1>
                Creating XHTML Tables
            </h1>
            <table border="1">
                <tr>
                    .
                    .
                    .
                </tr>
                <tr>
                    .
                    .
                    .
                </tr>
                <tr>
                    .
                    .
                    .
                </tr>
                <tr>
                    .
                    .
                    .
                </tr>
            </table>
        </center>
    </body>
</html>
```

Finally, you use the <td> element to create the data items in each column. Here are the legal attributes of the <td> elements:

- **abbr** Gives an abbreviated name for a cell. (XHTML 1.0 Strict, XHTML 1.0 Transitional, XHTML 1.0 Frameset, XHTML 1.1, 4)

- **align**   Sets the horizontal alignment of content in the table cell. Set to left, center, right, justify, or char. (XHTML 1.0 Strict, XHTML 1.0 Transitional, XHTML 1.0 Frameset, XHTML 1.1)

- **axis**   Contains a name for a cell (usually used only with table heading cells). Allows the table to be mapped to a tree hierarchy. (XHTML 1.0 Strict, XHTML 1.0 Transitional, XHTML 1.0 Frameset, XHTML 1.1)

- **bgcolor**   Deprecated in HTML 4.0. Sets the background color of table cells. (XHTML 1.0 Transitional, XHTML 1.0 Frameset)

- **char**   Specifies a character to align text on. (XHTML 1.0 Strict, XHTML 1.0 Transitional, XHTML 1.0 Frameset, XHTML 1.1)

- **charoff**   Sets the alignment offset to the first character to align on (which you set with char). (XHTML 1.0 Strict, XHTML 1.0 Transitional, XHTML 1.0 Frameset, XHTML 1.1)

- **class**   Style class of the element. (XHTML 1.0 Strict, XHTML 1.0 Transitional, XHTML 1.0 Frameset, XHTML 1.1)

- **colspan**   Specifies how many columns this cell should span. (XHTML 1.0 Strict, XHTML 1.0 Transitional, XHTML 1.0 Frameset, XHTML 1.1)

- **dir**   Sets the direction of text that doesn't have an inherent direction in which you should read it, called directionally neutral text. You can set this attribute to LTR, left-to-right text, or RTL, right-to-left text. (XHTML 1.0 Strict, XHTML 1.0 Transitional, XHTML 1.0 Frameset, XHTML 1.1)

- **headers**   Specifies a list of header cells that supply header information. (XHTML 1.0 Strict, XHTML 1.0 Transitional, XHTML 1.0 Frameset, XHTML 1.1)

- **height**   Deprecated in HTML 4.0. Sets the height of the cell in pixels. (XHTML 1.0 Transitional, XHTML 1.0 Frameset)

- **id**   You use the ID to refer to the element; set this attribute to a unique identifier. (XHTML 1.0 Strict, XHTML 1.0 Transitional, XHTML 1.0 Frameset, XHTML 1.1)

- **lang**   Specifies the base language used in the element. Only applies when the document is interpreted as HTML. (XHTML 1.0 Strict, XHTML 1.0 Transitional, XHTML 1.0 Frameset, XHTML 1.1)

- **nowrap**   Deprecated in HTML 4.0. Indicates that content should not be wrapped by the browser by adding line breaks. (XHTML 1.0 Transitional, XHTML 1.0 Frameset)

- **rowspan**   Specifies how many rows of the table this cell should span. (XHTML 1.0 Strict, XHTML 1.0 Transitional, XHTML 1.0 Frameset, XHTML 1.1)

- **scope**   Specifies a set of data cells for which the header cell provides header information. Set to: row, col, rowgroup, or colgroup. (XHTML 1.0 Strict, XHTML 1.0 Transitional, XHTML 1.0 Frameset, XHTML 1.1)

- **style**   Inline style indicating how to render the element. (XHTML 1.0 Strict, XHTML 1.0 Transitional, XHTML 1.0 Frameset, XHTML 1.1)

- **title**   Contains the title of the element. (XHTML 1.0 Strict, XHTML 1.0 Transitional, XHTML 1.0 Frameset, XHTML 1.1)

- **valign**   Sets the vertical alignment of the data in this cell. Set to top, middle, bottom, or baseline. (XHTML 1.0 Strict, XHTML 1.0 Transitional, XHTML 1.0 Frameset, XHTML 1.1)

- **width**   Deprecated in HTML 4.0. Gives the width of the header. (XHTML 1.0 Transitional, XHTML 1.0 Frameset)

- **xml:lang**   Specifies the base language for the element when the document is interpreted as an XML document. (XHTML 1.0 Strict, XHTML 1.0 Transitional, XHTML 1.0 Frameset, XHTML 1.1)

We can add the <td> element to our example like this:

```
<?xml version="1.0"?>
<!DOCTYPE html PUBLIC "-//W3C//DTD XHTML 1.0 Transitional//EN"
"http://www.w3.org/tr/xhtml1/DTD/xhtml1-transitional.dtd">
<html xmlns="http://www.w3.org/1999/xhtml" xml:lang="en" lang="en">
    <head>
        <title>
            Creating XHTML Tables
        </title>
    </head>

    <body>
        <center>
            <h1>
                Creating XHTML Tables
            </h1>
            <table border="1">
                <tr>
                    <td>Tic</td>
                    <td>Tac</td>
                    <td>Toe</td>
                </tr>
                <tr>
                    <td>O</td>
                    <td>X</td>
                    <td>O</td>
                </tr>
                <tr>
                    <td>X</td>
                    <td>O</td>
                    <td>X</td>
                </tr>
```

```
        <tr>
            <td>O</td>
            <td>X</td>
            <td>O</td>
        </tr>
    </table>
  </center>
 </body>
</html>
```

And there you have it—a complete XHTML table. You can see this table in Figure 8-10. Nice.

So as you can see, it you're comfortable with HTML, you can be comfortable with XHTML—as long as you know something about XML.

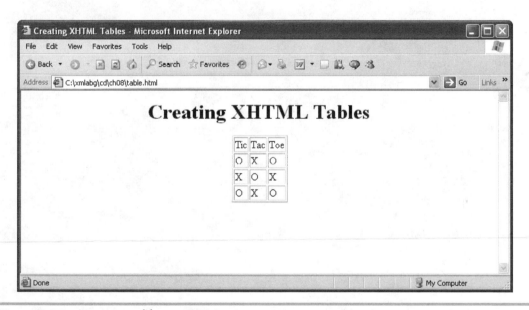

Figure 8-10   Creating tables in XHTML

Chapter 9

XML and Data Binding

Key Skills & Concepts

- Introducing data binding
- Binding HTML data
- Binding XML data
- Creating bound tables

In this chapter, we'll take a look at ways to display and handle XML without programming. As you saw in the chapter on XSLT, XSLT is a great way to extract data from XML documents without the hassle of writing programming code. This chapter focuses on the Data Source Objects (DSOs) you'll find built into Internet Explorer that also can extract XML data and work with it—all without programming.

Getting Started with DSOs

There are four data source objects in Internet Explorer—the Microsoft HTML (MSHTML) control, the tabular data control (TDC), the XML DSO, and XML data islands. Two of these DSOs, the XML DSO and XML data islands, support XML documents.

A DSO doesn't appear in a Web page. You use a DSO to read a document and make its data available to the rest of the page. In order for a DSO to read data from a document, that data must be formatted correctly.

Storing Data in HTML Format

DSOs can bind data in HTML or XML format, and to get started, we'll take a look at binding data in HTML format first, and then turn to XML. We'll start by saving some data—say a document holding information about some school students—in a document named students.html.

This is an HTML document, so we start with some HTML:

```
<html>
    <head>
        <title>
            Student Data
        </title>
    </head>

    <body>
        .
        .
        .
    </body>
</html>
```

How can you store data in an HTML document so that a DSO can extract it? You store that data in <span> elements, like this for the first student's name:

```html
<html>
    <head>
        <title>
            Student Data
        </title>
    </head>

    <body>
        Name: <span>Steve</span><br>
            .
            .
            .
    </body>
</html>
```

How will the DSO know that this <span> element contains the student's name? You can give the <span> element the ID "name":

```html
<html>
    <head>
        <title>
            Student Data
        </title>
    </head>

    <body>
        Name: <span id="name">Steve</span><br>
            .
            .
            .
    </body>
</html>
```

We can also store the student's ID like this:

```html
<html>
    <head>
        <title>
            Student Data
        </title>
    </head>

    <body>
        Name: <span id="name">Steve</span><br>
        ID: <span id="student_id">58704</span><br>
            .
            .
            .
```

```
    </body>
</html>
```

And we can store the student's graduation date:

```
<html>
    <head>
        <title>
            Student Data
        </title>
    </head>

    <body>
        Name: <span id="name">Steve</span><br>
        ID: <span id="student_id">58704</span><br>
        Graduation date: Date: <span id="grad_date">
            6/15/2009</span><br>
            .
            .
            .
    </body>
</html>
```

And the department the student is majoring in:

```
<html>
    <head>
        <title>
            Student Data
        </title>
    </head>

    <body>
        Name: <span id="name">Steve</span><br>
        ID: <span id="student_id">58704</span><br>
        Graduation date: Date: <span id="grad_date">
            6/15/2009</span><br>
        Department: <span id="department">
            Physics</span><br>
            .
            .
            .
    </body>
</html>
```

And, let's say, the student's faculty advisor:

```
<html>
    <head>
        <title>
```

```
            Student Data
        </title>
    </head>

    <body>
        Name: <span id="name">Steve</span><br>
        ID: <span id="student_id">58704</span><br>
        Graduation date: Date: <span id="grad_date">
            6/15/2009</span><br>
        Department: <span id="department">
            Physics</span><br>
        Advisor: <span id="advisor_name">Perkins</span><br>
        .
        .
        .

    </body>
</html>
```

Great, that completes the first student—now we can add others:

```
<html>
    <head>
        <title>
            Student Data
        </title>
    </head>

    <body>
        Name: <span id="name">Steve</span><br>
        ID: <span id="student_id">58704</span><br>
        Graduation date: Date: <span id="grad_date">
            6/15/2009</span><br>
        Department: <span id="department">
            Physics</span><br>
        Advisor: <span id="advisor_name">Perkins</span><br>

        Name: <span id="name">Britta</span><br>
        ID: <span id="student_id">58705</span><br>
        Graduation date: <span id="grad_date">
            6/15/2009</span><br>
        Department: <span id="department">
            Chemistry</span><br>
        Advisor: <span id="advisor_name">Grant</span><br>

        Name: <span id="name">Phoebe</span><br>
        ID: <span id="student_id">58706</span><br>
        Graduation date: <span id="grad_date">
            6/15/2009</span><br>
        Department: <span id="department">
            Physics</span><br>
        Advisor: <span id="advisor_name">Kramden</span><br>
```

```
Name: <span id="name">Mark</span><br>
ID: <span id="student_id">58707</span><br>
Graduation date: <span id="grad_date">
    6/15/2009</span><br>
Department: <span id="department">
    Physics</span><br>
Advisor: <span id="advisor_name">Thompson</span><br>

Name: <span id="name">Nancy</span><br>
ID: <span id="student_id">58708</span><br>
Graduation date: <span id="grad_date">
    6/15/2009</span><br>
Department: <span id="department">
    English</span><br>
Advisor: <span id="advisor_name">Smith</span><br>

    </body>
</html>
```

You can see students.html in Figure 9-1.

Okay, now let's work on using a DSO to read the data in students.html.

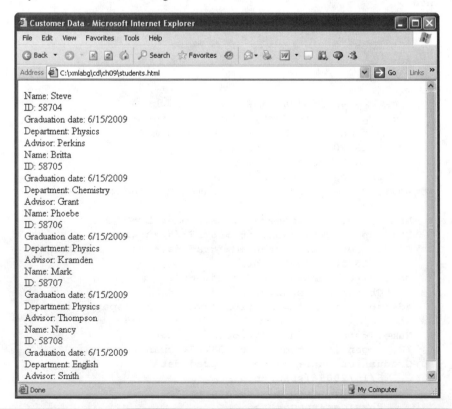

Figure 9-1   students.html

Binding Data in HTML Format

How do you bind data to HTML controls in Internet Explorer? You load the data into a DSO and then use the datasrc and datafld attributes of many HTML controls in Internet Explorer to connect to the DSO.

So what HTML elements can you bind to a DSO—and what property (like the text in a text field, or the check in a check box) is actually bound when you connect to a DSO (that is, how does the HTML control display the bound data? That data is displayed as text in a text field, as the image in an <img> element, and so on). Here's a list of HTML elements in Internet Explorer detailing what property is actually bound when you use their datasrc and datafld attributes:

- **a**   Will bind to the href property; does not update data.

- **applet**   Will bind to the param property; updates data.

- **button**   Will bind to the value property; does not update data.

- **div**   Will bind to the innerText and innerHTML properties; does not update data.

- **frame**   Will bind to the src property; does not update data.

- **iframe**   Will bind to the src property; does not update data.

- **img**   Will bind to the src property; does not update data.

- **input type=button**   Will bind to the value property; does not update data.

- **input type=checkbox**   Will bind to the checked property; updates data.

- **input type=hidden**   Will bind to the value property; updates data.

- **input type=password**   Will bind to the value property; updates data.

- **input type=radio**   Will bind to the checked property; updates data.

- **input type=text**   Will bind to the value property; updates data.

- **label**   Will bind to the value property; does not update data.

- **marquee**   Will bind to the innerText and innerHTML properties; does not update data.

- **object**   Will bind to the objects property; updates data.

- **param**   Will bind to the param property; updates data.

- **select**   Will bind to the text property of an option; updates data.

- **span**   Will bind to the innerText and innerHTML properties; does not update data.

- **table**   Constructs an entire table; does not update data.

- **textarea**   Will bind to the value property; updates data.

Let's see all this in an example, which will make what's going on clear. Our goal is to display the data in students.html in HTML elements like text fields, and let the user navigtate from student to student. We'll do that in a new Web page, studentsDSOHTML.html, that will use Internet Explorer's MSHTML DSO.

The studentsDSOHTML.html example is a standard Web page, so we can start it like this:

```
<html>
    <head>
        <title>
            Data Binding With the MSHTML DSO
        </title>
    </head>

    <body>

        <center>
            <h1>
                Data Binding With the MSHTML DSO
            </h1>
            .

            .

            .
        </center>
    </body>
</html>
```

Now we'll create the DSO. All that's necessary to create a DSO bound to the data in students.html is to use the <object> element, with the data attribute set to the URL of the HTML document holding the data. Since we're going to put students.html in the same directory as studentsDSOHTML.html, that URL is simply "students.html". DSOs can also display status messages, and we won't use that here, so we'll set the height and width of the DSO to 0. To let the other HTML elements in the page refer to the DSO, we have to give the DSO an id value, and we'll give it the ID dsoStudent. So the creation of the DSO looks like this:

```
<html>
    <head>
        <title>
            Data Binding With the MSHTML DSO
        </title>
    </head>

    <body>

        <center>
            <h1>
                Data Binding With the MSHTML DSO
            </h1>

            <object id="dsoStudent" data="students.html"
                height="0" width="0">
            </object>
```

```
            .
            .
            .
        </center>
    </body>
</html>
```

Great, that creates a DSO and connects it to the data in students.html. The DSO binds to that data in the form of *records*, and each student has their own record. That DSO feeds the data from the current record to the HTML elements it's bound to, and you can tell the DSO to move from record to record.

For example, let's display the name in the current record in a text field. You create text fields with the <input type="text"> element in HTML, and we can bind the text field to the DSO we've named dsoStudent this way—by assigning #dsoStudent (the # stands for "ID") to the text field's datasrc attribute (we're also giving the text field a size of 10 characters):

```
<html>
    <head>
        <title>
            Data Binding With the MSHTML DSO
        </title>
    </head>

    <body>

        <center>
            <h1>
                Data Binding With the MSHTML DSO
            </h1>

            <object id="dsoStudent" data="students.html"
                height="0" width="0">
            </object>

            Name: <input type="text" datasrc="#dsoStudent"
                size="10">
                .
                .
                .

        </center>
    </body>
</html>
```

That's fine, but how do we tell the text field to display the student's name? Each record is divided up into *fields*—name, student_id, grad_date, and so on—like this:

```
Name: <span id="name">Mark</span><br>
ID: <span id="student_id">58707</span><br>
Graduation date: <span id="grad_date">
    6/15/2009</span><br>
```

```
Department: <span id="department">
    Physics</span><br>
Advisor: <span id="advisor_name">Thompson</span><br>
```

So to display the name in the current record, you want the name field. You can tie the text field to the name field with its datafld attribute like this:

```
<html>
    <head>
        <title>
            Data Binding With the MSHTML DSO
        </title>
    </head>

    <body>

        <center>
            <h1>
                Data Binding With the MSHTML DSO
            </h1>

            <object id="dsoStudent" data="students.html"
                height="0" width="0">
            </object>

            Name: <input type="text" datasrc="#dsoStudent"
                datafld="name" size="10">
                .
                .
                .
        </center>
    </body>
</html>
```

And that's all it takes—now the text field will display the data in the name field of the current record in the DSO.

Let's also display the student's ID in a text field:

```
<html>
    <head>
        <title>
            Data Binding With the MSHTML DSO
        </title>
    </head>

    <body>

        <center>
            <h1>
                Data Binding With the MSHTML DSO
            </h1>
```

```
<object id="dsoStudent" data="students.html"
    height="0" width="0">
</object>

Name: <input type="text" datasrc="#dsoStudent"
    datafld="name" size="10">

<p>
ID: <input type="text" datasrc="#dsoStudent"
    datafld="student_id" size="5">
        .
        .
        .
        </center>
    </body>
</html>
```

We might just display the graduation date as plain text, as we can do with an HTML <span> element:

```
<html>
    <head>
        <title>
            Data Binding With the MSHTML DSO
        </title>
    </head>

    <body>

        <center>
            <h1>
                Data Binding With the MSHTML DSO
            </h1>

            <object id="dsoStudent" data="students.html"
                height="0" width="0">
            </object>

            Name: <input type="text" datasrc="#dsoStudent"
                datafld="name" size="10">

            <p>
            ID: <input type="text" datasrc="#dsoStudent"
                datafld="student_id" size="5">

            <p>
            Graduation date: <span datasrc="#dsoStudent"
                datafld="grad_date"></span>
```

```
          .
          .
          .
        </center>
    </body>
</html>
```

Let's do something different with the student's department, displaying that in a drop-down list control, which you create with the <select> HTML element. You just connect the <select> control to the DSO as you would if it were a text field, but then add <option> elements for all possible choices for the department—English, Physics, and so on. When the page is active, the drop-down list box will display the item that matches the value of the department field. Here's what the HTML looks like (note that we're also displaying the name of the student's advisor in another <span> element):

```
<html>
    <head>
        <title>
            Data Binding With the MSHTML DSO
        </title>
    </head>

    <body>

        <center>
            <h1>
                Data Binding With the MSHTML DSO
            </h1>

            <object id="dsoStudent" data="students.html"
                height="0" width="0">
            </object>

            Name: <input type="text" datasrc="#dsoStudent"
                datafld="name" size="10">

            <p>
            ID: <input type="text" datasrc="#dsoStudent"
                datafld="student_id" size="5">

            <p>
            Graduation date: <span datasrc="#dsoStudent"
                datafld="grad_date"></span>

            <p>
            Department: <select datasrc="#dsoStudent"
                datafld="department" size="1">
```

```
        <option value="Chemistry">Chemistry
        <option value="Physics">Physics
        <option value="English">English
    </select>

    <p>
    Advisor: <span datasrc="#dsoStudent"
      datafld="advisor_name">
    </span>
        .

        .

        .
    </center>
  </body>
</html>
```

That ties the HTML elements in the page to the current record in the DSO. When the page first loads, the first record in students.html is the current record. But that's not too exciting if you can only see one record. How can you navigate from record to record?

Navigating from Record to Record

So how do you navigate from record to record in the DSO? The current record is displayed in the HTML elements we've added, such as text fields, but how do you get to new records? When you move to a new record, the data in that record's fields (name, student_id) and so on will appear in the bound HTML elements.

It turns out that collectively the records in the DSO are called a record set, and you can access them as dsoStudent.recordset. Then you can move to the next record in the record set with the JavaScript dsoStudent.recordset.moveFirst(), or the previous record with dsoStudent. recordset.movePrevious(). Here's how you move around in record sets (yes, I know, I said no programming in this chapter, and this is JavaScript, but it's so little it barely counts):

- **dsoStudent.recordset.moveFirst()**   Moves to the first record.

- **dsoStudent.recordset.movePrevious()**   Moves to the previous record.

- **dsoStudent.recordset.moveNext()**   Moves to the next record.

- **dsoStudent.recordset.moveLast()**   Moves to the last record.

Here's something else—if we're at the beginning of the record set, we shouldn't try to move to a previous record. We can test if we're not at the beginning of the record set with the JavaScript if(!dsoStudent.recordset.BOF), which you can read as "if not at the beginning of the record set"—BOF stands for "beginning of file," and although there is no actual file here, that's the terminology that's used. And similarly, we can check if we're at the end of the record set with the keyword EOF, in which case we shouldn't try to go past it.

Here's what the JavaScript looks like, which we connect to the onclick event of four buttons to let the user move around the record set by clicking buttons:

```html
<html>
    <head>
        <title>
            Data Binding With the MSHTML DSO
        </title>
    </head>

    <body>

        <center>
            <h1>
                Data Binding With the MSHTML DSO
            </h1>

            <object id="dsoStudent" data="students.html"
                height="0" width="0">
            </object>

            Name: <input type="text" datasrc="#dsoStudent"
                datafld="name" size="10">

            <p>
            ID: <input type="text" datasrc="#dsoStudent"
                datafld="student_id" size="5">

            <p>
            Graduation date: <span datasrc="#dsoStudent"
                datafld="grad_date"></span>

            <p>
            Department: <select datasrc="#dsoStudent"
                datafld="department" size="1">
                <option value="Chemistry">Chemistry
                <option value="Physics">Physics
                <option value="English">English
            </select>

            <p>
            Advisor: <span datasrc="#dsoStudent"
              datafld="advisor_name">
            </span>

            <p>
            <button onclick=
                "dsoStudent.recordset.moveFirst()" >&lt;&lt;
            </button>
```

```
        <button onclick="if (!dsoStudent.recordset.BOF)
            dsoStudent.recordset.movePrevious()" >&lt;
        </button>
        <button onclick="if (!dsoStudent.recordset.EOF)
            dsoStudent.recordset.moveNext()" >&gt;
        </button>
        <button onclick=
            "dsoStudent.recordset.moveLast()">&gt;&gt;
        </button>
    </center>
  </body>
</html>
```

You might also notice that we gave each of the four buttons here captions to match what you might see on a stereo—<<, <, >, and >> using the HTML for > (>) and < (<). You can see the whole page, studentsDSOHTML.html, in Figure 9-2.

As you can see in Figure 9-2, the fields of the first record are displayed in the text fields and <span> elements in the page. To move to another page, just click a button—you can see the second record displayed in Figure 9-3. Cool!

That gives us an introduction to data binding—now let's see how to do it in XML.

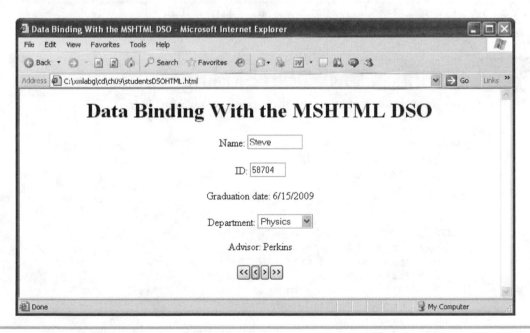

Figure 9-2   Binding HTML data

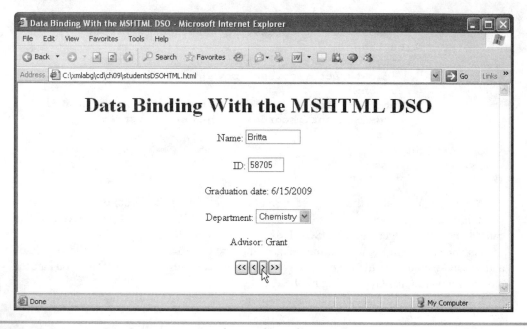

Figure 9-3 Navigating to a new record using bound HTML data

Try This Creating HTML Data Binding

Create your own version of students.html—but put your own data in it:

```
<html>
    <head>
        <title>
            Student Data
        </title>
    </head>

    <body>
        Name: <span id="name">Steve</span><br>
        ID: <span id="student_id">58704</span><br>
        Graduation date: Date: <span id="grad_date">
            6/15/2009</span><br>
        Department: <span id="department">
            Physics</span><br>
        Advisor: <span id="advisor_name">Perkins</span><br>
        .
        .
        .
    </body>
</html>
```

And try to get your data to show up in studentsDSOHTML.html. Next, create an HTML Web page that holds friend data (not student data) with fields like name, age, weight, and height, and modify studentsDSOHTML.html to display your new data.

Binding XML Data

Let's convert our students.html document into XML. In XML, we won't need any of that <span id="name"> stuff—if we want to store a student's name, we can just use an element named <name>, no <span> element needed.

Here's what students.html looks like translated into XML, students.xml:

```xml
<?xml version="1.0"?>
<students>

    <student>
        <name>Steve</name>
        <student_id>58704</student_id>
        <grad_date>6/15/2009</grad_date>
        <department>Physics</department>
        <advisor_name>Perkins</advisor_name>
    </student>

    <student>
        <name>Britta</name>
        <student_id>58705</student_id>
        <grad_date>6/15/2009</grad_date>
        <department>Chemistry</department>
        <advisor_name>Grant</advisor_name>
    </student>

    <student>
        <name>Phoebe</name>
        <student_id>58706</student_id>
        <grad_date>6/15/2009</grad_date>
        <department>Physics</department>
        <advisor_name>Kramden</advisor_name>
    </student>

    <student>
        <name>Mark</name>
        <student_id>58707</student_id>
        <grad_date>6/15/2009</grad_date>
        <department>Physics</department>
<advisor_name>Thompson</advisor_name>
    </student>
```

```
<student>
    <name>Nancy</name>
    <student_id>58708</student_id>
    <grad_date>6/15/2009</grad_date>
    <department>English</department>
    <advisor_name>Smith</advisor_name>
</student>

</students>
```

Okay, now how do we extract the data in students.xml by binding the <student> records to HTML elements? There are a couple of ways, and we'll start with the most popular: using XML data islands.

Using XML Data Islands

In Internet Explorer, you create an XML data island with the <xml> element (you use this element in HTML documents, not XML documents, in Internet Explorer). XML data islands can act as DSOs, and we'll create a data island with the ID "students" to do just that.

To create an XML data island DSO, you use the <xml> element's src attribute to point to the data source, which will be students.xml here, and its id attribute to give the XML data island the ID students. Here's how it goes in our new Web page, studentsXMLislands.html:

```
<html>
    <head>
        <title>Single Record Binding Using XML Data Islands</title>
    </head>

    <xml src="students.xml" id="students"></xml>
        .
        .
        .
</html>
```

That connects our XML data to a DSO—it was as easy as that.

Now we can use the same HTML elements as we used earlier in this chapter to connect to the DSO to display the fields of the current record, in just the same way as when we used HTML data:

```
<html>
    <head>
        <title>Single Record Binding Using XML Data Islands</title>
    </head>

    <xml src="students.xml" id="students"></xml>
```

```
<body>
    <center>
        <h1>
            Single Record Binding Using XML Data Islands
        </h1>

        Name: <input type="text" datasrc="#students"
            datafld="name" size=10>
        <p>

        Student ID: <input type="text" datasrc="#students"
            datafld="student_id" size=5>

        <p>
        Graduation date: <span datasrc="#students"
            datafld="grad_date"></span><p>
        Advisor: <span datasrc="#students"
          datafld="advisor_name"></span>

        <p>
        Department: <select datasrc="#students"
            datafld="department" size=1>

        <option value="Physics">Physics
        <option value="Chemistry">Chemistry
        <option value="English">English
        </select>
            .
            .
            .

    </center>
    </body>
</html>
```

And we can add navigation buttons, just as we did earlier:

```
<html>
    <head>
        <title>Single Record Binding Using XML Data Islands</title>
    </head>

    <xml src="students.xml" id="students"></xml>

    <body>
        <center>
            <h1>
                Single Record Binding Using XML Data Islands
            </h1>
```

```
Name: <input type="text" datasrc="#students"
    datafld="name" size=10>
<p>

Student ID: <input type="text" datasrc="#students"
    datafld="student_id" size=5>

<p>
Graduation date: <span datasrc="#students"
    datafld="grad_date"></span><p>
Advisor: <span datasrc="#students"
  datafld="advisor_name"></span>

<p>
Department: <select datasrc="#students"
    datafld="department" size=1>

<option value="Physics">Physics
<option value="Chemistry">Chemistry
<option value="English">English
</select>

<p>
<button onclick="students.recordset.moveFirst()" >
    &lt;&lt;
</button>
<button onclick="if (!students.recordset.BOF)
    students.recordset.movePrevious()" >
    &lt;
</button>
<button onclick="if (!students.recordset.EOF)
    students.recordset.moveNext()" >
    &gt;
</button>
<button onclick="students.recordset.moveLast()">
    &gt;&gt;
</button>
        </center>
    </body>
</html>
```

You can see this new HTML page, studentsXMLislands.html, in Figure 9-4. Excellent—it works just as our HTML-binding example did.

Great—now we've been able to extract XML data and display it in Internet Explorer—without any programming (okay, with a minimal amount of programming . . .).

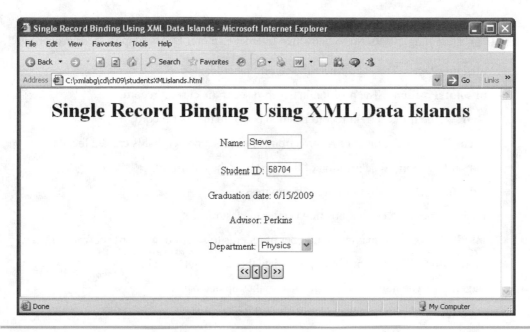

Figure 9-4 Using bound XML data

Try This Creating XML Data Binding

Create your own version of students.xml—but put your own data in it:

```
<?xml version="1.0"?>
<students>

    <student>
        <name>Steve</name>
        <student_id>58704</student_id>
        <grad_date>6/15/2009</grad_date>
        <department>Physics</department>
        <advisor_name>Perkins</advisor_name>
    </student>
        .
        .
        .
<students>
```

And try to get your data to show up in studentsXMLislands.html. Next, create an XML document that holds friend data (not student data) with elements like <name>, <age>, <weight>, and <height>, and modify studentsXMLislands.html to display your new data.

We've done all this with a minimum of programming, but if you're somewhat familiar with programming, it's useful to know that Internet Explorer DSOs support these properties:

- **absolutePage**   The page where the current record is.
- **absolutePosition**   The position in a record set of the current record.
- **BOF**   True if the current record position is before the first record.
- **cacheSize**   The number of records from a record set object that is cached locally.
- **cursorLocation**   The location of the cursor for the record set.
- **editMode**   Specifies if editing is in progress.
- **EOF**   True if the current position is after the last record.
- **maxRecords**   The maximum number of records to return to a record set from a query.
- **pageCount**   The number of pages of data the record set contains.
- **pageSize**   The number of records that makes up one page.
- **recordCount**   The number of records in the record set.
- **state**   The state of the record set (open or closed).
- **stayInSync**   Specifies if a hierarchical record set should remain in contact with the data source.

And they support these methods ("method" is the name given to functions built into objects—if that doesn't make any sense to you, it's best to take a look at a book on JavaScript before continuing):

- **addNew**   This method adds a new record to the record set.
- **cancel**   This method cancels execution of a pending Execute or Open request.
- **cancelUpdate**   This method cancels a pending update operation.
- **clone**   This method creates a copy of the record set.
- **close**   This method closes a record set.
- **delete**   This method deletes the current record (or group of records).
- **find**   This method searches the record set (although the Structured Query Language syntax required here is not supported in Internet Explorer yet).
- **getRows**   This method reads records and stores them in an array.
- **getString**   This method gets the record set as a string.

- **move**   This method moves the position of the current record.

- **moveFirst, moveLast, moveNext, movePrevious**   These methods let you navigate to various positions in the record set.

- **nextRecordSet**   This method clears the current record set object and returns the next record set. Used with hierarchical record sets.

- **open**   This method opens a database.

- **requery**   This method re-executes the query that created the record set.

- **save**   This method saves the record set in a file.

- **supports**   This method indicates the features the record set supports. You must pass long integer values that correspond to the various ADO methods, as defined in the Microsoft ADO documentation; for example, passing this method a value of 0x1000400 (0x specifies a hexadecimal value) returns a value of true, indicating that the record set supports the addNew method, but passing a value of 0x10000 returns a value of false, indicating the record set does not support the updateBatch method.

Okay, now you've seen how to bind data fields to HTML elements without a lot of programming, But what if you wanted to extract data from a DSO yourself? we'll take a brief dip into some programming to see how that works.

Extracting Data from DSOs Yourself

It turns out that you can address the individual fields in the current record in a DSO like this for the name field: student.recordset("name"). In other words, student.recordset("name") is how you extract the name of the current student.

That's very useful in case you want to work with data from your XML records yourself. Here's an example—we're getting into a little more programming here—named XMLall.html that extracts all the data from the students.xml document by looping over all the records and extracting all the fields when the user clicks a button.

Here's what the button—with the caption "View data"—looks like in XMLall.html:

```
<html>
    <head>
        <title>
            Accessing individual data fields
        </title>
            .
            .
            .
    </head>
```

```
    <body>
        <center>
            <h1>
                Accessing individual data fields
            </h1>
        </center>

        <form>
            <center>
                <input type="button" value="View data"
                    onclick="viewData()">
            </center>
        </form>
        <div id="div1">
        </div>
    </body>
</html>
```

This button will call a JavaScript function named viewData when it's clicked, so let's add that function:

```
<html>
    <head>
        <title>
            Accessing individual data fields
        </title>

        <script language="JavaScript">
            function viewData()
            {
            .
            .
            .
            }
        </script>
    </head>

    <body>
        <center>
            <h1>
                Accessing individual data fields
            </h1>
        </center>

        <form>
            <center>
                <input type="button" value="View data"
```

```
                       onclick="viewData()">
                </center>
            </form>
            <div id="div1">
            </div>
        </body>
</html>
```

Let's also add an XML data island that will make our XML-based data available to us:

```
<html>
    <head>
        <title>
            Accessing individual data fields
        </title>

        <xml id="student" src="students.xml"></xml>

        <script language="JavaScript">
            function viewData()
            {
                .
                .
                .
            }
        </script>
    </head>

    <body>
        <center>
            <h1>
                Accessing individual data fields
            </h1>
        </center>

        <form>
            <center>
                <input type="button" value="View data"
                    onclick="viewData()">
            </center>
        </form>
        <div id="div1">
        </div>
    </body>
</html>
```

In JavaScript, you can use a while loop to loop over all the records in our record set and display the data in them by writing to a <div> element like this:

```html
<html>
    <head>
        <title>
            Accessing individual data fields
        </title>

        <xml id="student" src="students.xml"></xml>

        <script language="JavaScript">
            function viewData()
            {
                while (!student.recordset.EOF) {
                    div1.innerHTML +=
                    student.recordset("name") +
                    "'s advisor is " +
                    student.recordset("advisor_name") +
                    " in the " +
                    student.recordset("department") +
                    " department.<br>"
                    student.recordset.moveNext()
                }
            }
        </script>
    </head>

    <body>
        <center>
            <h1>
                Accessing individual data fields
            </h1>
        </center>

        <form>
            <center>
                <input type="button" value="View data"
                    onclick="viewData()">
            </center>
        </form>
        <div id="div1">
        </div>
    </body>
</html>
```

You can see the results of XMLall.html in Figure 9-5.

Very nice—we've been able to extract the data we want from our XML document—and we still haven't used much programming.

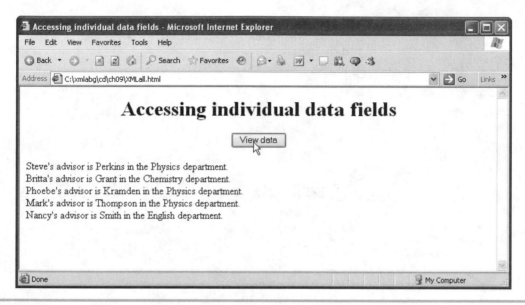

Figure 9-5   Extracting XML data

Try This Extracting XML Data

Modify XMLall.html to extract the data you've stored about your friends in your sample XML document, changing these field names as needed:

```html
<html>
    <head>
        <title>
            Accessing individual data fields
        </title>

        <xml id="student" src="students.xml"></xml>

        <script language="JavaScript">
            function viewData()
            {
                while (!student.recordset.EOF) {
                    div1.innerHTML +=
                    student.recordset("name") +
                    " bought " +
                    student.recordset("advisor_name") +
```

(continued)

```
                          " from the " +
                          student.recordset("department") +
                          " department.<br>"
                          student.recordset.moveNext()
                      }
                  }
              </script>
          </head>

          <body>
              <center>
                  <h1>
                      Accessing individual data fields
                  </h1>
              </center>

              <form>
                  <center>
                      <input type="button" value="View data"
                          onclick="viewData()">
                  </center>
              </form>
              <div id="div1">
              </div>
          </body>
      </html>
```

And check your work in Internet Explorer.

That gives us the chance to display all the data in our XML document, but it involves some programming. Want to display all the data in an XML document without any programming? Bind that data to a table, coming up next.

Binding XML Data into HTML Tables

An HTML table is the perfect way to display all the data in a record set, and here's an example, XMLtable.html, that does just that.

We'll start XMLtable.html as a normal HTML page, and add an XML data island connected to our students.xml document:

```
<html>
    <head>
        <title>
            Tabular Binding with XML Data Islands
        </title>
    </head>
```

```
    <body>
        <center>
            <h1>
                Tabular Binding with XML Data Islands
            </h1>

            <xml src="students.xml" id="students"></xml>
                .
                .
                .


    </body>
</html>
```

Now we'll start creating our table like this:

```
<html>
    <head>
        <title>
            Tabular Binding with XML Data Islands
        </title>
    </head>

    <body>
        <center>
            <h1>
                Tabular Binding with XML Data Islands
            </h1>

            <xml src="students.xml" id="students"></xml>

             <table cellspacing="10" border="1">
                .
                .

                .
            </table>
        </center>
    </body>
</html>
```

How do you tie the new table to the students DSO? You use the <table> element's datasrc attribute in Internet Explorer:

```
<html>
    <head>
        <title>
            Tabular Binding with XML Data Islands
        </title>
    </head>
```

```
    <body>
        <center>
            <h1>
                Tabular Binding with XML Data Islands
            </h1>

            <xml src="students.xml" id="students"></xml>

             <table datasrc="#students" cellspacing="10" border="1">
              .
              .
              .
            </table>
        </center>
    </body>
</html>
```

Okay, that connects our XML data to the table. Now we'll add a table header labeling the columns that will display the data fields, such as Name, Graduation Date, and so on:

```
<html>
    <head>
        <title>
            Tabular Binding with XML Data Islands
        </title>
    </head>

    <body>
        <center>
            <h1>
                Tabular Binding with XML Data Islands
            </h1>

            <xml src="students.xml" id="students"></xml>

             <table datasrc="#students" cellspacing="10" border="1">
                <thead>
                    <tr>
                        <th>Name</th>
                        <th>Student ID</th>
                        <th>Graduation Date</th>
                        <th>Department</th>
                        <th>Advisor</th>
                    </tr>
                </thead>
                 .
                 .
                 .
            </table>
```

```
            </center>
        </body>
</html>
```

So how do you populate a table's cells with data? For example, how do you display the student's name in a table cell? You can do that by inserting a <span> element into every table cell. The <span> elements are contained in the <table> element, so they'll use the same data source as the table itself, which means that you only have to specify the data field whose value you want to display in the <span> element. That looks like this for the name field:

```
<html>
    <head>
        <title>
            Tabular Binding with XML Data Islands
        </title>
    </head>

    <body>
        <center>
            <h1>
                Tabular Binding with XML Data Islands
            </h1>

            <xml src="students.xml" id="students"></xml>

             <table datasrc="#students" cellspacing="10" border="1">
                <thead>
                    <tr>
                        <th>Name</th>
                        <th>Student ID</th>
                        <th>Graduation Date</th>
                        <th>Department</th>
                        <th>Advisor</th>
                    </tr>
                </thead>

                <tbody>
                    <tr>
                        <td>
                            <span datafld="name">
                            </span>
                        </td>
                            .
                            .
                            .

                </tbody>
            </table>
        </center>
    </body>
</html>
```

And you can do the same for the other fields in the record set:

```html
<html>
    <head>
        <title>
            Tabular Binding with XML Data Islands
        </title>
    </head>

    <body>
        <center>
            <h1>
                Tabular Binding with XML Data Islands
            </h1>

            <xml src="students.xml" id="students"></xml>

            <table datasrc="#students" cellspacing="10" border="1">
                <thead>
                    <tr>
                        <th>Name</th>
                        <th>Student ID</th>
                        <th>Graduation Date</th>
                        <th>Department</th>
                        <th>Advisor</th>
                    </tr>
                </thead>

                <tbody>
                    <tr>
                        <td>
                            <span datafld="name">
                            </span>
                        </td>
                        <td>
                            <span datafld="student_id">
                            </span>
                        </td>
                        <td>
                            <span datafld="grad_date">
                            </span>
                        </td>
                        <td>
                            <span datafld="department">
                            </span>
                        </td>
```

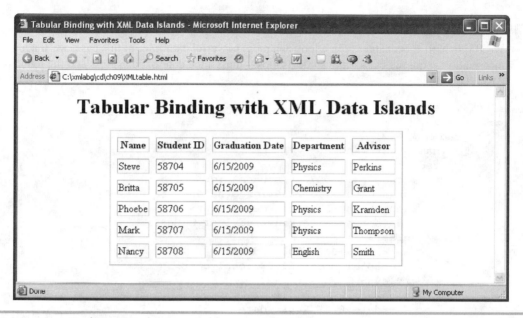

Figure 9-6 Binding XML data to a table

```
            <td>
                <span datafld="advisor_name">
                </span>
            </td>
        </tr>
    </tbody>
</table>
</center>
</body>
</html>
```

That completes the first row—that is, the data for the first record. How do you display all the data from all the records? It turns out that that's handled for you automatically—the <table> element will automatically loop over all the records in your record set, creating one row in the table for each record. Cool.

You can see the results in Figure 9-6.

Try This Binding XML Data to a Table

Modify XMLtable.html to extract the data you've stored about your friends in your sample XML document, changing these field names as needed: Then, as usual, check your results.

Handling Nested Records

We'll finish off this chapter with a look at a more powerful example. In this case, we'll add information about the classes the students took—that is, the date of each class and the total cost, like this:

```
<?xml version="1.0"?>
<students>
    <student>
        <name>Steve</name>
        <record>
            <student_id>58704</student_id>
            <grad_date>6/15/2009</grad_date>
            <department>Physics</department>
            <advisor_name>Perkins</advisor_name>
            <class>
                <date>10/20/2009</date>
                <total_cost>$2100</total_cost>
            </class>
            <class>
                <date>8/25/2009</date>
                <total_cost>$3450</total_cost>
            </class>
        </record>
    </student>
    <student>
        <name>Britta</name>
        <record>
            <student_id>58705</student_id>
            <grad_date>6/15/2009</grad_date>
            <department>Chemistry</department>
            <advisor_name>Grant</advisor_name>
            <class>
                <date>10/20/2009</date>
                <total_cost>$3000</total_cost>
            </class>
            <class>
                <date>8/25/2009</date>
                <total_cost>$2950</total_cost>
            </class>
        </record>
    </student>
    <student>
        <name>Phoebe</name>
        <record>
            <student_id>58706</student_id>
            <grad_date>6/15/2009</grad_date>
```

```xml
            <department>Physics</department>
            <advisor_name>Kramden</advisor_name>
            <class>
                <date>10/20/2009</date>
                <total_cost>$3100</total_cost>
            </class>
            <class>
                <date>8/25/2009</date>
                <total_cost>$3750</total_cost>
            </class>
        </record>
    </student>
    <student>
        <name>Mark</name>
        <record>
            <student_id>58707</student_id>
            <grad_date>6/15/2009</grad_date>
            <department>Physics</department>
            <advisor_name>Thompson</advisor_name>
            <class>
                <date>10/20/2009</date>
                <total_cost>$3150</total_cost>
            </class>
            <class>
                <date>8/25/2009</date>
                <total_cost>$3850</total_cost>
            </class>
        </record>
    </student>
    <student>
        <name>Nancy</name>
        <record>
            <student_id>58708</student_id>
            <grad_date>6/15/2009</grad_date>
            <department>English</department>
            <advisor_name>Smith</advisor_name>
            <class>
                <date>10/20/2009</date>
                <total_cost>$2100</total_cost>
            </class>
            <class>
                <date>8/25/2009</date>
                <total_cost>$2200</total_cost>
            </class>
        </record>
    </student>
</students>
```

Okay, now say that we wanted to create a table that displayed each student's name, as well as the date and cost of each of their classes. How could we extract just that information? We could start by extracting the name of each student like this in a bound table in a new example, XMLtablenested.html:

```
<table datasrc="#dsoStudent" border="1">
    <tr>
        <th><div datafld="name"></div></th>
        .
        .
        .
    </tr>
</table>
```

Now we've got to drill down to the data we need. That data is nested in <record> elements, so we can create a new, nested table, that uses <records> as the data field:

```
<table datasrc="#dsoStudent" border="1">
    <tr>
        <th><div datafld="name"></div></th>
        <td>
            <table datasrc="#dsoStudent"
            datafld="record">
            .
            .
            .
            </table>
        </td>
    </tr>
</table>
```

Now how do we refer to the <class> element inside the <record> element? You can refer to <class> elements by assigning a new nested table's datafld attribute the value "record.class"—that's the way you specify that you're looking for a nested element. Here's what it looks like in XMLtablenested.html:

```
<table datasrc="#dsoStudent" border="1">
    <tr>
        <th><div datafld="name"></div></th>
        <td>
            <table datasrc="#dsoStudent"
            datafld="record">
                <tr>
                    <td>
                    <table datasrc="#dsoStudent"
                        cellpadding = "5"
```

```
                        datafld="record.class">
                                   .
                                   .
                                   .
                    </table>
                  </td>
             </tr>
          </table>
        </td>
    </tr>
</table>
```

Now that we have the <class> elements targeted, we can extract the data we want and place that data into table cells using <span> elements as before (you can also use <div> elements) like this:

```
<table datasrc="#dsoStudent" border="1">
    <tr>
        <th><div datafld="name"></div></th>
        <td>
           <table datasrc="#dsoStudent"
           datafld="record">
               <tr>
                   <td>
                   <table datasrc="#dsoStudent"
                       cellpadding = "5"
                       datafld="record.class">
                       <tr align = "left">
                           <th>Date</th>
                           <th>Total Cost</th>
                       </tr>
                       <tr align = "left">
                           <td><span datafld="date">
                           </span></td>
                           <td><span
                           datafld="total_cost">
                           </span></td>
                       </tr>
                   </table>
                   </td>
               </tr>
           </table>
        </td>
    </tr>
</table>
```

Alright, now we've extracted the data we want—the student's name, as well as the date that student took a class and how much it cost. You can see the full table in Figure 9-7.

As you can see, with a little work, you can extract just the data you want from XML documents using data binding—next to no programming involved. Of course, there are some things you just can't do when it comes to handling your XML data without programming—and that's why we'll start looking at handling XML data with JavaScript in the next chapter.

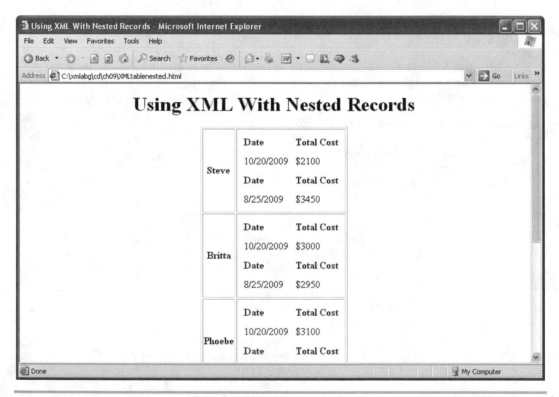

Figure 9-7 Binding nested XML data to a table

Chapter 10

XML and JavaScript

Key Skills & Concepts

- Introducing XML and JavaScript
- Using the W3C DOM
- Navigating through XML documents
- Searching for XML data

In this chapter, we'll take a look at working with XML using JavaScript—you'll need to have some familiarity with JavaScript to read this chapter. The World Wide Web Consortium, W3C, has set up a way of looking at XML documents that makes them easy to handle with JavaScript and other languages like Java (see the next chapter). The W3C model is called the Document Object Model, or DOM, and it views everything in an XML document as a *node*. Elements are nodes, attributes are nodes, text is a node, and so on.

Here are the legal nodes in the W3C DOM:

- Element
- Attribute
- Text
- CDATA section
- Entity reference
- Entity
- Processing instruction
- Comment
- Document
- Document type
- Document fragment
- Notation

For example, look at this XML document:

```
<?xml version="1.0" encoding="UTF-8"?>
<document>
    <greeting>
        Hello From XML
    </greeting>
```

```
    <message>
        Welcome to the wild and woolly world of XML.
    </message>
</document>
```

This document can be viewed as a tree of nodes, extending from the document element to the two element nodes to the two text nodes. Here's what that tree of nodes would look like (yes, I know it's an upside-down tree, but that's the way it's done in the W3C DOM):

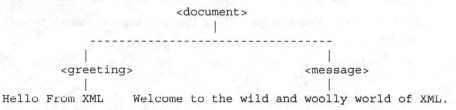

Here are the official W3C DOM objects, each corresponding to a node type:

- **Attr**   An attribute.
- **CDATASection**   ***
- **Comment**   The content of an XML comment.
- **Document**   The document object.
- **DocumentFragment**   Refers to a fragment of a document.
- **DocumentType**   Refers to the <!DOCTYPE> element.
- **Element**   An element.
- **Entity**   Stands for a parsed or unparsed entity in the XML document.
- **EntityReference**   A reference to an entity.
- **NamedNodeMap**   Allows iteration and access by name to the collection of attributes.
- **Node**   A single node in the document tree.
- **NodeList**   A list of node objects. Allows iteration and indexed access operations.
- **Notation**   Holds a notation.
- **ProcessingInstruction**   A processing instruction.
- **Text**   Text content of an element or attribute.

The Microsoft Internet Explorer is, so far, the only browser that supports the DOM in JavaScript—and it gives different names to all the W3C node types. Here are the objects—

accessible in JavaScript in Internet Explorer—that you can use with XML documents when you're treating them as a tree of nodes:

- **DOMDocument**   The top node of the XML DOM tree.

- **XMLDOMNode**   A single node in the document tree. Includes support for data types, namespaces, DTDs, and XML schemas.

- **XMLDOMNodeList**   A list of node objects. Allows iteration and indexed access operations.

- **XMLDOMNamedNodeMap**   Allows iteration and access by name to the collection of attributes.

- **XMLDOMParseError**   Information about the most recent error; includes error number, line number, character position, and a text description.

- **XMLDOMAttribute**   Stands for an attribute object.

- **XMLDOMCDATASection**   Handles CDATA sections so that text is not interpreted as markup language.

- **XMLDOMCharacterData**   Provides methods used for text manipulation.

- **XMLDOMComment**   The content of an XML comment.

- **XMLDOMDocumentFragment**   A lightweight object useful for tree insert operations.

- **XMLDOMDocumentType**   Holds information connected to the document type declaration.

- **XMLDOMElement**   Stands for the element object.

- **XMLDOMEntity**   Stands for a parsed or unparsed entity in the XML document.

- **XMLDOMEntityReference**   Stands for an entity reference node.

- **XMLDOMImplementation**   Supports general DOM methods.

- **XMLDOMNotation**   Holds a notation (as declared in the DTD or schema).

- **XMLDOMProcessingInstruction**   A processing instruction.

- **XMLDOMText**   Text content of an element or attribute.

Okay, enough talk. Let's put this to work reading in and deciphering some actual XML.

Reading XML and Extracting Data from It

Let's say that you had this simple XML document, people.xml, which records the details of a meeting named "XML In The Real World":

```
<?xml version="1.0"?>
<meetings>
   <meeting type="informal">
```

```
<meeting_title>XML In The Real World</meeting_title>
<meeting_number>2079</meeting_number>
<subject>XML</subject>
<date>6/1/2009</date>
<people>
    <person attendance="present">
        <first_name>Cary</first_name>
        <last_name>Grant</last_name>
    </person>
    <person attendance="absent">
        <first_name>Myrna</first_name>
        <last_name>Loy</last_name>
    </person>
    <person attendance="present">
        <first_name>Jimmy</first_name>
        <last_name>Stewart</last_name>
    </person>
</people>
    </meeting>
</meetings>
```

Now say that you wanted to use JavaScript, which Internet Explorer supports, to extract and display the name of the third person (Jimmy Stewart) when the user clicks a button in a Web page. How could you do that?

Try This   Creating Your Own people.xml

Create your own version of people.xml—but put your own friends in it, something like this:

```
<?xml version="1.0"?>
<meetings>
    <meeting type="informal">
        <meeting_title>XML In The Real World</meeting_title>
        <meeting_number>2079</meeting_number>
        <subject>XML</subject>
        <date>6/1/2009</date>
        <people>
            <person attendance="present">
                <first_name>Dan</first_name>
                <last_name>Peterson</last_name>
            </person>
            <person attendance="absent">
                <first_name>Frank</first_name>
                <last_name>Burns</last_name>
            </person>
```

(continued)

```
        <person attendance="present">
            <first_name>Ben</first_name>
            <last_name>Cartwright</last_name>
        </person>
      </people>
   </meeting>
</meetings>
```

Then try opening your people.xml in a browser to make sure it's well formed. We'll work on extracting the name of the third person in your people.xml document in this chapter.

Creating a DOMDocument Object

Our first step is to read the XML document people.xml in—and in Internet Explorer, that means creating a DOMDocument object. This object corresponds to the root node of our document—that is, the node at the *very beginning* of the document, even before the XML declaration (don't confuse the root node, which is before the very first character in the XML document, and the document element—also sometimes called the root element— which is the first element in the document).

Okay, now to see this in code. We're planning to navigate to the third <person> element and extract their first and last names here, so we'll call out JavaScript-enabled Web page navigator.html, and start it like this:

```
<html>
    <head>
        <title>
            Reading XML element values
        </title>
    </head>

    <body>
        <center>
            <h1>
                Reading XML element values
            </h1>

        </center>
    </body>
</html>
```

Next, we'll add an HTML button with the caption "Get the name of the third person", connecting that button's onclick event to a JavaScript function named readXMLDocument— that is, the JavaScript function readXMLDocument (which we have yet to write) will be called when this button is clicked:

```
<html>
    <head>
        <title>
            Reading XML element values
        </title>
    </head>

    <body>
        <center>
            <h1>
                Reading XML element values
            </h1>

            <input type="button"
                value="Get the name of the third person"
                onclick="readXMLDocument()">
            <p>
        </center>
    </body>
</html>
```

Now we add the <script> element to the Web page's <head> element to have a place to put the JavaScript we'll use:

```
<html>
    <head>
        <title>
            Reading XML element values
        </title>

        <script language="JavaScript">
            .
            .
            .
        </script>
    </head>

    <body>
        <center>
            <h1>
                Reading XML element values
            </h1>

            <input type="button"
                value="Get the name of the third person"
                onclick="readXMLDocument()">
            <p>
        </center>
    </body>
</html>
```

And we'll place the readXMLDocument function inside the <script> element—the code in this function will be executed when the user clicks the button:

```
<html>
    <head>
        <title>
            Reading XML element values
        </title>

        <script language="JavaScript">
            function readXMLDocument()
            {
                .
                .
                .
            }
        </script>
    </head>

    <body>
        <center>
            <h1>
                Reading XML element values
            </h1>

            <input type="button"
                value="Get the name of the third person"
                onclick="readXMLDocument()">
            <p>
        </center>
    </body>
</html>
```

Now, in the readXMLDocument function, we'll create a DOMDocument object named xmldoc with this line of code (note that we also declare the xmldoc object with the JavaScript var statement—that's good form, but it's not strictly necessary):

```
<html>
    <head>
        <title>
            Reading XML element values
        </title>

        <script language="JavaScript">
            function readXMLDocument()
            {
                var xmldoc
                xmldoc = new ActiveXObject("Microsoft.XMLDOM")
```

```
                    .
                    .
                    .
                }
            </script>
        </head>

        <body>
            <center>
                <h1>
                    Reading XML element values
                </h1>

                <input type="button"
                    value="Get the name of the third person"
                    onclick="readXMLDocument()">
                <p>
            </center>
        </body>
    </html>
```

This DOMDocument object, which we've named xmldoc, will serve as the container for our XML document, people.xml. This object, xmldoc, will represent the root node of our document, and everything else in the document is accessible from the root node.

You can load people.xml into xmldoc with the load method like this:

```
<html>
    <head>
        <title>
            Reading XML element values
        </title>

        <script language="JavaScript">
            function readXMLDocument()
            {
                var xmldoc, meetingsNode, meetingNode, peopleNode
                var first_nameNode, last_nameNode, outputText
                xmldoc = new ActiveXObject("Microsoft.XMLDOM")
                xmldoc.load("people.xml")
                    .
                    .
                    .
            }
        </script>
    </head>

    <body>
        <center>
```

```
      <h1>
          Reading XML element values
      </h1>

      <input type="button"
          value="Get the name of the third person"
          onclick="readXMLDocument()">
      <p>
    </center>
  </body>
</html>
```

That's fine—now our full XML document has been read into xmldoc, a DOMDocument object. Here are the JavaScript properties for DOMDocument objects that you can use in JavaScript:

- **attributes**   The list of attributes for this node. Read-only.

- **baseName**   The base name for the name qualified with the namespace. Read-only.

- **childNodes**   A node list containing the child nodes of the current node. Read-only.

- **dataType**   The data type for this node. Read/write.

- **definition**   The definition of the node in the DTD or schema. Read-only.

- **firstChild**   The first child of the current node. Read-only.

- **lastChild**   The last child of the current node. Read-only.

- **namespaceURI**   The URI for the namespace. Read-only.

- **nextSibling**   The next sibling of this node. Read-only.

- **nodeName**   Holds a qualified name for an element, attribute, or entity reference, or a string for other node types. Read-only.

- **nodeType**   The XML DOM node type. Read-only.

- **nodeTypedValue**   The node's value. Read/write.

- **nodeTypeString**   The node type in string form. Read-only.

- **nodeValue**   The text associated with the node. Read/write.

- **ownerDocument**   The root of the document. Read-only.

- **parentNode**   The parent node. Read-only.

- **parsed**   True if this node and all descendants have been parsed; false otherwise. Read-only.

- **prefix**   The namespace prefix. Read-only.

- **previousSibling**   The previous sibling of this node. Read-only.

- **specified**   Indicates if a node is explicitly given or derived from a default value. Read-only.

- **text**   The text content of the node and its subtrees. Read/write.

- **xml**   The XML representation of the node and all its descendants. Read-only.

Here are the JavaScript methods for DOMDocument objects:

- **appendChild**   Appends a new child as the last child of this node.

- **cloneNode**   Creates a new node that is a copy of this node.

- **hasChildNodes**   True if this node has children.

- **insertBefore**   Inserts a child node before the given node.

- **removeChild**   Removes the given child node.

- **replaceChild**   Replaces the given child node with the given new child node.

- **selectNodes**   Applies the given pattern-matching operation to this node's context, returning a list of matching nodes.

- **selectSingleNode**   Applies the given pattern-matching operation to this node's context, returning the first matching node.

- **transformNode**   Transforms this node and its children using the given XSL style sheet.

- **transformNodeToObject**   Transforms this node and its children using the given XSL style sheet, returning the result in an object.

Okay, so now we have an object, xmldoc, that represents the root node of our document, and contains all the data in the original XML document. How do we access that data in the document's elements? You begin by getting an object corresponding to the document's document element.

Getting a Document's Document Element

The document element in people.xml is the XML element that contains all the other XML elements—the <meetings> element. You can get an object corresponding to that document element with the root node's documentElement property like this in navigator.html—the document element is the <meetings> element node, so we'll call the object that contains the document element meetingsNode:

```
<html>
    <head>
        <title>
            Reading XML element values
        </title>
```

```
<script language="JavaScript">
    function readXMLDocument()
    {
        var xmldoc, meetingsNode
        xmldoc = new ActiveXObject("Microsoft.XMLDOM")
        xmldoc.load("people.xml")

        meetingsNode = xmldoc.documentElement
            .
            .
            .
    }
</script>
</head>
    .
    .
    .
</html>
```

This new node, meetingsNode, is an element node—in Internet Explorer, that's an XMLDOMElement object. How do we work with element nodes in JavaScript? Here are the properties of the XMLDOMElement object:

- **attributes**   The list of attributes for this node. Read-only.

- **baseName**   The base name for the name qualified with the namespace. Read-only.

- **childNodes**   A node list containing the children. Read-only.

- **dataType**   The data type for this node. Read/write.

- **definition**   The definition of the node in the DTD or schema.

- **firstChild**   The first child of this node. Read-only.

- **lastChild**   The last child node of this node. Read-only.

- **namespaceURI**   The URI for the namespace. Read-only.

- **nextSibling**   The next sibling of this node. Read-only.

- **nodeName**   Holds the qualified name of an element, attribute, or entity reference, or a string for other node types. Read-only.

- **nodeType**   Indicates the XML DOM node type. Read-only.

- **nodeTypeString**   The node type in string form. Read-only.

- **nodeValue**   The text associated with the node. Read/write.

- **ownerDocument**   The root of the document. Read-only.

- **parentNode**   The parent node of the current node. Read-only.

- **parsed**   True if this node and all descendants have been parsed; false otherwise. Read-only.

- **prefix**   The namespace prefix. Read-only.

- **previousSibling**   The previous sibling of this node. Read-only.

- **specified**   Indicates if the node is explicitly specified or derived from a default value in the DTD or schema. Read-only.

- **tagName**   Holds the element name. Read-only.

- **text**   Holds the text content of the node and its subtrees. Read/write.

- **xml**   Holds the XML representation of the node and all its descendants. Read-only.

Here are the methods of the XMLDOMElement object:

- **appendChild**   Appends a new child as the last child of the current node.

- **cloneNode**   Returns a new node that is a copy of this node.

- **getAttribute**   Gets the value of the named attribute.

- **getAttributeNode**   Gets the named attribute node.

- **getElementsByTagName**   Returns a list of all descendant elements which match the given name.

- **hasChildNodes**   True if this node has children.

- **insertBefore**   Inserts a child node before the given node.

- **normalize**   Normalizes all descendant elements, combining two or more text nodes next to each other into one text node.

- **removeAttribute**   Removes or replaces the named attribute.

- **removeAttributeNode**   Removes the given attribute from this element.

- **removeChild**   Removes the given child node.

- **replaceChild**   Replaces the given child node with the given new child node.

- **selectNodes**   Applies the given pattern-matching operation to this node's context, returning the list of matching nodes.

- **selectSingleNode**   Applies the given pattern-matching operation to this node's context, returning the first matching node.

- **setAttribute**   Sets the value of a named attribute.

- **setAttributeNode**   Adds or changes the given attribute node on this element.

- **transformNode**   Transforms this node and its children using the given XSL style sheet.

- **transformNodeToObject**   Transforms this node and its children using the given XSL style sheet and returns the resulting transformation as an object.

We have the <meetings> document element, and want to navigate to third <person> element's <first_name> and <last_name> elements. The first step, starting from the document element, is to get to the <meeting> element:

```xml
<?xml version="1.0"?>
<meetings>
    <meeting type="informal">
        <meeting_title>XML In The Real World</meeting_title>
        <meeting_number>2079</meeting_number>
        <subject>XML</subject>
        <date>6/1/2009</date>
        <people>
            <person attendance="present">
                <first_name>Cary</first_name>
                <last_name>Grant</last_name>
            </person>
            <person attendance="absent">
                <first_name>Myrna</first_name>
                <last_name>Loy</last_name>
            </person>
            <person attendance="present">
                <first_name>Jimmy</first_name>
                <last_name>Stewart</last_name>
            </person>
        </people>
    </meeting>
</meetings>
```

And because the <meeting> element is the first child of the <meetings> element, we can reach <meeting> with the document element's firstChild property:

```html
<html>
    <head>
        <title>
            Reading XML element values
        </title>

        <script language="JavaScript">
            function readXMLDocument()
            {
                var xmldoc, meetingsNode, meetingNode
                xmldoc = new ActiveXObject("Microsoft.XMLDOM")
                xmldoc.load("people.xml")

                meetingsNode = xmldoc.documentElement
                meetingNode = meetingsNode.firstChild
                    .
                    .
                    .
            }
```

```
        </script>
      </head>
          .
          .
          .
</html>
```

That's fine—now we have the <meeting> element. Next, we can reach the <people> element:

```
<?xml version="1.0"?>
<meetings
    <meeting type="informal">
        <meeting_title>XML In The Real World</meeting_title>
        <meeting_number>2079</meeting_number>
        <subject>XML</subject>
        <date>6/1/2009</date>
        <people>
            <person attendance="present">
                <first_name>Cary</first_name>
                <last_name>Grant</last_name>
            </person>
            <person attendance="absent">
                <first_name>Myrna</first_name>
                <last_name>Loy</last_name>
            </person>
            <person attendance="present">
                <first_name>Jimmy</first_name>
                <last_name>Stewart</last_name>
            </person>
        </people>
    </meeting>
</meetings>
```

The <people> node is the last child of the <meeting> element, so you can reach it like this:

```
<html>
    <head>
        <title>
            Reading XML element values
        </title>

        <script language="JavaScript">
            function readXMLDocument()
            {
                var xmldoc, meetingsNode, meetingNode, peopleNode
                var first_nameNode, last_nameNode, outputText
                xmldoc = new ActiveXObject("Microsoft.XMLDOM")
                xmldoc.load("people.xml")
```

```
                            meetingsNode = xmldoc.documentElement
                            meetingNode = meetingsNode.firstChild
                            peopleNode = meetingNode.lastChild
                              .
                              .
                              .
                        }
                  </script>
            </head>
            .
            .
            .
</html>
```

Now we've got to reach the third <person> element node:

```
<?xml version="1.0"?>
<meetings>
    <meeting type="informal">
        <meeting_title>XML In The Real World</meeting_title>
        <meeting_number>2079</meeting_number>
        <subject>XML</subject>
        <date>6/1/2009</date>
        <people>
            <person attendance="present">
                <first_name>Cary</first_name>
                <last_name>Grant</last_name>
            </person>
            <person attendance="absent">
                <first_name>Myrna</first_name>
                <last_name>Loy</last_name>
            </person>
            <person attendance="present">
                <first_name>Jimmy</first_name>
                <last_name>Stewart</last_name>
            </person>
        </people>
    </meeting>
</meetings>
```

The third <person> element is the last child of the <people> node, so we can reach it like this:

```
<html>
    <head>
        <title>
            Reading XML element values
        </title>
```

```
<script language="JavaScript">
    function readXMLDocument()
    {
        var xmldoc, meetingsNode, meetingNode, peopleNode
        var first_nameNode, last_nameNode, outputText
        xmldoc = new ActiveXObject("Microsoft.XMLDOM")
        xmldoc.load("people.xml")

        meetingsNode = xmldoc.documentElement
        meetingNode = meetingsNode.firstChild
        peopleNode = meetingNode.lastChild
        personNode = peopleNode.lastChild
            .
            .
            .

    }
</script>
</head>
    .
    .
    .

</html>
```

Great—now we're at the correct <person> node. The <first_name> element node is the first child of the <person> element, and the <last_name> element node is the last child of the <person> element, so we can access the correct <first_name> and <last_name> elements this way:

```
<html>
    <head>
        <title>
            Reading XML element values
        </title>

        <script language="JavaScript">
            function readXMLDocument()
            {
                var xmldoc, meetingsNode, meetingNode, peopleNode
                var first_nameNode, last_nameNode, outputText
                xmldoc = new ActiveXObject("Microsoft.XMLDOM")
                xmldoc.load("people.xml")

                meetingsNode = xmldoc.documentElement
                meetingNode = meetingsNode.firstChild
                peopleNode = meetingNode.lastChild
                personNode = peopleNode.lastChild
                first_nameNode = personNode.firstChild
                last_nameNode = first_nameNode.nextSibling
                    .
                    .
                    .
```

```
            }
        </script>
    </head>
        .
        .
        .
</html>
```

Whew. Are we done? We have the <first_name> element and the <last_name> element. But we still need to extract the actual first and last names, which are stored as text in these elements:

```
<first_name>Jimmy</first_name>
<last_name>Stewart</last_name>
```

In other words, we can't just use first_nameNode as the first name—we have to extract the text in that element, which is stored as a text node. And you can reach that text node as first_nameNode.firstChild.

Great, are we done? Nope—you have to read the actual value of the text node to determine the person's name. So if we have an object corresponding to the third person's first name, first_nameNode, you can reach the actual text using the nodeValue property like this: first_nameNode.firstChild.nodeValue. And the person's last name would be: last_nameNode.firstChild.nodeValue (that is, we're accessing the node value of the text node in the last_nameNode object). Here's what it looks like in code as we assemble the person's first and last names into a text string named outputText and then display that text in a <div> element with the ID "messagediv" :

```
<html>
    <head>
        <title>
            Reading XML element values
        </title>

        <script language="JavaScript">
            function readXMLDocument()
            {
                var xmldoc, meetingsNode, meetingNode, peopleNode
                var first_nameNode, last_nameNode, outputText
                xmldoc = new ActiveXObject("Microsoft.XMLDOM")
                xmldoc.load("people.xml")

                meetingsNode = xmldoc.documentElement
                meetingNode = meetingsNode.firstChild
                peopleNode = meetingNode.lastChild
                personNode = peopleNode.lastChild
                first_nameNode = personNode.firstChild
                last_nameNode = first_nameNode.nextSibling
```

```
                outputText = "Third name: " +
                      first_nameNode.firstChild.nodeValue + ' '
                    + last_nameNode.firstChild.nodeValue
                messagediv.innerHTML=outputText
              }
        </script>
    </head>

    <body>
        <center>
            <h1>
                Reading XML element values
            </h1>

            <input type="button"
                value="Get the name of the third person"
                onclick="readXMLDocument()">
            <p>
            <div id="messagediv"></div>
        </center>
    </body>
</html>
```

You can see this Web page—navigator.html—at work in Figure 10-1, where it's doing its stuff and retrieving the third person's name. Cool.

That gives us an introduction to extracting data from XML documents using JavaScript.

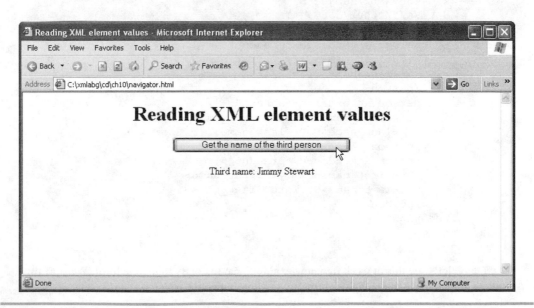

Figure 10-1 Extracting data from people.xml

Try This Get navigator.html to Work

Get navigator.html to work yourself on your own people.xml document. If you have added more than three people to your people.xml document, verify that navigator.html extracts the full name of the last person in Internet Explorer.

Okay, we've been able to access the third person's name, but it involved navigating from element to element laboriously. Isn't there an easier way? It turns out that there is.

Searching for XML Elements by Name

Although it's important to know how to navigate through XML documents using the firstChild and lastChild and other properties, there is a direct way to extract information from XML elements—you can access those elements by name with the getElementsByTagName method.

The getElementsByTagName method is a method of the root node object, and that method returns a node list of matching elements. For our purposes, a node list functions like an array. So if we searched for <first_name> elements, we'd get a node list of these three elements:

```
<?xml version="1.0"?>
<meetings>
    <meeting type="informal">
        <meeting_title>XML In The Real World</meeting_title>
        <meeting_number>2079</meeting_number>
        <subject>XML</subject>
        <date>6/1/2009</date>
        <people>
            <person attendance="present">
                <first_name>Cary</first_name>
                <last_name>Grant</last_name>
            </person>
            <person attendance="absent">
                <first_name>Myrna</first_name>
                <last_name>Loy</last_name>
            </person>
            <person attendance="present">
                <first_name>Jimmy</first_name>
                <last_name>Stewart</last_name>
            </person>
        </people>
    </meeting>
</meetings>
```

Okay, let's see this at work in a new example, navigatorByTagName.html. We start this new example as we did navigator.html, by reading in people.xml:

```
<html>
    <head>
        <title>
            Reading XML element values
        </title>

        <script language="JavaScript">
            function loadDocument()
            {
                var xmldoc

                xmldoc = new ActiveXObject("Microsoft.XMLDOM")
                xmldoc.load("people.xml")
                    .
                    .
                    .
            }
        </script>
    </head>

    <body>
        <center>
          <h1>
              Reading XML element values
          </h1>

          <input type="button" value="Get the name of the third person"
              onclick="loadDocument()">
          <p>
          <div id="messagediv"></div>
        </center>
    </body>
</html>
```

Now we can use the root node's getElementsByTagName method to get a node list of
<first_name> elements and another of <last_name> elements by passing the name of those
elements ("first_name" and "last_name") to getElementsByTagName like this:

```
<html>
    <head>
        <title>
            Reading XML element values
        </title>

        <script language="JavaScript">
            function loadDocument()
            {
                var xmldoc, listNodesFirstName, listNodesLastName
```

```
                xmldoc = new ActiveXObject("Microsoft.XMLDOM")
                xmldoc.load("people.xml")

                listNodesFirstName =
                  xmldoc.getElementsByTagName("first_name")
                listNodesLastName =
                  xmldoc.getElementsByTagName("last_name")
                    .
                    .
                    .

            }
         </script>
      </head>
        .
        .
        .

</html>
```

Now we have a node list of the three <first_name> elements in our document—listNodesFirstName—and another node list of the three <last_name> elements in our document—listNodesLastName. How do you extract the third <first_name> element and the third <last_name> element from these node lists? You can use the node list method item—here, for example, is how you get the third <first_name> element from the node list: listNodesFirstName.item(2) (why item(2) and not item(3)? Items are zero-based in node lists, so item(0) is the first item, item(1) the second item, and item(2) the third item).

After you've gotten the right <first_name> element, you still have to extract the text node in it, and then the value of the text node to recover the actual text of the person's first name like this: listNodesFirstName.item(2).firstChild.nodeValue. So here's how we recover the third person's first and last names and display the whole name:

```
<html>
    <head>
        <title>
            Reading XML element values
        </title>

        <script language="JavaScript">
            function loadDocument()
            {
                var xmldoc, listNodesFirstName, listNodesLastName

                xmldoc = new ActiveXObject("Microsoft.XMLDOM")
                xmldoc.load("people.xml")

                listNodesFirstName =
                  xmldoc.getElementsByTagName("first_name")
                listNodesLastName =
                  xmldoc.getElementsByTagName("last_name")
```

```
            outputText = "Third name: " +
              listNodesFirstName.item(2).firstChild.nodeValue
              + ' ' +
              listNodesLastName.item(2).firstChild.nodeValue
              messagediv.innerHTML=outputText
          }
      </script>
  </head>

  <body>
      <center>
        <h1>
            Reading XML element values
        </h1>

        <input type="button" value="Get the name of the third person"
            onclick="loadDocument()">
        <p>
        <div id="messagediv"></div>
      </center>
  </body>
</html>
```

And you can see this new example at work in Figure 10-2.

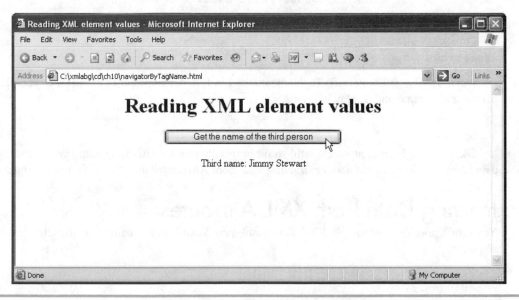

Figure 10-2   Extracting data from people.xml by searching for elements

Try This Extract Just the Data You're Looking For

Modify your sample XML document so that it includes a <nick_name> element for everyone:

```
<?xml version="1.0"?>
<meetings>
    <meeting type="informal">
        <meeting_title>XML In The Real World</meeting_title>
        <meeting_number>2079</meeting_number>
        <subject>XML</subject>
        <date>6/1/2009</date>
        <people>
            <person attendance="present">
                <first_name>Dan</first_name>
                <last_name>Peterson</last_name>
                <nick_name>Bo</nick_name>
            </person>
            <person attendance="absent">
                <first_name>Frank</first_name>
                <last_name>Burns</last_name>
                <nick_name>Frankie</nick_name>
            </person>
            <person attendance="present">
                <first_name>Ben</first_name>
                <last_name>Cartwright</last_name>
                <nick_name>Boss</nick_name>
            </person>
        </people>
    </meeting>
</meetings>
```

Next, use the getElementsByTagName method in Internet Explorer to extract the second person's nickname and display it.

Okay, we've been pretty successful so far in this chapter by extracting data from elements using JavaScript. But what about extracting data from XML attributes? That's coming up next.

Extracting Data from XML Attributes

You might note that our sample XML document, people.xml, uses an attribute, the attendance attribute:

```
<?xml version="1.0"?>
<meetings>
    <meeting type="informal">
        <meeting_title>XML In The Real World</meeting_title>
```

```
        <meeting_number>2079</meeting_number>
        <subject>XML</subject>
        <date>6/1/2009</date>
        <people>
            <person attendance="present">
                <first_name>Cary</first_name>
                <last_name>Grant</last_name>
            </person>
            <person attendance="absent">
                <first_name>Myrna</first_name>
                <last_name>Loy</last_name>
            </person>
            <person attendance="present">
                <first_name>Jimmy</first_name>
                <last_name>Stewart</last_name>
            </person>
        </people>
    </meeting>
</meetings>
```

How can you get the attributes of an XML element? It turns out that the attributes property of element nodes is a *named node map* of attribute objects (and we'll see how to work with attribute objects in a minute).

Attribute objects are actually XMLDOMAttribute objects in Internet Explorer, and here are the properties of the XMLDOMAttribute objects:

- **attributes**   The list of attributes for this node. Read-only.

- **baseName**   The base name for the name qualified with the namespace. Read-only.

- **childNodes**   A node list containing child nodes. Read-only.

- **dataType**   The data type of this node. Read/write.

- **definition**   The definition of the node in the DTD or schema. Read-only.

- **firstChild**   The first child of the current node. Read-only.

- **lastChild**   The last child of the current node. Read-only.

- **name**   The attribute name. Read-only.

- **namespaceURI**   The URI for the namespace. Read-only.

- **nextSibling**   The next sibling of this node. Read-only.

- **nodeName**   The qualified name for an element, attribute, or entity reference, or a string for other node types. Read-only.

- **nodeType**   The XML DOM node type. Read-only.

- **nodeTypedValue** The node's value. Read/write.

- **nodeTypeString** The node type in string form. Read-only.

- **nodeValue** The text associated with the node. Read/write.

- **ownerDocument** The root of the document. Read-only.

- **parentNode** Holds the parent node (for nodes that can have parents). Read-only.

- **parsed** True if this node and all descendants have been parsed; false otherwise. Read-only.

- **prefix** The namespace prefix. Read-only.

- **previousSibling** The previous sibling of this node. Read-only.

- **specified** Indicates whether the node (usually an attribute) is explicitly specified or derived from a default value. Read-only.

- **text** The text content of the node and its subtrees. Read/write.

- **value** The attribute's value. Read/write.

- **xml** The XML representation of the node and all its descendants. Read-only.

Here are the methods of the XMLDOMAttribute object:

- **appendChild** Appends a new child as the last child of this node.

- **cloneNode** Returns a new node that is a copy of this node.

- **hasChildNodes** True if this node has children.

- **insertBefore** Inserts a child node before the given node.

- **removeChild** Removes the given child node from the list.

- **replaceChild** Replaces the given child node with the given new child node.

- **selectNodes** Applies the given pattern-matching operation to this node's context, returning a list of matching nodes.

- **selectSingleNode** Applies the given pattern-matching operation to this node's context, returning the first matching node.

- **transformNode** Transforms this node and its children using the given XSL style sheet.

- **transformNodeToObject** Transforms this node and its children using the given XSL style sheet and returns the result in an object.

Let's put together an example, attributes.html, which checks the attendance of the third person, Jimmy Stewart.

We can start attributes.html as usual, with a button:

```
<html>
    <head>
        <title>
            Reading attribute values from XML documents
        </title>
            .
            .
            .
    </head>

    <body>
        <center>
            <h1>
                Reading attribute values from XML documents
            </h1>

            <input type="button"
                value="Get attendance of the third person"
                onclick="readXMLDocument()">
            <p>
        </center>
    </body>
</html>
```

When the button is clicked, the browser calls a JavaScript function named readXMLDocument, which does just that, loading people.xml into an object named xmldoc:

```
<html>
    <head>
        <title>
            Reading attribute values from XML documents
        </title>

        <script language="JavaScript">
            function readXMLDocument()
            {
                var xmldoc

                xmldoc = new ActiveXObject("Microsoft.XMLDOM")
                xmldoc.load("people.xml")
                    .
                    .
                    .
            }
        </script>
    </head>
```

```
          .
          .
          .
    </html>
```

Now we drill down to getting the <third <person> element, as well as that element's <first_name> and <last_name> child elements:

```
<html>
    <head>
        <title>
            Reading attribute values from XML documents
        </title>

        <script language="JavaScript">
            function readXMLDocument()
            {
                    var xmldoc, meetingsNode, meetingNode, peopleNode
                    var first_nameNode, last_nameNode, outputText
                    var attributes, attendancePerson

                    xmldoc = new ActiveXObject("Microsoft.XMLDOM")
                    xmldoc.load("people.xml")

                    meetingsNode = xmldoc.documentElement
                    meetingNode = meetingsNode.firstChild
                    peopleNode = meetingNode.lastChild
                    personNode = peopleNode.lastChild
                    first_nameNode = personNode.firstChild
                    last_nameNode = first_nameNode.nextSibling
                        .
                        .
                        .

            }
        </script>
    </head>
        .
        .
        .
</html>
```

We want to read the value of the attendance attribute, which is an attribute of the <person> element:

```
        <people>
            <person attendance="present">
                <first_name>Cary</first_name>
                <last_name>Grant</last_name>
            </person>
```

```
<person attendance="absent">
    <first_name>Myrna</first_name>
    <last_name>Loy</last_name>
</person>
<person attendance="present">
    <first_name>Jimmy</first_name>
    <last_name>Stewart</last_name>
</person>
</people>
```

Let's get a named node map of the <person> element's attributes and name that map attributes:

```
<html>
    <head>
        <title>
            Reading attribute values from XML documents
        </title>

        <script language="JavaScript">
            function readXMLDocument()
            {
                var xmldoc, meetingsNode, meetingNode, peopleNode
                var first_nameNode, last_nameNode, outputText
                var attributes

                xmldoc = new ActiveXObject("Microsoft.XMLDOM")
                xmldoc.load("people.xml")

                meetingsNode = xmldoc.documentElement
                meetingNode = meetingsNode.firstChild
                peopleNode = meetingNode.lastChild
                personNode = peopleNode.lastChild
                first_nameNode = personNode.firstChild
                last_nameNode = first_nameNode.nextSibling
                attributes = personNode.attributes
                     .
                     .
                     .
            }
        </script>
    </head>
         .
         .
         .
</html>
```

A "named node map" might sound scary, but all it means is that such maps support the getNamedItem, which allows us to extract information about the attribute we're interested in—the attendance attribute. We can get an XMLDOMAttribute object corresponding to the attendance attribute this way using getNamedItem on the named node map:

```
<html>
    <head>
        <title>
            Reading attribute values from XML documents
        </title>

        <script language="JavaScript">
            function readXMLDocument()
            {
                var xmldoc, meetingsNode, meetingNode, peopleNode
                var first_nameNode, last_nameNode, outputText
                var attributes, attendancePerson

                xmldoc = new ActiveXObject("Microsoft.XMLDOM")
                xmldoc.load("people.xml")

                meetingsNode = xmldoc.documentElement
                meetingNode = meetingsNode.firstChild
                peopleNode = meetingNode.lastChild
                personNode = peopleNode.lastChild
                first_nameNode = personNode.firstChild
                last_nameNode = first_nameNode.nextSibling
                attributes = personNode.attributes
                attendancePerson =
                  attributes.getNamedItem("attendance")
                  .
                  .
                  .

            }
        </script>
    </head>
    .
    .
    .
</html>
```

Swell, now we have an XMLDOMAttribute corresponding to the attendance attribute. How do you extract the value of that attribute? You can do that by using the value property of the XMLDOMAttribute object. We'll take that value and display it in a <div> element in the HTML page like this:

```
<html>
    <head>
        <title>
            Reading attribute values from XML documents
        </title>

        <script language="JavaScript">
            function readXMLDocument()
            {
                var xmldoc, meetingsNode, meetingNode, peopleNode
                var first_nameNode, last_nameNode, outputText
                var attributes, attendancePerson

                xmldoc = new ActiveXObject("Microsoft.XMLDOM")
                xmldoc.load("people.xml")

                meetingsNode = xmldoc.documentElement
                meetingNode = meetingsNode.firstChild
                peopleNode = meetingNode.lastChild
                personNode = peopleNode.lastChild
                first_nameNode = personNode.firstChild
                last_nameNode = first_nameNode.nextSibling
                attributes = personNode.attributes
                attendancePerson =
                    attributes.getNamedItem("attendance")
                outputText = first_nameNode.firstChild.nodeValue
                    + ' ' + last_nameNode.firstChild.nodeValue
                    + " is " + attendancePerson.value
                messagediv.innerHTML=outputText
            }
        </script>
    </head>

    <body>
        <center>
            <h1>
                Reading attribute values from XML documents
            </h1>

            <input type="button"
                value="Get attendance of the third person"
                onclick="readXMLDocument()">
            <p>
            <div id="messagediv"></div>
        </center>
    </body>
</html>
```

And you can see the results of attributes.html in Figure 10-3.

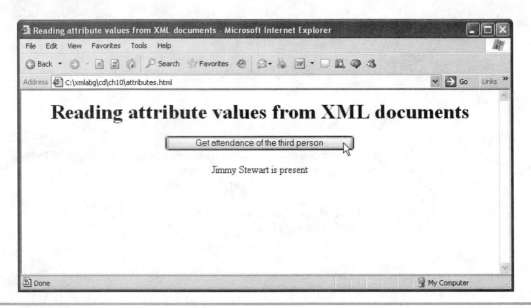

Figure 10-3 Extracting attribute values from people.xml

Try This Extract Attribute Values

Modify your sample XML document so that it includes a hair_color attribute for everyone:

```
<?xml version="1.0"?>
<meetings>
    <meeting type="informal">
        <meeting_title>XML In The Real World</meeting_title>
        <meeting_number>2079</meeting_number>
        <subject>XML</subject>
        <date>6/1/2009</date>
        <people>
            <person hair_color="brown">
                <first_name>Dan</first_name>
                <last_name>Peterson</last_name>
                <nick_name>Bo</nick_name>
            </person>
            <person hair_color="black">
                <first_name>Frank</first_name>
                <last_name>Burns</last_name>
                <nick_name>Frankie</nick_name>
            </person>
```

```
<person hair_color="white">
    <first_name>Ben</first_name>
    <last_name>Cartwright</last_name>
    <nick_name>Boss</nick_name>
</person>
        </people>
    </meeting>
</meetings>
```

Next, extract the hair color of the first person and display it.

Using XML Data Islands

It also turns out that you don't have to use the ActiveX object Microsoft.XMLDOM to work
with XML and JavaScript in Internet Explorer, as we've been doing:

```
xmldoc = new ActiveXObject("Microsoft.XMLDOM")
xmldoc.load("people.xml")
```

You can also use XML data islands, which we did in the preceding chapter, with the <xml>
element to access an XML document via JavaScript. Here's an example, attributesXMLisland.
html, showing how to do just that:

```
<html>
    <head>
        <title>
        Reading attribute values from XML documents using XML islands
        </title>

        <xml id="meetingsXML" src="people.xml"></xml>

        <script language="JavaScript">
            function readXMLDocument()
            {
                var xmldoc, meetingsNode, meetingNode, peopleNode
                var first_nameNode, last_nameNode, outputText
                var attributes, attendancePerson

                xmldoc= document.all("meetingsXML").XMLDocument

                meetingsNode = xmldoc.documentElement
                meetingNode = meetingsNode.firstChild
                peopleNode = meetingNode.lastChild
                personNode = peopleNode.lastChild
                first_nameNode = personNode.firstChild
                last_nameNode = first_nameNode.nextSibling
                attributes = personNode.attributes
                attendancePerson =
```

```
                    attributes.getNamedItem("attendance")
                outputText = first_nameNode.firstChild.nodeValue
                    + ' ' + last_nameNode.firstChild.nodeValue
                    + " is " + attendancePerson.value
                messagediv.innerHTML=outputText
            }
        </script>
    </head>

    <body>
        <center>
            <h1>
        Reading attribute values from XML documents using XML islands

            </h1>

            <input type="button"
                value="Get attendance of the third person"
                onclick="readXMLDocument()">
            <p>
            <div id="messagediv"></div>
        </center>
    </body>
</html>
```

And you can see attributesXMLisland.html at work in Figure 10-4.

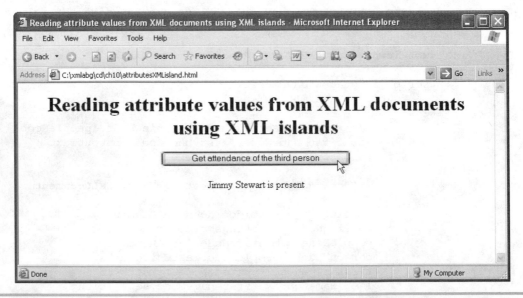

Figure 10-4 Extracting attribute values from people.xml using XML islands

Chapter 11

XML and Java

Key Skills & Concepts

- Introducing XML and Java
- Using the W3C DOM
- Navigating through XML documents with Java
- Searching for XML data

This is our heavy-lifting chapter on handling XML with programming—so if programming's not your bowl of chowder, feel free to skip this chapter. We're going to be using the Java programming language, because Java has exceptional support built into it for handling XML—and it supports the W3C DOM, which we saw in the preceding chapter (that's the way of treating XML documents as collections of node objects).

You can get Java for free at http://java.sun.com—just click the Java SE link and download the latest (non-beta) version of Java. We'll be using Java SE 6 in this chapter, which you can install easily and automatically from the Sun site. Note that you'll need some familiarity with programming in Java to get the most out of this chapter, so if you have an interest in working with XML and Java, take a look at a few free online tutorials on Java if you're not familiar with Java.

When you've downloaded and installed Java, you have all you need to work with XML. XML support was built into Java since Java version 1.4, so if you have at least version 1.4 on your computer, you're all set. Let's jump into some programming!

Working with Java and XML

Let's use the same XML document that we saw in the preceding chapter—people.xml, as our sample document in this chapter:

```
<?xml version="1.0"?>
<meetings>
    <meeting type="informal">
        <meeting_title>XML In The Real World</meeting_title>
        <meeting_number>2079</meeting_number>
        <subject>XML</subject>
        <date>6/1/2009</date>
        <people>
            <person attendence="present">
                <first_name>Cary</first_name>
                <last_name>Grant</last_name>
            </person>
```

```
        <person attendence="absent">
            <first_name>Myrna</first_name>
            <last_name>Loy</last_name>
        </person>
        <person attendence="present">
            <first_name>Jimmy</first_name>
            <last_name>Stewart</last_name>
        </person>
    </people>
  </meeting>
</meetings>
```

How shall we get started? Let's begin simply, by seeing if we can't just use the getElementsByTagName method to determine how many <person> elements are in person.xml.

We'll call this example program people.java, and it'll show to load an XML document into a Java program and start working with it. You start people.java with a public Java class; the name of this public class (there can be only one public class per Java file) must match the name of the Java file, so we'll call this class people:

```
public class people
{
      .
      .
      .

}
```

The "entry point" in Java programs—that is, the code that is called when the program starts—goes into the main method:

```
public class people
{
    public static void main(String[] args)
    {
          .
          .
          .

    }
}
```

We're going to be writing some sensitive code in our program, including creating various objects that can't be created if Java can't *parse* (that is, read and break into its component nodes) our XML document correctly, and Java is going to insist that we catch run-time errors—that is, exceptions—in our code (Java won't let us compile and run our code if we don't). To do that, and handle run-time errors—we surround our code in a try block:

```
public class people
{
    public static void main(String[] args)
    {
```

```
        try {
            .
            .
            .
        }
    }
}
```

A try block has a corresponding catch block to handle the actual run-time error, and here's our catch block, which follows the try block:

```
public class people
{
    public static void main(String[] args)
    {

        try {
            .
            .
            .
        } catch (Exception e) {
            .
            .
            .
        }
    }
}
```

Control is given to the catch block if there was a serious run-time error, and in the catch block, we'll just dump the error to the screen with some generic Java exception-handling code:

```
public class people
{
    public static void main(String[] args)
    {

        try {
            .
            .
            .
        } catch (Exception e) {
            e.printStackTrace(System.err);
        }
    }
}
```

Now we'll start making use of the built-in support for XML handling in Java, and that means using some packages (prebuilt code) that come with Java. That code is included with Java, but not available by default (Java does it that way to avoid burdening programs with prebuilt code you don't need), so we have to use the Java import statement, as you do in nearly all Java programs, to import the packages we want. To work with the Java support for the XML DOM, you import these packages:

```
import javax.xml.parsers.*;
import org.w3c.dom.*;

public class people
{
    public static void main(String[] args)
    {

        try {
            .
            .
            .
        } catch (Exception e) {
            e.printStackTrace(System.err);
        }
    }
}
```

Okay, so how do you read an XML document into a Java program? You read in XML documents with the parse method of a DocumentBuilder object. Alright, so we need to create a DocumentBuilder object first, right? Yep, that's right—and in order to create a DocumentBuilder object, you have to create a DocumentBuilder object *factory*.

Creating a Document Builder Factory

DocumentBuilder factories are objects that let you create DocumentBuilder objects (which, in turn, will read in and parse our XML document). Why this added level of abstraction—Java has a reputation of being needlessly complex and overly difficult to program—is it true?

Difficult or not, the reason you have to create Document Builder factories in order to create DocumentBuilder objects is that there are many different parsers available for XML in Java, and you might want to use your own parser rather than the built-in XML parser that comes with Java (for example, the parser you use to read in a specialized XML dialect might know how to use the height and width attribute you've added to XML elements to draw graphics figures). We're going to use the built-in parser that comes with Java here, so we just create a generic Document Builder factory with the DocumentBuilderFactory class's newInstance method:

```
import javax.xml.parsers.*;
import org.w3c.dom.*;

public class people
{
    public static void main(String[] args)
    {
```

```
        try {

            DocumentBuilderFactory dbf =
                DocumentBuilderFactory.newInstance();

                .

                .

                .

        } catch (Exception e) {
            e.printStackTrace(System.err);
        }
    }
}
```

The DocumentBuilderFactory class comes built into Java (it's in the javax.xml.parsers.* package) and has many built-in methods, as you can see in Table 11-1. (Table 11-1 uses standard Java terminology, listing the data type of data returned by each method in front of the method's name, and gives the data type of each argument you pass to the method in the same way.)

Method	Does This
protected DocumentBuilderFactory()	The default constructor.
abstract Object getAttribute(String *name*)	Returns specific attribute values.
boolean isCoalescing()	True if the factory is configured to produce parsers that convert CDATA nodes to Text nodes.
boolean isExpandEntityReferences()	True if the factory is configured to produce parsers that expand XML entity reference nodes.
boolean isIgnoringComments()	True if the factory will produce parsers that ignore comments.
boolean isIgnoringElementContentWhitespace()	True if the factory will produce parsers that ignore ignorable whitespace (such as that used to indent elements) in element content.
boolean isNamespaceAware()	True if the factory will produce parsers that can use XML namespaces.
boolean isValidating()	True if the factory will produce parsers that validate the XML content during parsing operations.
abstract DocumentBuilder newDocumentBuilder()	Creates a new DocumentBuilder object.

Table 11-1 Methods of the javax.xml.parsers.DocumentBuilderFactory Class

Method	Does This
static DocumentBuilderFactory newInstance()	Returns a new DocumentBuilderFactory object.
abstract void setAttribute(String *name*, Object *value*)	Sets specific attributes.
void setCoalescing(boolean *coalescing*)	Requires that the parser produced will convert CDATA nodes to Text nodes.
void setExpandEntityReferences(boolean *expandEntityRef*)	Requires that the parser produced will expand XML entity reference nodes.
void setIgnoringComments(boolean *ignoreComments*)	Requires that the parser produced will ignore comments.
void setIgnoringElementContentWhitespace(boolean *whitespace*)	Requires that the parsers created must eliminate ignorable whitespace.
void setNamespaceAware(boolean *awareness*)	Requires that the parser produced will provide support for XML namespaces.
void setValidating(boolean *validating*)	Requires that the parser produced will validate documents as they are parsed.

Table 11-1 Methods of the javax.xml.parsers.DocumentBuilderFactory Class *(continued)*

Swell, now we have a Document Builder factory. How do we create a DocumentBuilder object to read in our XML document?

Creating a Document Builder

DocumentBuilder objects let you read in and parse XML documents, and you create a DocumentBuilder object with the newDocumentBuilder method of a DocumentBuilderFactory object. We'll start by creating a variable, named db, to hold our DocumentBuilder object (we set it to null here so that if the Document Builder factory fails to build a DocumentBuilder object, db is left holding null and our program can't be confused into thinking there is a real object in the db variable):

```
import javax.xml.parsers.*;
import org.w3c.dom.*;

public class people
{
    public static void main(String[] args)
    {
```

```
        try {

            DocumentBuilderFactory dbf =
                DocumentBuilderFactory.newInstance();

            DocumentBuilder db = null;
                .
                .
                .

        } catch (Exception e) {
            e.printStackTrace(System.err);
        }
    }
}
```

Now we use our Document Builder factory's newDocumentBuilder method to create the new DocumentBuilder object—and enclose the creation process in a try block:

```
import javax.xml.parsers.*;
import org.w3c.dom.*;

public class people
{
    public static void main(String[] args)
    {

        try {

            DocumentBuilderFactory dbf =
                DocumentBuilderFactory.newInstance();

            DocumentBuilder db = null;
            try {
                db = dbf.newDocumentBuilder();
            }
                .
                .
                .

        } catch (Exception e) {
            e.printStackTrace(System.err);
        }
    }
}
```

If the DocumentBuilder creation process failed, Java causes a ParserConfigurationException exception. We won't do anything special with that exception here, but I'm breaking it out into its own try/catch block in case you want to display an error message specific to any custom parser you may be using. Here's what the catch block for this exception looks like in our code:

```java
import javax.xml.parsers.*;
import org.w3c.dom.*;

public class people
{
    public static void main(String[] args)
    {

        try {

            DocumentBuilderFactory dbf =
                DocumentBuilderFactory.newInstance();

            DocumentBuilder db = null;
            try {
                db = dbf.newDocumentBuilder();
            }
            catch (ParserConfigurationException pce) {}
            .
            .
            .
        } catch (Exception e) {
            e.printStackTrace(System.err);
        }
    }
}
```

Great—now we've created a DocumentBuilder object, and stored it in the variable db. The DocumentBuilder is what actually reads in and parses XML documents, and you can find the method of the DocumentBuilder class in Table 11-2 (including the parse method that we're about to use).

Method	Does This
protected DocumentBuilder()	The default constructor.
abstract DOMImplementation getDOMImplementation()	Returns a DOMImplementation object.
abstract boolean isNamespaceAware()	True if this parser is configured to understand namespaces.
abstract boolean isValidating()	True if this parser is configured to validate XML documents.
abstract Document newDocument()	Returns a new instance of a DOM Document object to build a DOM tree with.

Table 11-2 Methods of the javax.xml.parsers.DocumentBuilder Class

Method	Does This
Document parse(File f)	Parse the content of the file as an XML document and return a new DOM Document object.
abstract Document parse(InputSource *is*)	Parse the content of the specified source as an XML document and return a new DOM Document object.
Document parse(InputStream *is*)	Parse the content of the specified InputStream as an XML document and return a new DOM Document object.
Document parse(InputStream *is*, String *systemId*)	Parse the content of the specified InputStream as an XML document and return a new DOM Document object.
Document parse(String *uri*)	Parse the content of the specified URI as an XML document and return a new DOM Document object.
abstract void setEntityResolver(EntityResolver *er*)	Specify the EntityResolver object to be used to resolve entities.
abstract void setErrorHandler(ErrorHandler *eh*)	Specify the ErrorHandler to be used to report errors.

Table 11-2 Methods of the javax.xml.parsers.DocumentBuilder Class *(continued)*

Parsing an XML Document

You actually read in and parse an XML document using a DocumentBuilder object's parse method. That method returns a Document object that corresponds to the root node of the document, just as it did in JavaScript. We'll store our Document object in a variable named doc:

```
import javax.xml.parsers.*;
import org.w3c.dom.*;

public class people
{
    public static void main(String[] args)
    {

        try {

            DocumentBuilderFactory dbf =
                DocumentBuilderFactory.newInstance();
```

```
        DocumentBuilder db = null;
        try {
            db = dbf.newDocumentBuilder();
        }
        catch (ParserConfigurationException pce) {}

        Document doc = null;
            .
            .
            .
    } catch (Exception e) {
        e.printStackTrace(System.err);
    }
  }
}
```

How do we access the name of the XML document the user wants us to read? You can pass the name of the XML document, which is people.xml in this case, on the command line when you use Java to run the people.java program. That will look like this:

```
C:\>java people people.xml
```

In this case, the string "people.xml" will be passed to the people class's main method in an array we named args when we created the main method:

```
public class people
{
    public static void main(String[] args)
    {
        .
        .
        .
    }
}
```

Here, the name of the file the user wants to read will be accessible as the first element in the args array—that is, we can read it as args[0]. So here's how we read in and parse the XML document the user wants us to read:

```
import javax.xml.parsers.*;
import org.w3c.dom.*;

public class people
{
    public static void main(String[] args)
    {

        try {
```

```
        DocumentBuilderFactory dbf =
            DocumentBuilderFactory.newInstance();

        DocumentBuilder db = null;
        try {
            db = dbf.newDocumentBuilder();
        }
        catch (ParserConfigurationException pce) {}

        Document doc = null;
        doc = db.parse(args[0]);
            .

            .

            .
    } catch (Exception e) {
        e.printStackTrace(System.err);
    }
    }
}
```

Wow, now we've read in and parsed the XML document, and stored its data in the object we've named doc. In other words, the XML document's data is now available to the rest of our program. You can find the methods of the Document class in Table 11-3.

Method	Does this
Attr createAttribute(String *name*)	Creates an Attr object of the specified name.
Attr createAttributeNS(String *namespaceURI*, String *qualifiedName*)	Creates an attribute of the specified name and namespace.
CDATASection createCDATASection(String *data*)	Creates a CDATASection node whose value is the specified string.
Comment createComment(String *data*)	Creates a Comment node using the specified string.
DocumentFragment createDocumentFragment()	Creates an empty DocumentFragment object.
Element createElement(String *tagName*)	Creates an element of the type specified.
Element createElementNS(String *namespaceURI*, String *qualifiedName*)	Creates an element of the specified qualified name and namespace URI.
EntityReference createEntityReference(String *name*)	Creates an EntityReference object.
ProcessingInstruction createProcessingInstruction (String *target*, String *data*)	Creates a ProcessingInstruction node.
Text createTextNode(String *data*)	Creates a Text node specified by the specified string.

Table 11-3 Methods of org.w3c.dom.Document

Method	Does this
DocumentType getDoctype()	Returns the Document Type Declaration (DTD) for this document.
Element getDocumentElement()	Provides direct access to document element.
Element getElementById(String elementId)	Returns the Element whose ID is specified.
NodeList getElementsByTagName(String *tagname*)	Returns all the Elements with a specified tag name.
NodeList getElementsByTagNameNS(String *namespaceURI*, String *localName*)	Returns all the Elements with a specified name and namespace.
DOMImplementation getImplementation()	Gets the DOMImplementation object that handles this document.

Table 11-3   Methods of org.w3c.dom.Document *(continued)*

In this first example, we want to count the number of <person> elements in the XML document, and we can do that by seeing how many <person> elements are returned by the doc object's getElementsByTagName method, and that's coming up next.

Accessing XML Data That You've Read in

We want to use the getElementsByTagName method of the doc object (which corresponds to the root node of our document) to see how many <person> elements there are in the XML document. You can get a node list of all <person> elements in the XML document by calling getElementsByTagName like this:

```java
import javax.xml.parsers.*;
import org.w3c.dom.*;

public class people
{
    public static void main(String[] args)
    {

        try {

            DocumentBuilderFactory dbf =
                DocumentBuilderFactory.newInstance();

            DocumentBuilder db = null;
            try {
                db = dbf.newDocumentBuilder();
            }
            catch (ParserConfigurationException pce) {}
```

```
        Document doc = null;
        doc = db.parse(args[0]);

        NodeList nodelist = doc.getElementsByTagName("person");
        .

        .

        .
    } catch (Exception e) {
        e.printStackTrace(System.err);
    }
  }
}
```

Now we have a node list of all the <person> nodes in people.xml. The methods of NodeList appear in Table 11-4.

Note in particular the getLength method you see in Table 11-4. That method returns the number of nodes in the node list, and it's just what we need to determine the number of <person> elements in our node list. We can display that number with the System.out.println method:

```
import javax.xml.parsers.*;
import org.w3c.dom.*;

public class people
{
    public static void main(String[] args)
    {

        try {

            DocumentBuilderFactory dbf =
                DocumentBuilderFactory.newInstance();

            DocumentBuilder db = null;
            try {
                db = dbf.newDocumentBuilder();
            }
            catch (ParserConfigurationException pce) {}
```

Method	Summary
int getLength()	Gets the number of nodes in this list.
Node item(int index)	Gets the item at index *index* in the collection.

Table 11-4   NodeList Methods

```
        Document doc = null;
        doc = db.parse(args[0]);

        NodeList nodelist = doc.getElementsByTagName("person");
        System.out.println(args[0] + " has " +
            nodelist.getLength() + " <person> elements.");

    } catch (Exception e) {
        e.printStackTrace(System.err);
    }
  }
}
```

Great—that completes people.java. To run it, we have to compile it into a Java .class file with the Java compiler, javac. For example, in Windows, if javac is in your computer's path, and people.java is stored in a directory named c:\ch11, you can compile people.java by first opening a DOS window (by selecting Start | All Programs | Accessories | Command Prompt) and then moving to the directory that contains people.java:

```
C:\>cd \ch11
C:\ch11>
```

Then you can use javac to compile people.java, creating people.class:

```
C:\ch11>javac people.java
```

If the Java compiler is not in your path, you can give the full path to javac.exe in this command. For example, if you installed Java SE 6 to c:\java6, then javac.exe is in the c:\java6\ bin directory, so you can use this command to compile people.java:

```
C:\ch11>c:\java6\bin\javac people.java
```

Now you can run the newly created people.class with the java program (the first "people" here refers to people.class):

```
C:\ch11>java people people.xml
```

Or if the java program isn't in your path, you can do this:

```
C:\ch11>c:\java6\bin\java people people.xml
```

What happens? If everything is working correctly, the program should display the number of <person> elements your XML document has:

```
C:\xmlabg\cd\ch11>c:\java6\bin\java people people.xml
people.xml has 3 <person> elements.
```

Cool.

Try This   Counting XML Elements

Start with your own version of people.xml that you created in the preceding chapter:

```xml
<?xml version="1.0"?>
<meetings>
    <meeting type="informal">
        <meeting_title>XML In The Real World</meeting_title>
        <meeting_number>2079</meeting_number>
        <subject>XML</subject>
        <date>6/1/2009</date>
        <people>
            <person attendence="present">
                <first_name>Dan</first_name>
                <last_name>Peterson</last_name>
            </person>
            <person attendence="absent">
                <first_name>Frank</first_name>
                <last_name>Burns</last_name>
            </person>
            <person attendence="present">
                <first_name>Ben</first_name>
                <last_name>Cartwright</last_name>
            </person>
        </people>
    </meeting>
</meetings>
```

Try modifying people.java to count the number of <first_name> elements in your version of people.xml.

Okay, now we've seen how to load an XML document into Java code and how to use methods like getElementsByTagName to work with that data. What's the next step?

Next, we'll take a look at a program that shows how to read and extract *all* the data in peoplc.xml. Seeing how this example works will show us how to work with all the data in an XML document in Java.

This new Java example, parser.java, reads people.xml into a Document object and then shows how to extract all the elements, text, and attributes in that object, displaying the whole people.xml document to confirm that it's been able to read it in and handle all its data. Here's what parser.java looks like when you run it and parse people.xml—it reads in people.xml and deciphers it; then it prints it out on the screen like this:

```
C:\xmlabg\cd\ch11>c:\java6\bin\java parser people.xml
<?xml version="1.0" encoding="UTF-8"?>
```

```
<meetings>
    <meeting type="informal">
        <meeting_title>
            XML In The Real World
        </meeting_title>
        <meeting_number>
            2079
        </meeting_number>
        <subject>
            XML
        </subject>
        <date>
            6/1/2009
        </date>
        <people>
            <person attendence="present">
                <first_name>
                    Cary
                </first_name>
                <last_name>
                    Grant
                </last_name>
            </person>
            <person attendence="absent">
                <first_name>
                    Myrna
                </first_name>
                <last_name>
                    Loy
                </last_name>
            </person>
            <person attendence="present">
                <first_name>
                    Jimmy
                </first_name>
                <last_name>
                    Stewart
                </last_name>
            </person>
        </people>
    </meeting>
</meetings>
```

Okay, that's the goal—to read in XML documents and to show how to handle all the data in them, reading and displaying that data. Let's start digging into the code.

Extracting All the Data in an XML Document Yourself

Let's create parser.java. This is a substantial program, so get ready. The public class here will be named parser, and that class will start by running the code in a method named main:

```
import javax.xml.parsers.*;
import org.w3c.dom.*;

public class parser
{
    public static void main(String args[])
    {
        .
        .
        .
    }
}
```

The main method will call another method named parseDocument to actually parse the document, passing that method the name of the document the user wants to parse as args[0]:

```
import javax.xml.parsers.*;
import org.w3c.dom.*;

public class parser
{
    public static void main(String args[])
    {
        parseDocument(args[0]);
        .
        .
        .
    }
}
```

The parseDocument method will decode the XML document line by line, storing each line in an array named displayText (I'm using a simple array rather than any of the more esoteric Java data structures here so that parser.java will work under all Java versions that support XML parsing—Java 1.4, 1.5, and 6), and it will store the total number of lines in the document in a variable named numberOfLines:

```
import javax.xml.parsers.*;
import org.w3c.dom.*;

public class parser
{
    static String displayText[] = new String[1000];
    static int numberOfLines = 0;
```

```
public static void main(String args[])
{
    parseDocument(args[0]);
      .
      .
      .

}
}
```

The main method will loop over the displayText array, displaying each line on the screen like this:

```
import javax.xml.parsers.*;
import org.w3c.dom.*;

public class parser
{
    static String displayText[] = new String[1000];
    static int numberOfLines = 0;

    public static void main(String args[])
    {
        parseDocument(args[0]);

        for(int loopIndex = 0; loopIndex < numberOfLines;
          loopIndex++){
            System.out.println(displayText[loopIndex]);
        }
    }
}
```

Okay, that sets things up. The real meat of the program is all about extracting all the data from the XML document—that's the point of this program, to show how to extract all the data from an XML document—and to store that document, line by line, in the displayText array. To get started, we parse the XML document the user is requesting us to parse in the parseDocument method, and store that document in a Document object just named document by creating DocumentBuilderFactory and DocumentBuilder objects as before:

```
import javax.xml.parsers.*;
import org.w3c.dom.*;

public class parser
{
    static String displayText[] = new String[1000];
    static int numberOfLines = 0;

    public static void parseDocument(String uri)
    {
        try {
```

```
            DocumentBuilderFactory dbf =
                DocumentBuilderFactory.newInstance();

            DocumentBuilder db = null;
            try {
                db = dbf.newDocumentBuilder();
            }
            catch (ParserConfigurationException pce) {}

            Document document = null;
            document = db.parse(uri);
                .
                .
                .
        } catch (Exception e) {
            e.printStackTrace(System.err);
        }

    }
        .
        .
        .
    public static void main(String args[])
    {
        parseDocument(args[0]);

        for(int loopIndex = 0; loopIndex < numberOfLines;
          loopIndex++){
            System.out.println(displayText[loopIndex]);
        }
    }
}
```

Here's the clever part: Since we don't know what the structure of the document looks like before we start working on it, we'll create a new method to "walk" up and down each branch of the document's tree of nodes. Starting with the root node, we'll loop over all child nodes—and if those child nodes have child nodes themselves, we'll loop over those, and so on down. This walking over child nodes will be done by a method named walkNodes, and we just pass it the root node (held in the object we've named document) to get started. We'll also indent the output document, so we'll pass an indentation to walkNodes so that each successive level of the document can be indented appropriately. Because this is the root node, there is no indentation, so we pass an indentation string of just "" (the empty string):

```
import javax.xml.parsers.*;
import org.w3c.dom.*;

public class parser
{
```

```
    static String displayText[] = new String[1000];
    static int numberOfLines = 0;

    public static void parseDocument(String uri)
    {
        try {

            DocumentBuilderFactory dbf =
                DocumentBuilderFactory.newInstance();

            DocumentBuilder db = null;
            try {
                db = dbf.newDocumentBuilder();
            }
            catch (ParserConfigurationException pce) {}

            Document document = null;
            document = db.parse(uri);

            walkNodes(document, "");

        } catch (Exception e) {
            e.printStackTrace(System.err);
        }

    }
        .
        .
        .
    public static void main(String args[])
    {
        parseDocument(args[0]);

        for(int loopIndex = 0; loopIndex < numberOfLines;
          loopIndex++){
            System.out.println(displayText[loopIndex]);
        }
    }
}
```

Now let's write the walkNodes method, which you pass a node to walk (that is, to loop over the child nodes, recording them in the displayText array) and the current level of indentation:

```
import javax.xml.parsers.*;
import org.w3c.dom.*;

public class parser
{
    static String displayText[] = new String[1000];
    static int numberOfLines = 0;
```

```
public static void parseDocument(String uri)
{
    try {

        DocumentBuilderFactory dbf =
            DocumentBuilderFactory.newInstance();

        DocumentBuilder db = null;
        try {
            db = dbf.newDocumentBuilder();
        }
        catch (ParserConfigurationException pce) {}

        Document document = null;
        document = db.parse(uri);

        walkNodes(document, "");

    } catch (Exception e) {
        e.printStackTrace(System.err);
    }

}

public static void walkNodes(Node node, String indent)
{
    .
    .
    .
}

public static void main(String args[])
{
    parseDocument(args[0]);

    for(int loopIndex = 0; loopIndex < numberOfLines;
      loopIndex++){
        System.out.println(displayText[loopIndex]);
    }
}
}
```

Walking over XMLNodes

In the walkNodes method, we'll start by checking if the node passed to us to walk is not really a node—if it's null, we just return without storing it in the displayText array:

```
public static void walkNodes(Node node, String indent)
{
    if (node == null) {
        return;
    }
    .
    .
    .
}
```

Okay, so far, so good. Now we'll have to handle all different types of nodes in the XML document—element nodes, text nodes, and so on. What kind of node are we dealing with? You can determine the node's type with its getNodeType method like this:

```
public static void walkNodes(Node node, String indent)
{
    if (node == null) {
        return;
    }

    int type = node.getNodeType();
    .
    .
    .
}
```

What possible values can the node type be? These are the possible values, as defined by these constants in Java:

- Node.ATTRIBUTE_NODE
- Node.CDATA_SECTION_NODE
- Node.COMMENT_NODE
- Node.DOCUMENT_FRAGMENT_NODE
- Node.DOCUMENT_NODE
- Node.DOCUMENT_TYPE_NODE
- Node.ELEMENT_NODE
- Node.ENTITY_NODE
- Node.ENTITY_REFERENCE_NODE
- Node.NOTATION_NODE
- Node.PROCESSING_INSTRUCTION_NODE
- Node.TEXT_NODE

In the remainder of the walkNodes method, we'll check what type of node we're dealing with—element node, text node, CDATA node, and so on—and handle each appropriately. We'll do that with a Java switch statement that will have one contained case statement for every type of node:

```
public static void walkNodes(Node node, String indent)
{
    if (node == null) {
        return;
    }

    int type = node.getNodeType();

    switch (type) {
        .
        .
        .
    }
}
```

We'll start by handling the root node itself.

Handling the Root Node

The root node corresponds to node type Node.DOCUMENT_NODE, and when we get that node, we know we're at the very beginning of the document. In that case, we'll just place a representative XML declaration into the output text. Here's how it works—we start by creating a case statement to handle document nodes:

```
public static void walkNodes(Node node, String indent)
{
    if (node == null) {
        return;
    }

    int type = node.getNodeType();

    switch (type) {
        case Node.DOCUMENT_NODE: {
            .
            .
            .
        }
        .
        .
        .
    }
}
```

And start by placing the current indentation into the output text (that is, the current element of the displayText array):

```java
public static void walkNodes(Node node, String indent)
{
    if (node == null) {
        return;
    }

    int type = node.getNodeType();

    switch (type) {
        case Node.DOCUMENT_NODE: {
            displayText[numberOfLines] = indent;
                .
                .
                .
        }
            .
            .
            .
    }
}
```

Next, we'll store the representative XML declaration and increment the number of lines of the document we've stored by one:

```java
public static void walkNodes(Node node, String indent)
{
    if (node == null) {
        return;
    }

    int type = node.getNodeType();

    switch (type) {
        case Node.DOCUMENT_NODE: {
            displayText[numberOfLines] = indent;
            displayText[numberOfLines] +=
              "<?xml version=\"1.0\" encoding=\""+
              "UTF-8" + "\"?>";
            numberOfLines++;
                .
                .
                .
        }
            .
            .
            .
    }
}
```

That's fine—now we have to skip on to the next node to handle, and that's the document element, which we can get with the root node's getDocumentElement method. We want to walk through the child nodes of the document element, so we call walkNodes again, this time passing it the document element:

```
public static void walkNodes(Node node, String indent)
{
    if (node == null) {
        return;
    }

    int type = node.getNodeType();

    switch (type) {
        case Node.DOCUMENT_NODE: {
            displayText[numberOfLines] = indent;
            displayText[numberOfLines] +=
                "<?xml version=\"1.0\" encoding=\""+
                "UTF-8" + "\"?>";
            numberOfLines++;
            walkNodes(((Document)node).getDocumentElement(), "");
            break;
        }
        .
        .
        .
    }
}
```

Calling the same method that you're currently inside is called *recursion,* and it's perfectly legal in Java. So now we have to start working with element nodes, and that's coming up next.

Handling the Opening Tag of Element Nodes

If we've come across an element node, we want to begin by placing the current indentation and the element's opening tag into the output text. You can find the name of the current element with the element node's getNodeName method like this—note that we're adding the < and > markup manually:

```
public static void walkNodes(Node node, String indent)
{
    if (node == null) {
        return;
    }

    int type = node.getNodeType();
```

```
    switch (type) {
        .
        .
        .

        case Node.ELEMENT_NODE: {
            displayText[numberOfLines] = indent;
            displayText[numberOfLines] += "<";
            displayText[numberOfLines] +=
                node.getNodeName();
            displayText[numberOfLines] += ">";

            numberOfLines++;
            .
            .
            .

        }
    }
}
```

Okay—but what if the element contained child nodes, such as other element nodes or text nodes? We want to loop over them too, passing them to the walkNodes method. And because they're child nodes of the current node, we'll increase the indentation by four spaces. You can get a node list of the current node's child nodes with the getChildNodes method, and you can loop over all those child nodes, passing them to walkNodes like this:

```
public static void walkNodes(Node node, String indent)
{
    if (node == null) {
        return;
    }

    int type = node.getNodeType();

    switch (type) {
        .
        .
        .

        case Node.ELEMENT_NODE: {
            displayText[numberOfLines] = indent;
            displayText[numberOfLines] += "<";
            displayText[numberOfLines] +=
                node.getNodeName();
            displayText[numberOfLines] += ">";

            numberOfLines++;

            NodeList childNodes = node.getChildNodes();
            if (childNodes != null) {
```

```
                length = childNodes.getLength();
                indent += "    ";
                for (int loopIndex = 0; loopIndex < length;
                    loopIndex++ ) {
                        walkNodes(childNodes.item(loopIndex), indent);
                }
            }
            break;
        }
    }
}
```

Great—we've handled the opening tags of element nodes. Or have we? What if the element has attributes? Those should be displayed in the opening tag as well.

Handling Attribute Nodes

Let's add some code now to handle an element's attributes, if it has any. You can get an element's attributes with an element node's getAttributes method, which returns a node list of attribute nodes (their type is Attr in Java). Here's how we get all the attributes an element has, store them in an array, and add them to the element's opening tag:

```
public static void walkNodes(Node node, String indent)
{
    if (node == null) {
        return;
    }

    int type = node.getNodeType();

    switch (type) {
        .
        .
        .
        case Node.ELEMENT_NODE: {
            displayText[numberOfLines] = indent;
            displayText[numberOfLines] += "<";
            displayText[numberOfLines] +=
                node.getNodeName();

            int length = (node.getAttributes() != null) ?
                node.getAttributes().getLength() : 0;
            Attr attributes[] = new Attr[length];
            for (int loopIndex = 0; loopIndex < length;
                loopIndex++) {
                    attributes[loopIndex] =
                        (Attr)node.getAttributes().item(loopIndex);
            }
```

```
              for (int loopIndex = 0; loopIndex <
                attributes.length; loopIndex++) {
                  Attr attribute = attributes[loopIndex];
                  displayText[numberOfLines] += " ";
                  displayText[numberOfLines] +=
                    attribute.getNodeName();
                  displayText[numberOfLines] += "=\"";
                  displayText[numberOfLines] +=
                    attribute.getNodeValue();
                  displayText[numberOfLines] += "\"";
              }
              displayText[numberOfLines] += ">";

              numberOfLines++;

              NodeList childNodes = node.getChildNodes();
              if (childNodes != null) {
                  length = childNodes.getLength();
                  indent += "     ";
                  for (int loopIndex = 0; loopIndex < length;
                    loopIndex++ ) {
                      walkNodes(childNodes.item(loopIndex), indent);
                  }
              }
              break;
          }
      }
}
```

And that, finally, handles the parsing of element node's opening tags.

Handling CDATA Nodes

What if the node we're asked to handle is a CDATA section? How can we handle that? It turns out that we can get the contents of the CDATA section with the getNodeValue method, and adding the <![CDATA[and]]> markup, we can add the CDATA section to the output text like this:

```
public static void walkNodes(Node node, String indent)
{
    if (node == null) {
        return;
    }

    int type = node.getNodeType();

    switch (type) {
        .
        .
        .
```

```
        case Node.CDATA_SECTION_NODE: {
            displayText[numberOfLines] = indent;
            displayText[numberOfLines] += "<![CDATA[";
            displayText[numberOfLines] +=
                node.getNodeValue();
            displayText[numberOfLines] += "]]>";
            numberOfLines++;
            break;
        }
    }
}
}
```

Handling Text Nodes

Sometimes the contents of elements is text, and in that case, the node we'll be handling is of type Node.TEXT_NODE. This type of node is easy to handle—you just get the actual text with the getNodeValue method and store it in the output text like this (note that we also test for "newline" characters, which are denoted "\n" in Java, to avoid text nodes that are used only to indent the original document):

```
public static void walkNodes(Node node, String indent)
{
    if (node == null) {
        return;
    }

    int type = node.getNodeType();

    switch (type) {
        .
        .
        .

        case Node.TEXT_NODE: {
            displayText[numberOfLines] = indent;
            String newText = node.getNodeValue().trim();
            if(newText.indexOf("\n") < 0 && newText.length() > 0)
            {
                displayText[numberOfLines] += newText;
                numberOfLines++;
            }
            break;
        }
    }
}
}
```

Handling Processing Instruction Nodes

If the node you're dealing with is a processing instruction, you can get the processing instruction name with the getNodeName method and the processing instruction's data with the getNodeValue method. So you can handle processing instructions like this in our code:

```
public static void walkNodes(Node node, String indent)
{
    if (node == null) {
        return;
    }

    int type = node.getNodeType();

    switch (type) {
        .
        .
        .

        case Node.PROCESSING_INSTRUCTION_NODE: {
            displayText[numberOfLines] = indent;
            displayText[numberOfLines] += "<?";
            displayText[numberOfLines] +=
                node.getNodeName();
            String text = node.getNodeValue();
            if (text != null && text.length() > 0) {
                displayText[numberOfLines] += text;
            }
            displayText[numberOfLines] += "?>";
            numberOfLines++;
            break;
        }
    }
}
```

Great—we're almost done. We've handled the opening tag of elements, attributes, CDATA sections, text, and processing instructions. All that's left in our example is handling the closing tag of elements.

Handling the Closing Tag of Element Nodes

How do you handle the closing tag of elements, which will appear on a different line from the opening tag—and possibly be separated from the opening tag by child elements and/or text content? We can add an if statement after our switch statement to handle the closing tag of elements, where we test if the node is of the element type. If it is, we need to supply a closing tag, and we can get the element's name with the getNodeName method, reduce the indentation by four spaces, and store the closing tags in the output text like this:

```
public static void walkNodes(Node node, String indent)
{
    if (node == null) {
```

```
            return;
        }

        int type = node.getNodeType();

        switch (type) {
        .
        .
        .
        }

        if (type == Node.ELEMENT_NODE) {
            displayText[numberOfLines] = indent.substring(0,
              indent.length() - 4);
            displayText[numberOfLines] += "</";
            displayText[numberOfLines] += node.getNodeName();
            displayText[numberOfLines] += ">";
            numberOfLines++;
            indent += "    ";
        }
    }
```

And that's it—that completes parser.java. Here's the whole program for reference:

```
import javax.xml.parsers.*;
import org.w3c.dom.*;

public class parser
{
    static String displayText[] = new String[1000];
    static int numberOfLines = 0;

    public static void parseDocument(String uri)
    {
        try {

            DocumentBuilderFactory dbf =
                DocumentBuilderFactory.newInstance();

            DocumentBuilder db = null;
            try {
                db = dbf.newDocumentBuilder();
            }
            catch (ParserConfigurationException pce) {}

            Document document = null;
            document = db.parse(uri);

            walkNodes(document, "");
```

```java
    } catch (Exception e) {
        e.printStackTrace(System.err);
    }

}

public static void walkNodes(Node node, String indent)
{
    if (node == null) {
        return;
    }

    int type = node.getNodeType();

    switch (type) {
        case Node.DOCUMENT_NODE: {
            displayText[numberOfLines] = indent;
            displayText[numberOfLines] +=
            "<?xml version=\"1.0\" encoding=\""+
            "UTF-8" + "\"?>";
            numberOfLines++;
            walkNodes(((Document)node).getDocumentElement(), "");
            break;
        }

        case Node.ELEMENT_NODE: {
            displayText[numberOfLines] = indent;
            displayText[numberOfLines] += "<";
            displayText[numberOfLines] +=
              node.getNodeName();

            int length = (node.getAttributes() != null) ?
              node.getAttributes().getLength() : 0;
            Attr attributes[] = new Attr[length];
            for (int loopIndex = 0; loopIndex < length;
              loopIndex++) {
                attributes[loopIndex] =
                  (Attr)node.getAttributes().item(loopIndex);
            }

            for (int loopIndex = 0; loopIndex <
              attributes.length; loopIndex++) {
                Attr attribute = attributes[loopIndex];
                displayText[numberOfLines] += " ";
                displayText[numberOfLines] +=
                  attribute.getNodeName();
                displayText[numberOfLines] += "=\"";
                displayText[numberOfLines] +=
                  attribute.getNodeValue();
                displayText[numberOfLines] += "\"";
```

```java
        }
        displayText[numberOfLines] += ">";

        numberOfLines++;

        NodeList childNodes = node.getChildNodes();
        if (childNodes != null) {
            length = childNodes.getLength();
            indent += "    ";
            for (int loopIndex = 0; loopIndex < length;
              loopIndex++ ) {
                walkNodes(childNodes.item(loopIndex), indent);
            }
        }
        break;
    }

    case Node.CDATA_SECTION_NODE: {
        displayText[numberOfLines] = indent;
        displayText[numberOfLines] += "<![CDATA[";
        displayText[numberOfLines] +=
          node.getNodeValue();
        displayText[numberOfLines] += "]]>";
        numberOfLines++;
        break;
    }

    case Node.TEXT_NODE: {
        displayText[numberOfLines] = indent;
        String newText = node.getNodeValue().trim();
        if(newText.indexOf("\n") < 0 && newText.length() > 0)
        {
            displayText[numberOfLines] += newText;
            numberOfLines++;
        }
        break;
    }

    case Node.PROCESSING_INSTRUCTION_NODE: {
        displayText[numberOfLines] = indent;
        displayText[numberOfLines] += "<?";
        displayText[numberOfLines] +=
          node.getNodeName();
        String text = node.getNodeValue();
        if (text != null && text.length() > 0) {
            displayText[numberOfLines] += text;
        }
        displayText[numberOfLines] += "?>";
```

```
                        numberOfLines++;
                        break;
                }
        }

        if (type == Node.ELEMENT_NODE) {
            displayText[numberOfLines] = indent.substring(0,
                indent.length() - 4);
            displayText[numberOfLines] += "</";
            displayText[numberOfLines] += node.getNodeName();
            displayText[numberOfLines] += ">";
            numberOfLines++;
            indent += "    ";
        }
    }

    public static void main(String args[])
    {
        parseDocument(args[0]);

        for(int loopIndex = 0; loopIndex < numberOfLines;
            loopIndex++){
                System.out.println(displayText[loopIndex]);
        }
    }
}
```

That gives us a good introduction to using the XML DOM in Java to navigate around XML documents and extract the data from them. There are other ways to parse XML documents in Java (such as the Simple API for XML—SAX—which is a lightweight, read-only, forward-reading-only parser), but the DOM parser is the big one. Not only can you move around in XML documents, you can also use DOM methods to edit the document and even add your own new elements.

Try This   Parsing XML Processing Instructions

Add an XML-processing instruction to your sample XML document:

```
<?xml version="1.0"?>
<?xml-stylesheet href="style.xsl" ?>
<meetings>
  <meeting type="informal">
      <meeting_title>XML In The Real World</meeting_title>
      <meeting_number>2079</meeting_number>
      <subject>XML</subject>
      <date>6/1/2009</date>
```

(continued)

```
        <people>
            <person attendence="present">
                <first_name>Dan</first_name>
                <last_name>Peterson</last_name>
            </person>
            <person attendence="absent">
                <first_name>Frank</first_name>
                <last_name>Burns</last_name>
            </person>
            <person attendence="present">
                <first_name>Ben</first_name>
                <last_name>Cartwright</last_name>
            </person>
        </people>
    </meeting>
</meetings>
```

And check if parser.java correctly displays that processing instruction.

Chapter 12

Ajax and XQuery

Key Skills & Concepts

- Introducing Ajax
- Creating XMLHttpRequest objects
- Fetching Text
- Fetching XML
- Working with XQuery

One of the most exciting topics when it comes to XML is Ajax—asynchronous JavaScript and XML. Using Ajax, browsers can download data from the server behind the scenes and pop that data into a Web page—without refreshing that Web page.

That's great, because it gives the Web page more of the feeling of a desktop application—there's no flickering on the screen as your whole Web page is refreshed. Ajax is one of the components of Web 2.0—making the Internet a seamless part of the computer experience.

Using Ajax, you can download data in either text or XML format—we'll start with text because it's easier and demonstrates how Ajax works. Also in this chapter, we're going to see how to work with XQuery—XML's way of working with data much as if you were connected to a database system.

Getting Started with Ajax

We're going to start with an Ajax example, ajax.html, that downloads a text document, data.txt, in the background, and displays the data in that document in a Web page when the user clicks a button—all without refreshing the Web page.

Let's see this at work, and then go through the code. Here's what ajax.html looks like:

```
<html>
  <head>
    <title>Ajax at Work</title>

    <script language = "javascript">
      var XMLHttpRequestObject = false;

      if (window.XMLHttpRequest) {
        XMLHttpRequestObject = new XMLHttpRequest();
      } else if (window.ActiveXObject) {
        XMLHttpRequestObject = new
          ActiveXObject("Microsoft.XMLHTTP");
      }
```

```
      function getData(dataSource, divID)
      {
        if(XMLHttpRequestObject) {
          var obj = document.getElementById(divID);
          XMLHttpRequestObject.open("GET", dataSource);

          XMLHttpRequestObject.onreadystatechange = function()
          {
            if (XMLHttpRequestObject.readyState == 4 &&
              XMLHttpRequestObject.status == 200) {
                obj.innerHTML = XMLHttpRequestObject.responseText;
            }
          }

          XMLHttpRequestObject.send(null);
        }
      }
    </script>
  </head>

  <body>

    <H1>Ajax at Work</H1>

    <form>
      <input type = "button" value = "Fetch the text"
        onclick = "getData('data.txt', 'targetDiv')">
    </form>

    <div id="targetDiv">
      <p>The fetched text will appear here.</p>
    </div>

  </body>
</html>
```

And here's the text data in data.txt:

```
Hello from Ajax!
```

When the user clicks a button in ajax.html, that Web page will download data.txt and display the "Hello from Ajax!" message. Note that in this example, both ajax.html and data.txt are stored in the same directory on a Web server. You can't just place these two files in a simple directory on your computer—ajax.html has to be server to your browser via a Web server, because ajax.html fetches the data using an XMLHttpRequest object, which needs to connect to a server.

You can see ajax.html in a browser in Figure 12-1.

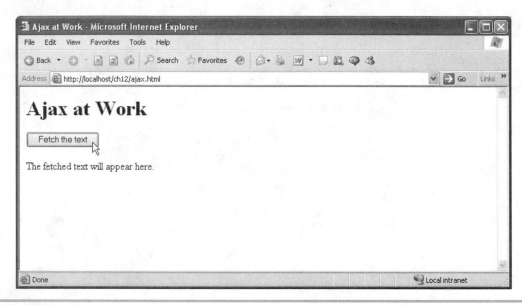

Figure 12-1   ajax.html

When the user clicks the button you see in Figure 12-1, the JavaScript code in the Web page makes the browser download data.txt behind the scenes. The JavaScript code then reads the data in data.txt and displays that data in the Web page, as you can see in Figurer 12-2—all without a single browser refresh.

Okay, let's get ajax.html working with text, and then see how to work with XML data.

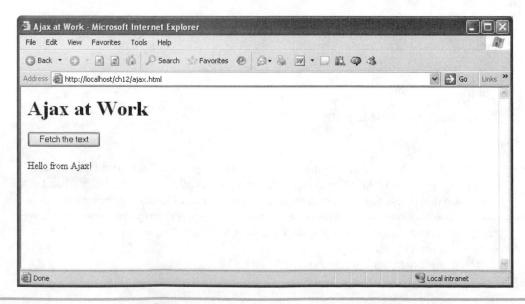

Figure 12-2   Fetching text from a server using Ajax

Understanding ajax.html

The ajax.html example starts with the button:

```html
<html>
  <head>
    <title>Ajax at Work</title>
            .
            .
            .
  </head>

  <body>

    <H1>Ajax at Work</H1>

    <form>
      <input type = "button" value = "Fetch the text"
        onclick = "getData('data.txt', 'targetDiv')">
    </form>

  </body>
</html>
```

When the user clicks the button, the browser calls a JavaScript function named getData with the parameters 'data.txt', which is the file it's supposed to download from the server, and 'targetDiv', which is the name of the HTML <div> element in which the data in data.txt is supposed to be displayed within the Web page:

```html
<html>
  <head>
    <title>Ajax at Work</title>
          .
          .
          .
  </head>

  <body>

    <H1>Ajax at Work</H1>

    <form>
      <input type = "button" value = "Fetch the text"
        onclick = "getData('data.txt', 'targetDiv')">
    </form>
```

```
<div id="targetDiv">
  <p>The fetched text will appear here.</p>
</div>

</body>
</html>
```

Let's get started with the JavaScript part of this page—the part that actually connects to the server to download text and will ultimately allow us to download XML. We add the getData function like this:

```
<html>
  <head>
    <title>Ajax at Work</title>

    <script language = "javascript">

      function getData(dataSource, divID)
      {
        .
        .
        .
      }
    </script>
  </head>

<body>

  <H1>Ajax at Work</H1>

  <form>
    <input type = "button" value = "Fetch the text"
      onclick = "getData('data.txt', 'targetDiv')">
  </form>

  <div id="targetDiv">
    <p>The fetched text will appear here.</p>
  </div>

</body>
</html>
```

In the getData function, we're going to use an XMLHttpRequest object—a built-in object accessible in browsers like Internet Explorer, Firefox, and Apple Safari—that you use to connect to the Web server behind the scenes and download data.

So how do you create an XMLHttpRequest object when you need one?

Creating an XMLHttpRequest Object

XMLHttpRequest objects are what makes Ajax possible. Using these objects, you can contact Web servers without causing a page refresh, and download (as well as upload) data. The ajax. html page actually creates this object when it first loads—before the getData function is called.

How's that work? We'll create a JavaScript variable named XMLHttpRequestObject to hold our XMLHttpRequest object:

```
<script language = "javascript">
  var XMLHttpRequestObject = false;
      .
      .
      .
  function getData(dataSource, divID)
  {
      .
      .
      .
  }
</script>
```

In browsers other than Internet Explorer, you can check if there's support for new XMLHttpRequest objects by checking if window.XMLHttpRequest exists, in which case you can create a new XMLHttpRequest object like this (this JavaScript code is outside any function, so it's run automatically when the page first loads):

```
<script language = "javascript">
  var XMLHttpRequestObject = false;

  if (window.XMLHttpRequest) {
    XMLHttpRequestObject = new XMLHttpRequest();
  }
      .
      .
      .
  function getData(dataSource, divID)
  {
      .
      .
      .
  }
</script>
```

On the other hand, if window.XMLHttpRequest doesn't exist, but window.ActiveXObject does, you're dealing with Internet Explorer, and you create an XMLHttpRequest object like this:

```
<script language = "javascript">
  var XMLHttpRequestObject = false;
```

```
if (window.XMLHttpRequest) {
  XMLHttpRequestObject = new XMLHttpRequest();
} else if (window.ActiveXObject) {
  XMLHttpRequestObject = new
    ActiveXObject("Microsoft.XMLHTTP");
}

function getData(dataSource, divID)
{
    .
    .
    .
}
</script>
```

With this added JavaScript code, the browser creates an XMLHttpRequest object when the page first loads—and that XMLHttpRequest object, stored in the variable named XMLHttpRequestObject, is ready to be used in the getData function when the user clicks the button and that function is called.

What are the properties and methods of XMLHttpRequest objects? That varies by browser. You can see the properties of the Internet Explorer XMLHttpRequest object in Table 12-1, and its methods in Table 12-2. The properties of this object for Mozilla, Netscape Navigator, and Firefox appear in Table 12-3, and the methods in Table 12-4. As yet, Apple hasn't published a full version of the properties and methods for its XMLHttpRequest object, but it has published a set of commonly used properties, which appear in Table 12-5, and commonly used methods, which appear in Table 12-6.

Event Handler	Does This
onreadystatechange	Contains the name of the event handler that should be called when the value of the readyState property changes. Read/write.
readyState	Contains the state of the request. Read-only.
responseBody	Contains a response body, which is one way HTTP responses can be returned. Read-only.
responseStream	Contains a response stream, a binary stream to the server. Read-only.
responseText	Contains the response body as a string. Read-only.
responseXML	Contains the response body as XML. Read-only.
status	Contains the HTTP status code returned by a request. Read-only.
statusText	Contains the HTTP response status text. Read-only.

Table 12-1 XMLHttpRequest Object Properties for Internet Explorer

Event Handler	Does This
abort	Aborts the HTTP request.
getAllResponseHeaders	Returns all the HTTP headers.
getResponseHeader	Returns the value of an HTTP header.
open	Opens a request to the server.
send	Sends an HTTP request to the server.
setRequestHeader	Sets the name and value of an HTTP header.

Table 12-2 XMLHttpRequest Object Methods for Internet Explorer

Event Handler	Does This
channel	Contains the channel used to perform the request. Read-only.
readyState	Contains state of the request. Read-only.
responseText	Contains the response body as a string. Read-only.
responseXML	Contains the response body as XML. Read-only.
status	Contains the HTTP status code returned by a request. Read-only.
statusText	Contains the HTTP response status text. Read-only.

Table 12-3 XMLHttpRequest Object Properties for Mozilla, Firefox, and Netscape Navigator

Event Handler	Does This
abort	Aborts the HTTP request.
getAllResponseHeaders	Returns all the HTTP headers.
getResponseHeader	Returns the value of an HTTP header.
openRequest	Native (nonscript) method to open a request.
overrideMimeType	Overrides the MIME type the server returns.

Table 12-4 XMLHttpRequest Object Methods for Mozilla, Firefox, and Netscape Navigator

Event Handler	Does This
onreadystatechange	Contains the name of the event handler that should be called when the value of the readyState property changes. Read/write.
readyState	Contains the state of the request. Read-only.
responseText	Contains the response body as a string. Read-only.
responseXML	Contains the response body as XML. Read-only.
status	Contains the HTTP status code returned by a request. Read-only.
statusText	Contains the HTTP response status text. Read-only.

Table 12-5 XMLHttpRequest Object Properties for Apple Safari

Event Handler	Does This
abort	Aborts the HTTP request.
getAllResponseHeaders	Returns all the HTTP headers.
getResponseHeader	Returns the value of an HTTP header.
open	Opens a request to the server.
send	Sends an HTTP request to the server.
setRequestHeader	Sets the name and value of an HTTP header.

Table 12-6 XMLHttpRequest Object Methods for Apple Safari

Okay, we've created our XMLHttpRequest object. Now what do we do with it?

Opening an XMLHttpRequest Object

To configure an XMLHttpRequest object, telling it what data to fetch, you use its open method (note: the open method does not open any connection to the Web server—that comes later). You open the XMLHttpRequest object when you're about to use that object in the getdata function (called when the user clicks the button to fetch the data from the server). First in the getData function, we check if we were successful in creating an XMLHttpRequest object:

```
<script language = "javascript">
  var XMLHttpRequestObject = false;

  if (window.XMLHttpRequest) {
    XMLHttpRequestObject = new XMLHttpRequest();
  } else if (window.ActiveXObject) {
    XMLHttpRequestObject = new
      ActiveXObject("Microsoft.XMLHTTP");
  }

  function getData(dataSource, divID)
  {
    if(XMLHttpRequestObject) {
      .
      .
      .
    }
  }
</script>
```

If we have been successful in creating an XMLHttpRequest object (when the page first loaded), we can now configure it using its open method to get data.txt, which is passed to the getData function as the dataSource parameter. We also indicate to the XMLHttpRequest object that we want to access the Web server using the GET HTTP method (as opposed to the POST HTTP method) like this:

```
<script language = "javascript">
  var XMLHttpRequestObject = false;

  if (window.XMLHttpRequest) {
    XMLHttpRequestObject = new XMLHttpRequest();
  } else if (window.ActiveXObject) {
    XMLHttpRequestObject = new
      ActiveXObject("Microsoft.XMLHTTP");
  }

  function getData(dataSource, divID)
  {
    if(XMLHttpRequestObject) {
      XMLHttpRequestObject.open("GET", dataSource);
      .
      .
      .
    }
  }
</script>
```

Okay, now when we connect to the server, the XMLHttpRequest object knows that it's supposed to fetch data.txt. So how do we actually connect to the server and download data.txt?

Connecting to the Server

You connect to the server *asynchronously* with Ajax. That means that the server answers back when it's ready—you don't wait for it. To implement that kind of connection, you set up a *callback* function that will be called when your data has been downloaded.

You connect the callback function to the XMLHttpRequest object using that object's onreadystatechange property—in particular, you can simply assign a JavaScript function to that property like this:

```
<script language = "javascript">
  var XMLHttpRequestObject = false;

  if (window.XMLHttpRequest) {
    XMLHttpRequestObject = new XMLHttpRequest();
  } else if (window.ActiveXObject) {
    XMLHttpRequestObject = new
      ActiveXObject("Microsoft.XMLHTTP");
  }
```

```
function getData(dataSource, divID)
{
  if(XMLHttpRequestObject) {
    XMLHttpRequestObject.open("GET", dataSource);

    XMLHttpRequestObject.onreadystatechange = function()
    {
      .
      .
      .
    }
  }
}
</script>
```

The code in this new function will be called when your data has been downloaded from the server. How do you know if the download was completed successfully? You start by checking the XMLHttpRequest object's readyState property.

Here are the possible values for this property—a value of 4 is what you want to see, because that means that the data has been fully downloaded:

- 0 uninitialized
- 1 loading
- 2 loaded
- 3 interactive
- 4 complete

Here's how we check if the download is complete:

```
<script language = "javascript">
  var XMLHttpRequestObject = false;

  if (window.XMLHttpRequest) {
    XMLHttpRequestObject = new XMLHttpRequest();
  } else if (window.ActiveXObject) {
    XMLHttpRequestObject = new
      ActiveXObject("Microsoft.XMLHTTP");
  }

  function getData(dataSource, divID)
  {
    if(XMLHttpRequestObject) {
      XMLHttpRequestObject.open("GET", dataSource);

      XMLHttpRequestObject.onreadystatechange = function()
```

```
    {
        if (XMLHttpRequestObject.readyState == 4 &&
            .
            .
            .
        }
    }

  }
}
</script>
```

In addition, you check that the download is in good shape by checking the XMLHttpRequest object's status property. This is the normal HTTP status code that you get when you try to download Web pages—for example, if the data you're looking for wasn't found, you'd get a value of 404 in the status property. Here are some of the possible values—note that you'll want to see a value of 200 here, which means that the download completed normally:

- 200 OK

- 201 Created

- 204 No Content

- 205 Reset Content

- 206 Partial Content

- 400 Bad Request

- 401 Unauthorized

- 403 Forbidden

- 404 Not Found

- 405 Method Not Allowed

- 406 Not Acceptable

- 407 Proxy Authentication Required

- 408 Request Timeout

- 411 Length Required

- 413 Requested Entity Too Large

- 414 Requested URL Too Long

- 415 Unsupported Media Type

- 500 Internal Server Error

- 501 Not Implemented

- 502 Bad Gateway

- 503 Service Unavailable

- 504 Gateway Timeout

- 505 HTTP Version Not Supported

Here's how we check the status property:

```
<script language = "javascript">
  var XMLHttpRequestObject = false;

  if (window.XMLHttpRequest) {
    XMLHttpRequestObject = new XMLHttpRequest();
  } else if (window.ActiveXObject) {
    XMLHttpRequestObject = new
      ActiveXObject("Microsoft.XMLHTTP");
  }

  function getData(dataSource, divID)
  {
    if(XMLHttpRequestObject) {
      XMLHttpRequestObject.open("GET", dataSource);

      XMLHttpRequestObject.onreadystatechange = function()
      {
        if (XMLHttpRequestObject.readyState == 4 &&
        XMLHttpRequestObject.status == 200) {
          .
          .
          .
        }
      }

    }
  }
</script>
```

Displaying the Download

Now that you've downloaded the data—and checked it twice—how do you access that data? We want to display that downloaded data in the target <div> element in the Web page, and the ID of that <div> element is passed to us in the getData function as the parameter divID, so we get a JavaScript object corresponding to that <div> element like this:

```
<script language = "javascript">
  var XMLHttpRequestObject = false;
```

```
  if (window.XMLHttpRequest) {
    XMLHttpRequestObject = new XMLHttpRequest();
  } else if (window.ActiveXObject) {
    XMLHttpRequestObject = new
      ActiveXObject("Microsoft.XMLHTTP");
  }

  function getData(dataSource, divID)
  {
    if(XMLHttpRequestObject) {
      var obj = document.getElementById(divID);
      XMLHttpRequestObject.open("GET", dataSource);

      XMLHttpRequestObject.onreadystatechange = function()
      {
        if (XMLHttpRequestObject.readyState == 4 &&
          XMLHttpRequestObject.status == 200) {
          .
          .
          .
        }
      }

    }
  }
</script>
```

Now we want to display the downloaded text in the <div> element, and we can access that text using the XMLHttpRequest object's responseText property—that's the property you read downloaded text from. Here's how we display the downloaded text:

```
<script language = "javascript">
  var XMLHttpRequestObject = false;

  if (window.XMLHttpRequest) {
    XMLHttpRequestObject = new XMLHttpRequest();
  } else if (window.ActiveXObject) {
    XMLHttpRequestObject = new
      ActiveXObject("Microsoft.XMLHTTP");
  }

  function getData(dataSource, divID)
  {
    if(XMLHttpRequestObject) {
      var obj = document.getElementById(divID);
      XMLHttpRequestObject.open("GET", dataSource);
```

```
XMLHttpRequestObject.onreadystatechange = function()
{
  if (XMLHttpRequestObject.readyState == 4 &&
    XMLHttpRequestObject.status == 200) {
      obj.innerHTML = XMLHttpRequestObject.responseText;
  }
}


  }
}
</script>
```

And there you have it—now ajax.html downloads and displays the data in data.txt. Very nice. On the other hand, there still is one crucial step left: we actually have to connect to the Web server and make the download happen.

Making the Download Happen

How do you actually connect to the server now that we've configured the XMLHttpRequest object to handle that download? You use the XMLHttpRequest object's send method to connect to the server and initiate the download. Since we're using the HTTP GET method for this download, you pass a value of null (meaning zero in this case) to the send method—if you were using the POST method, you could pass data to the server (or more correctly, code on the server) by passing that data to the send method. Here's how we make the download happen in our case:

```
<script language = "javascript">
  var XMLHttpRequestObject = false;

  if (window.XMLHttpRequest) {
    XMLHttpRequestObject = new XMLHttpRequest();
  } else if (window.ActiveXObject) {
    XMLHttpRequestObject = new
      ActiveXObject("Microsoft.XMLHTTP");
  }

  function getData(dataSource, divID)
  {
    if(XMLHttpRequestObject) {
      var obj = document.getElementById(divID);
      XMLHttpRequestObject.open("GET", dataSource);

      XMLHttpRequestObject.onreadystatechange = function()
      {
        if (XMLHttpRequestObject.readyState == 4 &&
          XMLHttpRequestObject.status == 200) {
            obj.innerHTML = XMLHttpRequestObject.responseText;
        }
      }
```

```
        XMLHttpRequestObject.send(null);
    }
  }
</script>
```

And that's it—now ajax.html is fully functional and works just as expected.

Try This Download Text Using Ajax

Get ajax.html working for yourself—but change the text in data.txt to this:

```
Ajax does it again!
```

Make sure you upload ajax.html and data.txt to the same directory on a Web server, and then make sure ajax.html fetches the contents of data.txt as it's supposed to.

However, the data in data.txt is simple text data—and Ajax stands for Asynchronous JavaScript and XML. Let's see if we can't start downloading some XML next.

Downloading Some XML

Let's say you had an XML document, flavors.xml, that listed primary ice cream flavors—strawberry, chocolate, and, of course, garbanzo. You could give flavors.xml a document element of <flavors>:

```
<?xml version = "1.0" ?>
<flavors>
    .
    .
    .
</flavors>
```

And then list each of the primary three flavors in <flavor> elements like this:

```
<?xml version = "1.0" ?>
<flavors>
  <flavor>strawberry</flavor>
  <flavor>chocolate</flavor>
  <flavor>garbanzo</flavor>
</flavors>
```

Okay, now how do you download flavors.xml and display the three flavors in an HTML page? This isn't simply text we're dealing with anymore—it's XML. How do you handle that? The process is similar to working with Ajax and text, but with a couple of other things to consider.

Our new example is going to be called ajaxxml.html, and it'll download and display the flavors in flavors.xml when the user clicks a button, as you can see in Figure 12-3.

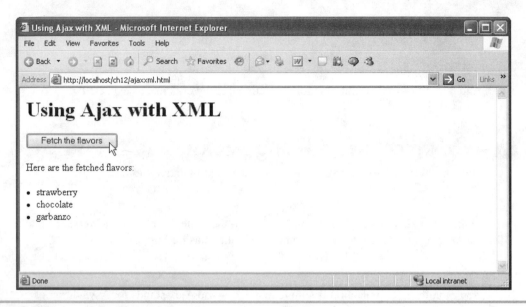

Figure 12-3 Fetching XML from a server using Ajax

Now let's build ajaxxml.html.

Writing ajaxxml.html

The HTML part of ajaxxml.html is easy enough—there's a button that the user can click to call the getData function, which is passed the name of the XML file to download—flavors. xml—and the ID of the <div> element to display the downloaded data in:

```
<html>
  <head>

    <title>Using Ajax with XML</title>
        .
        .
        .
  </head>

  <body>

    <h1>Using Ajax with XML</h1>

    <form>
      <input type = "button" value = "Fetch the flavors"
        onclick = "getData('flavors.xml', 'targetDiv')">
    </form>
```

```
<div id="targetDiv" width =100 height=100>
The list of flavors will appear here.</div>

</body>

</html>
```

The interesting part is in the getdata function, and that's coming up next.

Configuring XMLHttpRequest Objects to Handle XML

As with ajax.html, we start the JavaScript code by attempting to create an XMLHttpRequest object:

```
<script language = "javascript">

  var XMLHttpRequestObject = false;

  if (window.XMLHttpRequest) {
    XMLHttpRequestObject = new XMLHttpRequest();
  } else if (window.ActiveXObject) {
    XMLHttpRequestObject = new ActiveXObject("Microsoft.XMLHTTP");
  }

  function getData(dataSource, divID)
  {
    .
    .
    .
  }

</script>
```

In fact, there's one more step we need to take—if you're working with the Firefox brand of browsers, it's recommended that you also override the MIME type of the incoming data to make sure the browser knows it's XML, because under some circumstances, those browsers can default to plain text:

```
<script language = "javascript">

  var XMLHttpRequestObject = false;

  if (window.XMLHttpRequest) {
    XMLHttpRequestObject = new XMLHttpRequest();
    XMLHttpRequestObject.overrideMimeType("text/xml");
  } else if (window.ActiveXObject) {
    XMLHttpRequestObject = new ActiveXObject("Microsoft.XMLHTTP");
  }
```

```
function getData(dataSource, divID)
{
    .
    .
    .
}
```

```
</script>
```

Now we can configure the XMLHttpRequest object to download our file just as we did in ajax.html:

```
<script language = "javascript">

  var XMLHttpRequestObject = false;

  if (window.XMLHttpRequest) {
    XMLHttpRequestObject = new XMLHttpRequest();
    XMLHttpRequestObject.overrideMimeType("text/xml");
  } else if (window.ActiveXObject) {
    XMLHttpRequestObject = new ActiveXObject("Microsoft.XMLHTTP");
  }

  function getData(dataSource, divID)
  {
    if(XMLHttpRequestObject) {
      XMLHttpRequestObject.open("GET", dataSource);

      XMLHttpRequestObject.onreadystatechange = function()
      {
        if (XMLHttpRequestObject.readyState == 4 &&
          XMLHttpRequestObject.status == 200) {
          .
          .
          .
        }
      }
    }
  }

</script>
```

Great—at this point, we've downloaded the XML. How do we read it?

Recovering the Downloaded XML

When you're downloading text, you access that text with the XMLHttpRequest object's responseText property. When you're downloading XML, however, you use the responseXML property, which holds your downloaded XML in JavaScript document object form:

```
<script language = "javascript">

  var XMLHttpRequestObject = false;

  if (window.XMLHttpRequest) {
    XMLHttpRequestObject = new XMLHttpRequest();
    XMLHttpRequestObject.overrideMimeType("text/xml");
  } else if (window.ActiveXObject) {
    XMLHttpRequestObject = new ActiveXObject("Microsoft.XMLHTTP");
  }

  function getData(dataSource, divID)
  {
    if(XMLHttpRequestObject) {
      XMLHttpRequestObject.open("GET", dataSource);
      var obj = document.getElementById(divID);

      XMLHttpRequestObject.onreadystatechange = function()
      {
        if (XMLHttpRequestObject.readyState == 4 &&
          XMLHttpRequestObject.status == 200) {
          var xmlDocument = XMLHttpRequestObject.responseXML;
          .
          .
          .

        }
      }
    }
  }

</script>
```

Excellent, now you have a JavaScript document object that holds your XML. We
know how to handle such objects from Chapter 10—for example, you can get a node
list of all the <flavor> elements in the downloaded XML using the document object's
getElementsByTagName method:

```
<script language = "javascript">

  var XMLHttpRequestObject = false;

  if (window.XMLHttpRequest) {
    XMLHttpRequestObject = new XMLHttpRequest();
    XMLHttpRequestObject.overrideMimeType("text/xml");
  } else if (window.ActiveXObject) {
    XMLHttpRequestObject = new ActiveXObject("Microsoft.XMLHTTP");
  }

  function getData(dataSource, divID)
  {
    if(XMLHttpRequestObject) {
```

```
     XMLHttpRequestObject.open("GET", dataSource);
     var obj = document.getElementById(divID);

     XMLHttpRequestObject.onreadystatechange = function()
     {
       if (XMLHttpRequestObject.readyState == 4 &&
         XMLHttpRequestObject.status == 200) {
         var xmlDocument = XMLHttpRequestObject.responseXML;
         flavors = xmlDocument.getElementsByTagName("flavor");
         .
         .
         .
       }
     }

   }
 }

</script>
```

Now we have a node list of <flavor> elements—and we need to extract the actual text from each <flavor> element:

```
<?xml version = "1.0" ?>
<flavors>
  <flavor>strawberry</flavor>
  <flavor>chocolate</flavor>
  <flavor>garbanzo</flavor>
</flavors>
```

We can start by displaying the text "Here are the fetched flavors:", followed by an HTML unordered list (created with the <ul> element) to display a bulleted list of the flavors. We'll create that bulleted list by looping over the <flavor> elements this way:

```
<script language = "javascript">

  var XMLHttpRequestObject = false;

  if (window.XMLHttpRequest) {
    XMLHttpRequestObject = new XMLHttpRequest();
    XMLHttpRequestObject.overrideMimeType("text/xml");
  } else if (window.ActiveXObject) {
    XMLHttpRequestObject = new ActiveXObject("Microsoft.XMLHTTP");
  }

  function getData(dataSource, divID)
  {
    if(XMLHttpRequestObject) {
```

```
      XMLHttpRequestObject.open("GET", dataSource);
      var obj = document.getElementById(divID);

      XMLHttpRequestObject.onreadystatechange = function()
      {
        if (XMLHttpRequestObject.readyState == 4 &&
          XMLHttpRequestObject.status == 200) {
          var xmlDocument = XMLHttpRequestObject.responseXML;
          flavors = xmlDocument.getElementsByTagName("flavor");
          obj.innerHTML = "Here are the fetched flavors:<ul>";
          for (loopIndex =0; loopIndex < flavors.length;
            loopIndex++)
          {
            .
            .
            .
          }
          obj.innerHTML += "</ul>";
        }
      }


    }
  }

</script>
```

The text in each <flavor> element goes into a <li> (list item) element. That text is in a text node inside each <flavor> element, which is the first child of each <flavor> element, and you can reach the actual text in each text node with the text node's data property, so the code looks like this:

```
<script language = "javascript">

  var XMLHttpRequestObject = false;

  if (window.XMLHttpRequest) {
    XMLHttpRequestObject = new XMLHttpRequest();
    XMLHttpRequestObject.overrideMimeType("text/xml");
  } else if (window.ActiveXObject) {
    XMLHttpRequestObject = new ActiveXObject("Microsoft.XMLHTTP");
  }

  function getData(dataSource, divID)
  {
    if(XMLHttpRequestObject) {
      XMLHttpRequestObject.open("GET", dataSource);
      var obj = document.getElementById(divID);
```

```
    XMLHttpRequestObject.onreadystatechange = function()
    {
      if (XMLHttpRequestObject.readyState == 4 &&
        XMLHttpRequestObject.status == 200) {
        var xmlDocument = XMLHttpRequestObject.responseXML;
        flavors = xmlDocument.getElementsByTagName("flavor");
        obj.innerHTML = "Here are the fetched flavors:<ul>";
        for (loopIndex =0; loopIndex < flavors.length;
          loopIndex++)
        {
          obj.innerHTML += "<li>" +
            flavors[loopIndex].firstChild.data + "</li>";
        }
        obj.innerHTML += "</ul>";
      }
    }

    XMLHttpRequestObject.send(null);
  }
}

</script>
```

Note that we also used the XMLHttpRequest object's send method to send a value of null to the server, and so initiate the data downloading.

Whew. That shows how to download and display XML using Ajax. Note that in this example, we just downloaded a static XML file, but you can also connect to programs like PHP scripts on the server, and the data they send you may vary. For more details, take a look at a good book on Ajax, such as my *Ajax: A Beginner's Guide* (McGraw-Hill, 2008).

Here's the full listing of ajaxxml.html for reference:

```
<html>
  <head>

    <title>Using Ajax with XML</title>

    <script language = "javascript">

      var flavors;

      var XMLHttpRequestObject = false;

      if (window.XMLHttpRequest) {
        XMLHttpRequestObject = new XMLHttpRequest();
        XMLHttpRequestObject.overrideMimeType("text/xml");
      } else if (window.ActiveXObject) {
        XMLHttpRequestObject = new ActiveXObject("Microsoft.XMLHTTP");
      }
```

```
      function getData(dataSource, divID)
      {
        if(XMLHttpRequestObject) {
          XMLHttpRequestObject.open("GET", dataSource);
          var obj = document.getElementById(divID);

          XMLHttpRequestObject.onreadystatechange = function()
          {
            if (XMLHttpRequestObject.readyState == 4 &&
              XMLHttpRequestObject.status == 200) {
              var xmlDocument = XMLHttpRequestObject.responseXML;
              flavors - xmlDocument.getElementsByTagName("flavor");
              obj.innerHTML = "Here are the fetched flavors:<ul>";
              for (loopIndex =0; loopIndex < flavors.length;
                loopIndex++)
              {
                obj.innerHTML += "<li>" +
                  flavors[loopIndex].firstChild.data + "</li>";
              }
              obj.innerHTML += "</ul>";
            }
          }

          XMLHttpRequestObject.send(null);
        }
      }

    </script>
  </head>

<body>

  <h1>Using Ajax with XML</h1>

  <form>
    <input type = "button" value = "Fetch the flavors"
      onclick = "getData('flavors.xml', 'targetDiv')">
  </form>

  <div id="targetDiv" width =100 height=100>
  The list of flavors will appear here.</div>

</body>

</html>
```

Try This Download XML Using Ajax

Modify flavors.xml into friends.xml, something like this:

```
<?xml version = "1.0" ?>
<friends>
  <friend>Jeff</friend>
  <friend>Karen</friend>
  <friend>Sammy</friend>
</friends>
```

Next, modify ajaxxml.html to read and extract the names of your friends from friends.xml. Test your results out to make sure you've got it right.

Okay, that completes our look at Ajax. Next, we'll take a look at working with XML Query Language (XQuery).

Using XQuery

XML Query Language (XQuery) is an XML-based language that lets you interact with XML documents, databases—in fact, it's designed to interface with just about any data source. The idea is to let you avoid programming (such as with Java) by writing your own programming in XQuery. However, XQuery has been very slow to be adopted—perhaps because it doesn't seem to let you avoid any complexity. The W3C recommendation for XQuery is 227 pages alone, and you have to read it with another document, XQuery 1.0 and XPath 2.0 Functions and Operators, which itself is 183 pages long. That's a total of over 400 pages, and few amateurs seem willing to make the effort. For that reason, XQuery hasn't taken off like XSLT has, so we'll mostly get an overview of XQuery here, along with some examples, and refer the interested reader to the W3C documentation.

The official W3C recommendation for XQuery 1.0 is at www.w3.org/TR/xquery/, and the recommendation for XQuery 1.0 and XPath 2.0 Functions and Operators is at www.w3.org/TR/xpath-functions. You might want to take a look, but it takes some effort to get through those documents.

There are some public uses of XQuery available, such as "Liam's Pictures from Old Books" site, which is at www.fromoldbooks.org/. This site, which appears in Figure 12-4, lets you search old books for figures—and it uses XQuery to perform the search, as indicated in Figure 12-5.

Let's take a look at some XQuery examples.

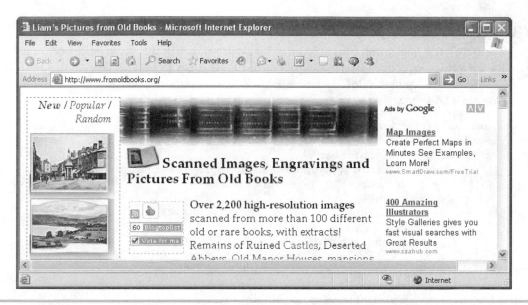

Figure 12-4   "Liam's Pictures from Old Books" site

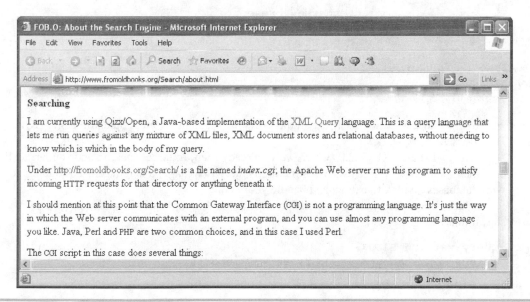

Figure 12-5   Searching for figures

Putting XQuery to Work

There are a few implementations of XQuery 1.0 available, such as the Saxon processor, available for www.saxonica.com/. Saxon comes packaged ready to use with Java (as Java .jar files).

We'll need a sample XML document to work on to demonstrate XQuery, so let's use our people.xml document:

```
<?xml version="1.0"?>
<meetings>
    <meeting type="informal">
        <meeting_title>XML In The Real World</meeting_title>
        <meeting_number>2079</meeting_number>
        <subject>XML</subject>
        <date>6/1/2009</date>
        <people>
            <person attendance="present">
                <first_name>Cary</first_name>
                <last_name>Grant</last_name>
            </person>
            <person attendance="absent">
                <first_name>Myrna</first_name>
                <last_name>Loy</last_name>
            </person>
            <person attendance="present">
                <first_name>Jimmy</first_name>
                <last_name>Stewart</last_name>
            </person>
        </people>
    </meeting>
</meetings>
```

Now say that we want to extract all the <person> elements from people.xml using XQuery. How does XQuery work?

XQuery 1.0 uses XPath 2.0 (which we've already seen) to target specific nodes in an XML document, and an SQL-like (SQL is Structured Query Language, a language used to interact with databases) syntax to extract and handle your data.

XQuery documents have the extension .xq, and this example will be called people.xq. We start it this way:

```
xquery version "1.0";
declare copy-namespaces no-preserve, inherit;
        .
        .
        .
```

Now we're going to loop over all <person> elements, which we can refer to using XPath as //meetings/meeting/people/person elements:

```
xquery version "1.0";
declare copy-namespaces no-preserve, inherit;

for $b in //meetings/meeting/people/person
        .
        .
        .
return
```

We can order the results alphabetically by peoples' first names like this:

```
xquery version "1.0";
declare copy-namespaces no-preserve, inherit;

for $b in //meetings/meeting/people/person
order by $b/first_name return
        .
        .
        .
```

Then we supply a template for the results to be displayed with:

```
xquery version "1.0";
declare copy-namespaces no-preserve, inherit;

for $b in //meetings/meeting/people/person
order by $b/first_name return
<person>
   { $b/first_name }
   { $b/last_name }
</person>
```

Okay, that's what people.xq looks like. You can use the Saxon Java class net.sf.saxon.
Query to apply this XQuery document to people.xml using the -q and -s switches like this:

```
C:\saxon>java net.sf.saxon.Query -q:people.xq -s:people.xml
        .
        .
        .
```

And here's what you get when you run this example:

```
C:\saxon>java net.sf.saxon.Query -q:people.xq -s:people.xml
<?xml version="1.0" encoding="UTF-8"?>
<person>
   <first_name>Cary</first_name>
   <last_name>Grant</last_name>
</person>
```

```
<person>
   <first_name>Jimmy</first_name>
   <last_name>Stewart</last_name>
</person>
<person>
   <first_name>Myrna</first_name>
   <last_name>Loy</last_name>
</person>
```

As you can see, the various <person> elements were indeed extracted, and sorted by the first name. Cool.

Using XQuery Functions

There are many functions you can use in both XSLT 2.0 and XQuery 1.0, and you can see a sample of them in Table 12-7. We'll show how to use those functions next.

Function	Meaning
fn:abs	Results in the absolute value of the parameter.
fn:boolean	Results in the effective boolean value of the parameter sequence.
fn:ceiling	Results in the smallest number with no fractional part that is greater than or equal to the parameter.
fn:collection	Results in a sequence of nodes retrieved using the specified URL or the nodes in the default collection.
fn:compare	Results in −1, 0, or 1, depending on whether the value of the first parameter is respectively less than, equal to, or greater than the value of the second parameter.
fn:concat	Concatenates two or more parameters.
fn:contains	Indicates whether one string contains another string.
fn:day-from-date	Results in the day from a date value.
fn:day-from-dateTime	Results in the day from a dateTime value.
fn:days-from-duration	Results in the days component of a duration value.
fn:distinct-values	Results in a sequence in which all but one of a set of duplicate values have been deleted.
fn:doc	Results in a document node retrieved using the specified URL.
fn:doc-available	Results in true if a document node can be retrieved using the specified URL.
fn:empty	Indicates whether or not the provided sequence is empty.
fn:encode-for-uri	Results in the string parameter with certain characters escaped to enable the resulting string to be used as a path segment in a URL.

Table 12-7 XQuery Functions

Function	Meaning
fn:ends-with	Indicates whether the value of one string ends with another string.
fn:escape-html-uri	Results in the string parameter with certain characters escaped in the manner that html user agents handle attribute values that expect URLs.
fn:exists	Indicates whether or not the provided sequence is empty.
fn:floor	Results in the largest number with no fractional part that is less than or equal to the parameter.
fn:hours-from-dateTime	Results in the hours from a dateTime value.
fn:hours-from-duration	Results in the hours component of a duration value.
fn:hours-from-time	Results in the hours from a time value.
fn:id	Results in the sequence of element nodes having an ID value matching the one or more of the supplied IDREF values.
fn:idref	Results in the sequence of element or attribute nodes with an IDREF value matching one or more of the supplied ID values.
fn:index-of	Results in a sequence of integers, each of which is the index of a member of the sequence specified as the first parameter that is equal to the value of the second parameter.
fn:insert-before	Inserts an item or sequence of items at a specified position in a sequence.
fn:iri-to-uri	Results in the string parameter with certain characters escaped to enable the resulting string to be used as a URL.
fn:lang	Results in true or false, depending on whether the language of the given node or the context node, as defined using the xml:lang attribute, is the same as, or a sublanguage of, the language specified by the parameter.
fn:local-name	Results in the local name of the context node.
fn:lower-case	Results in the lowercased value of the parameter.
fn:matches	Results in a boolean value that indicates whether the value of the first parameter is matched by the regular expression that is the value of the second parameter.
fn:minutes-from-dateTime	Results in the minutes from a dateTime value.
fn:minutes-from-duration	Results in the minutes component of a duration value.
fn:minutes-from-time	Results in the minutes from a time value.
fn:month-from-date	Results in the month from a date value.
fn:month-from-dateTime	Results in the month from a dateTime value.
fn:months-from-duration	Results in the months component of a duration value.
fn:name	Results in the name of the context node or the specified node as a string.
fn:normalize-space	Results in the whitespace-normalized value of the parameter.

Table 12-7   XQuery Functions (continued)

Function	Meaning
fn:normalize-unicode	Results in the normalized value of the first parameter in the normalization form specified by the second parameter.
fn:number	Results in the numeric value of the context item.
fn:remove	Removes an item from a specified position in a sequence.
fn:replace	Results in the value of the first parameter with every substring matched by the regular expression that is the value of the second parameter replaced by the replacement string that is the value of the third parameter.
fn:reverse	Reverses the order of items in a sequence.
fn:root	Results in the root of the tree to which the node parameter belongs.
fn:round	Rounds the parameter to the nearest number with no fractional part.
fn:round-half-to-even	Takes a number and a precision and returns a number rounded to the given precision.
fn:seconds-from-dateTime	Results in the seconds from a dateTime value.
fn:seconds-from-duration	Results in the seconds component of a duration value.
fn:seconds-from-time	Results in the seconds from a time value.
fn:starts-with	Indicates whether the value of one string begins with another string.
fn:string-join	Results in the string produced by concatenating a sequence of strings using an optional separator.
fn:string-length	Results in the length of the parameter.
fn:subsequence	Results in the subsequence of a given sequence, identified by location.
fn:substring	Results in the string located at a specified place within a parameter string.
fn:substring-after	Results in the substring that follows another string.
fn:substring-before	Results in the substring that precedes another string.
fn:timezone-from-date	Results in the timezone from a date value.
fn:timezone-from-dateTime	Results in the timezone from a dateTime value.
fn:timezone-from-time	Results in the timezone from a time value.
fn:translate	Results in the first string parameter with occurrences of characters contained in the second parameter replaced by the character at the corresponding position in the third parameter.
fn:unordered	Results in the items in the given sequence in a nondeterministic order.
fn:upper-case	Results in the uppercased value of the parameter.
fn:year-from-date	Results in the year from a date value.
fn:year-from-dateTime	Results in the year from a dateTime value.
fn:years-from-duration	Results in the year component of a duration value.

Table 12-7 XQuery Functions (*continued*)

For example, say that you wanted to sort the <person> elements according to the lengths of their first names. You could use the fn:string-length function for that like this:

```
xquery version "1.0";
declare copy-namespaces no-preserve, inherit;

for $b in //meetings/meeting/people/person
order by fn:string-length($b/first_name) return
<person>
   { $b/first_name }
   { $b/last_name }
</person>
```

And here's the result when you sort the <person> elements this way in people.xml:

```
C:\saxon>java net.sf.saxon.Query -q:people.xq -s:people.xml
<?xml version="1.0" encoding="UTF-8"?>
<person>
    <first_name>Cary</first_name>
    <last_name>Grant</last_name>
</person>
<person>
    <first_name>Myrna</first_name>
    <last_name>Loy</last_name>
</person>
<person>
    <first_name>Jimmy</first_name>
    <last_name>Stewart</last_name>
</person>
```

Great—that's got our example working. And that completes our look at XQuery. If you want more details, take a gander at the W3C XQuery 1.0 and XPath 2.0 documentation.

Index

Note: Page numbers referencing figures are italicized and followed by an "*f*". Page numbers referencing tables are italicized and followed by a "*t*".

Symbols

- (minus sign), 7
!= operator, 238
(sharp symbol), 148
& (ampersand), 256
* (asterisk), 213, 216
* operator, 240, 243
. operator, 243
.. operator, 243
/ (closing slash), 250
// (double slashes), 64
/> characters, 256
@* wildcard, 223, 243
@units, 217, 243
../@units operator, 244
[ ] (square brackets), 230–234
+ (plus sign), 7
+ operator, 240
< (<) element, 295
< operator, 238
<= operator, 238
= operator, 238
> (>) element, 295
> operator, 238
>= operator, 238
© symbol, 29
– operator, 240

A

a | b symbol, 44
a property, 287
a? symbol, 44
a symbol, 44
a* symbol, 44
a+ symbol, 44
<a> element, 256
abbr attribute, 276
abort event handler, *397t–398t*
absolute location path, 234
absolutePage property, 302
absolutePosition property, 302
abstract boolean
    isNamespaceAware( )
    method, *361t*
abstract boolean isValidating( )
    method, *361t*
abstract Document
    newDocument( ) method, *361t*
abstract Document
    parse(InputSource is)
    method, *362t*
abstract DocumentBuilder
    newDocumentBuilder( )
    method, *358t*
abstract DOMImplementation
    getDOMImplementation( )
    method, *361t*
abstract Object
    getAttribute(String name)
    method, *358t*
abstract void setAttribute(String
    name, Object value)
    method, *359t*
abstract void setEntityResolver
    (EntityResolver er)
    method, *362t*
abstract void setErrorHandler
    (ErrorHandler eh)
    method, *362t*
<account> element, 49–50

:active class, 155
ActiveX object, 351
addNew method, 302
address type, 128
addressData group, 129
ADO methods, 303
<age> element, 177, 219,
    228–229, 301
AJAX (asynchronous JavaScript
    and XML)
    ajax.html, 393–394
    ajaxxml.html, writing,
        406–407
    connecting to server,
        399–402
    downloading
        displaying
            downloaded data,
            402–404
        process of, 404–405
        XML, 405–406
    overview, 390–392
    recovering downloaded
        XML, 408–414
    XMLHttpRequest object
        configuring to
            handle XML,
            407–408
        creating, 395–398
        opening, 398–399
Ajax: A Beginner's Guide, 412
ajax.html, 390, *392f*, 393–394,
    404, 408
ajaxxml.html, 406–407, 412
<alias> element, 124, 126
align attribute
    <h1> to <h6> elements, 263
    <img> element, 271
    <table> element, 272
    <td> element, 277
    <tr> element, 275
alignments, 167–168
alink attribute, 260
all element, *77t*
all groups, 131
Allow Blocked Content setting, 8
alt attribute, 271
Amaya browser, 13, *71f*
&amp entity reference, 30
ampersand (&), 256
annotating schemas, 133–135
annotation element, *77t*
anonymous types, 97–101, 127

ANY content model, 41
any element, *77t*
anyAttribute element, *77t*
anyURI type, *120t*
&apos entity reference, 30
appendChild method
    XMLDOMAttribute
        object, 344
    XMLDOMElement
        object, 331
appendChild property, 329
appinfo element, *77t*
Apple Safari browser, *397t–398t*
applet element, 287
applicable facets, *120t–122t*
applications, XML, 12–13
args array, 363
args[0] parse, 370
asterisk (*), 213, 216
asynchronous JavaScript and
    XML. *See* AJAX
attendance attribute, 342, 346, 348
<!ATTLIST> element, 52
Attr createAttributeNS(String
    namespaceURI, String
    qualifiedName) method, *364t*
Attr createAttribute(String name)
    method, *364t*
Attr object, 321
attribute axis, 234
attribute element, *77t*
attribute names, 28–29, 68, 256
attribute values, 256
attribute::childname
    expression, 236
attributeGroup element, *77t*
attributes
    declaring in schemas
        adding attribute,
        112–113
    overview, 106–112
    in DTDs
        overview, 52–55
        setting attribute
            types, 60–62
        setting default
            values, 55–60
    extracting data from,
        342–351
    fixing, 115
    groups of, creating,
        129–131
    matching, 217–223

matching values of,
    232–233
nodes, handling with Java,
    380–381
overview, 26–29
specifying use of, 113–115
attributes property
    JavaScript, 328
    XMLDOMAttribute
        object, 343
    XMLDOMElement
        object, 330
attributes.html, 344–345, 348
attributesXMLisland.html, 351–352
<author> element, 139, 141, 146
axes, XPath, 234–236
axis attribute, 277

B

b symbol, 44
<b> element, 266–267
background attribute, 260
background-attachment
    property, 162
background-color property, 162
background-image property,
    162, 166
background-position property, 162
background-repeat property,
    162, 167
<base> element, 258
base64Binary type, *120t*
baseName property
    JavaScript, 328
    XMLDOMAttribute
        object, 343
    XMLDOMElement
        object, 330
beginning of file (BOF)
    property, 302
bgcolor attribute
    <h1> to <h6> elements, 262
    <head> element, 260
    <table> element, 272
    <td> element, 277
    <tr> element, 275
binding XML data. *See also* DSOs
    in HTML format, 287–293
    into HTML tables, 308–313
    overview, 297–298

block elements, 157

blue class, 150

<body> element, 4–5, 190, 246, 255, 257, 260–263

BOF (beginning of file) property, 302

bold text, 266–267

boolean isCoalescing( ) method, *358t*

boolean isExpandEntityReferences( ) method, *358t*

boolean isIgnoringComments( ) method, *358t*

boolean isIgnoringElementContentWhitespace( ) method, *358t*

boolean isNamespaceAware( ) method, *358t*

boolean isValidating( ) method, *358t*

boolean type, *120t*

border attribute
<img> element, 271
<table> element, 273

border-bottom-width style, 171

border-color style, 171

border-left-width style, 171

border-right-width style, 172

borders, 171–173

border-style style, 172

border-top-width style, 172

borrowDate attribute, 87, 107–108

<Borrower> element, 87–88, 108, 112, 131

bound HTML data, *296f*

bound XML data, *301f*

 element, 250

businessAddress type, 128, 130

<button> element, 256, 287

byte type, *120t, 122t*

C

cacheSize property, 302

callback function, 399

cancel method, 302

cancelUpdate method, 302

Cascading Style Sheets. *See* CSS

case statement, 376

catalogID type, 116–117

catch block, 355

catch-all templates, empty, 228–229

CDATA sections
handling with Java, 381–382
overview, 31–32

CDATA type, 53, 60

<![CDATA[and]]> markup, 381

CDATASection createCDATASection(String data) method, *364t*

CDATASection object, 321

cdata.xml, 31

ceiling( ) function, 241

cellpadding attribute, 273

cellspacing attribute, 273

channel event handler, *397t*

char attribute
<td> element, 277
<tr> element, 275

character sets, 17

characters, 17

charoff attribute
<td> element, 277
<tr> element, 275

ChemML documents, 13

child element nodes, matching, 214–217

child elements, 43, 85

child elements content model
multiple, 43–47
overview, 41–42

child nodes, 373, 379

child::childname expression, 236

childNodes property
JavaScript, 328
XMLDOMAttribute object, 343
XMLDOMElement object, 330

choice element, *77t*

choices
DTD, 49–52
schema, 123–126

circle class, 170

<city> element, 91, 127

class attribute
<b> element, 266
<font> element, 268
<h1> to <h6> elements, 263
<head> element, 260
<i> element, 267
<img> element, 271
<table> element, 273
<td> element, 277
<tr> element, 275

<class> element, 316–317

classes, selecting styles by, 150–155

clone method, 302

cloneNode property
JavaScript, 329
XMLDOMAttribute object, 344
XMLDOMElement object, 331

close method, 302

closing slash (/), 250

closing tags, 383–388

color attribute
<font> element, 268
<h1> to <h6> elements, 262

color class, 165

color property, 162, 164

colors, styling with, 162–167

colspan attribute, 277

comment( ) node test, 236

Comment createComment(String data) method, *364t*

Comment object, 321

comments
extracting, *225f, 228f*
matching, 224–229
overview, 17–18

complex elements, declaring in schemas, 85–95

complex type address, 90–91

complexContent element, *77t*

complexType element, *77t*

concat(string1, string2, …) function, 242

contains(string1, string2) function, 241

content models
ANY, 41
child elements, 41–42
EMPTY, 47–49
multiple children, 43–47
overview, 40–41
text, 42–43

context node, 234

count( ) function, 241

count(node-set) function, 237

Courier font, 270

<creationDate> child element, 99–100

CSS (Cascading Style Sheets)
alignments, 167–168
block elements, creating, 157
borders, 171–173

CSS (Cascading Style Sheets)
(*cont.*)
colors, 162–167
connecting to XML
documents, 142–144
example of, 138–140
formatting text, 157–161
indentations, 167–168
inline styles, 155–156
lists, 168–171
margins, 167–168
overview, 9, 140–141,
144–145
style sheet selectors, creating
grouping elements,
146
overview, 145
selecting by class,
150–155
selecting by element,
145–146
selecting by ID,
148–150
selecting by pseudo-
element, 146–147
styles, 157
current element, 207
cursorLocation property, 302
<customer> element, 20, 26–27,
31, 42, 44, 49–50, 52
customersDefault.xml, 55
customersDTD.xml, 35, 39, 41, 43
customersFixed.xml, 58
customers.xml document, 16,
28f, 65

D

data binding. *See also* DSOs
in HTML format, 287–293
into HTML tables, 308–313
overview, 297–298
data islands, XML
overview, 298–303
using with JavaScript,
351–352
data property, 411
data source objects, DSOs
datafld attribute, 287, 290, 316
dataSource parameter, 398

datasrc attribute, 287, 289, 309
data.txt, 391, 404
dataType property
JavaScript, 328
XMLDOMAttribute
object, 343
XMLDOMElement
object, 330
date type, *120t, 122t*
<date> element, 14, 21, 40, 42
dateTime type, *120t, 122t*
<day_of_the_week> element, 15
db variable, 359, 361
decimal type, *120t, 122t*
declarations, XML, 16–17
declaring
anonymous types, 97–101
attributes in schemas
adding attribute,
112–113
overview, 106–112
elements in DTDs
ANY content
model, 41
child elements
content model,
41–42
EMPTY content
model, 47–49
multiple children
content model,
43–47
overview, 40–41
text content model,
42–43
elements in schemas
complex elements,
85–95
overview, 84–95
by reference,
101–103
simple elements,
84–85
default attribute, 115
default namespace, 69
default values, 52, 55–60
definition property
JavaScript, 328
XMLDOMAttribute
object, 343
XMLDOMElement
object, 330

delete method, 302
descendant axis, 234
descendant-or-self axis, 234
/descendant-or-self::node( )/
expression, 236
descendants, 216
dialects, XML, 12–13
dir attribute
<b> element, 266
<font> element, 268
<h1> to <h6> elements, 263
<head> element, 258–260
<html> element, 257
<i> element, 267
<table> element, 273
<td> element, 277
<tr> element, 275
displaying AJAX downloads,
402–404
displayText array, 370,
373–374, 376
<distance> element, 208
div operator, 240
<div> element, 287, 306, 336,
348, 393, 402–403, 406
divID parameter, 402
doc object, 365
<!DOCTYPE> element, 39–40,
64, 75, 248, 255–256
Document class, 364
document element, 6, 19, 190,
324, 329–338
Document object, 321, 362
Document Object Model
(DOM), 320
Document parse(File f)
method, *362t*
Document parse(InputStream is)
method, *362t*
Document parse(InputStream is,
String systemId) method, *362t*
Document parse(String uri)
method, *362t*
document type definitions.
See DTDs
<document> element, 6, 19, 41,
43, 50, 164
<DOCUMENT> tag, 20
documentation element, *77t*
DocumentBuilder
creating, 359–362
factories, 357–359

DocumentBuilder object, 357, 359, 362, 371

DocumentBuilderFactory class, 358–359, 371

documentElement property, 329

DocumentFragment createDocumentFragment( ) method, *364t*

DocumentFragment object, 321

documents, XML. *See* well-formed XML documents

DocumentType getDoctype( ) method, *365t*

DocumentType object, 321

document.xml, 74, 79, 106

DOM (Document Object Model), 320

DOM parser, 387

DOMDocument object, 322, 324–329

DOMImplementation getImplementation( ) method, *365t*

dotted border, 172

double slashes (//), 64

double type, *120t, 122t*

downloading
 displaying AJAX downloads, 402–404
 process of, 404–405
 recovering downloaded XML, 408–414
 XML, 405–406

DSOs (data source objects)
 binding XML data into HTML tables, 308–313
  overview, 297–298
 extracting data from, 303–308
 HTML format
  binding data in, 287–293
  storing data in, 282–286
 methods, 302–303
 navigating from record to record, 293–297
 nested records, handling, 314–318
 overview, 282
 properties, 302
 XML data islands, 298–303

dsoStudent.recordset.moveFirst( ) record set, 292–293

dsoStudent.recordset.moveLast( ) record set, 293

dsoStudent.recordset.moveNext( ) record set, 293

dsoStudent.recordset.movePrevious( ) record set, 293

DTDs (document type definitions)
 checking syntax with, 18–19
 choices in, 49–52
 creating, 39–40
 declaring elements in
  ANY content model, 41
  child elements content model, 41–42
  EMPTY content model, 47–49
  multiple children content model, 43–47
  overview, 40–41
  text content model, 42–43
 external, 62–66
 handling attributes in
  overview, 52–55
  setting attribute types, 60–62
  setting default values, 55–60
 namespaces, 66–71
 overview, 15, 34–35
 validating XML documents with, 35–39
 XHTML, 248

duration type, *120t, 122t*

E

editMode property, 302

either/or expressions, 230

Element createElementNS(String namespaceURI, String qualifiedName) method, *364t*

Element createElement(String tagName) method, *364t*

element element, *77t*

Element getDocumentElement( ) method, *365t*

Element getElementById(String elementId) method, *365t*

element group, 128

element names, 256

element nodes, 213–214, 321, 375

Element object, 321

element selectors, 145–146

element wildcards, 223

<!ELEMENT> element, 40, 42, 77

elements
 block, 157
 closing tags, 383–388
 counting, 368
 declaring
  in DTDs, 40–47
  in schemas, 84–95, 101–103
 empty, creating, 126–127
 extracting multiple values, 205–209
 groups of, creating, 127–129
 opening tags, 378–380
 searching for elements by name, 338–342
 specifying number of occurrences of, 95–97
 storing data in, 19–25
 in XML schemas, 77

empty catch-all templates, 228–229

EMPTY content model, 47–49

empty elements, 25, 47, 126–127

empty template, 226

encoding attribute, 17

end of file (EOF) property, 302

ENTITIES type, 53, *120t*

entities.xml, 30

Entity object, 321

entity references, 29–30

ENTITY type, 53, *120t*

EntityReference createEntityReference(String name) method, *364t*

EntityReference object, 321

entry point, 355

Enumerated type, 53

EOF (end of file) property, 302

Extensible Hypertext Markup Language. *See* XHTML

Extensible Markup Language.
  See XML
Extensible Stylesheet Language
  Transformations. *See* XSLT
extension element, *77t*
external DTDs, 62–66
external.dtd, 62, 65
extracting data
  from DSOs, 303–308
  from XML, 10–12, 370–374
<eyecolor> element, 204

F

face attribute, 268
factories, DocumentBuilder,
  357–359
#ff7f50 value, 162
field element, *77t*
fields, 289–290
figures, searching for, *415f*
File | Open menu, 8
find method, 302
Firefox browser, *397t*
<first_name> element, 16, 21, 34,
  332, 335, 338–340, 346, 368
first_nameNode text node, 336
first_nameNode.firstChild text
  node, 336
first_nameNode.firstChild
  .nodeValue node, 336
:first-child class, 155
firstChild property
  JavaScript, 328
  XMLDOMAttribute
    object, 343
  XMLDOMElement
    object, 330
first-letter pseudo-element, 147
first-line pseudo-element, 147
fixed attributes, 59–60, 115
#FIXED VALUE type, 53
<flavor> element, 177, 193–195,
  197–198, 231, 233, 237, 405,
  409–411
flavors.xml, 405, 414
float text style, 157
float type, *121t–122t*
floor( ) function, 241
fn:abs function, *418t*
fn:boolean function, *418t*

fn:ceiling function, *418t*
fn:collection function, *418t*
fn:compare function, *418t*
fn:concat function, *418t*
fn:contains function, *418t*
fn:day-from-date function, *418t*
fn:day-from-dateTime
  function, *418t*
fn:days-from-duration
  function, *418t*
fn:distinct-values function, *418t*
fn:doc function, *418t*
fn:doc-available function, *418t*
fn:empty function, *418t*
fn:encode-for-uri function, *418t*
fn:ends-with function, *418t*
fn:escape-html-uri function, *419t*
fn:exists function, *419t*
fn:floor function, *419t*
fn:hours-from-dateTime
  function, *419t*
fn:hours-from-duration
  function, *419t*
fn:hours-from-time function, *419t*
fn:id function, *419t*
fn:idref function, *419t*
fn:index-of function, *419t*
fn:insert-before function, *419t*
fn:iri-to-uri function, *419t*
fn:lang function, *419t*
fn:local-name function, *419t*
fn:lower-case function, *419t*
fn:matches function, *419t*
fn:minutes-from-dateTime
  function, *419t*
fn:minutes-from-duration
  function, *419t*
fn:minutes-from-time
  function, *419t*
fn:month-from-date function, *419t*
fn:month-from-dateTime
  function, *419t*
fn:months-from-duration
  function, *419t*
fn:name function, *419t*
fn:normalize-space function, *419t*
fn:normalize-unicode
  function, *420t*
fn:number function, *420t*
fn:remove function, *420t*
fn:replace function, *420t*
fn:reverse function, *420t*

fn:root function, *420t*
fn:round function, *420t*
fn:round-half-to-even function, *420t*
fn:seconds-from-dateTime
  function, *420t*
fn:seconds-from-duration
  function, *420t*
fn:seconds-from-time function, *420t*
fn:starts-with function, *420t*
fn:string-join function, *420t*
fn:string-length function, *420t*, 421
fn:subsequence function, *420t*
fn:substring function, *420t*
fn:substring-after function, *420t*
fn:substring-before function, *420t*
fn:timezone-from-date
  function, *420t*
fn:timezone-from-dateTime
  function, *420t*
fn:timezone-from-time
  function, *420t*
fn:translate function, *420t*
fn:unordered function, *420t*
fn:upper-case function, *420t*
fn:year-from-date function, *420t*
fn:year-from-dateTime
  function, *420t*
fn:years-from-duration
  function, *420t*
:focus class, 155
<font> element, 268–270
font-family property, 157, 160
font-size property, 158
font-stretch property, 158
font-style property, 158
font-variant property, 158
font-weight property, 158–159
<form> element, 256
formal public identifier (FPI), 64
format10.css, *169f*
format11.css, 172
format1.xsl, 187, 190, 192, 221
format2.xsl, 194, 198–199,
  224, 227
format3.xls, 231
format3.xsl, 199, 204, 231
format4.css, 150
format4.xsl, 209
format5.css, 165
format5.xsl, 239
format6.css, 159–160
format8.css, 166

format9.css, 168
format.css, 141, 144, 157
format-number(number1, string2,
    string3) function, 242
formatted.css, 9
formatting, 9–10. *See also*
    CSS; XSLT
formatting tags, 4
format.xsl, 183–185
FPI (formal public identifier), 64
frame attribute, 273
frame element, 287
<frameset> element, 255, 257
//friend operator, 243
*/friend operator, 243
.//friend operator, 243
friend operator, 243
friend[@language and @units]
    operator, 244
friend[3] operator, 243
friend[6][@units = "inches"]
    operator, 244
friend[first( )] operator, 243
friend[name] operator, 244
friend[name="Paige Turner"]
    operator, 244
//friend/name operator, 243
<friends> element, 187, 196, 214
friends1.xml, 190
friends3.xml, 231
friends4.xml, 205
friends5/xml, 240
friends//friend operator, 243
/friends/friend[3]/name[2]
    operator, 243
friends.xml, 176, 184, 414
functions, XQuery, 418–421

G

gDay type, *121t–122t*
gender attribute, 26, 231
generic font family, 161
GET HTTP method, 399
getAllResponseHeaders event
    handler, *397t–398t*
getAttribute method, 331
getAttributeNode method, 331
getAttributes method, 380
getChildNodes method, 379
getData function, 394–396, 398,
    402, 406

getDocumentElement method, 378
getElementsByTagName method,
    331, 338–339, 342, 355, 365,
    368, 409
getNamedItem attribute, 348
getNodeName method, 378, 383
getNodeType method, 375
getNodeValue method, 381, 383
getResponseHeader event handler,
    397t–398t
getRows method, 302
getString method, 302
gMonth type, *121t–122t*
gMonthDay type, *121t–122t*
grandchildren, 216
green class, 153, 165
<greeting> element, 6, 9, 14
group elements, *77t*, 146
groups
    attribute, 129–131
    creating all, 131
    element, 127–129
&gt entity reference, 30
gYear type, *121t–122t*
gYearMonth type, *121t–122t*

H

<h1> to <h6> elements, 157,
    262–263
hair_color attribute, 350
hasChildNodes property
    JavaScript, 329
    XMLDOMAttribute
        object, 344
    XMLDOMElement
        object, 331
<head> element, 189, 246, 249,
    257–260, 325
headers attribute, 277
headings, XHTML, 263–265
height attribute
    <img> element, 271
    <td> element, 277
height[@units = "inches"]
    operator, 244
<height> element, 219, 226, 301
hello.xml document, 7
hexBinary type, *121t*
:hover class, 155
href attribute, 183
hspace attribute, 271

HTML (Hypertext Markup
    Language)
    binding data in, 287–293
    data binding into tables,
        308–313
    overview, 2, *3f*, 66–67
    storing data in, 282–286
    use of, 4–5
    XHTML versus, 255–256
<html> element, 189, 195, 200,
    246, 248, 255, 257
html.html document, 247
HTTP GET method, 404
Hypertext Markup Language.
    See HTML

I

<i> element, 267–268
IANA (Internet Assigned
    Numbers Authority), 17
id attribute
    <b> element, 266
    <font> element, 269
    <h1> to <h6> elements, 263
    <head> element, 260
    <i> element, 267
    <img> element, 271
    matching by, 223–224
    selecting by, 148–150
    <table> element, 273
    <td> element, 277
    <tr> element, 275
ID type, 53, *121t*
IDREF type, 53, *121t*
IDREFS type, 53, *121t*
id(string ID) function, 237
iframe element, 287
images, displaying in XHTML,
    271–272
<img> element, 20, 126,
    271–272, 287
#IMPLIED type, 53
import element, *78t*
include element, *78t*
indentations, 167–168
inline styles, 155–156
input type=button element, 287
input type=checkbox element, 287
input type=hidden element, 287
input type=password element, 287
input type=radio element, 287

input type=text element, 287, 289
insertBefore property
    JavaScript, 329
    XMLDOMAttribute
        object, 344
    XMLDOMElement
        object, 331
int getLength( ) method, 366
int type, *121t–122t*
integer type, *121t–122t*
Internet Assigned Numbers
    Authority (IANA), 17
Internet Explorer browser, 8, *163t,*
    396t–397t
<isindex> element, 258
ismap attribute, 271
italics, 267–268
<item> element, 21, 26, 34, *38f*

J

Java
    attribute nodes, 380–381
    CDATA nodes, 381–382
    closing tags, 383–388
    Document Builder factory,
        357–359
    Document Builder objects,
        359–362
    opening tags, 378–380
    overview, 354–357
    processing instruction
        nodes, 383
    root node, 376–378
    text nodes, 382
    walkNodes method,
        374–376
    XML data, accessing,
        365–369
    XML documents
        extracting all data,
            370–374
        parsing, 362–365
javac.exe command, 367
JavaScript
    document element,
        329–338
    DOMDocument object,
        creating, 324–329

example, *11f*
extracting data
    from XML, 322–324
    from XML attri-
        butes, 342–351
    overview, 320–322
    XML data islands,
        351–352
    XML elements, searching
        for, 338–342
JavaScript function, 345
javascript.html, 11
JavaServer Page (JSP), 184
javax.xml.parsers.Document-
    Builder class, *361t–362t*
javax.xml.parsers.DocumentBuild-
    erFactory class, *358t–359t*
JSP (JavaServer Page), 184
Jungle Book, The, 139–140
junglebook.xml, 139

K

key element, *78t*
keyref element, *78t*
Kipling, Rudyard, 138

L

<label> element, 256, 287
lang attribute
    <b> element, 266
    <font> element, 269
    <h1> to <h6>
        elements, 263
    <head> element, 258–260
    <html> element, 257
    <i> element, 267
    <img> element, 271
    <table> element, 274
    <td> element, 277
    <tr> element, 275
language attribute, 58, 108
language type, *121t*
last( ) function, 237, 239
<last_name> element, 16, 21, 34,
    40, 332, 335, 340, 346
last_nameNode object, 336

lastChild property
    JavaScript, 328
    XMLDOMAttribute
        object, 343
    XMLDOMElement
        object, 330
<Lender> element, 87–89, 108,
    112, 131
"Liam's Pictures from Old Books"
    site, *415f*
line-height property, 158, 167
link attribute, 260
:link class, 155
<link> element, 259
list element, *78t*
list-item property, 168
listNodesFirstName method, 340
listNodesFirstName.item(2) node
    list, 340
listNodesFirstName.item(2).first-
    Child.nodeValue node list, 340
listNodesLastName method, 340
lists, 168–171
list-style-image property, 168
list-style-type property, 168
local-name(node-set)
    function, 237
location path, 234
location steps, 234
long type, *121t–122t*
longdesc attribute, 271
&lt entity reference, 30

M

main method, 370
margin-left property, 167
margin-right property, 168
margins, 167–168
margin-top property, 161, 168
markup languages
    HTML, 4–5
    overview, 3
    using XML, 5–9
marquee element, 287
match attribute
    attributes, 217–223
    child element nodes,
        214–217

either/or expressions, 230
element nodes, 213–214
matching
     with [ ], 230–234
     by ID, 223–224
overview, 212–213
root node, 213
XML comments, 224–229
XML processing instructions, 229
matched elements, 216
MathML documents, 12–13,
     66–67, 70–71, 133
<maxDaysOut> element, 99–100
maxOccurs attribute, 95
maxRecords property, 302
<meeting> element, 332–333
<meetings> element, 329, 332
meetingsNode object, 329–330
message element, 6–7, 9, 14
<meta> element, 259
Microsoft HTML (MSHTML), 282
Microsoft Internet Explorer
     browser, 8, *163t*, *396t–397t*
Microsoft.XMLDOM object, 351
MIME type, 407
minOccurs attribute, 96
minus sign (−), 7
mod operator, 240
modular, 255
move method, 303
moveFirst method, 303
moveLast method, 303
moveNext method, 303
movePrevious method, 303
Mozilla Firefox browser, *397t*
MSHTML (Microsoft HTML), 282
multiple children content model,
     43–47
multiple elements values,
     extracting, 205–209

N

name, searching for elements
     by, 338–342
name attribute, 256
name property, 343
Name type, *121t*
<name> element, 21, 34, 42,
     91, 123, 126, 199–202, 206,
     216, 226, 229, 232–233, 237,
     297, 301

named node map, 343, 348
NamedNodeMap object, 321
name(node-set) function, 237
namespace nodes, 235
namespace prefix, 67, 83
namespaces
     overview, 66–71
     schemas and, 132–133
namespaceURI property
     JavaScript, 328
     XMLDOMAttribute
          object, 343
     XMLDOMElement
          object, 330
namespace-uri(node-set)
     function, 237
navigating, in DSOs, 293–297
navigation buttons, 299
Navigator browser, 256, *397t*
navigatorByTagName.html, 338
navigator.html, 324, 329, 338
NCName type, *121t*
negativeInteger type, *121t–122t*
nested element, 316
nested records, 314–318
nested XML data, *318f*
nesting errors, *29f*
Netscape Navigator browser,
     256, *397t*
net.sf.saxon class, 417
newDocumentBuilder method,
     359–360
newInstance method, 357
nextRecordSet method, 303
nextSibling property
     JavaScript, 328
     XMLDOMAttribute
          object, 343
     XMLDOMElement
          object, 330
<nickname> element, 126, 342
NMTOKEN type, 53, *121t*
NMTOKENS type, 53, *121t*
node( ) node test, 236
Node item(int index)
     method, 366
Node object, 321
node tests, XPath, 234, 236
Node.DOCUMENT_NODE
     node type, 376
NodeList getElementsByTagNa
     meNS(String namespaceURI,
     String localName)
     method, *365t*

NodeList getElementsByTagName
     (String tagname) method, *365t*
NodeList object, 321
nodeName property
     JavaScript, 328
     XMLDOMAttribute
          object, 343
     XMLDOMElement
          object, 330
nodes, 7, 234, 320
node-sct predicates, 237–238
Node.TEXT_NODE type, 382
nodeType property
     JavaScript, 328
     XMLDOMAttribute
          object, 343
     XMLDOMElement
          object, 330
nodeTypedValue property
     JavaScript, 328
     XMLDOMAttribute
          object, 344
nodeTypeString property
     JavaScript, 328
     XMLDOMAttribute
          object, 344
     XMLDOMElement
          object, 330
nodeValue property
     JavaScript, 328
     XMLDOMAttribute
          object, 344
     XMLDOMElement
          object, 330
nonNegativeInteger type,
     121t–122t
nonPositiveInteger type,
     121t–122t
normalize method, 331
normalizedString type, *121t*
normalize-space(string1)
     function, 242
<noscript> element, 259
notation element, *78t*
Notation object, 321
NOTATION type, 53, *121t*
<note> element, 79, 84–85, 88,
     102–103, 131
nowrap attribute, 277
<number> element, 22
numberOfLines variable, 370
numeric simple types, 122
numerical predicates, 240–241

O

<object> element, 259, 287–288
online validator, *37f*
onreadystatechange event
    handler, *397t*
open event handler, *397t–398t*
open method, 303
opening tags, 378–380
openRequest event handler, *397t*
<option> element, 292
optional value, 113
ordered simple types, *122t*
<orders> element, 21, 27, 34, 40, 42
org.w3c.dom.Document, *364t–365t*
output document, 226
outputText text string, 336
overrideMimeType event
    handler, *397t*
ownerDocument property
    JavaScript, 328
    XMLDOMAttribute
        object, 344
    XMLDOMElement
        object, 330

P

<p> element, 139, 147, 152–153,
    159, 168, 201
packages, 357
pageCount property, 302
pageSize property, 302
<painting> element, 97, 109, 131
paintingID attribute, 109–110, 116
paintings type, 93
<paintings> element, 87–88,
    93–94
<paintingTitle> child element, 99
param element, 287
parentheses, 46
parent::node( ) expression, 236
parentNode property
    JavaScript, 328
    XMLDOMAttribute
        object, 344
    XMLDOMElement
        object, 330
parse method, 357, 361
parsed character data, 43

parsed property
    JavaScript, 328
    XMLDOMAttribute
        object, 344
    XMLDOMElement
        object, 330
parseDocument method, 370
ParserConfigurationException
    exception, 360
parser.java program, 368, 384
parsing
    defined, 355
    XML documents, 362–365
    XML processing
        instructions, 387–388
<pays_on_time/> element, 25
#PCDATA content model, 43
<people> element, 333
people.class, 367
people.java program, 363, 367
people.xml document, 323–324,
    327, *337f*, 338, *341f*, 345,
    350f, *352f*, 368, 416
<person> element, 324, 334–335,
    346–347, 355, 365, 367, 416,
    418, 421
p:first-letter element, 147
phone attribute, 113
PHP scripts, 412
plain text, 265
plus sign (+), 7
position( ) function, 237
positiveInteger type, *121t–122t*
POST HTTP method, 399
POST method, 404
<pre> element, 256
predefined entity references,
    29–30
predicates
    matching with, 230–234
    node-set, 237–238
    numerical, 240–241
    overview, 236–237
    string, 241–243
    true/false, 238–240
prefix property
    JavaScript, 329
    XMLDOMAttribute
        object, 344
    XMLDOMElement
        object, 331

previousSibling property
    JavaScript, 329
    XMLDOMAttribute
        object, 344
    XMLDOMElement
        object, 331
<price> element, 23
processing instructions
    handling nodes with
        Java, 383
    matching, 229
    overview, 18
    parsing, 387–388
processing-instruction( )
    expression, 229
processing-instruction( ) node
    test, 236
ProcessingInstruction createPro-
    cessingInstruction (String tar-
    get, String data) method, *364t*
ProcessingInstruction object, 321
<product> element, 22
profile attribute, 258
prohibited value, 113
prologs, 17
protected DocumentBuilder( )
    method, *361t*
protected DocumentBuilderFac-
    tory( ) method, *358t*
pseudo-elements, 146–147
public class, 355, 370
public DTDs, 62
PUBLIC keyword, 40, 62, 64

Q

QName type, *121t*
-q switches, 417
&quot entity reference, 30

R

readXMLDocument function,
    324, 326
readyState event handler,
    397t, 400
<record> element, 316
recordCount property, 302

records, 289

\<records\> element, 316

recovering downloaded XML, 408–414

recursion, 378

redefine element, *78t*

reference_number attributes, 26

references, declaring elements by, 101–103

regular expressions, 110

relative location path, 234

removeAttribute method, 331

removeAttributeNode method, 331

removeChild property
    JavaScript, 329
    XMLDOMAttribute object, 344
    XMLDOMElement object, 331

replaceChild property
    JavaScript, 329
    XMLDOMAttribute object, 344
    XMLDOMElement object, 331

\<replacementValue\> child element, 99–100

requery method, 303

required attributes, 57–59

#REQUIRED type, 53, 57

required value, 113

responseBody event handler, *396t*

responseStream event handler, *396t*

responseText property, *396t, 397t,* 403, 408

responseXML property, *396t, 397t,* 408

restricting simple types, 116–122

restriction element, *78t*

root node, 213, 234, 324, 376–378

round( ) function, 241

rowspan attribute, 277

$rrggbb format, 162

rules attribute, 274

S

Safari browser, *397t–398t*

save method, 303

schema element, *78t*

schema facet, 117

schema validators, 78

schemas
    all groups, creating, 131
    annotating, 133–135
    attributes
        declaring, 106–113
        groups of, 129–131
        specifying use, 113–115
    creating, 83–84
    elements
        declaring, 84–95, 101–103
        empty, 126–127
        groups of, 127–129
        multiple choices for, 123–126
        specifying number of occurrences of, 95–97
    namespaces, 132–133
    overview, 74–79, 106
    types
        declaring anonymous, 97–101
        restricting simple, 116–122
    validating XML documents using, 79–83

schema.xsd type, 111

Scholarly Technology Group, 37

scope attribute, 277

\<script\> element, 259, 325

searching for XML elements by name, 338–342

\<section\> element, 146, 153, 159, 172

security bar, 8

\<select\> element, 287, 292

selectNodes property
    JavaScript, 329
    XMLDOMAttribute object, 344
    XMLDOMElement object, 331

selector element, *78t*

selectors
    element, 145–146
    grouping elements, 146
    overview, 145
    pseudo-elements, 146–147

selecting
    by class, 150–155
    by id attribute, 148–150

selectSingleNode property
    JavaScript, 329
    XMLDOMAttribute object, 344
    XMLDOMElement object, 331

self::node( ) expression, 236

send event handler, *397t–398t*

sequence element, *78t*

servers, connecting to, 399–402

setAttribute method, 331

setAttributeNode method, 331

setRequestHeader event handler, *397t–398t*

setting, 157

sharp symbol (#), 148

short type, *121t–122t*

sibling axis, 235

simple elements, declaring, 84–85

simple types, restricting, 116–122

simpleContent element, *78t*

simpleType element, *78t*

size attribute, 269

span element, 287

\<span id="name"\> element, 297

\<span\> element, 283–285, 290, 295, 297, 311, 317

specified property
    JavaScript, 329
    XMLDOMAttribute object, 344
    XMLDOMElement object, 331

SQL (Structured Query Language), 416

square brackets ([ ]), 230–234

src attribute, 127, 271

-s switches, 417

standalone attribute, 17

starts-with(string1, string2) function, 241

state property, 302

\<state\> element, 91, 127

static DocumentBuilderFactory newInstance( ) method, *359t*

status event handler, *396t, 397t,* 401–402

statusText event handler, *396t, 397t*
stayInSync property, 302
storing data
      in HTML format, 282–286
      in XML elements, 19–25
<street> element, 91, 127
string predicates, 241–243
string type, *121t*
string-length(string1) function, 242
Structured Query Language
      (SQL), 416
<student> element, 298
studentsDSOHTML.html, 288, 297
students.html, *286f*
students.xml document, 308
studentsXMLislands.html, 298, 301
style attribute
      <b> element, 266
      <font> element, 269
      <h1> to <h6> elements, 263
      <head> element, 260
      <i> element, 268
      <img> element, 271
      <table> element, 274
      <td> element, 278
      <tr> element, 275
style property, 157
style rules, 9, 145
style sheets. *See* CSS; XSLT
<style> element, 259, 262
styling XHTML documents,
      262–263
substring-after(string1, string2)
      function, 242
substring-before(string1, string2)
      function, 241
substring(string1, offset, length)
      function, 241
sum( ) function, 241
summary attribute, 274
supports method, 303
switch statement, 376
syntax, checking, 18–19
SYSTEM keyword, 40

T

<table> element, 218, 272, 287,
      309, 311, 313
tables
      data binding into HTML,
            308–313
      XHTML, 272–279

tabular data control (TDC), 282
tag names, 19, 67
tagName property, 331
tags, overview, 4–5
targetNamespace attribute, 132
<td> element, 272, 276–278
TDC (tabular data control), 282
templates
      empty catch-all, 228–229
      XSLT
            applying, 188–193
            new, 195–198
<term> element, 114–115
text, formatting, 157–161
text( ) function, 243
text( ) node test, 236
text attribute, 260
text content model, 42–43
Text createTextNode(String data)
      method, *364t*
text nodes, 375, 382, 411
Text object, 321
text property
      JavaScript, 329
      XMLDOMAttribute
            object, 344
      XMLDOMElement
            object, 331
text-align property, 158, 168
textarea element, 287
text-decoration property, 155,
      158, 160
text-indent property, 158, 168
text-transform property, 158
<third <person> element, 346
Tidy utility, 37
time type, *121t–122t*
title attribute
      <b> element, 266
      <font> element, 269
      <h1> to <h6>
            elements, 263
      <head> element, 261
      <i> element, 268
      <img> element, 271
      <table> element, 274
      <td> element, 278
      <tr> element, 275
<title> element, 139, 141, 146,
      259–260
token type, *121t*
<tr> element, 272, 275
<transaction> element, 86–87,
      89–90, 102, 107, 120

transactionType type, 88, 108, 131
transformNode property
      JavaScript, 329
      XMLDOMAttribute
            object, 344
      XMLDOMElement
            object, 331
transformNodeToObject property
      JavaScript, 329
      XMLDOMAttribute
            object, 344
      XMLDOMElement
            object, 331
translate(string1, string2, string3)
      function, 242
true/false predicates, 238–240
try block, 355–356, 360
type attribute, 57, 142

U

<ul> element, 410
Unicode Transformation Format 8
      (UTF-8), 17
union element, *78t*
unique element, *78t*
unsignedByte type, *121t–122t*
unsignedInt type, *121t–122t*
unsignedLong type, *121t–122t*
unsignedShort type, *121t–122t*
use attribute, 113
usemap attribute, 272
UTF-8 (Unicode Transformation
      Format 8), 17

V

Validate button, 37, 78
validating. *See also* DTDs
      XHTML, 252–254
      XML documents
            overview, 14–15
            process of, 34–35
            using schemas,
                79–83
valign attribute
      <td> element, 278
      <tr> element, 275
value property, 344
VALUE type, 53
version attribute, 17

vertical-align property, 158, 168
viewData function, 304
:visited class, 155
vlink attribute, 261
void setCoalescing(boolean
    coalescing) method, 359t
void setExpandEntityReferences
    (boolean expandEntityRef)
    method, 359t
void setIgnoringComments
    (boolean ignoreComments)
    method, 359t
void setIgnoringElementContent
    Whitespace(boolean
    whitespace) method, 359t
void setNamespaceAware(boolean
    awareness) method, 359t
void setValidating(boolean
    validating) method, 359t
vspace attribute, 272

W

W3C (World Wide Web Consor-
    tium), 5, 83, 176, 246, 320
W3C CSS validator, 141
W3C DOM objects, 321
W3C TIDY program, 141
W3C XML validator, 36
walkNodes method, 372, 374–376,
    378–379
<weight> element, 179, 219, 226,
    228, 301
well-formed XML documents
    checking syntax, 18–19
    comments, adding, 17–18
    overview, 14–16
    predefined entity
        references, 29–30
    processing instructions,
        handling, 18
    prologs, 17
    XML attributes, adding,
        26–29
    XML declaration, 16–17
    XML elements, storing data
        in, 19–25
well-formedness errors, 16
well-formedness rules, 16, 29
width attribute
    <img> element, 272
    <table> element, 274
    <td> element, 278

window.XMLHttpRequest
    object, 395
WordPad, 17
World Wide Web Consortium
    (W3C), 5, 83, 176, 246, 320

X

XHTML (Extensible Hypertext
    Markup Language)
    <body> element, 260–263
    bold text, 266–267
    <font> element, 268–270
    <head> element, 258–259
    headings, 263–265
    HTML versus, 255–256
    <html> document
        element, 257
    <img> element, 271–272,
        273f
    italics, 267–268
    mixing MathML and, 70–71
    namespaces, 66–67
    overview, 246–251,
        254–255
    plain text, 265
    tables, creating, 272–279
    <title> element, 259–260
    validating, 252–254
XHTML 1.0 DTDs, 254–255
XHTML validator, 252
xhtml.html document, 247, 250
xhtmlmathml.html, 70
XML (Extensible Markup
    Language)
    applications, 12–13
    CDATA sections, 31–32
    extracting data from, 10–12
    formatting, 9–10
    markup languages, 3–9
    overview, 2–3
    validating
        overview, 14–15
        process of, 34–35
        using schemas,
            79–83
    writing well-formed
        documents
        checking syntax,
            18–19
        comments, adding,
            17–18
        overview, 14–16

predefined entity ref-
    erences, 29–30
processing instruc-
    tions, handling, 18
prologs, 17
XML attributes,
    adding, 26–29
XML declaration,
    16–17
XML elements,
    storing data in,
    19–25
XML declaration, 5
.xml extension, 8
XML Path (XPath) Language.
    See XPath Language
XML processors, 15, 34
xml property
    JavaScript, 329
    XMLDOMAttribute
        object, 344
    XMLDOMElement
        object, 331
XML Query Language. See
    XQuery
XML Schema Definition (XSD)
    Language, 75, 77–78, 81t–82t
<xml> element, 298, 351
XMLall.html, 303, 308
xmldoc object, 326–327, 345
XMLDOMAttribute objects
    JavaScript, 322
    properties, 343–344
XMLDOMCDATASection
    object, 322
XMLDOMCharacterData
    object, 322
XMLDOMComment object, 322
XMLDOMDocumentFragment
    object, 322
XMLDOMDocumentType
    object, 322
XMLDOMElement objects
    JavaScript, 322
    methods, 331
    properties, 330–331
XMLDOMEntity object, 322
XMLDOMEntityReference
    object, 322
XMLDOMImplementation
    object, 322
XMLDOMNamedNodeMap
    object, 322
XMLDOMNode object, 322

XMLDOMNodeList object, 322
XMLDOMNotation object, 322
XMLDOMParseError object, 322
XMLDOMProcessingInstruction
    object, 322
XMLDOMText object, 322
XMLHttpRequest object, 391,
    394–399, 404, 407–408, 412
XMLHttpRequestObject
    variable, 395
xml:lang attribute
        <b> element, 266
        <font> element, 269
        <h1> to <h6> elements, 263
        <head> element,
            258–259, 261
        <html> element, 257
        <i> element, 268
        <img> element, 272
        <table> element, 274
        <td> element, 278
        <tr> element, 275
xmlns attribute, 257
<?xml-stylesheet?> element, 9,
    18, 142, 183, 185, 192, 228
XMLtable.html, 308, 313
XMLtablenested.html, 316
XPath (XML Path) Language
    axes, 234–236
    examples, 243–244
    node tests, 236
    overview, 234
    predicates
        node-set, 237–238
        numerical, 240–241
        overview, 236–237
        string, 241–243
        true/false, 238–240
XPath expression, 213
XPath operators, 238
.xq (XQuery document)
    extension, 416
XQuery (XML Query Language)
    functions, 418–421
    overview, 390, 414–415
    putting to work, 416–418

XSD (XML Schema Definition)
    Language, 75, 77–78, *81t–82t*
xsd prefix, 79
<xsd:all> element, 88, 131
<xsd:annotation> element,
    133–134
<xsd:appInfo> element, 134
<xsd:attribute> element, 90, 107,
    109, 111–114, 129
<xsd:attributeGroup> element, 130
<xsd:choice> element, 124, 126
<xsd:complexType> element, 88,
    97–99, 117, 128
xsd:date type, 107
<xsdd:attribute> element, 107
<xsd:documentation> element, 134
<xsd:element> element, 79, 85,
    95, 98, 102, 126
<xsd:enumeration> facet, 118–120
<xsd:facet> facet, 118
<xsd:group> element, 128–129
xsd:integer type, 109, 118
<xsd:maxInclusive> schema
    facet, 118
<xsd:minInclusive> schema
    facet, 118
<xsd:pattern> element, 117
<xsd:restriction> element, 117–118
<xsd:schema> element, 83, 132
<xsd:sequence> element, 88, 131
xsd:string type, 79, 80, 87, 92,
    109, 119
xsl namespace prefix, 187
<xsl:apply-templates> element,
    195–196, 200, 212, 218
<xsl:copy-of> element, 212
<xsl:for-each> element, 206, 212
<xsl:sort> element, 212
<xsl:stylesheet> element, 187
XSLT (Extensible Stylesheet
    Language Transformations)
        extracting
            multiple elements
                values, 205–209
            value of <name>
                elements, 199–201

<friend> elements,
    replacing, 193–195
match attribute
        attributes, 217–223
        child element nodes,
            214–217
        either/or
            expressions, 230
        element nodes,
            213–214
        matching by ID,
            223–224
        matching with [ ],
            230–234
        overview, 212–213
        root node, 213
        XML comments,
            224–229
        XML processing
            instructions, 229
    overview, 176, 212
    sample XML document
        creating, 176–182
        formatting, 183–186
    style sheets, creating,
        187–188
    templates, applying
        new, 195–198
        overview, 188–191
        replacing data in
            sample document,
            192–193
    XPath
        axes, 234–236
        examples, 243–244
        node tests, 236
        overview, 234
        predicates, 236–243
    <xsl:value-of>, 201–205
<xsl:template> element,
    188, 212
<xsl:text> element, 221
<xsl:value-of select="2 + 3"/>
    element, 240
<xsl:value-of> element, 201–205,
    207, 212